Michael Montgomery is Professor Emeritus of English and Linguistics at the University of South Carolina. For the past twenty years he has read widely in the archives and museums of Ireland, Scotland, and the U.S. to find the material for this book. His has written widely on Irish and Scottish links to American English as well as on the English of his native southern United States. His most recent book is *Dictionary of Smoky Mountain English* (2004). He is Honorary President of the Ulster-Scots Language Society.

From Ulster To America

The Scotch-Irish Heritage
of American English

From Ulster To America

The Scotch-Irish Heritage
of American English

Michael Montgomery

ULSTER HISTORICAL FOUNDATION

First published 2006
by Ulster Historical Foundation
12 College Square East, Belfast BT1 6DD
www.ancestryireland.com

Cover: Edwin Hayes: *An Emigrant Ship, Dublin Bay, Sunset, 1853*
Oil on Canvas, 58 x 86cm. Courtesy of the National Gallery of Ireland.

© Michael Montgomery 2006

ISBN 13: 978 1 903688 61 8
ISBN 10: 1903688 61 2

Printed by ColourBooks Ltd
Design by December Publications

CONTENTS

ACKNOWLEDGEMENTS

This volume was begun, in effect, more than fifteen years ago, in that it brings together my two principal scholarly interests during the intervening period: the language of Ulster emigrants to North America (the speech of my ancestors) and that of southern Appalachia (the speech I heard growing up in Tennessee). Any work of lexicography, as Dr Johnson discovered, aims to subdue the unruliness of language by combining the scientist's passion for order with the artist's intuition for selection. In this volume I have wrestled with this challenge in seeking a type of transatlantic picture that had never been attempted, at least for English a picture achieved by individual dictionary entries that cumulatively present as full and accurate a record as possible of what American English inherited from one small corner of the world an ocean away.

To accomplish this task required immersion in two different scholarly and cultural worlds, one of which was entirely new to me. In the summer of 1988 I first went to Northern Ireland to begin research on Ulster speech. The friendships forged then and since, along with long hours at libraries, archives and bookshops, introduced me to sources which no one in North America could ever have been aware of or had access to, even in this electronic age, no matter how adept or diligent their interlibrary loan staffs might be. Only by extended, regular visits to Northern Ireland could I have discovered and mined many of the sources from which I have drawn citations to produce reasonably complete dictionary entries. Often they were unknown outside the province. Such colleagues as Philip Robinson, John Erskine, Robert Heslip, John Kirk and Ivan Herbison brought many works to my attention. I am grateful to them and many others who have been my eyes and ears for sources that reflected or related to local speech patterns. I owe a great debt to staff members of the Ulster Folk and Transport Museum in Cultra, who put that institution's holdings at my disposal over the course of many years. In the library of the Museum I consulted amateur glossaries, local historical journals (from many of Northern Ireland's one hundred local history societies), novels, two and a half centuries of poetry, and countless other publications. Unpublished sources were also extremely rich, especially glossaries in the Museum's Dialect Archive, initiated in the 1960s by G. Brendan Adams, who arranged for much of this material to be preserved and deposited there for generations of researchers he would never know. To Adams and all those whose interest in local speech prompted them to donate and preserve such material I express my gratitude. I could never have contemplated this volume without the Museum's incomparable collections, which as my own research was beginning were being fortuitously organised for the commencement of the *Concise Ulster Dictionary* project (1989–94) and were made available to me to consult at the same time. I am profoundly grateful to Sally Skilling, Ronnie Adams and Roger Dixon of the Museum's library staff for help accessing the sources providing citations to enrich, and in many cases to form the core of, the Ulster evidence in this dictionary. Most especially I thank Anne Smyth, who on countless occasions has provided material from the Museum's electronic dialect database that was compiled during and for the *CUD* project, fielded queries from afar about bibliography, documentation and much else, checked items in the library for me, and ensured in so many ways the exactness of detail a work of lexicography requires. Caroline Macafee reviewed a draft of this dictionary and, as editor of the *CUD*, gave suggestions and made available printouts from the dictionary's database. More important, during the editing of the *CUD* a decade earlier, she was a source of guidance and inspiration on innumerable occasions and taught me more about the discipline and practice of lexicography than she can imagine. James Fenton permitted me to draw liberally from his own dictionary, *The Hamely Tongue*, responded to numerous queries about local usage, and offered always helpful corrections to an earlier draft.

The other institution whose help was instrumental in assembling this volume is my own, the University of South Carolina. Special recognition goes to the interlibrary loan staff at the university's Thomas Cooper Library, who tracked down and borrowed obscure items for me to read and excerpt. Jo Cottingham in particular deserves praise for her indefatigable efforts as the chief of these trackers. Two academic units at my university, the Department of English and the Linguistics Program, generously provided research assistants both before and after my retirement in 1999 who were invaluable in carrying out library and editorial tasks connected with my on-going projects on Ulster and southern mountain speech. Only in 2002 did I realise that years of extensive notes and other material amassed from both sides of the water had laid the foundation for a dictionary such as the present publication. From that time work progressed rapidly. During the 2003–04 academic year, when I undertook an extensive reading programme of books obtained through interlibrary loan and when most of the typing and proofing of this volume were accomplished, I was especially fortunate to have the help of Melissa Stockstill Jantz, a graduate student in linguistics, to keep the project moving rapidly along and to enable me to process borrowed items in the timeliest manner. Indeed, her to-ing and fro-ing of books can politely be described as academic weight training. She also provided reliable proofreading and other assistance that ensured the accuracy of the final typescript. Without her help this book would have been delayed for at least another year, and I look forward to putting my first copy of it into her hands.

Many American citations featured in this dictionary are taken directly from my *Dictionary of Smoky Mountain English* (2004, co-edited with Joseph Sargent Hall) because they were readily accessible and dated. It is almost certainly the case that the English of the Appalachian region reflects a stronger linguistic imprint from Ulster than other parts of the United States. The present volume's reliance on Appalachian citations no doubt exaggerates this inheritance somewhat, but the selection of citations has been based on convenience, not an implicit bias, and for any given entry the citations cannot be taken collectively to suggest the regional dimensions of a term in the United States. Where *DSME* citations proved inadequate for early dating, clarity, or some other reason, they were supplemented mainly by ones drawn from the *Dictionary of American Regional English*, either from its published volumes (which now encompass from A through Sk-) or from files at the dictionary office being edited for the remainder of the alphabet, which were put at my disposal on two visits in 1996 and 1997. For many entries the earliest, and sometimes the only, citation is from *DARE*. I am grateful to its Editor-in-Chief, Frederic G. Cassidy, for this access and to editors George Goebel and Joan Houston Hall for generously and with consummate alacrity responding whenever I have had a question or implied a need for evidence. They and their colleagues epitomise how a dictionary project can contribute to the work of others while in the throes of their own editing. From his vast personal knowledge of varieties of English, Robert Easton made helpful suggestions of several terms to include, and Peter Gilmore's '*Scots-Irish*' *Words from Pennsylvania's Mountains*, terms with Ulster connections taken from the collections of Pennsylvania folklorist Henry Shoemaker, identified other items I would have missed. Bruce D. Boling has been a 'Celticist on call' on matters of Irish etymology. However, none of these persons cited here or earlier bear responsibility for gaps, lapses, or any other matters in the volume. The entry format is of my own devising, as is the selection of terms and all other facets of the final work.

Like any dictionary, this volume represents work in progress, the product of one scholar's collection and sifting over many years. More historical evidence can, and doubtless will, come to light for many of its nearly four hundred items, and numerous others (particularly ones attested in Scotland but not yet on record for

Ulster) will be added to the total. I wish not to imply to have provided the final word on any one, and it is the privilege of readers to question the inclusion of some or the exclusion of others. Nor do I wish to suggest that American English's debt to Ulster is not shared in part with other regions of the British Isles, especially Scotland and northern England. My aim has always been to advance the lexicographical record towards the completion that William Craigie so enthusiastically and so justifiably called for nearly a century ago as the *Oxford English Dictionary* neared its completion.

Michael Montgomery
June 2006

PREFATORY NOTE
The Term *Scotch-Irish*

In the title and text of this book *Scotch-Irish* (not *Scots-Irish*) is used because it is the predominant term in the United States by which colonial-era emigrants from Ulster have been called for more than three hundred years and the one by which their descendants have known themselves since at least the middle of the nineteenth century. For many years I have collected authentic examples of the two labels from seventeenth- and eighteenth-century American documents; twenty-four of these are of *Scotch-Irish*, but only three are of *Scots-Irish*. While *Scots-Irish* has gained some popularity in recent years and some in both Northern Ireland and the United States object to *Scotch-Irish*, the latter continues to be the sole term which most Americans are familiar with or identify with. For them it is a respectable label that never suggests an alcoholic beverage or is objectionable on any other grounds. As the exclusive term I knew when growing up in Tennessee to refer to my own ancestry, I employ it here with pride.

FOREWORD

In his Presidential address to the American Dialect Society in January of 2005, Michael Montgomery outlined for his colleagues the research he had been doing over the previous seventeen years, reading obscure or hitherto unknown documents chronicling the English and Scots of the historical province of Ulster. Montgomery's talk was remarkable not only because of the wealth of new sources he identified, but especially because of his rather severe criticisms of two of lexicography's most revered icons, the *Oxford English Dictionary* (*OED*) and the *Dictionary of American Regional English* (*DARE*). These two projects, he said, had very seriously neglected the contributions of northern Ireland to the English of North America, particularly the broad Appalachian Mountain region of the United States. He demonstrated that while both dictionaries had copious etymological references to Scots and northern English dialect terms, they rarely specified that the words were also to be found in Ulster.

Montgomery tempered his criticisms by acknowledging that the sources he had been reading had not been available to the readers for the *OED* and *DARE*; but he challenged other lexicographers to make a conscientious effort to attribute to Ulster the words that are Ulster's. Such words might be discoverable through quotations that antedate existing evidence, quotations that postdate current citations (showing that words thought to be obsolete in English still hang on in Ulster), or through documentation demonstrating the transportation of lexical or grammatical forms across the Atlantic, especially to Pennsylvania and its secondary settlement areas.

The present volume makes it easier for lexicographers to do just that. By presenting examples of usage in both Ulster and America, Montgomery provides evidence of, if not ultimate Ulster origins, at least strong Ulster influence. That influence is particularly evident in American regional terms (especially those found in the South and South Midland), because Ulster immigrants were an early and tenacious force and because they were often the dominant group in the interior areas they settled. For such regional items as *backset* 'a relapse', *bedfast* 'bed-ridden', and *chimbley/chimley* as pronunciations for *chimney*, for example, both the *OED* and *DARE* mention Scots and/or English dialect origins; but these terms were doubtless reinforced in American use by Ulster speakers, and that contribution should be acknowledged in etymological explanations. For *DARE*, which concentrates on regional lexicon, to be able to provide both a geographic label and an etymological suggestion that correlates language with settlement history is highly satisfying. The editors of *DARE* are grateful for the work Montgomery has done in pointing out the many Ulster contributions to American regional English. His work will allow ours to be both more precise and more inclusive.

Examining the eclectic list of sources that Montgomery consulted illustrates the wide variety of documents that can be valuable in tracing language influences. His bibliography includes items ranging from moral and religious poems, to church records (on both sides of the Atlantic), to collections of humor, to contemporary Ulster newspaper articles, to recent works of Irish lexicography. (The dictionaries and glossaries provide useful reference materials, but they do not contribute materials for the historical record; it is his other sources that make Montgomery's work so rich.) His bibliography is a tantalizing reminder of how much more is yet to be discovered in the archives, museums, and basements or attics of the world.

Montgomery's pioneering effort to point out the contributions of Ulster immigrants to the English of the United States will surely spur other researchers to continue the exploration of neglected resources—distinguished or quotidian—in Ulster and elsewhere. For lexicographers, that prospect is extremely gratifying, since dictionary staffs lack the time and resources to conduct such investigations on their own. Together, we can puzzle out many more of the individual word histories that make the study of American English such a challenge and satisfaction.

Joan Houston Hall
Chief Editor, *Dictionary of American Regional English*

INTRODUCTION

1. Background and Genesis

This volume is the first lexicographic work devoted specifically to linguistic connections between the British Isles and North America. When the author went to Ireland and Scotland on the first of many visits to explore transatlantic language links in 1988, he found a deep conviction, especially in the historical province of Ulster,[1] of their having contributed to the culture of the United States. Soon he even began encountering one persistent comment: 'Did you know that the word *hillbilly* came from here?' People in Ulster believe (not without considerable reason) that the province put a stamp on America, especially on the large interior region known as Appalachia,[2] and that belief has been buttressed in the literature of popular historians for over a century. For example, their conviction that American country and bluegrass music has local roots, though based more on intuition than solid evidence, is palpable. The notion of a linguistic legacy, if only with respect to *hillbilly* (a generally derogatory label in the United States for a native of the southern Appalachian or Ozark mountains), seems equally embedded in the popular mind but equally difficult to pin down. At least two etymologies are possible for it: (1) *hill* + either *billie* (a Scots word meaning 'fellow, comrade' that is known to have been brought by Ulster emigrants to Pennsylvania); or (2) *billy* (short for *billy boy* 'a follower of King William III'). The only written account of either of these derivations the author can find comes from a book by Ian Adamson, and it is unknown whether his statement is based on the popular belief (it almost certainly contributes to it):

> Although the Scotch-Irish were merging quickly into the American Nation, the Ulster speech itself was to stay alive in the hill-country of Appalachia and beyond, where Scotch-Irish traditional music may still be heard. Among the earliest songs were ballads of King William of Orange, so those who sung them became known as Billy-boys of the hill-country or 'hillbillies'.[3]

The light of scholarship offers little reason to link either *billie* or *billy* to *hillbilly*. The earliest known example of the American compound is from Alabama in 1898, not in reference to archetypal mountaineers of southern Appalachia, and this is several generations removed from the time when Ulster emigrants first populated the region. By contrast, this dictionary documents two other eighteenth-century terms for groups in the American backwoods, *cracker* and *cohee*, which lack the iconic status of *hillbilly* and have no popular accounts giving them a transatlantic derivation, but which came unambiguously from Ulster.

Hillbilly may not be an authentic Ulsterism, but nearly four hundred other usages and expressions have been contributed to the English language of the United States in large part or in a few cases wholly by emigrants from the province. This book documents these in dictionary entries having dated citations from both sides of the Atlantic. The linguistic heritage brought by this group, who are generally referred to as the 'Ulster Scots' in the British Isles and as the 'Scotch-Irish' in North America,[4] was almost entirely unrecognized a few years ago. Given the numbers who left Ulster for America in the colonial period (at least 150,000)[5] in a migration that one historian states 'represented the single largest movement of any group from the British Isles to British North America during the eighteenth century',[6] a linguistic inheritance should not be surprising.

The first linguist to propose a substantial Ulster input to American speech was Hans Kurath, one of the foremost linguists of his generation, who wrote in a 1928 essay that linguistic evidence for it was almost certainly to be found in Pennsylvania and its secondary settlements (Ohio, Kentucky, West Virginia and western Virginia)[7]. His belief was based on the work of historians (e.g. Frederic Jackson Turner)[8] on the settlement of the eastern seaboard and migration patterns inland. Shortly afterwards he was to become the first director of the Linguistic Atlas of the United States and Canada project, which was designed to survey the whole of English-speaking North America using a standard questionnaire to collect vocabulary and pronunciation. He was to be given the opportunity to search for evidence on the ground in the speech of older individuals native to their communities. In his early essay on American regional pronunciation he had broadly stated that

> Like the seaboard of New England, the tide-water region of Virginia received most of its early population from Southeastern England, and therefore has Southern English speech habits. But the Piedmont of Virginia and the Carolinas, and the Great Valley [of Virginia], were largely settled, during the half-century preceding the Revolution, by the Scotch-Irish, who spoke a quite different dialect, namely, the English of the Lowlands of Scotland or the North of England as modified by the Southern English Standard. They neither dropped their r's nor did they pronounce their long mid-vowels diphthongal fashion. The large German

element from Pennsylvania ultimately acquired this type of English.[9]

Research on American settlement history gave Kurath early optimism, but after nearly twenty years of collecting he could identify very few terms, leading him to a conclusion quite different from the one he anticipated:

> After 1720 large flocks of Ulster Scots and Palatine Germans arrived on Delaware Bay and spread out into the back country of Philadelphia and then westward to the Alleghenies and the Ohio Valley, and then southward through western Maryland and Virginia to the Carolinas ... The influence of the English-speaking Ulster Scots upon the speech of certain sections of Pennsylvania and of the southern upland cannot be doubted, but it is surprisingly intangible. The Dutch and the Germans, who spoke their own language for many generations and passed through a stage of bilingualism before they gave up their native language, have left a much more tangible impress upon the English of their areas of concentration.[10]

To be sure, Kurath identified a few terms that were traceable to Ulster input (e.g. *hippin* 'diaper, nappy', *hap* 'coverlet', the preposition *till* (in *quarter till*, etc.), *piece* 'distance', and *you'ns* 'you (plural)'). These sufficed for him not only to believe that a much larger component would eventually be found, but to employ these and other terms to posit a Midland dialect region,[11] the map for which will be immediately recognizable to anyone familiar with American settlement patterns, showing as it does how the region widens from the Delaware Valley into the interior of Pennsylvania and then turns sharply south into the Shenandoah Valley of Virginia and beyond. This was the path taken by many Ulster emigrants who landed in Philadelphia, Pennsylvania or in Newcastle, Delaware.

Kurath's paucity of evidence led others to come to a very different conclusion: that the Ulster element in twentieth-century American English was either trivial or no longer discernible. The present book presents a very different picture. The fundamental handicap that Kurath would not overcome was the lack of dictionaries and other sources on Ulster speech at his disposal. The *English Dialect Dictionary* and *Scottish National Dictionary* included some Ulster material, but it was sparse, uneven, and difficult to extract from these multi-volume works (and the *SND* only completed publication in 1976). He would not know whether many items collected in the course of his atlas project could be found in Ulster or not. Given that he cites no source on language, one wonders whether he might have relied largely on personal acquaintance for what connections he did identify.[12]

The literature on Ulster-America historical connections is so extensive that it is rather surprising that virtually nothing was written on ones for language until very recently. Standard treatments, whether of the heroic genre chronicling prominent individuals and events[13] or works presenting broader pictures of social and economic developments[14] have said nothing about language. Historians have not shied away from other, much less tangible cultural phenomena, discussing the transfer of such entities as habits of mind and claiming that these uniquely suited, and indeed even molded, Ulster emigrants for life in America, especially in the backwoods.

The lack of attention began to change in the 1980s. Two events in particular prompted broader awareness of an Ulster element in American speech and culture. One was 'The Guid Scots Tongue', an episode in the BBC's *The Story of English* series (1986); it argued for the transplantation of language from Scotland to Ulster to the interior of America, most prominently southern Appalachia, in the seventeenth and eighteenth century.[15] Though the program was far more cultural panorama than linguistic case study, it had an audience of millions. The second event was historian David Hackett Fischer's widely reviewed and acclaimed monograph *Albion's Seed: Four British Folkways in America* (1989), which for twenty-four cultural 'ways' connected four regions of the British Isles to four others in the United States.[16] One of these linkages he called 'north Britain to the backcountry', arguing that a large and relatively homogeneous cultural region comprising northern England, Scotland and much of Ireland produced the primary founding population and cultural foundations for the interior of the mid-Atlantic colonies. What has become known as the American 'back country'. Like the BBC series, Fischer's work was based on secondary scholarship, used with enthusiasm but not always with the greatest discrimination. For the most part he was on target, but some of his 'north British' linguistic items were either in general usage in Britain (and thus came to the United States from other of his regions), and some cannot be associated with Ulster speech either today or in the past (e.g. *deef* 'deaf', *sartin* 'certain', *a-goin* 'going', *nigh* 'near'). Still others are more recent developments arising in America (*far* 'fire', *fixin to* 'getting ready to'). Although such examples vitiated Fischer's case somewhat, it at the same time highlighted the work that linguists needed to do, and his volume kindled much interest in transatlantic connections. He has been vindicated in his contention that many American terms having Ulster roots are, or at one time were, shared with Scotland and northern England.

Meanwhile two researchers on language were laying a broader and more systematic foundation. In 1984 Alan Crozier published an article in the journal

American Speech linking thirty-one Pennsylvania terms to Ulster.[17] More recently Peter Gilmore produced '*Scots-Irish' Words from Pennsylvania's Mountains*, a distillation of terms with Ulster connections taken from the collection of Henry Shoemaker, an early twentieth-century Pennsylvania folklorist.[18] Both works used great care to expand the knowledge of Scotch-Irish contributions and were important for their methodology as well as their substantive findings. What they lacked in Fischer's intrepidness and grand sweep they more than compensated for in the quality and detail of their evidence.[19]

In his comparison Crozier follows, though does not name, the 'principle of regionalization',[20] whereby an item is first circumscribed or determined to be generally restricted to a certain part of the British Isles before transatlantic evidence for it is sought. This seemingly simple step has very often been ignored by scholars. Crozier recognizes that most transatlantic language connections are relative, based on predominant but not exclusive evidence from Ulster. The sources at hand, not to mention the nature of the evidence, do not permit simple cross-Atlantic correlation, no matter how direct the emigration patterns might appear to have been, because American colonial settlements normally had quite mixed populations; this was certainly true for the areas to which Ulster emigrants went in the eighteenth century, though they often predominated in them. As instructive and as well directed as they were, Crozier's and Gilmore's steps are limited ones, both confined to Pennsylvania and neither undertaking a reading program or using available resources to full advantage. They leave us well short of a comprehensive assessment of the Ulster contribution to American English.

2. Approach and Methodology

In the form of dictionary entries this volume shows what one stream of settlers gave to American English, a contribution that was one of the most—arguably *the* most—substantial from all of Europe except when Britain is taken as a whole. Why it sets out what American English owes to *Ulster* rather than more broadly to *Ireland* requires some explanation. There are four principal reasons for this special focus. First of all, a dialect history manifestly binds together an area roughly corresponding to that defined by the historical border of Ulster.[21] Second, a transatlantic settlement history distinguishes Ulster from the rest of Ireland. Altogether only a minority—perhaps only a quarter—of the seven million[22] emigrants from Ireland were from the northern province, but the great bulk of those from Connacht, Munster and Leinster came after 1830 (especially in the famine years of the late 1840s and immediately thereafter) and principally to northern cities of the United States. Third (as a consequence), the linguistic component from Ulster was far larger and more fundamental than that from other provinces. The English (or sometimes Irish) of nineteenth-century emigrants apparently made little contribution to American speech in those northern parts of the new nation, most likely because emigrants from Ireland were a relatively late-arriving group to areas where English had already been spoken.[23] Only a small proportion of terms in American English traceable to Ireland (or from Ireland to Britain) are documented beyond Ulster, and these few are often of Irish Gaelic origin.[24] Fourth, the component from Ulster often penetrated into the American hinterland, in contrast to that from elsewhere in Ireland, and sometimes played a role in distinguishing American regional and social dialects. Colonial-era emigrants from Ireland to America were by and large from Ulster (mainly Presbyterians of Scottish heritage) and went to interior areas where their numbers made them a strong and often the dominant group. They routinely mixed with people of English, German, African or other extraction who borrowed from their speech.

If the foregoing presents something of the *why* of this book, a more practical question concerns *how* it was made possible and came about. A conviction that the Ulster element in American English has been under-appreciated or unaccounted for hardly ensures adequate or sufficient documentation of it. Several circumstances have enabled this presentation of that Ulster element. First has been an surge of lexicography in Ireland. Dictionaries and glossaries on England and Scotland have been available for decades, especially in the form of the *English Dialect Dictionary* and the *Scottish National Dictionary*.[25] The contrast can hardly have been more striking to the English of Ireland, where until recently there was no volume comparable even to Jamieson's *Etymological Dictionary of the Scottish Language* of two centuries ago, outside Patterson's *A Glossary of Words in Use in the Counties of Antrim and Down* (the *EDD*'s principal source for Ireland) and Traynor's *English Dialect of Donegal: A Glossary*, both covering only one or two counties.[26] Since 1995 five dictionaries have been published in Ireland, providing a much fuller record of the island's English and Scots. The three of these based outside Ulster (Ó Muirithe's *Dictionary of Anglo-Irish: Words and Phrases from Gaelic in the English of Ireland*, Share's *Slanguage: A Dictionary of Irish Slang*, and Dolan's *Dictionary of Hiberno-English*) concentrate to one degree or another on what Irish English has borrowed from Irish, and relatively few terms in them have been attested in the United States.[27] The two others, which are based on Ulster, feature much greater correspondence to American sources: Fenton's *The Hamely Tongue: A Personal Record of Ulster-Scots in County Antrim* and Macafee's *Concise Ulster Dictionary*.[28]

These sources individually and collectively remain a long way from a historical, citation-based dictionary such as the *Scottish National Dictionary*, and such a work is badly needed for the island of Ireland. However, they do assist comparisons of various kinds, including transatlantic ones, given the advent of the *Dictionary of American Regional English* (four volumes published to date) for filling in the American side.[29] *DARE*'s national scope has enabled its editors to identify the regional distribution of forms and meanings in many thousands of cases, and these determinations are reflected in labels (e.g. 'chiefly South, South Midland' for *backset* 'relapse of an illness', 'chiefly Appalachians' for *beal* 'of a sore: to fester'). *DARE* is far and away the most comprehensive and authoritative compilation of American regional terminology. It provides only thumbnail linkage of terms to different parts of the British Isles and does not claim definitiveness in doing so (for all intents and purposes, for instance, *DARE* does not employ Ulster sources). Researchers can take the raw material in it and begin identifying and categorizing more detailed historical connections for themselves. Or at least they can do so for the American side. A thorough job pinning down Ulster connections requires going far beyond works now in print. Knowledge of and in many cases access to the pertinent sources was possible only by the author's extended stints in repositories abroad, such as the Ulster Folk and Transport Museum. The Museum's Dialect Archive (established in the 1960s), its electronic database (assembled to support the *Concise Ulster Dictionary*, edited at the Museum between 1989 and 1994) and the Museum's library, which holds local journals and glossaries (many unpublished)[30] and other specialized literature unknown outside Northern Ireland were all invaluable to this project. In 2003 and much of 2004 the author undertook an intensive reading program of approximately 150 volumes (novels, plays, collections of stories, and so on, as many as possible from the nineteenth century), to excerpt these for citations for possible inclusion. The resulting large harvest shows how much can still be found by a reading program of local sources, even by one individual. Gradually he amassed sufficient documentation and citations for 379 terms (418 if multiple senses or uses are counted) for what he hopes is a proper compilation and assessment.

To provide an accurate and informative historical perspective on the material, two basic principles have been adopted: to date all citations, and to supply an etymological summary within square brackets following each definition. Each summary suggests or identifies, if possible, the antecedents of a term or sense by cross-referencing it to historical dictionaries, especially the *Oxford English Dictionary* (*OED*), *Dictionary of the Older Scottish Tongue* (*DOST*) or *Scottish*

National Dictionary (*SND*).[31] These are used to cite evidence from Scotland or England from the eighteenth century or before, including the date of earliest attestation and its form in Middle English, Middle Scots, or Old English if such is deemed of interest. Among dictionaries used occasionally are the *Dictionary of Hiberno-English* (*DHE*) and the *Dictionary of Newfoundland English* (*DNE*).[32] The *English Dialect Dictionary* and *Concise Ulster Dictionary* are not cited in the etymologies, but nonetheless have played pivotal roles, as explained below, serving as the basis on which most items were selected. They deserve special comment.

It is always well to recall the historical geography of the North Atlantic English-speaking world and that Ulster has been a crossroads of peoples and languages between Scotland and Ireland for centuries, just as more recently it has often been a bridge to North America. Ulster itself was a seventeenth-century colony from Britain from which two tongues, English and Scots, were transplanted a millennium after developing on the larger island of the archipelago, the settlers coming overwhelmingly from Scotland, northern England, and the north-west Midlands of England in King James I's plantation of Ulster (1610–25).[33] Relatively few terms (e.g. positive *anymore, all the* + adverb) originated in Ulster, compared with the great many that were brought from across the Irish Sea. With all this in mind, more than one thousand terms considered for inclusion in the present work were checked against the *English Dialect Dictionary*, whose coverage of Scotland and England (in contrast to that of Ireland) is roughly equal in intensity, to gauge their traditional distribution in Britain. If it was attested by the *EDD* primarily in Scotland and in England north of the River Humber, and if it met the criteria of having a *bona fide* citation from Ulster and a manifestly related form and meaning in the United States, it was adopted. If it was attested by the *EDD* in equal or greater proportion south of the Humber, it was eliminated, no matter how numerous or interesting were the citations at hand from Ulster (e.g. *knowed, blowed*), although it was undoubtedly brought to North America in part by Ulster emigrants. Some items included (e.g. *hit* 'it') are well known in Old and Middle English, but had largely disappeared in England by the seventeenth century.[34]

The approach just outlined has the virtue of transparent and consistent, if somewhat crude, application. But it also has the inevitable vices of both under- and over-representation. The provision of citations herein from Ulster, very often from well back in the nineteenth century, makes it highly unlikely that any items in the present work were brought exclusively from Scotland or England to America. At the same time, this volume does not claim that these items did not arrive in the speech of emigrants directly from Scotland or England, only that the large influx from Ulster to North America in the eighteenth century meant that forms traceable ultimately to the northern half of Britain can be attributed mainly to the Irish province. Even with a seemingly objective criterion governing the use of the *EDD*, the complexities of linguistic migration from Britain to Ireland make the selection of entries and the isolation of a reasonable version of the Ulster heritage subject to judgment and relativity. For example, the *EDD* may give a reliable view of regional currency, but like most dictionaries it is silent about how broadly a usage was found within a community, or indeed whether it was the usual choice over alternatives with the same meaning. In any case, it makes no sense to characterize as the 'distinct' heritage from Ulster only the few terms originating in the province.

Because the *Concise Ulster Dictionary* was compiled from existing sources (mainly on deposit at the Ulster Folk and Transport Museum in Cultra, Northern Ireland) rather than from a new reading or collection program, and because it was prepared for secondary schools and thus lacked dated citations, the *CUD* could play no role in etymologies complementary to historical works like the *OED* and *SND*. To cite the date of the dictionary itself (1996) would have been to obscure rather than to clarify. However, the circumstances of the volume's preparation make it an ideal portal to a large number of word-lists and glossaries that could be systematically consulted to fill gaps in defining and illustrating terms. Although the overwhelming majority of items in the present work are to be found in the *CUD* and its debt to the *CUD* is incalculable, it was logical to take the next step of going beyond that work to cite original, dated sources and not the *CUD per se*.

3. Format of Entries
Each entry consists of five parts:

(1) the headword and any variant forms. The headword reflects either the main form as found in other dictionaries (usually the one with the soundest historical basis) or, if this is not possible, the form most often found in the citations provided herein. Especially on the Ulster side writers of fiction often modify spelling to portray local speech, sometimes on a semi-phonetic basis, and it must be remembered that writers in Ulster had three different spelling traditions to draw upon: English, Scottish and Irish (the last used for terms that are borrowed from the Irish language, such as *dornog* 'small, round stone', or perceived to have been, such as *craic* 'entertaining talk'). Variant forms are listed in alphabetical order after the headword and number as many as nine for *yous*

and *donsie* and twelve for *fornent*. Each variant is to be found in at least one citation.

(2) the part of speech. When appropriate citations have been found from both Ulster and the United States, parts of speech are differentiated by sub-entries (e.g. *afore* is documented as an adverb, conjunction and preposition on both sides, *mizzle* as a noun and verb on both). When they have not, the parts of speech are subsumed together (e.g. *granny* is documented as a noun in Ulster but also a verb in the United States, *skiff* as a noun and verb in Ulster but only a noun across the water), pending the future provision of evidence.

(3) the definition, indicating both what is shared between Ulster and America and is not (e.g. *blink*).

(4) the etymological summary. As indicated previously, the *OED*, *DOST* and *SND* are used routinely to document the earlier form and sense of items and the date of first attestation if possible. It is safe to assume that if any of these three works is not cited in a given summary, the term is not to be found in those three works. Used for the spelling and definition of Irish terms is Ó Dónaill's *Foclóir Gaeilge–Béarla*,[35] for Scottish Gaelic ones Dwelly's *Facloir Gaidhlig gu Beurla le Dealbhan*.[36] Summaries also cross-reference items to American sources (principally three sources: (1) the *Dictionary of American Regional English*; (2) the *Linguistic Atlas of the United States and Canada* (*LAUSC*), as found in works deriving from the project;[37] and (3) *Webster's Third New International Dictionary*)[38] in order to show their regional distribution in the United States. Cumulative consideration of what *DARE*'s labels indicate about the persistence of Ulster-derived terms from a geographical point of view is presented below.

(5) the citations. These are of two principal types. First are excerpts from texts. These illustrate and occasionally comment on a form in context. On the Ulster side nearly all of this material is from written sources, in the main from local literature, especially fiction. From the United States much written material is cited as well, but a significant proportion comes from oral sources, taken from a previous dictionary co-edited by the author, *Dictionary of Smoky Mountain English*.[39] Second are citations from glossaries (especially from Fenton's *Hamely Tongue* and Traynor's *English Dialect of Donegal*) and other descriptive works, consisting of a definition and usually an illustrative example. The two matched sets of citations show forms and meanings that are identical or similar enough to make a case that the American usage was the outgrowth of the Ulster one.[40] If they are available, up to eight (in a few cases more) citations are provided from each side, in order to display as much chronological spread as possible. In addition to confirming the existence of each term, citations bring it to life and

give flavor to local speech and the culture it so often encapsulates. The citations taken from writings left by known eighteenth-century emigrants are assigned to Ulster except when they clearly portray a usage in America.[41]

4. Assessment of the Ulster Heritage

The entries in this volume present individual snapshots, but we may reasonably ask what larger picture they reveal. Though allegedly present in music and other cultural phenomena, the Ulster heritage in modern America has been persistently difficult to demonstrate, in large part because of the lack of documentation from the emigration and intervening periods. Language is the best candidate for overcoming this problem. Words have intrinsic structure and are shared possessions of a community, meaning that they are not as subject to change or deliberate manipulation as a traditional story or tune is, for example. When they shift in form or meaning, this is usually according to well-known principles. The strenuous efforts made to locate and include eighteenth- and nineteenth-century citations have in many cases avoided the extrapolation from evidence two hundred or more years removed in time from the period of emigration. American citations from before the twentieth century have also been assiduously sought. This twofold internal reconstruction of linguistic history has been necessary to avoid fallacious connections based on coincidental occurrence (as is shown by *hillbilly*) or the coincidental existence of remarkably similar terms.[42] Perhaps it was apprehension of these and other methodological challenges that have led academic historians of the Ulster diaspora to be so reticent about cultural elements, especially non-material ones.

In pronunciation the Ulster influence on American English has been minimal and limited to barely a dozen or so individual terms, rather to than general patterns.[43] These include *becase* [bŕkez] 'because', *beyont* 'beyond', *chimbley/chimley*, *drap* 'drop', *drouth* 'drought', *lenth* 'length', *massacre+e* (with the final syllable pronounced [kri]), *saft* 'soft', *on-* 'un-' (as in *oncertain* 'uncertain'), *strenth* 'strength', *ye* 'you', and *yo* 'ewe', all of which can be characterized as unabsorbed relics in American English, consistent with what other scholars have found.[44] By contrast, grammatical items are more numerous (between forty-five and fifty, depending on how broadly one defines 'grammatical') and often more prominent in American English. Here the Ulster influence is very often not in the forms themselves so much as in their functions (e.g. the adverbial conjunction *whenever*) or syntax (e.g. the pronoun phrase *who all*). While much has been written about the structure, functions, and in some cases the semantics of grammatical features entered here as they appear in modern American English, these dimensions can be understood only imperfectly without the historical perspective that the present work provides.[45]

If the evidence here confirms existing linguistic literature in pointing to a modest Ulster contribution to American pronunciation and an extensive one to American grammar, the lexical inheritance of American English from Ulster has, by contrast, been heretofore a much more open question. Why this is so has in part been suggested already: the unfamiliarity of American linguists with documentation in the British Isles, compounded by its lack of availability. Complicating these factors is an often inadequate understanding of the historical relationship between Ulster and Britain in the Early Modern Period (the sixteenth through the eighteenth centuries). One cannot view Ulster as one of several parts of the British Isles from which early American settlers came, all of which parts can be used independently in seeking simple and direct correspondences of terms between British and American regions. (Such an exercise could more justifiably be undertaken between Britain and Ireland for the seventeenth and eighteenth centuries). Scotland and northern England in many ways formed a general speech area with Ulster because the latter's speech is by and large derived from them, as a result of events of the seventeenth century, As demonstrated by the present volume, these difficulties can be addressed and partially overcome when good linguistic spadework is done. Works on the history of American English rarely say anything about how much of it can be traced to various parts of the British Isles or even raise the question. For example, Marckwardt's *American English*, one of the fullest accounts of Old World roots, presents the inheritance from a number of European languages and even touches on contributions from African ones, but has nothing on regional varieties of British or Irish English.[46] From standard treatments, it is as if regional speech from the British Isles played a trivial role in dialect formation in the history of American English, owing to leveling processes in the eighteenth century or for other reasons. This view, though undoubtedly reflecting Kurath's failure to demonstrate the transatlantic correlations that he once anticipated finding (for which he has been chastised)[47] is quite unfounded. Good examples are how German and Scotch-Irish speech patterns merged and reinforced one another in Pennsylvania or how Scotch-Irish speech influenced Pennsylvania German.[48] *DARE* often suggests something about the British regional ancestry of terms brought to America, but employs only broad demarcations (such as 'northern England' or 'Scotland', never 'Ulster' and rarely 'nIrel[and]'), and these are based on the *EDD* and *SND*. Use of the latter work enables the dictionary to give an unprecedented register of items of immediate or ultimate Scottish provenance, but, as shown below, causes it to under-represent significantly the contribution from Ireland, especially from Ulster.

Beyond entries included to show connections in pronunciation and grammar, this work contains approximately 320 lexical items attributable primarily (and sometimes exclusively) to Ulster. A closer look at this large and quite diverse set of terms is justified. The majority are nouns, but conjunctions, prepositions, adverbs, adjectives, pronouns, verbs, and even interjections (e.g. *sook* [a feeding call to livestock]) are also well represented. The semantic domains into which they fall are many, and one certainly cannot conclude that they were preponderantly connected with folk culture and attribute their obsolescence to this. In distillery the Ulster contribution is particularly marked, with *double/doubling, first shot, flake stand, mountain dew, run* (of liquor), *singling* and *worm* having crossed the Atlantic. Even so, it did not involve the simple transportation of vocabulary; these terms pertain in Ireland to the making of poteen, but in America to the distillation of whiskey. The two processes are closely related, but by no means identical.

The regional distribution of the Ulster-derived vocabulary in the United States is overwhelmingly Midland, the settlement-based territory outlined and defined by Kurath, stretching from east-central Pennsylvania to north-east Georgia.[49] Many terms are found primarily in Pennsylvania (e.g. *dinge* 'dent', *hap* 'bedspread', *nebby* 'nosey', *slippy* 'slippery', and *want* + past participle) and may have hardly passed beyond this primary settlement area. Twenty-nine items have only a single citation, from Shoemaker's glossary from the central Pennsylvania mountains (e.g. *bole* 'small recess in a wall, *crusie* 'small oil-burning house-lamp'). If we consider the first four volumes of *DARE* (letters A–Sk), we find that they assign labels to 138 of the 306 items contained in the present work for the same part of the alphabet. These labels indicate the regional distribution of the 138, if this is coherent or discernible, in the late twentieth century: South Midland 77, South 66, Midland 20, Appalachia 18, Pennsylvania 7, Northeast 4, New England 3, North Central 3, Mid Atlantic 2, Ohio Valley 2, Ozarks 2, South Atlantic 2, West 2, Central Atlantic 1, Great Lakes 1, Maryland 1, North 1, North Atlantic 1, North Carolina 1, North Central 1, North Midland 1, Ohio 1, Oklahoma 1, Texas 1, Upper Midwest 1, West Midland 1, West Virginia 1.[50] These labels reflect both where terms were planted and where they survived. Only five of 138 items labeled by *DARE* were not found in the Midland region: e.g. *fleech* 'to coax, wheedle, flatter', identified by *DARE* as South Atlantic. The large number assigned to the South (54) is deceptive, because none of these were found in that region alone (e.g. 52 are labeled 'South, South Midland').

The earlier history of items is mixed, but even counting those for which this cannot be determined, they are predominantly (more than 60 percent) from Scotland and northern England (e.g. *barefoot(ed)* 'having no spare ingredients', *body* 'person', *childer* 'children', *first foot* 'New Year's Eve custom', *flit* 'to move house', *galluses* 'suspenders', *gumption* 'common sense, shrewdness', *ill* 'vicious', *infare* 'wedding feast', *leave* 'to allow (to)', *piece* 'distance', and *reel foot* 'club foot'). Perhaps surprisingly, only eight are from Irish Gaelic (*bonny clabber* 'curdled sour milk', *clabber* 'mud, mire', *donsie* 'sickly, frail', *dornick* 'small, round stone', *moiley/muley* 'hornless cow', *streal* 'to trail along the ground', *striffin* 'membrane, thin skin', and *suggan*), suggesting little contact between incoming plantation settlers and the native Irish, and some of these terms might have been borrowed into Lowland Scots from Scottish Gaelic before then being taken to Ireland and being reinforced there by Irish. Terms indigenous to Ulster include *diamond* 'town square', and quite possibly positive *anymore* (which may be based on an underlying Irish structure).

This work turned up many items whose historical record in the *OED* now requires revision in three regards. Cases in which *OED* evidence needs to be postdated include *for why* 'why' (documented in that work only until 1710), *aneath* 'beneath' (documented there only until 1825), and others that are attested in Ulster down to the present day. Antedatings include *clabber* (documented by the *OED* only from 1824, eleven years after this work) and others. These two types of shortcomings only begin to show the inadequacy of the *OED*'s coverage of Ireland, which can be overcome only by launching a full-scale reading program for the on-going work for its third edition. Although English has been spoken there since the twelfth century and by the majority of the population for approximately two hundred years, Ireland remains a land without a comprehensive historical dictionary of its English for the *OED* to bank on. As a result, any examination finds innumerable gaps (either of dated citations or of terms altogether) for which evidence from Ireland has been missed. The result of this situation is a third shortcoming: erroneous geographical labels. For example, the *OED* identifies as 'Scottish and United States' terms such as *back* 'address a letter', *residenter* 'older member of a community', *sook* (feeding call to animals), *stay* 'reside', and others attested herein for Ireland. It labels as 'Scottish' *backset* 'relapse of an illness', *gab* 'mouth', *rue back* 'regret', *scrunt* 'runt of a litter' and so on that have been well known in Ireland and documented herein for Ulster. Other items are labeled by the *OED* as 'Scottish and northern [English]' (*fornent* 'nearby, opposite', *hantle* 'large amount', *hippin* 'diaper, nappy', *scunner* 'to disgust', and *what for* 'why') or as 'Scottish, northern English and United States' (*infare* 'wedding feast', *jag* 'to prick'), or 'United States' (*dornick* 'small, round stone', *doubletree* 'double horizontal bar at the front of a wagon', *who all* 'who'). That the *OED* has not yet found any of these in Ireland calls into question the basic reliability of its labeling practices.

Quite a few of the forms inherited from Ulster are simple retentions from the old country that maintained the same meaning in the new. These include *backset*, *bad man* 'the Devil', *doless* 'lazy, shiftless, dilatory', *galluses* and *residenter*. Sometimes it was a minority sense that was transplanted to America, as *banter* 'to challenge, taunt, dare to fight' or *blackguard* 'to abuse verbally, especially with profanity'. Retentions are only part of the story, however, and probably not the most interesting one. Many of the vocabulary items traceable to Ulster shifted semantically in one way or another. For example, in Ulster *backing(s)* refers to 'refuse from the production of flax, cloth or wool', but in the United States to 'refuse from the distillation of whiskey'. *Bannock* in Ulster is a hard bread usually made from oats, in America usually from corn meal. Sometimes the shift was quite rapid and dramatic, in no case more so than with *cracker*, which in Ulster meant/means 'boaster, brash talker', but in America early on became applied to back-country inhabitants who were not only brash but often unsavory (see relevant citations).

In the United States the meaning of some terms broadened or became generalized. *Clabber*, for example, refers to mud or mire in Ulster, but in America also to curdled milk (perhaps under the influence of *bonny clabber*). *Meeting house* 'house of worship' in Ulster was limited to Presbyterian and Quaker traditions, but in the United States was adopted by Baptists and Methodists. Other terms narrowed in meaning or function. As a verb *blink* in Ulster has meant 'to bewitch' and by extension 'to cause to sour (presumably under the influence of a spell)', but in America only 'of milk: to sour (from lack of being kept cool)' (soured milk is called *blinked milk* or *blinky* in the United States, terms apparently unknown in Ireland). *Hap* 'coverlet' in Ulster is also a verb meaning 'to cover, enclose'. Examples of functional shift from one part of speech to another include *brogue* ('a heavy shoe' in Ulster, but also 'to walk or wander about' in America) and *spang* (in Ulster only a noun or verb meaning 'a sudden leap or bound, to leap or bound suddenly', but in America only an adverb meaning 'directly, absolutely, completely'). Further research may turn up the missing links on one side of the Atlantic or the other for such terms. At least one shifted form owing to folk etymology: *moiley* 'hornless cow' in America became *muley*, presumably under the influence of *mule*.

A major goal of this volume has been to address gaps not only in the *OED* but also in *DARE*. One very large one, shown by *DARE's* indexes,[51] is the striking disparity in the number of terms it connects to Scotland and Ireland. Several times as many emigrants came from Ireland, but *DARE* identifies 522 items as 'Scotland', 'Scots', or 'Scottish' and barely one-ninth of this number (59) as 'Ireland', 'Irish', or 'nIrel[and]'. For all *DARE's* vastness and wonder, these figures show quite dramatically that any dictionary can be only as good or as complete as its sources. *DARE* had at hand two magnificent multi-volume dictionaries from Scotland (*DOST* and *SND*), while the impoverished lexicographical record from Ireland has provided little guidance. A similar disparity in *DARE* is revealed by another comparison. The 306 items listed here in the A–Sk section are more than five times as identified by *DARE* as 'Ireland', 'Irish', or 'nIrel[and]' (59). *DARE* contains nearly all 306, but references only 14 to Ireland (e.g. *dinge*, *need* + past participle), as compared with 80 to Scotland.

It should therefore not come as a surprise that the Scotch-Irish inheritance is not clearly seen in *DARE*, or in this regard that the larger picture of earlier American English suggested by *DARE* is out of focus. The comparative proportion of its terms connected to Scotland and Ireland, the reverse of what emigration history would predict, has a simple and elegant resolution once we take into account the internal history of the British Isles, that Ulster was a colony of Britain and that North America was a colony of both. The 522 items that *DARE* connects to Scotland are therefore too many, the 59 that it connects to Ireland far too few. This is why the debt American English has to Ulster can be reckoned to be as substantial and important as any other from the British Isles and rivaled by few, if any, from mainland Europe. Revisions of major historical dictionaries should now follow suit and rectify this situation, and historical accounts of English, especially American English, should take due notice of both the extensive record of English in Ireland and the fundamental role of Ulster in particular in providing input to varieties of American English.

Notes

1   Herein 'Ulster' refers to the historical nine-county province rather than to present-day six-county Northern Ireland. Emigrants to America were particularly prominent from one of the three historical counties (Donegal) now in the Republic of Ireland.

2   Appalachia is a large region defined in various ways. Geologically it stretches from New England to Alabama, socio-economically from New York State to Mississippi (according to the Appalachian Regional Commission, an agency of the United States federal government), and culturally from western Pennsylvania to northern Alabama. Throughout the United States (and increasingly in Ireland and Scotland) the core part of the region, from West Virginia to north Georgia, is often considered a highly valued repository of traditional music, language, storytelling, and so on.

3 Ian Adamson, *The Identity of Ulster: The Land, the Language, and the People* (Bangor: Pretani, 1982), 44. Adamson does not indicate his source for this information and, upon personal inquiry from the author, was unable to recall it.

4 For further information on the historical currency and validity of this term see Michael Montgomery, 'Nomenclature for Ulster Emigrants: *Scotch-Irish* or *Scots-Irish?*', *Familia* 20 (2004): 16–36.

5 Using various indices and methodologies, historians have sought for well over a century to estimate the pre-revolutionary emigrants from Ulster. The minimum number of 150,000 was the consensus (reached at its meeting in Staunton, Virginia, in September 2003) of the United States Scholarship Panel commissioned by the Ulster American Folk Park to advise it on developing a new outdoor exhibit. This team comprised eight American academics, including several historians of emigration: Katharine Brown, Warren Hofstra, Kenneth Keller, Richard MacMaster, Kerby A. Miller, Michael Montgomery, Anita Puckett and Marianne Wokeck. It agreed that the figure may have been much higher, but that 150,000 was a minimum for those coming from Ulster between 1718 and 1776 and 500,000 for those coming between 1680 and 1830.

6 Patrick Griffin, *The People with No Name: Ireland's Ulster Scots, America's Scots Irish and the Creation of a British Atlantic World, 1689–1764* (Princeton, N.J.: Princeton University Press, 2001), 1.

7 Hans Kurath, 'The Origin of Dialectal Differences in Spoken American English', *Modern Philology* 25 (1928): 385–95.

8 Frederick Jackson Turner, 'The Old West', in *The Frontier in American History* (New York: Holt, 1920), 67–125.

9 Kurath, *op. cit.*, 391–2.

10 Hans Kurath, *Word Geography of the Eastern United States* (Ann Arbor: University of Michigan Press, 1949), 3–4.

11 Kurath, *op. cit.*, 1949, 91.

12 He almost certainly did use the *English Dialect Dictionary*, but does not indicate this.

13 John Harrison, *The Scot in Ulster: Sketch of the History of the Scottish Population of Ulster* (Edinburgh: Blackwood, 1888); Charles A. Hanna, *The Scotch-Irish or the Scot in North Britain, North Ireland, and North America*, 2 vols (New York, N.Y.: Putnam, 1902); Henry Jones Ford, *The Scotch-Irish in America* (Princeton, N.J.: Princeton University Press, 1915); Rory Fitzpatrick, *God's Frontiersmen: The Scots-Irish Epic* (London: Weidenfeld & Nicolson, 1989); Billy Kennedy, *The Scots-Irish in the Hills of Tennessee* (Londonderry: Causeway, 1995).

14 James G. Leyburn, *The Scotch-Irish: A Social History* (Chapel Hill, N.C.: University of North Carolina Press, 1962); R. J. Dickson, *Ulster Emigration to Colonial America, 1718–1775* (London: Routledge & Kegan Paul, 1966; repr. Belfast: Ulster Historical Foundation, 1987); David N. Doyle, *Ireland, Irishmen and Revolutionary America, 1760–1820* (Dublin: Mercier, 1981); Kerby A. Miller, *Emigrants and Exiles* (New York: Oxford University Press, 1985).

15 Robert McCrum, William Cran and Robert MacNeil, *The Story of English* (New York: Viking. 1986), 127–61.

16 David Hackett Fischer, *Albion's Seed: Four British Folkways in America* (New York: Oxford University Press, 1989).

17 Alan S. Crozier, 'The Scotch-Irish Influence on American English', *American Speech* 59 (1984): 310–31.

18 Peter Gilmore, ed., 'Scots-Irish' Words from Pennsylvania's Mountains taken from the Shoemaker Collection (Bruceton Mills, W.V.: Scotpress, 1999).

19 For example, where appropriate (which is often), they employ 'perhaps' in positing a connection, a qualifying word for all intents and purposes not in Fischer's vocabulary.

20 For this concept as applied to reconstructing language patterns see Michael Montgomery, 'British and Irish Antecedents', in John Algeo, ed. Cambridge History of the English Language, Vol. 6: English in North America (Cambridge: Cambridge University Press, 2001), 95.

21 Michael V. Barry, 'The Southern Boundaries of Northern Hiberno-English Speech', in Aspects of English Dialects in Ireland 1 (Belfast: Institute of Irish Studies, 1981), 52–95; John Harris, 'English in the North of Ireland', in Peter Trudgill, ed., Language in the British Isles (Cambridge: Cambridge University Press, 1994), 115–34; Michael Montgomery, 'The Position of Ulster Scots', Ulster Folklife 45 (1999): 86–107.

22 This figure is estimated by Miller, op. cit., 3.

23 It must be granted that this topic warrants further investigation. Although folk etymologies from Irish are legion (e.g. so long from slán), scholarly assessment of what Irish emigrants might have contributed to local urban varieties of American English, or to American slang generally, remains to be undertaken. See Michael Montgomery, 'The Celtic Element in American English', in Hildegard Tristram, ed., Celtic Englishes II (Heidelberg: Winter, 2001), 231–64.

24 For example, compare Bernard Share, Slanguage (Dublin: Gill & Macmillan, 1997; 2nd ed. 2004) and Terence P. Dolan, ed., Dictionary of Hiberno-English (Dublin: Gill & Macmillan, 1998; 2nd ed. 2004) with Caroline Macafee, ed., A Concise Ulster Dictionary (Oxford: Oxford University Press, 1996).

25 Joseph Wright, ed., English Dialect Dictionary, 6 vols (London: Henry Frowde, 1898–1905); William Grant and David Murison, eds, The Scottish National Dictionary, 10 vols. (Edinburgh: Scottish National Dictionary Association, 1931–76).

26 John Jamieson, Etymological Dictionary of the Scottish Language (Edinburgh: Creech, 1808); William H. Patterson, A Glossary of Words in Use in the Counties of Antrim and Down (London: English Dialect Society, 1880); Michael Traynor, ed., The English Dialect of Donegal: A Glossary, incorporating the Collections of H. C. Hart, etc. (Dublin: Royal Irish Academy, 1953).

27 Diarmaid Ó Muirithe, Dictionary of Anglo-Irish: Words and Phrases from Gaelic in the English of Ireland (Dublin: Four Courts, 1996); Share, op. cit.; Dolan, op. cit.

28 James Fenton, The Hamely Tongue: A Personal Record of Ulster-Scots in County Antrim (Newtownards: Ulster-Scots Academic Press for the Ulster-Scots Language Society, 1995; 2nd. ed. 2000, Belfast: Ullans Press for the Ulster-Scots Language Society); Macafee, op. cit.

29 Frederic G. Cassidy and Joan Houston Hall, eds, Dictionary of American Regional English (Cambridge, Mass.: Belknap Press of Harvard University, 1985–).

30 John W. Byers, 'Glossary', typescript on deposit at Ulster Folk and Transport Museum, Cultra, c1910; R. H. Montgomery, 'Heard in Ulster', manuscript on deposit at Ulster Folk and Transport Museum, Cultra, c1955.

31 The second and third of these are now merged electronically in the online Dictionary of the Scots Language (www.dsl.ac.uk).

32 Dolan, *op. cit.*; George Story, John Widdowson and William Kirwin, eds, *Dictionary of Newfoundland English* (Toronto: University of Toronto Press, 1982).

33 Philip Robinson, *The Plantation of Ulster: British Settlement in an Irish Landscape, 1600–1670* (Dublin: Gill & Macmillan, 1984; repr. Belfast: Ulster Historical Foundation, 1993).

34 The *OED* characterizes *hit* as moribund by the sixteenth century except in north Britain; the *EDD* labels it 'Scotland, Northumberland, America'.

35 Niall Ó Dónaill, *Foclóir Gaeilge–Béarla* (Baile Átha Cliath: Oifig na tSolathair, 1992[1977]).

36 Edward Dwelly, *Facloir Gaidhlig gu Beurla le Dealbhan* (Glasgow: Gairm, 1994).

37 Kurath, *op. cit.*, 1949; Hans Kurath and Raven I. McDavid, Jr., *The Pronunciation of English in the Eastern United States* (Ann Arbor: University of Michigan Press, 1961).

38 Philip Gove, ed., *Webster's Third New International Dictionary* (Springfield, Mass.: Merriam–Webster, 1961).

39 Michael B. Montgomery and Joseph S. Hall, eds, *Dictionary of Smoky Mountain English* (Knoxville: University of Tennessee Press, 2004).

40 Exceptions are *crack, the*, and *yous ones* (not attested in the United States) and *hillbilly, brogan*, and *all the* (+ a comparative and superlative form of an adverb or adjective), not attested in Ulster. *Hillbilly* is included—perhaps perversely—to indicate, for the historical record, a lack of connection. In the other cases the attestation of related forms led the editor to believe that evidence will eventually be found. In a number of further cases terms are attested in one part of speech in Ulster but an entirely different one in the United States (e.g. *spang*).

41 For example, Charles Woodmason, *The Carolina Backcountry on the Eve of the Revolution*, ed. and introduced by Richard J. Hooker (Chapel Hill, N.C.: University of North Carolina Press, 1953).

42 For example, the copula / auxiliary verb *be* (less frequently *bes*, as 'She bes working in the shop') is found in both vernacular African American English and Vernacular Irish English to express a frequent event or habitual activity. A number of linguistic historians, on the presumption of sufficient early dialect contact between African American slaves and emigrants from Ireland, argue that Irish English was the original source (see John R. Rickford, 'Social Contact and Linguistic Diffusion', *Language* 62 (1986): 245–90). However, this possibility is now seen as unlikely because the feature cannot be documented before the mid-nineteenth century, after the period of presumed contact. As tantalizing a hypothesis as the connection may be, it remains in want of convincing early evidence (see Michael Montgomery and John Kirk, 'The Origin of the Habitual Verb *be* in American Black English: Irish or English or What?' *Belfast Working Papers in Linguistics* 11 (1996): 308–33).

43 For the sake of classification, these are limited to forms in which the incidence of phonemes differs from general English. Hence, this category excludes forms such as *afore* 'before'.

44 Roger Lass, *The Shape of English: Structure and History* (London: Dent, 1987), 275. Interestingly, Lass also attributes the merger of /ɑ/ and /ɔ/ in *cot* and *caught* to Ulster influence: 'Despite its recent spread into new areas, the merger itself is clearly an old one and ties in well with settlement geography. The most likely source is Ulster Scots'. (Roger Lass, 'Where do Extraterritorial Englishes Come from? Dialect Input and Recodification

in Transported Englishes', in Sylvia Adamson, ed., *Papers from the 5th International Conference on English Historical Linguistics* (Amsterdam: Benjamins, 1990), 245–80). Complicating this scenario is the fact that the merger is to a different vowel in American English (/ɑ/ or /a/) than it is in Scotland and Ulster today /ɔ/ (Lass, *op. cit.*, 1987, 286).

45 Much of the work on grammatical patterns has been undertaken by the present author. See Michael Montgomery, 'Exploring the Roots of Appalachian English'. *English World-Wide* 10 (1989): 227–78; Michael Montgomery, 'The Scotch-Irish Influence on Appalachian English: How Broad? How Deep?' in H. Tyler Blethen and Curtis W. Wood, eds. *Ulster and North America: Transatlantic Perspectives on the Scotch-Irish* (Tuscaloosa: University of Alabama Press, 1997), 189–212; Michael Montgomery, 'Solving Kurath's Puzzle: Establishing the Antecedents of the American Midland Dialect Region', in Raymond Hickey, ed., *The Legacy of Colonial English: The Study of Transported Dialects* (Cambridge: Cambridge University Press, 2004), 410–25.

46 Albert C. Marckwardt, *American English* (New York: Oxford University Press, 1958).

47 J. L. Dillard, *A History of American English* (London: Longman, 1992).

48 Michael Adams, 'Lexical Doppelgängers', *Journal of English Linguistics* 28 (2000): 295–310; Carroll Reed, 'English Archaisms in Pennsylvania German', *Publication of the American Dialect Society* 19 (1953): 3–7.

49 Kurath, *op. cit.*, 1949, 3–4.

50 Some items are labeled by *DARE* as found in more than one region or state. For the states encompassed by these regions see Cassidy and Hall, *op. cit.*, 1985–, xxxii.

51 *An Index by Region, Usage, and Etymology to the Dictionary of American Regional English, Volumes I and II*, Publication of the American Dialect Society 77 (Tuscaloosa: University of Alabama Press, 1993); *An Index by Region, Usage, and Etymology to the Dictionary of American Regional English, Volume III*, Publication of the American Dialect Society 82 (Tuscaloosa: University of Alabama Press, 1999).

ABBREVIATIONS

adj	adjective		McMillan, 1998; 2nd
adj phr	adjective phrase		ed., 2004)
adv	adverb	Dial	dialect
adv phr	adverb phrase	Dict	dictionary
Affirm	affirmative	DNE	*Dictionary of*
Amer	American		*Newfoundland English*,
Anniv	anniversary		ed. George Story, John
Appal	Appalachia		Widdowson and
Arch	archaeology		William Kirwin
Ark	Arkansas		(Toronto: University of
Atl	Atlantic		Toronto Press, 1982)
CCC	Civilian Conservation	DOST	*Dictionary of the Older*
	Corps		*Scottish Tongue*, ed.
Cent	central, century		William Craigie, A. J.
cf	compare		Aitken et al. (Chicago:
Co	County		University of Chicago
Coll	Collection		Press, and Oxford:
conj	conjunction		Oxford University
conj phr	conjunctive phrase		Press, 1931–2002)
Contrib	contributions	Engl	English
CSD	*Concise Scots Dictionary*,	Geog	geography
	ed. Mairi Robinson et	GSMNP	Great Smoky Mountains
	al. (Aberdeen: Aberdeen		National Park
	University Press, 1985)	GSMNPOHP	
CUD	*Concise Ulster Dictionary*,		Great Smoky Mountains
	ed. Caroline Macafee		National Park Oral
	(Oxford: Oxford		History Project
	University Press, 1996)	High	highlanders
DARE / DARE		interj	interjection
	Dictionary of American	Intl	international
	Regional English, ed.	Jour	Journal
	Frederic G. Cassidy and	LANE	Linguistic Atlas of New
	Joan Houston Hall		Englamd
	(Cambridge, Mass.:	LAUSC	Linguistic Atlas of the
	Belknap Press of		United States and
	Harvard University,		Canada
	1985–)	Lex	lexicon
def art	definite article	Lg	language
DHE	*Dictionary of Hiberno-*	Misc	miscellaneous
	English, ed. Terence P.	Mt, Mts	Mountain, Mountains
	Dolan (Dublin: Gill &	Mtneer	mountaineer

n	noun	SED	Survey of English
n phr	noun phrase		Dialects, ed. Harold
Natl	national		Orton et al. (Leeds:
NC	North Carolina		University of Leeds,
NITCS	Northern Ireland		1962–68)
	Transcribed Corpus of	SF	Sinn Féin
	Speech	SND	*Scottish National*
N.p.; n.p.	No place; no publisher		*Dictionary*, ed. William
NW	north-west		Grant and David
NY	New York		Murison (Edinburgh:
OED	*Oxford English*		Scottish National
	Dictionary, ed. James A.		Dictionary Association,
	H. Murray et al.		1931–76)
	(Oxford: Oxford	Sthn	southern
	University Press,	s.v.	*sub voce*
	1884–1928)	SW	south-west
Penn	Pennsylvania	Tenn	Tennessee
phr	phrase	Univ	University
prep	preposition	U.S.	United States
prep phr	prepositional phrase	vb	verb
Presby	Presbyterian	vbl n	verbal noun
pron	pronoun	vb phr	verb phrase
Pron	pronunciation	Virg	Virginia
pron phr	pronoun phrase	WEB3	*Webster's Third New*
Ques	questionnaire		*International Dictionary*,
q.v.	*quod vide*		ed. Philip Gove et al.
rel pron	relative pronoun		(Springfield, Mass.:
SC	South Carolina		Merriam-Webster,
SE	south-east		1961)

A

aback of See **back of**

abain, abane, abeen, abin See **aboon**

able *adj* Well-to-do, rich. [OED *able* 6 →1863, obsolete]
ULST.: **1953** Traynor *Donegal Glossary* 1 = well-to-do, prosperous.
1990 Todd *Words Apart* 20 They may be able enough now but I mind them when they hadn't tuppence.
U.S.: **1899** Green *Virginia Word-Book* 37 = wealthy: 'He is an able man'.
1952 Wilson *Folk Speech NC* 512 = rich, possessing considerable means.

aboon, abain, abane, abeen, abin, abune *prep, adv* Above (in the U.S. only *aboon* is attested and only as a prep). [< Middle English *aboven* < Old English *abufan/onbofan*; OED *aboon* 16th century→; DOST *abone* prep 'above, over, higher up than' 1386→, adv 4 'in (or into) the higher place or position'; DARE *aboon* prep, adv 'above, higher than' western North Carolina]
1 *prep* Above, higher than.
ULST.: **1804** Orr *Poems* 170 The herd's aboon me on the laft.
1811 Boyle *Poems* 77 Now Jock, tak' care what ye do wi't, / An' buy claith for my winnin' sheet / An' ae slit deal aboon six feet, / To mak' my coffin; / An' whan my neighbour wives do greet, / Let nane be scoffin'.
1885 Lyttle *Robin Gordon* 38 The Meer [is] the man that's aboon a' the megistrates, an' sogers an' polis.
1902 McIlroy *Druid's Island* 40 Sic talent's only wasted in the country, an' far abune ordinary people's heids.
1953 Traynor *Donegal Glossary* 1 He came from abeen Churchill.
c1955 Montgomery *Heard in Ulster* 3 He's abane that sort of thing.
1985 Gregg *Scotch-Irish* The form *abeen* dominates in south Down and Donegal, *abane* in north Antrim and Londonderry, and *aboon* elsewhere.
1991 O'Kane *You Don't Say* 1 *abeen* = often used to indicate geographical position: 'He was workin' in the field abeen the house'.
U.S.: **1944** Wilson *Word-list* 38 *aboon* = above, to think oneself superior: 'That [woman's] aboon her own kinnery'.
2 *adv* Above, overhead, upstairs.
ULST.: **1733** *North Country Description* 25 This Place was amest foo o' Foke; as weel aboon as whar I was, this they cad the Kirk.
1753 *Scotch Poems* 371 Ye'd think that a' the starns abeen, / Were gath'ring round their passing queen.
1902 McIlroy *Druid's Island* 33 'The hoose abane?' she cried oot in response tae some remark he had made.
c1910 Byers *Glossary*, *abeen, abin, aboon* = overhead, in the sky, aloft, upstairs.
1942 *Bangor Words* 1 *aboon* = above, higher up.
2000 Fenton *Hamely Tongue* 2 the Man abain = God.

acause *conj* Because. [OED *acause* < *a-* + *(be)cause*]
ULST.: **1886** Lyttle *Ballycuddy* 35 A guid wheen fowk in Ballycuddy thinks me waur than an infidel acause A want them till get a harmoneyum fur oor meetin'-hoose.

1928 Ervine *Mountain* 54 'Ye shud do a thing', he would say, 'acause ye like doin' it, not acause ye're paid t' do it!'

2003 Dodds *Newry Nyuck* It happened acause a his mistake.

U.S.:   **1922** Rollins *Cowboy* 191 I've warmed up this bit, acause I'm riding the finest little cow horse this State has ever seen.

1997 Andrews *Mt Vittles* 82 Some folks called the little varmints [i.e. ground hogs] whistle pigs a'cause of the noise they make.

account See **on account of**

ache *transitive vb* To pain, cause to hurt. [OED *ache* vb 2 'to make ache' obsolete, rare]

ULST.:   **1953** Traynor *Donegal Glossary* 2 I'll ache your head.

U.S.:   **2001** Lowry *Expressions* 18 Those breathing pills ache up my heart when I take them.

afeard, afeared, afeered *predicate adj* Afraid, frightened. Same as **feard**. [< Middle English *afered* < Old English *afēred*, past participle of *afǣran*, attested since c1000; DARE *afear(e)d* adj 'afraid' once widespread in the U.S., but now somewhat old-fashioned, chiefly South and Midland]

ULST.:   **1801** Bruce *Poems* 44 Is there ony proud Laird, / To mak ye afeard, / To wham ye maun haud off yer hat.

1840 Boyce *Shandy Maguire* 6 Am not afeered to say mony a guid wallet o' siller, I hae carried ahint me in the wee-bit saddle-bags.

1845 Carleton *Irish Peasantry* 14 May the holy Mother keep and guard us, Ned, but I'm afeard that's no Christian crather, at all at all!

1895 MacManus *Leadin' Road* 111 Masther, sir, it's afeared I am that I'm not able to make more of it.

1931 Bratton *Turf Fire* 20 Whatever other people might think about ghosts, I wasn't afeared of them anyway.

1981 Pepper *Ulster-English Dict* 7 She's afeard of her own skin.

U.S.:   **1843** Hall *New Purchase* 227 Sker'd Pete ... so powerful he was afeer'd to come down.

1871 Eggleston *Hoosier Schoolmaster* 128 'Well, I'll gin you the upper side, but come on', cried Bud, 'ef you a'n't afeared to fight somebody besides a poor, little, sickly baby or a crippled soldier.'

1937 Hall *Coll* I ain't nary bit afeared of him.

1989 Smith *Flyin' Bullets* 244 That Charles had a lot of nerve, he wasn't afeared of them in the least bit.

afore *adv, conj, prep* Of position: before, preceding, in front of. Of time: before, previous, earlier than. [< Old English *on-* 'on' + *foran* 'in front, in advance'; OED *afore* represents Old English prep *on foran, ætforan* 'in front of' c1000→ as adv, 1205→ as prep, 1340→ as conj; DOST *afore* A adv 1 'at an earlier time or date, preceding' 1494→, B prep 1 'before; earlier than' 1541→, C conj 'before' 1536→; DARE once widespread, now chiefly South, Midland]

1 *adv*

ULST.:   **1824** McHenry *Insurgent Chief* 13 I had na' sae muckle this twalmonth afore.

1895 MacManus *Leadin' Road* 15 The lake of what's goin' on in thondher I nivir rested me eyes on afore and trust I nivir may again.

1928 McKay *Oul' Town* 55 Nobody iver accused me, Paddy, of bein' backward at maletime afore.

1935 Megaw *Carragloon* 108 I know now a wee thing I didn't know afore.

1942 *Bangor Words* 1 = before: 'I have heard that afore'.

U.S.:   **1849** Lanham *Allegheny Mts* 89 Now, the way the thing happened was this, and I reckon you never heard sich like afore.

1975 Chalmers *Better* 37 I 'lowed I'd send fer you, but I done what you told me afore, and it holp me some.

2 *prep*

ULST.:   **1893** Bullock *Awkward Squad* 96 As I wus sayin', afore this interruption, these twenty or thirty blaggards took possession av the castle.

1897 McIlroy *Lint in Bell* 118 Ye'r nae man ava', that can stan' tae the yin side and let anither snap up the lass frae afore ye'r face.

c1955 Montgomery *Heard in Ulster* 5 He didnae dee afore his time.

2000 Fenton *Hamely Tongue* 3 It lucks that bad afore folk.

U.S.:   **1844** Thompson *Major Jones' Courtship* 75 She gin her galls a rite good talkin to rite afore me.

1899 Green *Virginia Word-Book* 61 A little afore day.

1937 Hall *Coll* I allowed he'd return afore this.

1955 Parris *Roaming Mts* 77 I heard the dogs a-comin' and knowed without askin' that the bear was afore them.

3 *conj*

ULST.:   **1838** McIlwham *McIlwham Papers* 15 It was lang afore the bairn got weel, an' its illness put a' ither things oot o' my head.

1895 MacManus *Leadin' Road* 22 I'll make it hot for ye afore ye go home to Susy again.

1910 Russell *Language of Ulster* 32 The word 'afore' is common in Ulster. It is used equally as meaning before in time: e.g. 'He was there afore I kem up'; or as before in place, as, 'He stud up afore him'.

c1955 Montgomery *Heard in Ulster* 3 I'll ax ye yin question afore I leave.

1983 Marshall *Drumlister* 106 I knowed a man in the mountain, / And afore he dug the spuds / He coorted a great big woman / With sweets an' cinnamon buds.

2000 Fenton *Hamely Tongue* 3 Ye could see anither war afore al's by.

U.S.:   **1871** Eggleston *Hoosier Schoolmaster* 28 Twas when my Jack, him as died afore Bud was born, was a baby.

1937 Hall *Coll* That happened afore I left the Smoky [Mountains].

1973 *GSMNP*-83:26 I was special deputy afore I was deputy under [the] high sheriff of Sevier County two year.

after *prep* (in phrase *be after* + verb + *-ing* to express an action just completed (thus *I'm after eating* = I have just eaten). [based on a pattern in Irish (for details, see **1998** Dolan *Dict Hiberno-English* 3-4); this construction rarely, if ever, survived beyond the speech of emigrants in the U.S., but it is still found in Newfoundland, cf DNE s.v. *after* prep)]

ULST.:   **1845** Carleton *Irish Peasantry* 125 'I'll warrant', observed Katty, 'we'll soon be after seein' John O'Callaghan ... sthrolling afther them, at his ase.'

c1910 Byers *Glossary* = when used with a progressive tense indicates ... completed action: 'I am after telling him' = I have just told him.

> 1955 Murphy *Culprit of Shadows* 8 Isn't that what I'm after saying?
> 1993 Montgomery *Barnish* 63 'I'm only after doing it' = I have just done that.

U.S.: 1815 Brackenridge *Modern Chivalry* 104 Teague gave his account of the matter; adding, if he had had a shillelah, he 'would have been after making him know dat the paple in dis country, could curry a horse, or a cow, or a sheep, as well as any Englishman in de world'.

again, against, agen, agin, gin *conj, prep* By the time that or of, in case of, before, in time for, in anticipation of. [these senses represent three sources that have fallen together; OED *again* B11 'against the time that, before the' obsolete; *against* prep A19 'in view of; in anticipation of, in preparation for, in time for' c1350→, conj Bb, c1300→, archaic or dialect; *gin* prep 'against (or by) a certain time' Scottish; DARE *again* prep C2 'by, before, in anticipation of' chiefly South, Midland, *against* conj C1 'at the time (that); before' chiefly southern Appalachians, Ozarks, *gin* conj² 'before, by the time that; when' chiefly South, South Midland]

1 *conj*

ULST.: 1942 *Bangor Words* 1 Have my tea ready agin I come back.

U.S.: 1814 (in 1956 Eliason *Tarheel Talk* 258) I expecte to get up the two Lower fiedds against you get these few Lines.
1875 (in 1983 Heap *Bucks Co Word List* 21) I think snow around here must have been nearly six inches deep against it was done snowing.
1908 Payne *Word-list East Alabama* 314 You better be thu that work gin I get back.
1937 Hall *Coll* We'd oughta do plenty of fishin' against the season closes.
1937 Hall *Coll* I'm goin' to get a whole lot of work done agin the week's out.
1970 *GSMNP*-26:11 He took his knife and cut him ... just cut him till he bled to death again they could get him home.
1976 *GSMNP*-113:10 Gin he got to me it was summer, you know.
1983 Broaddus and McAtee *Estill Co Word List* 29 I'll have dinner ready agin you get back.

2 *prep*

ULST.: 1881 Hart *Mere Irish* 142 I'll be back to ye again dusk, to hear that ye've got it.
c1910 Byers *Glossary* The lamp'll be out agin the morn; He'll be here against 10 o'clock.
1930 Shiels *Mt Dew* 19 What am I to do agen to-morrow? If I can't pay the fine they'll gaol me.
1942 *Bangor Words* 1 *agin* = again or against, when the time comes: 'That'll come in useful agin Christmas'.
1953 Traynor *Donegal Glossary* 119 He'll be ten years old gin March.
c1955 Montgomery *Heard in Ulster* 4 Put bye again a rainy day.
2000 Fenton *Hamely Tongue* 85 A should hae daen gin Seterday.

U.S.: 1830 (in 1956 Eliason *Tarheel Talk* 258) 4 bsls. of wheet at $1.00. If paid again Christmas if not $1.25.
1899 Green *Virginia Word-Book* 160 = against a certain time, by, as 'I'll be there gin five o'clock'.
1939 Hall *Coll* He'll be in town against nine o'clock.
1973 *GSMNP*-87:2:28 He didn't make it back again the night.

agg See **egg**

agin See **again**

ahind, ahin, ahine, ahint *prep, adv* Behind, at the back of. [reduced form of *at*) + -*hind*; < Middle English *a-hind* < Old English *at-hindan*; OED *ahind* prep 'behind'; SND *ahint* 1768→; DARE *ahind* 'behind' chiefly Midland]

1 *prep*

ULST.:   **1840** Boyce *Shandy Maguire* 6 Am not afeered to say mony a guid wallet o' siller, I hae carried ahint me in the wee-bit saddle-bags.
    1885 Lyttle *Robin Gordon* 52 A'll warrant you'll no' be far ahint her.
    1901 Savage-Armstrong *Ballads of Down* 119 The sun's ahint the brae; / A can nae langer stay, noo.
    1902 McIlroy *Druid's Island* 27 A'll sweer there are some commit-tees that are no' very far ahin' them.
    1930 MacNeill *Told to Reverence* 87 When the door's closed ahind me I slip back and creep into the wee pig-house over thonder in the corner.
    c1955 Montgomery *Heard in Ulster* 5 There is something ahint the dour.
    1993 Montgomery *Barnish* 5 ahint, ahine.
    2002 Gillen *Wizard's Quill* 1 Whun iver I got near the hall I already hard the band / So I fired the oul bicycle ahint the cream'ry stan'.

U.S.:   **1871** Eggleston *Hoosier Schoolmaster* 32 He's been and gone and pulled back the board that you have to step on to git ahind your desk.
    1884 Murfree *In Tenn Mts* 250 He war a-ridin' a-hint him.

2 *adv*

ULST.:   **1900** Given *Poems* 235 The tentless, trailin' on ahint, / Are scarcely worth disdainin'.
    1901 Savage-Armstrong *Ballads of Down* 189 They're moanin' there, they're jibberin' here, / Ahint, afore, they're flittin', / They're getherin' far, they're crowdin' near, / Or cloak'd an' dumb they're sittin'.

U.S.:   **1958** Wood *Words from Tenn* 6.

all See **what all; who all**

all the *adj phr*

1 (before a singular count noun or the pronoun *one*) The only (thus, *all the one/a' the yin* = the only one). [SND *all the one* (at *all* (4)); DARE *all* adj[1] chiefly South, Midland]

ULST.:   **1880** Patterson *Antrim/Down Glossary* 2 *all the one* = the only one: 'Is this all the one you have?'
    1881 Hart *Mere Irish* 80 Teague was well to do in the world; and maybe that was all the reason that Peggy Phelan had for marrying him.
    c1910 Byers *Glossary* He's all the son he has.
    1920 McCallin *Fireside Tales* 86 The girl didn't come up till her standard in worl'ly gear—and that was all the fault she had.
    1921 O'Neill *More Songs of Glens* 29 You were all the daughter she had, an' faith, twas just as well!
    1948 Marshall *Planted by River* 43-44 It's all the road we have for ourselves, barrin' we take a roundabout.
    1982 Glassie *Folk History* 41 Well, do ye see, in them days all the part of Ireland that was free from English rule was the province of Ulster.

2000 Fenton *Hamely Tongue* 1 A wush A could gie ye a better yin, but that's a' the yin A hae.

U.S.: **1814** Hartsell *Journal* 143 he was all the purson that Dyed out of our ridgement yet.

1871 Eggleston *Hoosier Schoolmaster* 100 Mr. Pearson, you're all the friend I've got, and I want you to save my boy.

1959 Hall *Coll* (Newport TN) [H]e had about eight or ten on [the string], speckled trout—that's all the kind they was back in what they called Laurel Creek.

1973 *GSMNP*-74:14 In Sugarlands that's all the one I know anything about.

1974 *GSMNP*-50:1:23 That was all the job I ever could get then.

1981 *GSMNP*-117:35 We didn't know nothin', all the thing we knowed was what the teacher told us around the school.

2 (modifying nouns or the positive form of adverbs, to express extent) As ... as (thus, *all the far* = how far, all the distance that, as far as; *all the height* = as high as). [DARE *all the* chiefly South, South Midland]

ULST.: **c1910** Byers *Glossary* That's all the far I can go.

1932 Quinn *Quiet Twelfth* 101-02 Is that all the far ye've got? Didn't I tell you to slip out by the bedroom window?

2000 Fenton *Hamely Tongue* 1 Efter a' these years, is that a' the weel ye know me?; For a' the far it is, there's naethin tae hinther ye tae trevel.

2003 Dodds *Newry Nyuck* Six feet—is that all the height it is?

U.S.: **1908** Payne *Word-list East Alabama* 286 = as ... as. This is a very common usage, found even among the well educated in such expressions as 'all the far', 'all the high', 'all the fast', etc.: 'That's all the fast I can run'.

1975 Montgomery *File* That's all the far I want to go.

3 In the U.S. the pattern in §2 has been extended to comparative and superlative forms of adverbs or adjectives, to express extent (thus *all the faster* = as fast as; *all the best* = as good as). [DARE *all the* chiefly Inland North, North Midland]

U.S.: **1931** Maxfield *Speech SW Penn* 19 *all the bigger* = as big as: 'Is that all the bigger they get?'

1956 McAtee *Some Dial NC* 2 Is that all the faster you can run?

1968 *DARE Coll* This is all the further we can go.

1982 Barrick *Coll, all the farther* = as far as: 'This is all the farther it went'.

1996 Montgomery *Coll* Is that all the best you can do?

2004 *Pittsburgh Dictionary* I started driving to Philadelphia but it started to snow and Harrisburg was all the further I got.

2004 Wellman *Underground Railroad* It's slippery kind of evidence, but it's all the best we've got.

alow, alo *adv, prep* Below; downwards. [*a-* < Old English *on-* + *low*; OED *alow* adv 1 'of position: low down, below'; SND *alow* 'below' formed by analogy with *afore*]

ULST.: **1885** Lyttle *Robin Gordon* 75 'Look yonner', an' he pointed to a gentleman stannin' doon alow us in a nice karpeted place.

1900 McIlroy *Craig-Linnie Burn* 36 Thir's nae doot they're no' vera conseederate doon 'alow.

1902 McIlroy *Druid's Island* 34 He's in alow the h'y.

2002 Gillen *Wizard's Quill* 1 I sprayed alo mae oxters an' poothered a' mae feet / In case that they got scadded wi' dancin' in the heat.

U.S.: 1945 Colcord *Sea Language* 23 = down, downwards. The word is now obsolete except in the phrase, alow and aloft, meaning completely.

anayth See **aneath**

and *conj*
  1 (introducing a nominative absolute phrase, usually with ellipsis of the non-finite verb form *being*) What with, while at the same time, because, despite the fact. [probably from influence of Irish and Scottish Gaelic *agus*, used as both a co-ordinating and subordinating conjunction; DOST *and* conj 1c 'seeing that' late 15th century→; see also DHE]
  ULST.: 1840 Boyce *Shandy Maguire* 77 He's a bad man, Miss Ellen, to brak a poor girl's heart that way, an' her not doin' any harm.
    1889 Hart *Derryreel* 159 It's far for me to travel, and me with a beeled toe.
    1920 Ervine *Mrs Martin's Man* 32 It's quare to think of my da lyin' there, with your child on the top of him, an' him hadn't a word to say to you, an' him dyin'.
    1928 Ervine *Mountain* 150 A fine young fella like meself has to lave his country an' go til a strange lan' fur to earn a livin'! ... An' me willin' an' able til work, an' not a han's turn can I get til do.
    1933 Foster *Tyrone among Bushes* 86 'I never knew till you're standin' fornenst me', she said reproachfully, 'an' me sittin' here my lone an' frettin' meself to death over a cow.'
    1955 Murphy *Culprit of Shadows* 6 I don't know how a body could be content to sit an' smoke behind that jamb-wall at the fire an' it so dark.
    1982 Glassie *Folk History* 103 They could play cards and them sittin at the fire.
    1998 Dolan *Dict Hiberno-English* 9 = this word has a much wider range of use in [Hiberno-English] than in [Standard English], because in Irish the conjunction *agus* (and) commonly functions as a subordinating adverbial conjunction (e.g. 'when', 'because', 'although', 'if') followed by a pronoun and the non-finite part of the verb and an infinitive.
    2000 Fenton *Hamely Tongue* 6 ... expectin me tae work, an me kilt wae pens.
  U.S.: 1834 Crockett *Narrative* 40 [I] was, of course, left with no money, and but very few clothes, and them very indifferent ones.
    1939 Hall *Coll* That woman is doin' too much work, and her in a family way.
    1976 Carter *Little Tree* 75 Granpa said that he couldn't have done any better hisself, and him going on seventy odd years.
  2 If. [OED *and* C1(a) 'if, suppose that, provided that' 1205→1711]
  ULST.: 1942 *Bangor Words* 2 And I catch you there again, I'll warm your ears.
    1953 Traynor *Donegal Glossary* 5 An it please your honor.
  U.S.: 1973 GSMNP-2 And they'd found able bodied men that wasn't in the service, bang, they'd kill 'em.

ane See **one**

aneath, anayth *adv, prep* Beneath, under. [*a-* (< Old English *on-*) + *neath*; OED *aneath* 'below' 1801→1825; SND *aneath* 'beneath; below; under' formed by analogy with *afore* 1540→]
  ULST.: 1722 Starrat *Epistle* 70 I in the Beild of yon auld Birk-tree Side / Poor cauldrife Coly whing'd aneath my Plaid.

1753 *Scotch Poems* 375 And what's far mair, for there's the joak, / You'll think the pig's aneath his cloak.
c1800 Thomson (in **1992** Scott and Robinson *Samuel Thomson* 89) I kenna how, aneath the sin, / Ye cou'd a kept a house within.
1825 McHenry *Hearts of Steel* 53 I ha'e the comfort, therefore, to think that it's likely my head will lie aneath the grass before that day comes.
1901 Savage-Armstrong *Ballads of Down* 52 He plunged through the gep in his glee; / But whun he got intil the loanin' anayth, / De'il a glimpse o' the hare cud he see!
c1910 Byers *Glossary, aneath* = beneath.
2003 Dodds *Newry Nyuck* Shove them boxes aneath the table outa the way.
U.S.:   **1952** Wilson *Folk Speech NC* 515 = beneath.

anent *prep* Close to, near, against, beside; in front of, opposite; concerning, about. [< Middle English *onevent, anent* < Old English *on efen* 'on even ground'; OED *anent* 'fronting, opposite, over against, close against, close to' 13th century→, archaic or dialect, now literary but old-fashioned; DOST *anent* prep 'over against, opposite, in front of' 1375→, 3 'with respect or reference to' 14th century→]
ULST.:   **1813** Porter *Glossary Poetical Attempts* = against.
            c1910 Byers *Glossary* = opposite, in front of: 'We stopped anent the gate'.
            1942 *Bangor Words* 2 = over against, opposite to.
            1953 Traynor *Donegal Glossary* 6 = near to, alongside: 'Sit ye anent me'.
            1993 Montgomery *Barnish* 6 = in a line with; concerning, about.
            1998 Dolan *Dict Hiberno-English* 10 = concerning, opposite.
U.S.:   **1895** Edson and Fairchild *Tenn Mts* 370 It was anent two houses.
            1930 Shoemaker *1300 Penn Words* 2 = opposite.
            1939 Hall *Coll* I fell back into the river and just took up right up in the water and was wet all over and got up anent them.
            1974 Fink *Bits Mt Speech* 1 = close to or by: 'His house stood anent the church house'.

antic, antick *adj* Usually of a person: clownish, amusing, animated, odd. [DARE chiefly South Midland]
ULST.:   **1880** Patterson *Antrim/Down Glossary* 3 = funny, droll: 'He's very antic'.
            c1910 Byers *Glossary* 'He's an antic boy that' = an oddity, either in dress or behaviour.
            1932 Quinn *Quiet Twelfth* 106 If ye start any of yer antic capers here, Joe Anderson, Oul' Johnny won't put wan fut over the threshold this day.
            1953 Traynor *Donegal Glossary* 6 He's an antic lad.
            1964 Braidwood *Ulster/Elizabethan English* 93 *Antic* as an adjective is now archaic. The Ulster Dialect Archive records it in the sense of 'funny, droll', which is merely a slight weakening of its original force, 'fantastic, ludicrous, even grotesque'.
            2000 Fenton *Hamely Tongue* 6 a rail antic wee boy.
U.S.:   (also **anticky**)
            1930 Shoemaker *1300 Penn Words* 1 *antic* = odd, full of tricks.
            1937 Haun *Cocke Co* 2 Piedy cows sometimes get contrarious, and calves pert-nigh always have on antic spells.
            c1945 Haun *Hawk's Done* 260 Long Boy got to looking puny and not being very anticky.
            1953 Randolph and Wilson *Down in Holler* 223 *antick* = playful, 'fresh',

sometimes wild or ungovernable: 'Charley's gettin' too antick round them Burton gals' generally means only that he pinched the girls' leg, or something of the sort.
1974 Fink *Bits Mt Speech* 1 He was an antic sort of fellow.

anunder See **in under**

anymore, any more *adv* (in positive constructions) In Ulster used predominantly in the future tense to mean 'from now on', a usage unknown in the U.S., where the form occurs in the present tense with the meaning 'now, nowadays, at present', i.e. to indicate a contrasting state of affairs to the past. For the Irish source of the Ulster construction see **1984** Crozier citation. [OED (at *more* C4) 'from now on' 1898→; DARE *anymore* 'in positive constructions: nowadays, now' scattered, but least frequent New England]
ULST.:   **1953** Traynor *Donegal Glossary* 7 I think it'll be fine any more; The water in the well is better and I'll go there any more.
      1984 Crozier *Scotch-Irish Influence* 318 = this usage is of Gaelic origin: Irish *feasta* in affirmative sentences means 'from now on' and in negative sentences '(not) any more'.
      1995 Montgomery *Ulster File* The Orange marches have become increasingly working class. If they have money, middle-class people go on holiday for the Twelfth anymore.
      1998 Dolan *Dict Hiberno-English* 11 I swear I'll do it any more.
U.S.:   **1931** Malone *Any More in Affirm* 460 People used to shop a lot in the morning, but any more the crowd comes in about three o'clock.
      1931 Maxfield *Speech SW Penn* 19 *anymore* 19 = at present, now: 'It's quite warm anymore', or 'It's pretty poor anymore'.
      1978 Montgomery *White Pine Coll* III-1 Politics moves so fast and in such mysterious ways anymore, it's hard to keep up with it.
      1982 Ginns *Snowbird Gravy* 16 [W]e called it 'hog' all the time. Anymore, they call it 'pork'.
      1982 McCool *Pittsburghese* 2 = signifies a prevailing condition or situation, as in 'Anymore there's so many new buildings, you can't tell which is which'.
      1996 Montgomery *File* Anymore I want Christmas to be a quiet time.
      2004 *Pittsburgh Dictionary* Anymore, the traffic on Liberty Avenue moves so slow, it's quicker to walk.

appearant *adj* Apparent. Hence **appearantly, appearingly, appearinly** *adv* Apparently. [cf SND *appearandly* adv; DARE *appearantly* adv chiefly Midland]
ULST.:   **1905** Marshall *Dial of Ulster* 66 *appearantly* = apparently.
      c1910 Byers *Glossary*, *appearantly, appearingly* It's a lively day appearingly.
      1930 McCurry *Ulster Village* 134 It's a wee song made by somebody raired in Co. Tyrone who went t'Australia and made a fortune, an' appearantly it has not made him happy, for he's aye thinkin' long for the place he come from.
      2000 Fenton *Hamely Tongue* 6 *appearinly*.
U.S.:   **1908** Payne *Word-list East Alabama* 287 *appearant*.
      1952 Wilson *Folk Speech NC* 515 *appearant* = apparent.
      1956 Hall *Coll* She was a big woman and awful scary appearantly.

argufy *vb* To argue, dispute, haggle, contend, especially in a petty way. [*argue* + *-ify* verb-forming suffix; OED *argufy* vb 2 'to argue, dispute, wrangle' 1753→, now colloquial or dialect; DARE *argufy* vb 2 'to contend, wrangle; to dispute or debate (a point or topic)' now chiefly South, South Midland]

ULST.:   1895 MacManus *Leadin' Road* 233 I'll not argufy the point with ye, for I don't intend axin' ye to ait him.

1900 Irvine *Lady Chimney Corner* 120 I don't want to argufy or palaver with a dacent man.

c1910 Byers *Glossary* 'He's always argufyin" = in argument, wrangling.

1953 Traynor *Donegal Glossary* 7 = to argue, especially heatedly.

U.S.:   1848 Bartlett *Americanisms* = to argue. This word has a place in several of the English glossaries. In this country it is only heard among the most illiterate.

1899 Green *Virginia Word-Book* 45 = to argue, signify.

1963 Hooper *Unwanted Boy* 231 Of course, a husband gains nothing by arguing with his wife, especially if she has two or three different streaks of argufying blood in her veins.

as *conj* Than. [OED *as* conj B4, 1460→, obsolete except dialect; DOST *as* conj 6, 15th century→; DARE *as* conj B3 now chiefly Midland, South]

ULST.:   1880 Patterson *Antrim/Down Glossary* 3 = than: 'I'd rather sell as buy'.

1953 Traynor *Donegal Glossary* 8 I'd sooner travel as drive.

2000 Fenton *Hamely Tongue* 7 They wud rather sell as buy (once said to be true of Cullybackey men holding turkeys on Boxing Day).

U.S.:   1895 Edson and Fairchild *Tenn Mts* 376 I would rather see you as him.

1937 Hall *Coll* I'd rather work as go to school.

1939 Aurand *Idioms and Expressions* 22 She'd rather be married to him AS (than) to keep house for him.

1973 *GSMNP*-74:12 And he said he'd rather die as to go.

aside *prep* Beside, next to. [*a*- (reduced form of *on*) + *side*; OED *aside* prep 'at the side of, beside' 1615→, still in Scotland: SND *aside* prep 1 'at, on, or to the side of, alongside of']

ULST.:   1885 Lyttle *Robin Gordon* 40 He sut doon on a cher aside me.

1901 Savage-Armstrong *Ballads of Down* 122 O, nestle close aside my heart, / An' A thy life shall shield.

c1910 Wier *Bab McKeen* 91 I interviewed yin o' these stick carriers on her wye hame, wi' a bundle on her back, and twa youngsters aside her.

1930 MacNeill *Told to Reverence* 77 I'm to be buried wi' ma own ones, for I have no wish to lie aside him.

U.S.:   (also **aside of**)

1838 Kemper *Trip Wisconsin* 437 The Stockbridges ... have a reservation aside of the Brothertowns.

1976 Garber *Mountain-ese* 4 In the classroom the boys were often seated aside the girls.

1982 Ginns *Snowbird Gravy* 188 They said something got on to 'em, and the mother said she saw the awfullest face lookin' in at the window, aside of the old chimney.

ask See **ax**

at, 'at *rel pron* That, who. [OED *atl 'at* rel pron B 'that, who, which, what' , c1300→, perhaps from Old Norse ... still in regular use in northern dialect speech; DOST *at*

rel pron A1 'that, which, who' 1375→]

ULST.: **1861** Hume *Rabbin's Ollminick* 4 Them 'at hes tuck pains, an' examined into things, an' wrote down notes maybe knows more nor sich as only gets things in books, an' nivver wos a-mile from a cow's tail in their lives.
1897 McIlroy *Lint in Bell* 19 Whor's the use o' his learnin' the names o' a wheen o' places 'at he's never likely tae see?
c1910 Wier *Bab McKeen* 49 It's a pity he did that for it cast a reflection on the nice lass, 'at'll stick to her while gress grows or water rins.
2000 Fenton *Hamely Tongue* 7 It's him 'at daen it.

U.S.: **1894** Riley *Little Mock-Man* 533 He mocks the man at picks the pears.
1939 Hall *Coll* And we had some old trained bear hounds 'at turned off in the roughs, the laurel on the Bear Creek side, and picked up a cold trail.

at oneself *adj phr* (usually expressed in the negative) In one's right mind or usual health, in full possession of one's wits, at one's best (thus, *not at myself* = not my usual self, not feeling well, not at one's best). [DARE *at oneself* adj phrase 'at one's best; in full possession of one's physical or mental powers' chiefly South, Midland]

ULST.: **1840** Boyce *Shandy Maguire* 6 As for auld Duncan here, he's no at himsel jist so weel as he used to be.
1880 Patterson *Antrim/Down Glossary* 73 *not at himself* = mad, not in health.
1923 Lutton *Montiaghisms* 9 = a person who is said to be labouring under some temporary aberration of intellect, is said to be 'not at himself'.
1936 White *Mrs Murphy* 25 I wasn't at myself for a long time, and at last I sent for the doctor.
1948 Marshall *Planted by River* 30 He lay back again, and observed wearily and bitterly: 'If I was only at myself, I would go and wring his neck'.
1990 McIntyre *Some Handlin'* 63 'Since she had measles she hasn't been at herself' = has not been feeling completely well.
1993 Montgomery *Barnish* 58 'Ah'm no at myself' = I'm not too well.
2000 Fenton *Hamely Tongue* 7 Ir ye at yersel, wumman?

U.S.: **1872** Thompson *Major Jones' Courtship* 189 I do b'lieve if they hadn't brung little Henry Clay to her, ... she never would got her senses agin. She aint more'n half at herself yit.
1908 Payne *Word-list East Alabama* 287 = up to one's full strength or ability: 'I can easily pick 300 pounds of cotton when I am at myself'.
1993 Ison and Ison *Whole Nother Lg* 3 *at himself* = is fully awake and is thinking all right.

atween *prep* Between. [< Old English *a-* + *-tween, -twene*; OED *atween* prep c1400→, archaic and dialect; SND *atween* 1721→]

ULST.: **c1800** Thomson (in **1992** Scott and Robinson *Samuel Thomson* 55) The road is lang an' unco dreigh, / And roaring seas do intervene; / And cauld-rife mountains, wild an' heigh, / Erect their joyless brows atween.
1840 Boyce *Shandy Maguire* 6 It's no much grass he'd let grow to his heels atween Stranorlar and Donegal.
1898 MacManus *Humours of Donegal* 60 Atween you an' me an' the bedpost, there's them an' their prayers isn't maybe as often answered as Father Luke's.
c1910 Wier *Bab McKeen* 97 A farmer'll come forrit to a likely lad or lass, an' mak' enquiries, an' sometimes a conversation's carriet on atween them.
1933 MacNeill *Reverence Listens* 43 'I seen ye', says I, 'comin' home from the

Soiree, the two o' yees, and there wasn't a patch of moonshine atween ye.'
1949 Mac Airt *Tyrone Folktales* 37 Atween the eating and drinking and all it came to ten shillings.

U.S.:   **1834** Downing *Life Andrew Jackson* 103 He therefore retired tu a narrow pass atween the swamp and the Missippi.
1913 Kephart *Our Sthn High* 225 Atween the shoulders I've got a pain.

ax, axe *vb* To ask. [a form in variation with *ask* for the past thousand years; Old English had both *acsian/axian* and *ascian* as forms of the verb; DARE *ask* vb A1a formerly especially New England, now chiefly South, Midland]

ULST.:   **1635** Hamilton *Letter* I hewe got sum informasioune since my cuming into this cuntry that I dar mor boldly ax for my oune.
1804 Orr *Poems* 158 The hen-pecket taupie, wha'd wiss to be happy, / Sud ax nane wha ken / what the wife does at hame.
1840 Boyce *Shandy Maguire* 6 Where, might a body ax, were you spending the night?
1886 Lyttle *Ballycuddy* 3 Sur, if it wudnae be makin' ower free, A wud ax ye yer name, fur nether o' us kens ye.
1939 Paterson *Country Cracks* 84 All the sorrows of Ireland come be the weemin an' if ye ax me, they're the cause of many a heart burn still.
c1955 Montgomery *Heard in Ulster* 3 I'll ax ye yin question afore I leave.
1991 O'Kane *You Don't Say* 3 = old form of the verb to ask: 'I axed him if he would give me a hand'.

U.S.:   **1837** Sherwood *Georgia Provincialisms* 118 *axd* = asked.
1930 Shoemaker *1300 Penn Words* 1 *axe* = to ask.
1939 Hall *Coll* They axed him how he ever got away from there, axed him where he stayed all night.
1953 Atwood *Verbs East US* 5 In N.C. [*ax*] becomes much more common, reaching considerable concentrations in the western one fourth of the state, where nearly all Type I informants use it.

ayond, ayont *prep, adv* Beyond, on the other side of. [< *a-* (< *on-*) + *yond*; OED *ayond/ayont* 'beyond' 1724→, Scottish and northern English; SND *ayont* A prep 'on the further side of; past, later than' 1750→]

ULST.:   **1753** *Scotch Poems* 371 The twa ald wives ayont the fire / Are settled to their hearts desire.
c1800 Thomson (in **1992** Scott and Robinson *Samuel Thomson* 109) Thou'll ne'er be sic a tree / As Billy Shakespeare's mulberry, / Nor e'er ayont the parish be / A thing to brag on.
1886 Lyttle *Ballycuddy* 36 He said he wuz a loyal Presbyterian, an' had nae earthly desire in this life ayont the weel bein' o' the Newtoonbreda Kirk.
1935 Megaw *Carragloon* 190 It's all right for them's childer that's near the new school, but it's a sarious paddle for the wee wans that lives ayont the moss.
1942 *Bangor Words* 3 = beyond or past: 'The wee sma hours ayont the twal'.
c1955 Montgomery *Heard in Ulster* 4 The duck hoose is ayont the pig hoose.
2002 Reynolds *Granfeyther's Tunge* 6 In a wee cottar hoose on tha tap o' tha brae, / Ayont Kilmoyle school is whaur I did lay.

U.S.:   **1843** Hall *New Purchase* 433 Strate ayond is near about whare Bill first seed the wolf or fox.

B

baby-clout See **clout**

back *vb* To address a letter or endorse a document. This usage was carried over from days before envelopes, when a letter was folded and the address written on the reverse side. It was then sealed with wax or folded before being mailed. [OED *back* vb 12b Scottish and U.S.; SND *back* vb 2(4); DARE *back* vb 3 'to endorse a document; especially to address an envelope or letter' chiefly South, South Midland]

ULST.: 1879 Lyttle *Paddy McQuillan* 74 The skule-mester backit the envilopes fur them.
1953 Traynor *Donegal Glossary* 11 = of a letter: to write the address.

U.S.: 1859 Bartlett *Americanisms* 2 To back a letter, is Wesstern for to 'direct' it.
1913 Kephart *Our Sthn High* 32 In the group that gathered at mail time I often was solicited to 'back' envelopes.
1988 Kosier *Maggie* 25 Sometimes they would 'back' letters for customers—letters were folded over and addressed on the back when there were no envelopes.

backing, backings *vbl n* Refuse (in Ulster from the production of flax, cloth or wool; in the U.S. from the distillation of whiskey, where the terms refer to the weaker alcohol at the end of a **run**, too low in proof properly to be considered whiskey). [OED *backing* vbl n 11 'refuse of wool or flax, or what is left after dressing it'; SND *backings* 'refuse of tow, wool, etc.'; DARE *backings* South Midland]

ULST.: c1910 Byers *Glossary* = refuse of flax, cloth or wool.
U.S.: 1911 Shearin *East Kentucky Dialect* 537 *backings* = a grade a whiskey intermediate between 'first shot' ... and 'singlings'.
1949 Maurer *Argot of Moonshiner* 7 *backings* = low-proof liquor, not containing enough alcohol to be considered whiskey; usually low-proof distillate at the end of a run.
1977 Shields *Cades Cove* 79f It was sort of a custom to have a party after a 'run off' of moonshine whiskey. Sometimes called backins parties, these featured a quantity of the mash 'backins' or spent beer, heated with spices and served along with food ... The alcoholic content of the drink is not high, but enough of it can elevate the drinkers' spirits.

backjaw *n* Backtalk, insolent or impudent replies. [cf SND *backjaw* n 'impudence, abusive language']

ULST.: c1910 Byers *Glossary* = saucy replies to a superior (as from a child or an inferior).
U.S.: 1952 Wilson *Folk Speech NC* 517 Don't give me no backjaw, big boy!

back of, aback of *prep phr* Of position: behind, beyond. Of time: earlier than. [OED (at *back* adv 15) 'back from, behind' 1694→]

ULST.: 1949 Mac Airt *Tyrone Folktales* 38 There's an old torn quilt there and clap it about you and go round there aback of the house and come up that lea field before the door.

1975 Murphy *You're Talking* 63 She run and put the hen back under the bowl and put the whiskey aback of the plates on the dresser.
1983 Marshall *Drumlister* 17 Back of there the sun is shining, and the riverside is cheery.
1997 Robinson *Grammar* 105 'To the back of' is *behinn, ahint,* or *a-bak o.*

U.S.:   **1939** Hall *Coll* They was out of hearing a-going out just a-back of Round Top.
1969 *GSMNP*-46:5 Back of that, he just minded every word I said to him.
1970 *GSMNP*-26:4 Now the road comes back of the Ephraim house, but it did come in front of it.

backset *n* (especially in phr *take a backset*) The relapse of an illness or ailment. [perhaps a reversal of *setback*; OED *backset* n 1 'a reverse, check, relapse' 1721→, Scottish; SND *backset* n 1 'anything that checks one's course or causes a relapse: of health, worldly circumstances, vegetation, etc.' 1721→; DARE *backset* n 1b 'a relapse during convalescence' chiefly South, South Midland, *take a backset* especially Appalachians]

ULST.:   **c1910** Byers *Glossary* = always used of a relapse after illness, never in a moral sense.
1923 Lutton *Montiaghisms* 9 = a relapse into sickness; anything that checks the growth of plants or animals.
1939 Paterson *Country Cracks* 119 'He's got a back-set' = He has got a relapse.
1953 Traynor *Donegal Glossary* 11 She had a bad backset.
1990 Todd *Words Apart* 25 She was doin' rightly an' we thought she'd have another wee go but she took a backset an' now she's a-waitin on (expected to die).

U.S.:   **1816** Calhoun *Works* 2.170 It would give a back set, and might ... endanger their ultimate success.
1939 Hall *Coll* He tuck the whooping cough along about Christmas time and was out of school for a month, and then he tuck a back set and was out of school again.
1996 *GSMNPOHP* 1:4 They'd get up too early and try to take care of somebody and take a backset.

back suggan See **suggan**

backward(s) *adj* Shy, diffident. [OED *backward* adj B6a 'turning or hanging back from activity; disinclined to advance or make advances; reluctant, loath, chary, shy, bashful' 1599→]

ULST.:   **1738** Ray *Letter* Ye kend aways whare to find me, whom ye know was never backward to assist ye upon aw occasions.
1919 MacGill *Glenmornan* 39 He's never been backwards in sendin' some money home to his own people.
1920 Doyle *Ballygullion* 111 But Mrs Magorrian is a quiet wee woman, an' wi' all the crowd there, an' him callin' her madam, she was too backward to get up out av the corner she was in.
1936 White *Mrs Murphy* 68 He had nobody to give him a hand, poor chap, and he was always terrible backward.
1942 *Bangor Words* 3 = shy or modest: 'She's a bit backward with strangers'.

U.S.:   **1859** Bartlett *Americanisms* 18 = sometimes used in the West for *bashful,* unwilling to appear in company, on the same principle as 'forward' in correct language means the very contrary.

1969 *GSMNP*-38:95 They'd tell you right at once what they believed. They wasn't a bit backward about talking.
1999 Montgomery *File* A lot of mountain people are kind of backward, but I don't care to talk to nobody.

(the) bad man *n* The Devil; a demon or hobgoblin (used especially to admonish children against misbehavior). [SND *bad man* 'a child's name for the devil'; DARE *bad man* n 2 (usually preceded by *the* or *old*) 'the Devil' chiefly South, South Midland]
ULST.: **1880** Patterson *Antrim/Down Glossary* 4 = the devil.
2000 Fenton *Hamely Tongue* 129 = the devil.
U.S.: **1884** Harrison *Negro English* 277 = the Devil.
1952 Wilson *Folk Speech NC* 517-18 = the devil. usually to children to induce good behavior: 'If you don't stop crying the (old) *bad man* will get you'.
1977 Hamilton *Mt Memories* 56 So when Leona and I fussed, we would often say, 'I know you'll go to the Bad Place', or 'The Bad Man will get you for that'.

(the) bad place *n* Hell (used especially to admonish children against misbehavior). [OED *bad place* n 'hell'; SND *bad place* n 'hell'; DARE *bad place* n 'hell' chiefly South, Midland]
ULST.: **1880** Patterson *Antrim/Down Glossary* 4 = hell.
1983 Marshall *Drumlister* 78 Sez I, 'Ye may go till the bad place, / I'm as good just as she is, or you'.
U.S.: **1859** Bartlett *Americanisms* 322 = the little finger. A very common term in New York, especially among small children, who, when making a bargain with each other, are accustomed to confirm it by interlocking the little finger of each other's right hands, and repeating the following doggerel: *Pinky, pinky, bow-bell, / Whoever tells a lie / Will sink down to the bad place, / And never rise up again.*
1899 Green *Virginia Word-Book* 49 = hell. Children are warned against the 'bad place'.
1977 Hamilton *Mt Memories* 56 'Hell' was always called the 'Bad Place' ... So when Leona and I fussed, we would often say, 'I know you'll go to the Bad Place', or 'The Bad Man will get you for that'.

bad'un See **one**

bannock, bonnick, bonnock *n* In Ulster, originally an oatmeal cake baked on a griddle, now a home-baked cake of any kind. In the U.S., a thin bread, usually made of cornmeal and cooked on a griddle; also a hard bread made from flour and fried in a pan. [related to Irish *bannóg/bannach/bonnóg*, Scottish Gaelic *bannoch*, and Old English *bannuc*, all ultimately possibly < Latin *paniculum* 'little bread'; DOST *bannok* n 1 'a flat round of cake, usually of barley, oat, or pease meal, and baked on a girdle or "back"' 16th century→; SND *bannock* 1 'a round, flat, thickish cake of oatmeal, barley, pease or flour, baked on a girdle'; DARE chiefly North, especially New England]
ULST.: **1804** Orr *Poems* 33 Wives baket bonnocks for their men, / Wi' tears instead o' water.
1880 Patterson *Antrim/Down Glossary* 5 bannock, bonnock = a cake baked on a griddle.

c1910 Byers *Glossary* = a cake composed of oatmeal or less commonly of barley, mixed with water and baked on a griddle.

1919 MacGill *Glenmornan* 196 In one hand he carried a strong ash-plant, in another a bundle of bannocks wrapped in a dotted hankerchief.

1942 *Bangor Words* 5 = a circular piece of soda bread, baked on a griddle.

1945 Murphy *Gullion's Foot* 24 It is this crane, and crooks, which have been so responsible for the famous Irish griddle-cakes. The bread can be seen as it bakes, and can be lowered or raised as the woman of the house deems necessary. Round bonnicks are seldom made on a griddle; the bread is cut in four parts known as farls.

1975 Murphy *You're Talking* 101 His wife was making a bonnick of bread at the time, and she lifted off the fire and put it in the middle of the bonnick and threw the cake of bread in a scouder across the tongs of the fire when the Scotch giant walks in.

1980 McClean *Ulster Words I* 3 *bonnicks* = griddle scones.

1993 Montgomery *Barnish* 7 *bannock* = bread baked on a griddle.

U.S.: 1859 Bartlett *Americanisms* 21 = In Scotland, a cake of oatmeal, baked on an iron plate ... In New England, cakes of Indian meal, fried in lard, are called *bannocks*.

1872 Schele de Vere *Americanisms* 439 *bannock* = in Scotland, a round cake of oatmeal, kneaded in water only, and baked against a stone, called bannock-stone, while the same cake is called a girdle-cake if baked on an iron plate, means in America a cake of Indian meal, fried in lard.

1982 *Smokies Heritage* 37 A special camp bread of flour and sugar, bannock bread, was most often baked in Dutch ovens.

banter *vb*, *n* [origin obscure; OED *banter* vb 6 'to challenge'; cf SND *banter* 'rebuke, scold, drive away by scolding' 1820→; DARE *banter* vb 2 'to challenge, dare; goad' chiefly South, Midland] (Note: the senses 'light conversation' and 'to engage in light conversation' are standard.)

1 *vb* To dare, taunt, challenge to fight.

ULST.: 1880 Patterson *Antrim/Down Glossary* 5 = to taunt a person to fight: 'He bantered me to fight him'.

1920 Doyle *Ballygullion* 127 He was afeard I might banther him into buyin' better.

1953 Traynor *Donegal Glossary* 14 I'll banter ye to a fight.

1991 O'Kane *You Don't Say* 6 = to challenge to fisticuffs. Often the one doing the bantering has no wish for the challenge to be taken up, and usually picks for his target a placid type of man on whom to unleash a mixture of bluster and vicious threats. Occasionally, though, the bantering exceeds the limits and is rewarded with a richly deserved thrashing.

2000 Fenton *Hamely Tongue* 11 = challenge to fight: '[I] bantered him up an doon, but he wudnae shape'.

U.S.: 1855 *Pawpaw Hollow Minutes* 161 Arming himself with a revolver and bantering and dunning his brother to go into a fight with him.

1859 Bartlett *Americanisms* 21 = to challenge, defy; namely, to a race, a shooting-match, etc.

1899 Green *Virginia Word-Book* 51 = to challenge to a contest: 'He bantered him to a contest'.

1974 Fink *Bits Mt Speech* 2 John bantered him for a race.

2 *n* A challenge, taunting.

ULST.:   1948 Marshall *Planted by River* 119 He had to swallow a full measure of banter and jibe from his betters as they strolled past him to begin another row.

U.S.:   1834 Crockett *Narrative* 57 But I couldn't help thinking, that she intended what she had said as a banter for me to court her!

1872 Schele de Vere *Americanisms* 439 = in the West, means not merely to joke and jest good-humoredly, but also to challenge to a match, and to provoke a wager: 'We had a fine banter, but the match was postponed till spring'.

banty, bantie *n* A type of miniature chicken, a bantam; by extension, an undersized animal or person. [SND (at *bantim*) Scottish form of English *bantam*; DARE widespread, especially east of Mississippi River]

ULST.:   1880 Patterson *Antrim/Down Glossary* 5 = a bantam fowl.

c1910 Byers *Glossary* = a small, strutting, conceited person.

1921 Irvine *Poor Folk* 68 He can believe if he takes that a banty hen can lay swan's eggs, and out of thim hatch a flock of nice big whales.

1942 *Bangor Words* 5 = a bantam hen; anything small.

1953 Traynor *Donegal Glossary* 14 = of fowl of any kind: small.

c1955 Montgomery *Heard in Ulster* 18 = bantam or small fowl; also an undersized person: 'He's only a banty'.

1974 Braidwood *Crowls and Runts* 75 *Banty* is recorded in one instance for 'the weakling of the litter', from Tyrone (Gortin).

2000 Fenton *Hamely Tongue* 11 = a bantam; *banty-cock* = a male bantam, a small, ridiculously posturing person; *banty-hen* = a female bantam.

2004 Cromie *M'Craidy's Monkey* 112 As a result o this, their back gairden wus foo o aa an assoartment o banties, hens, geese - aye, an even an al sookin pig at times.

U.S.:   1936 Stanley *Speech East Texas* 161 Banty is almost as widely used as the standard form in the phrase 'bantam rooster'.

barefoot, barefooted, barefut, barefutted *adj* Of a food or beverage: made of basic or bare ingredients, having nothing added; thus, unsweetened, undiluted or unmixed (often applied to tea or coffee without sugar or cream/milk). In the U.S. the term has been extended to various foodstuffs. [SND *bar(e)fit broth* (at *barefit*) 'broth made without meat'; DARE chiefly Mid and Central Atlantic, Ohio Valley]

ULST.:   1921 O'Neill *More Songs of Glens* 37 The drink we get is barefut tea, an' not for gold or love, / Could ye rise an' post a letter here as ye would in Cushendun.

1922 McKay *Mts of Mourne* 93 Ye darn't set down a barefutted cup of tay to Felix. He wud luk at ye—nothing but beef for him.

1953 Traynor *Donegal Glossary* 14 = of spirits: raw, neat: 'I'll take it barefoot'.

U.S.:   1867 Lowell *Biglow Papers* lxi-lxii 'I take my tea barfoot', said a backwoodsman when asked if he would have cream and sugar.

1953 Randolph and Wilson *Down in Holler* 225 *barefoot bread* = hard cornbread, made without eggs or shortening.

1992-97 Montgomery *Coll*, *barefoot* = any food made with basic ingredients; *barefoot bread* = hard bread, lacking such ingredients as eggs or lard; *barefoot(ed) coffee* = without cream or sugar: 'I'll take my coffee barefoot'; *barefoot dumpling* = made from water, grease, and salt.

bawsie, bawsay *n* A favorite cow, or the pet name for one. [< Old French *bausant* 'white-spotted, piebald'; DOST *bawsant* adj 'having a blaze, a white spot or streak on the face, brindled'; SND *bawsey* 'a horse or a cow having a white stripe or patch on the face (Jamieson)' 1789→]

> ULST.:   c1800 Thomson (in 1992 Scott and Robinson *Samuel Thomson* 115) Howe'er his Bawsay to the fair, / Took crafty, sleekit Sim. / A noble naig he did declare, / But didna answer him.
>
> U.S.:   1930 Shoemaker *1300 Penn Words* 8 *bawsie* = a white faced horse or bovine animal, a favorite name for a pet cow.

beal, beel *vb* Of a sore, especially one on the ear: to fester, become infected or abscessed. Hence **bealing, beeling** *vbl n* Pus; a sore. [probably originally a variant of *boil*; OED *beal* vb obsolete or dialect, still in regular use in Scotland; DOST *bele* vb 1b 'to swell with morbid matter' 15th century→; DARE *beal* chiefly Appalachians]

> ULST.:   1861 Hume *Rabbin's Ollminick* 32 Aftther awhile, the wound got worse an' worse; an' beel'd twice, an' run a power.
>
> 1880 Patterson *Antrim/Down Glossary* 6 *beal* = to suppurate; *bealing* = a suppuration, sore.
>
> 1889 Hart *Derryreel* 159 It's far for me to travel, and me with a beeled toe.
>
> 1933 MacNeill *Reverence Listens* 42 I heard no more till the poor sowl took a beelin' jaw. It riz and it riz.
>
> 1953 Traynor *Donegal Glossary* 18 – of a sore: to fester, become septic: 'If you don't look after that cut it'll beal'.
>
> 1981 Pepper *Ulster-English Dict* 12 I kept the wee lad from school for his finger was beelin.
>
> 1991 O'Kane *You Don't Say* 8 *beeling* = pus, the discharge from a boil, wound or pimple.
>
> U.S.:   1800 Osborn *Diary* (7 Mar) I am near hardly able for to walk with a Bealing in my Left Leg.
>
> 1967 DARE *Coll* 'His head's bealed' = he has pus come out of his ear.
>
> 1974 Fink *Bits Mt Speech* 2 I had a bealed ear.
>
> 1975 Jackson *Unusual Words* 158-59 Many a person has suffered a *jumpin' toothache*, an abscess; or his *year* has *beeled*—has an abscess in his ear.

beastings, beaslins, beastlings, beeselins, beeslings, beeslins, beesnings, beesnins, beestings, beslings *n* (construed as plural) The first milk given by a cow after calving. [< Old English *biesting* 1000→; cf OED *beest* n² 1 'the first milk drawn from a mammal, especially a cow, after parturition']

> ULST.:   1880 Patterson *Antrim/Down Glossary* 6 *beeslings* = the milk got from a cow the first three milkings after she has calved.
>
> 1891 Simmons *Armagh Words and Phrases* 3 *beastlings* = strong milk yielded by a cow after calving.
>
> 1923 Lutton *Montiaghisms* 10 *beeselins* = the first milk given by a cow after calving.
>
> 1939 Paterson *Country Cracks* 39 The first churnin' after the calvin' too wus always called the beastlin'.
>
> 1942 *Bangor Words* 7 *beesnins, beesnings, beastings* = the first milk given by a cow after calving. When boiled it sets like cheese, and is cut in slices and eaten like cheese, with or without bread.

1945 Murphy *Gullion's Foot* 75 This first [milk] taken from a cow after calving which is known as 'beeslins' was either tipped on to the fairy 'forth' or left in a cup or bowl.

1993 Montgomery *Barnish* 8 *beestings* = cow's milk after calving.

U.S.: **1899** Green *Virginia Word-Book beestlings, beeslings, beaslins, beslings* = first milk of a cow with her first calf. Generally poured on her rump to make gentle and a good milch cow.

1927 Woofter *Dialect West Virginia* 348 Do not milk the beaslings on the ground or the cow will grow dry.

1984 Wilder *You All Spoken* 135 = colostrum, the first breast milk let down by cows and other animals after birthing.

becase, becaise, bekase, kase *conj* Because. [DARE South, South Midland; LAUSC South, South Midland]

ULST.: **1829** McSparran *Irish Legend* 244 I wouldn't like to pick a quarrel with Mister O'Neill, bekase as I may safely say he's an ould cronie of yours, master.

1845 Carleton *Irish Peasantry* 10 The thief o' the world baffled him from day to day, and wouldn't give him a penny—bekase he knew, the blaggard, that the Square was then poor as a church mouse, and hadn't money enough to try it at law with him.

1899 MacManus *Chimney Corners* 90 Bekase he had neither money nor means.

1900 Irvine *Lady Chimney Corner* 17 'It's a mortial pity she's a girl', said Bridget, 'bekase she might hev been an althar boy before she goes.'

1904 Marshall *Dial of Ulster* 124 *becaise*.

1921 Irvine *Poor Folk* 126 'Ov coorse', he said, 'a maan isn't quare, jist bekase he cyant whustle wi' a hot pirta in his mouth.'

U.S.: **1837** Sherwood *Georgia Provincialisms* 118 *becase* = because.

1871 Eggleston *Hoosier Schoolmaster* 118 I'd picked her out kase, not bein' Flat Crick born herself, she might help a feller to do better!

1905 Miles *Spirit of Mts* 112 Mis' Beaver hated her, if anything, a little wuss'n the old man did, bekase old Nance was always a tawmentin' the children.

1961 Kurath and McDavid *Pron Engl Atl Sts* 162 *Because* with the vowel /e/ of *eight* occurs in the folk speech of the South and the South Midland; it is sharply recessive.

1969 *GSMNP*-37:2:6 I believe that his daddy used to live on Coopers Creek, for becase after my brother married, my oldest one, by God he moved up there and they called it Grandpaw's place.

bed See **the 1**

bedfast *adj* Bed-ridden, usually temporarily. [< *bed* + *fast* 'firm, fixed'; OED *bedfast* 'confined to bed' c1639→, northern dialect and Scottish; DOST *bedfast* adj 'bedridden' 16th century→; DARE chiefly Midland, West]

ULST.: c1910 Byers *Glossary* = bed-ridden.

1991 O'Kane *You Don't Say* 8 = to be bedridden, usually said of a person who is temporarily indisposed and would prefer to be up and about: 'Johnny won't like to be bedfast with all this good weather and the hay ready to cut'.

1997 Share *Slanguage* 17 = temporarily confined to bed.

U.S.: **1873** (in **1983** Heap *Bucks Co Word List* 22) We found Elizabeth Warner bed fast with a broken knee.

1927 Dingus *Mt Words* 468 = confined to bed, bed-ridden.

bed-happin's See **hap**

beel See **beal**

beeselins See **beastings**

bee skep See **scape**

beeslings, beeslins, beesnings, beesnins, beestings See **beastings**

be for *vb phr* In favor of, intending to, proposing to (do something).
ULST.:   1824 McHenry *Insurgent Chief* 47 Some o' them may be for takin' my life.
1912 Gregory *Ulster Folk* 36 Then suddenly he turned, an' axed: 'Are ye for ower the hill, the day?'
1933 Foster *Tyrone among Bushes* 20 I'm not for sittin' at present.
1936 White *Mrs Murphy* 197 I thought you were never for comin'.
1975 Murphy *You're Talking* 38 Anyway the girl was for having the blacksmith and she told the tailor what she had in mind and he said she was foolish.
1983 Marshall *Drumlister* 74 But I'm for tacklin' Sarah Ann; no matter if the snow / Is everywhere shebowin'; when the morra comes I'll go.
2000 Fenton *Hamely Tongue* 79 A'm for startin noo.
U.S.:   1937 Thornborough *Great Smoky Mts* 134 I was fur leavin' again, but the men laughed at me and said they hadn't heard nothin' and we'd only fish a little longer.
1963 Edwards *Gravel* 30 'Well, I'm for making him pay for it then', said Genuwine, and he was supported by all present.

behint *prep, adv* Behind. [DOST *behint* prep/adv 'behind' 1375→]
ULST.:   c1800 Thomson (in 1992 Scott and Robinson *Samuel Thomson* 87) Grim Calumny wad never crack / Your character behint your back.
1825 McHenry *Hearts of Steel* 70 It does na noo appear as I wad lang remain behint her in this world.
1881 Hart *Mere Irish* 53 When Saint Columb heerd them makin' a gowk of him behint his back, and them sitting forenenst his very own nose, he was sore vexed.
1900 Irvine *Lady Chimney Corner* 84 Dead entirely was I but fur th' eyes an' th' wit behint thim.
1910 Russell *Language of Ulster* 26 The word 'behind' may either be called 'behine' or 'behint', or probably be reformed altogether into 'ahin" or 'ahint'.
U.S.:   1895 Crane *Badge of Courage* 2 We're goin' way up the river, cut across, an' come around in behint 'em.
1942 Thomas *Blue Ridge* 285 I'm a-feard of that 'mobile. I'd ruther ride behint Old Nell in the jolt wagon.
1960 Hall *Smoky Mt Folks* 27 She was up behint a man on a mule.

bekase See **becase**

betimes, by times *adv* Occasionally, from time to time. [< *be-* 'by' + *times*; DOST *betimes* adv 1 'occasionally, at certain times' late 15th century→]
ULST.:   1829 McSparran *Irish Legend* 81 An old woman that sat close to the fire, on what in the Scottish tongue is called the hab, scourged three handfuls of salt over all their heads, muttering at the same time some incomprehensible

chronan, then down on her seat, slipping the end of the tongs into the fire, and began to spin on a rock and spindle, keeping the tail of her eye glancing betimes over at the strangers.

1900 Given *Poems* 159 I try betimes tae haud her in, / But just as sure as I begin, / Some apostolic sage, / Wae upturned e'en in holy glare / Invites the world tae see him there, / Which puts her in a rage.

1906 MacDermott *Foughilotra* 5 Des ye hear talkin' in it betimes?

c1910 Byers *Glossary* = at times, occasionally: 'I'm bad betimes'.

U.S.: **1795** Smith *Letter* he tells me he sees you by times.

1930 Maurer *Schoonerisms* 389 *betimes* = now and then.

beyont, beyant *prep, adv* Beyond, over and above. [SND *beyont* 1724→; DARE chiefly South, South Midland]

ULST.: **1840** Boyce *Shandy Maguire* 5 If the walls i' the auld barracks beyont could spake, it's many the quare story they'd tell.

1880 Patterson *Antrim/Down Glossary* 7 *beyont the beyons* = some very out of the way place.

1904 Byers *Sayings of Ulster* 52 When a place ... is out of the way and hard to reach, and altogether uninteresting, it is said to be 'at the back of beyant' (beyond), that is, it is even more distant than 'beyant (beyond) the beyants', a phrase more expressive than 'a God-forsaken spot', or the 'back of God-speed'.

c1910 Byers *Glossary* 'Ye wud think he was nobody beyont the common' = said of a person of distinction.

1919 MacGill *Glenmornan* 39 He went away beyont the water and stayed there for short on five years and came back and bought old Columb Beag's farm.

1939 Paterson *Country Cracks* 24 Finn was on the hill above when he saw a giant the spit of himself but a far bigger man restin' 'tween the two oul' teeth on Carrick beyant.

c1955 Montgomery *Heard in Ulster* 7 There's nathin' beyont what ye see.

U.S.: **1837** Sherwood *Georgia Provincialisms* 118 *beyant* = beyond.

1931 Rawlings *Jacob's Ladder* 453 Iffen they do float, they'll dreeft on beyant where we could ketch 'em at.

biddable *adj* Especially of a child or animal: obedient, docile, submissive. [< *bid* 'to command, enjoin' + *-able*; OED *biddable* adj 1 'ready to do what is bidden, obedient, willing, docile'; SND *biddable* adj 'obedient' 1768→; DARE *biddable* 'obedient, tractable, docile' chiefly South, South Midland]

ULST.: **1889** Hart *Derryreel* 35 The Princess had grown as biddable as ye plaze.

c1910 Byers *Glossary* 'He's a biddable waen (or child)' = obedient, docile, does what he is told.

1923 Lutton *Montiaghisms* 10 = obedient to orders given by a superior, submissive.

1948 Marshall *Planted by River* 200 I've engaged a wee girl of the cotter man's; she's only twelve year oul', but she's willin' and biddable, an' she's makin' a grand shape at the housekeepin'.

1953 Traynor *Donegal Glossary* 22 = obedient, easily managed, usually a *biddable* child.

U.S.: **1859** Bartlett *Americanisms* 31 = this Irish word is in use in the West: 'White servants are not biddable', that is, manageable, obedient to order.

1886 Smith *Southernisms* 36 *biddableness* = disposition to obey. I have been familiar with the word in this sense in South Carolina all my life, and it is so used in East Tennessee, Georgia, and no doubt elsewhere (Ohio).
1940 Simms *Coll* Nice dog, as biddable as a child.

bide *vb* To wait, stay. [OED *bide* vb I 1 'to remain in expectation, to wait' c1000→, chiefly northern; DOST *bide* vb 1 'to remain or stay (especially temporarily), to continue to be in a place' late 14th century→]

ULST.:   **1753** *Scotch Poems* 372 For death, or fate, it maksna whither, / Ne'er lets them bide o'erlang the gither.
    1830 McMillan *Poems* But ai' she bides through thick and thin, / In spite o' a'.
    1880 Patterson *Antrim/Down Glossary* 7 = to wait.
    1920 McCallin *Ulster Plenishing* 73 May the plates be let bide on the dresser, where they were got for.
    1921 O'Neill *More Songs of Glens* 13 Ye'll often hear them say a woman cannot bide her lone.
    1933 *North Antrim* 45 The lass that I met at the fair / Is mine noo, an' bidin' wi' me.
    1948 Marshall *Planted by River* 9-10 You must bide till you can steal it.
    1993 Montgomery *Barnish* 8 = to wait.
U.S.:   **1918** Steadman *NC Word List* 20 *bide a wee* = stay a while.

billie See **hillbilly**

blackguard, blaggard, blaggart *vb* To vilify, curse, use profane or obscene language. Hence *n* Such language; a person using such language. [Note: the sense 'to behave in an ugly or dishonest manner' is standard.]

ULST.:   **1884** McFadyen and Hepburn *Lays and Legends* 84 So they started, none iver knew which wis till blame ... Till blaggard ach other, an' curse, an' upbraid.
    c1910 Byers *Glossary* = applied in Ulster in a restricted sense, to a person obscene either in words (language) or actions.
    1932 Quinn *Collecting Rent* 111 Most of them paid something, with the exception of the one or two women that blackguarded us from the top windows.
    1939 Paterson *Country Cracks* 66 It was she [who had] the bad luck, all her cows dyin' of disorders an' she claimin' compensation off two townlan's and blackguardin' all her neighbours.
    2000 Fenton *Hamely Tongue* 19 *owl blaggart tak* = obscene talk of a sexual nature.
U.S.:   **1953** Randolph and Wilson *Down in Holler* 227 *blackguard* = to use vulgar or obscene language, or to tell smutty stories: 'Them Toliver gals just sets around an' blackguards all day long'; 'I'm ag'in this here blackguard talk right here in the church-house!'
    n.d. Berry and Repass *Grandpa Says* 19 'I heard you been blackguardin' me' = insulting.

blather See **blether**

blatherkumskite See **bletherkumskite**

blatherskite See **bletherskite**

blether(s), **blather(s)** *n* (sometimes plural in form) Nonsense, idle talk, one who talks nonsense. Hence *vb* To talk nonsense, especially at length; *interj* Nonsense! [< Old Norse *blaðra* 'to utter inarticulately, talk stupidly'; OED *blether* vb 1 'to talk nonsense loquaciously' 1524→, Scottish and northern dialect; DOST *bladder* vb 'to stammer; to talk nonsense' 1540→; SND *blether* vb 'to talk foolishly, or loquaciously; to brag']

ULST.:   **1813** Porter *Glossary Poetical Attempts* = idle talk.
1886 Lyttle *Ballycuddy* 41 Whun they say that they're jest talkin' blethers.
1917 Walsh *Guileless Saxon* 42 I hold ye it's the Temperance woman that he was blatherin' about, the night he came.
1920 McCallin *Fireside Tales* 141 When something unexpected happens all of a suddent t'yer benefit, it's only blethers yer apt to talk at yer best.
1921 Irvine *Poor Folk* 49 I don't pay gomerals to blether with the girls.
1925 McKay *Mourne Folk* 19 Och, Dandy, ye're a blether; but I forgive ye, for ye're too ould to take any notice of.
1932 Quinn *McConaghy's Money* 83 Yer nathin' but my poor oul' Da sent back to me to look after. I felt it there when ye wur blatherin' away.
1935 Megaw *Carragloon* 145 Ye needn't think that I'm goin' till listen till your blethers.
c1950 Doyle *Polis Protection* 10 I'm too busy a man to be standin' here blethering to a loafer like you.
1980 McClean *Ulster Words I* 2 *blether* = incessant idle talk.
U.S.:   **1859** Bartlett *Americanisms* 35 = the Irish pronunciation of *bladder*; figuratively, idle, windy talk.

bletherskite, **bletherkumskite**, **blatherskite**, **blatherkumskite** *n* A foolish person, one who talks nonsense. Hence *vb* To talk nonsense. [variant of *bletherskate* < *blether* + *skate* ' a mean or contemptible person'; cf OED *bletherskate* a 'a noisy, talkative fellow, talker of blatant nonsense' 1650→; b 'foolish talk, nonsense' 1825→, dialect and U.S. colloquial; cf SND *bladderskate* n 1(1) 'a silly foolish person, a babbler', 1(3) 'nonsense']

ULST.:   **1801** Bruce *Poems* 20 I'm nae mair than a bletherskyte / Compar'd wi' him.
1897 MacManus *Dhroll Donegal* 41 'Go to pot', says she, 'for a blatherskite. I don't believe a word of it that he has the sthrength he lets on'.
1903 MacManus *Lad of O'Friels* 192 What is it ye're bletherskitin' about?
1924 (in *Northern Whig*, as cited in **1931-76** Grant and Murison *SND*) 'A sore bletherkumskite' = one who talks nonsense.
1932 Quinn *Quiet Twelfth* 103 It's that blatherskite of an eedjit out there.
1998 Dolan *Dict Hiberno-English* 30 = a non-stop talker of nonsense.
2000 Fenton *Hamely Tongue* 19 *bletherskite* = one who habitually talks nonsense.
U.S.:   **1859** Bartlett *Americanisms* 35 *bletherskite* = a blustering, noisy, talkative fellow. the Irish pronunciation of *bladder*; figuratively, idle, windy talk.
1957 Justus *Other Side* 39 Glory always laughed at this speech, and so did Mammy and Grandy, although Grandy called it 'tomfoolery', and Matt a 'blatherskite'.

blink *vb* To bewitch, exercise an evil influence (over) by a glance of the 'evil eye', cast a spell or curse over; especially of milk: to spoil, turn sour. Hence *n* One who exercises an evil influence; an unlucky or jinxed person; a jinx or spell. In the U.S. the term is associated only with the souring of milk from being left warm, or with the milk so soured (usually called **blinky** or **blinked milk**). Hence **blinker** *n* One who exercises such an evil power. [OED *blink* vb I originally 'to deceive, elude, turn away', 7a 'to turn (milk, beer, etc.) slightly sour' 1616→, 7b 'to turn slightly sour' c1648→; DOST *blenk* v 1 'to give a glance or sudden look'; SND *blink* vb 3 'to glance at with the evil eye, to bewitch' (often as participial adj *blinkit* 'bewitched; turned sour'; DARE *blink* vb 1 'of milk: to turn sour' chiefly Midland]

ULST.:   1829 McSparran *Irish Legend* 247 He intended to go to Banagher for a little of the sacred sand, to cast over the Bimmagh to save him from witchcraft, or the blink of an ill eye, said he.
1880 Patterson *Antrim/Down Glossary* 9 = cow's milk is said to be blinked when it does not produce butter, in consequence of some supposed charm having been worked—a counter charm is required to bring it right.
1891 Simmons *Armagh Words and Phrases* 3 = to exercise an evil influence, to bewitch, to overlook, to deceive.
1910 Joyce *English in Ireland* 217 = to exercise an evil influence by a glance of 'the evil eye', to 'overlook', hence 'blinked', blighted by the eye. When the butter does not come in churning, the milk has been *blinked* by someone.
1929 Morrison *Modern Ulster* 53 On no account was a 'gentle bush' to be disturbed, for the fairies could 'blink', as they had for their defence the 'evil eye', or ability to secure that punishment would fall on whom they would.
1935 Megaw *Carragloon* 148 I'll say no more, Mr McElvey, but I'll say this that she's a witch and she blinked every egg I set this spring.
1937 Rowley *Tales of Mourne* 42 Mary's desprit feared they'll put the blink on the weans, an' bad as I am, I wouldn't want any ill-turn to happen to the childre.
1939 Paterson *Country Cracks* 43 Cows that wur blinked kept roarin' from morn till dusk an' there wur only two ways of curin' them. One wus till git the charm, and was slow, an' not always sure—an' the other, till keep the blinkers away.
1953 Traynor *Donegal Glossary* 26 = to exercise the powers of the evil eye, to overlook. If a cow gives symptons of illness, moans, give little milk, she had been blinked by someone. Also said of milk if it fails to produce butter ... remedy, which is still seen, is to tie a red ribbon on the horns of the animal.
1956 Bell *Orange Lily* 96-97 Today, in some parts of Ulster, men and women still twine red thread into the tails of their cattle before they drive them to market. It is a periapt. They would be politely surprised at your surprise. They could show you the stretch of road where the animals might be 'blinked'. To protect their animals is the sensible and commonplace thing to do.
1971 St. Clair *Folklore Ulster* 86 In most Ulster counties it was thought that if a person suspected of being able to 'blink' cattle offered to buy a beast off you, it was as well to sell it, for you would never have any good of her afterwards.
1981 Pepper *Ulster-English Dict* 13 Don't ast him to come along. He's the blink.
2000 Fenton *Hamely Tongue* 19 = to put the blink on, put a curse (the evil eye) on.

U.S.:   1895 *Word-lists* 384 blink, blinky = sour milk.

1905 Carr *Words NW Ark* 70 = to turn sour, used of milk only: 'It was so warm that the milk blinked'.
1953 Randolph and Wilson *Down in Holler* 227 That milk'll blink sure if you leave it settin' out in the sun that-a-way.
1997 *GSMNPOHP* 1:2 The milk was put in the spring house to keep the milk cool. If you didn't, it'd blink on you.

blow *vb* To speak loudly, brag; mislead by exaggeration or deceive. Hence *n* A boast; one who brags or misleads by exaggeration. [OED *blow* vb I 6(a) 'to boast, brag' chiefly regional; SND (at *blaw* vb II.1) 'to boast, brag; to exaggerate']
ULST.: **1898** MacManus *Humours of Donegal* 19 There must have been something in it, or he wouldn't have made such a blow out of nothing.
1932 Quinn *McConaghy's Money* 16 A woman that's always blowin' of the fine man ma Da was when she met him first workin' at the main drainage.
1942 *Bangor Words* 9 Don't heed him, he's only a blow.
1991 O'Kane *You Don't Say* 13 = to boast or brag, especially about oneself: 'I heard him blowin' about how well he played'.
2000 Fenton *Hamely Tongue* 20 = brag, talk at length of one's ability, achievements or possessions (especially *bum an blow*); = a braggart, a boastful person.
U.S.: **1859** Bartlett *Americanisms* = to boast, brag; to 'talk big. 'You blow behind my back, but not dare not say any thing to my face'.
c1945 Haun *Hawk's Done* 218 He wouldn't be blowing when he told his boys how he fit for the woman he got.
1975 Jackson *Unusual Words* 153 If one man says of another, 'Hay-lo, you gotta watch 'im; he'll blow you', the listener is being warned about an excessive bragger.

boady See **body**

boal See **bole**

body, boady, bodey, buddy *n* A person, someone, certain person. [DOST *body* n 3 'a person' 15th century→; DARE widespread, but especially Midland]
ULST.: **1840** Boyce *Shandy Maguire* 35 Well, every thing a body hears isn't true, for all that.
1885 Lyttle *Robin Gordon* 29 A lauched at the puir, simple buddy, although, indeed, she wuz nae mair ignorant nor A wuz mysel' yince.
1902 McIlroy *Druid's Island* 71 'Aye, there's nae doot ava', said Geordie, 'but the weemen are curious, kittle bodies.'
c1910 Byers *Glossary* = an impersonal pronoun; a person, anyone, oneself; implying that the person indicated belongs to the humbler classes, or is in some way inferior.
1912 Gregory *Ulster Folk* 3 Anither body owns it now, / But she's—jist like m'self—grown grey.
1935 Megaw *Carragloon* 78 'It's this way', says the beggar body, 'the cure lies nearder the disease nor folks thinks'.
1938 McCallin *Killywhapple* 35 A body might reasonably a-thought that by-gones would a-been let be by-gones with them.
c1955 Montgomery *Heard in Ulster* 38 He's a dae-less bodey.
1955 Murphy *Culprit of Shadows* 6 I don't know how a body could be content to sit an' smoke behind that jamb-wall at the fire an' it so dark.

2000 Fenton *Hamely Tongue* 20 = a person: 'Ye couldnae meet a dacenter
boady'.

U.S.:   **1843** Hall *New Purchase* 68 How in creation is a body to have dinner if a body
aint time cook it?
1895 Edson and Fairchild *Tenn Mts* 370 A body can't git along here.
1899 Green *Virginia Word-Book* 63 = a person: 'Why cant you let a body
alone?'
1939 Hall *Coll* One-armed Jim is right feeble. I reckon a body'll find him dead
somewheres.
1930 Shoemaker *1300 Penn Words* 1 *body* = a person.
1940 Haun *Hawk's Done* 48 There wasn't anything a body could say to Barshia
that would do him any good.

bole, boal, bole-hole *n* A small hole in the wall for holding articles. [possibly
imitative; OED *bole* 'a small square hole in the recess of a room for holding articles'
1728→, Scottish; DOST *bowall* n 'a recess in the wall' 16th century→; SND *bole* 1 'a
small recess or cupboard in the wall of an apartment']

ULST.:   **1900** Given *Poems* 251 I hid like a frog in a hole, / While fearing the critic's
effusion / I flung my pen intae the bole.
1953 Traynor *Donegal Glossary* 29 *bole* = a round or square air-hole in the side
of a byre.
1957 Evans *Irish Folk-Ways* 65 Wooden or stone seats are often built in near
the hearth, and the wall behind the fire, protected by a flagstone or a built-up
hob, usually has a keeping hole on each side of the fire. Known as boles in
Antrim and coves in Cavan, these may be elaborated into two- or three-tier
wall-dressers whose ancestry lies in the stone house tradition of the mountain
country.
1980 McClean *Ulster Words* I 3 *bole-holes* = cavities set in the wall by the
fireplace.
2000 Fenton *Hamely Tongue* 22 *bole* = a recess in a wall used as a pigeon-hole,
etc.; a small opening in a wall (usually for ventilation).

U.S.:   **1930** Shoemaker *1300 Penn Words* 5 *boal* = a small press, or cupboard in the
wall.

bonnick, bonnock See **bannock**

bonny clabber, bonny clobber *n* Clotted sour milk; milk that has begun to sour
and curdle. See also **clabber**. [< Irish *bainne* 'milk' + *clabar* (usually taken as an
extended meaning of Irish *clábar* 'mud, mire', but for an alternative etymology see
1960 Malone *Bonnyclabber*, which defines the term as 'milk of the dasher (i.e. of a
stage fit to be churned)' and derives it from Irish *bainne* 'milk' + *clabaire* 'inverted
cup through which the churndash passes'); OED *bonnyclabber* n 'milk naturally
clotted or coagulated on souring' 1634→, Anglo-Irish; DARE chiefly North Atlantic]

ULST.:   c**1910** Byers *Glossary, bonny clabber* = sour milk that has become thick.
1990 Todd *Words Apart* 34 When ye get cruds on the milk, that's
bonnyclobber.
1998 Dolan *Dict Hiberno-English* 35 *bonny clabber* = thick milk that could be
used for churning.

U.S.:   **1807** Janson *Stranger in America* 187 The morning's milk turns to curd in the
evening ... This they call 'bonny-clabber', and eat it with honey, sugar, or
molasses.

1859 Bartlett *Americanisms* 43 = milk turned sour and thick. It is sometimes called simply *clabber*. The etymology shows that the sense in which the term is used in America is the true and original one, although it is usually explained in dictionaries as meaning 'sour buttermilk'.

1949 Kurath *Word Geog East US* 70 *Bonny-clabber* is still common in the Philadelphia area [and] appears in scattered fashion in central and western Pennsylvania and from there southward to North Carolina, an area in which it has been largely replaced by other terms.

botheration *n* A nuisance, petty source of trouble or vexation. Hence *interj* A mild oath. [OED *botheration* 'petty vexation or annoyane; often used as an exclamation'; DARE as exclamation chiefly North]

ULST.:   1840 Boyce *Shandy Maguire* 38 Botheration to me, but I'll take the tongs to ye, if ye don't hold yer tongue.
1920 Doyle *Ballygullion* 'Bad cess to it, Milly', sez I to the wife, 'here's more botheration.'
1921 Irvine *Poor Folk* 142 'Botheration!', he would say, 'I hate the—things.'
1923 Lutton *Montiaghisms* 11 = a person, thing or circumstance that causes trouble or annoyance.
1953 Traynor *Donegal Glossary* 31 = bother, trouble.
1991 O'Kane *You Don't Say* 15 = trouble, nuisance, annoyance: 'The new money is a terrible botheration'.
2000 Fenton *Hamely Tongue* 23 = a pest or nuisance: 'a botheration haein tae change yer claes ivery fart's-en'.

U.S.:   1834 Smith *Life Jack Downing* 49 The people are growing pretty mad at all this botheration.
1938 Justus *No-End Hollow* 35 But Jessie is a botheration, making fun the way she does, and Granny fusses at the noise.
1970 Vincent *More of Best* 41 He does have one little botheration now.

bottom(s), **bottom land** *n* A stretch of low-lying, well-drained, usually fertile land along a river or stream. [OED *bottom* n 4b 'low-lying land, a valley, a dell, an alluvial hollow'; SED northern English; DARE *bottom* n 1a 'alluvial land, especially low-lying land near a stream; the soil in such an area' chiefly South, West Midland, *bottomland* chiefly South, Midland]

ULST.:   1891 Simmons *Armagh Words and Phrases* 4 bottom = a low-lying field.
c1910 Byers *Glossary*, bottoms = low-lying land, meadow or holmland, subject to inundation.
1919 MacGill *Glenmornan* 52 From the river to the road the bottom land is a level strip. From the road to the top of the hill, the land stands on end.
c1955 Montgomery *Heard in Ulster* 14 bottoms = low-lying fields or land.

U.S.:   1816 Pickering *American Vocabulary* 51 In Pennsylvania and some other States [*bottom lands*] is given to rich flat lands on the banks of rivers, which in New England is generally called *interval-land*, or simply *interval*.
1834 Crockett *Narrative* 111 It was very dark, and the river was so full that it overflowed the banks and the adjacent low bottoms.
1859 Bartlett *Americanisms* 45 bottom = low land with a rich soil formed by alluvial deposits, and formerly the bottom or bed of a stream or lake.
1871 Eggleston *Hoosier Schoolmaster* 28 You see this ere bottom land was all Congress land in them there days.

1943 Peattie *Indian Days* 41 Level alluvial land among the mountains is usually a bottom.
1949 Kurath *Word Geog East US* 61 In the Midland and the South *bottom lands* and *bottoms* are the most common expressions for low-lying flat meadow lands and fields along large and small watercourses. *Bottom lands* is more common in the North Midland, *bottoms* in the South and South Midland.
1982 Parris *Here's How* Level land fit for farming is a 'bottom', and if it's located beside a major stream it's called a 'river bottom'.

brash *n* A slight attack of sickness, especially indisposition brought on by indigestion. [perhaps imitative; OED *brash* 2 'a slight attack of sickness or indisposition, especially one arising from a disorder of the alimentary canal' chiefly dialect; DOST *brasche* n 2 'an attack or fit of illness' 1622→]

ULST.:   **1880** Patterson *Antrim/Down Glossary* 12 = an attack of illness.
1892 *Ballymena Observer* (in **1898-1905** Wright *Engl Dial Dict*) I have got over that brash.
1904 Byers *Sayings of Ulster* 58 While proceeding to visit the patient the doctor may be told by the Ulsterman that the member of his family who is ill (it may be his wife) has a 'bad brash' (attack).
1953 Traynor *Donegal Glossary* 33 = an attack of illness, any bout of sickness: 'He'd a bad brash a few years gone and he never mended all out'.

U.S.:   **1872** Schele de Vere *Americanisms* 446 In southern New Jersey and Pennsylvania an acid taste rising in the mouth is frequently called *brash*, and an indisposed person is said to be *brashy*.
1899 Green *Virginia Word-Book* 67 = sudden nausea, with acid rising in the mouth, as in heartburn.

brickle, brickly, bruckle *adj* Brittle, easily broken; of weather: changeable, uncertain. In Ulster only the form *bruckle* is attested (although both it and *brickle* are documented in Scotland); in the U.S. only *brickle* and *brickly* are attested [the forms represent two etymological sources that have at some point fallen together; OED *brickle* adj 2b 'liable to break, easily broken' < Middle English *bruchel* 1468→, obsolete or dialectal, *bruckle* 'liable to break, fragile, brittle' 1513→, chiefly Scottish and dialect; DOST *brukill* adj 'easily broken, brittle; unstable'; SND *bruckle, brickle* 'brittle, easily broken, crumbling'; DARE *brickle* adj 1 'brittle, crisp' chiefly South, Midland]

ULST.:   **1861** Hume *Rabbin's Ollminick* 10 Goin' out on the watther's dangersome these bruckle days.
1880 Patterson *Antrim/Down Glossary* 13 *bruckle* = brittle: 'That's bruckle ware ye'r carryin'".
1904 Marshall *Dial of Ulster* 125 *bruckle* = brittle, short-grained, easily broken.
1923 Lutton *Montiaghisms* 12 *bruckle* = applied to the weather, signifies changeable and showery.
1942 *Bangor Words* 12 *bruckle* = easily broken into small pieces, brittle: 'Oaten bread when well harned is gye and bruckle'; 'His temper is a bit bruckle in the morning'.
1953 Traynor *Donegal Glossary* 37 *bruckle* = (1) brittle: 'The bread is getting bruckle'; (2) of weather: unstable, changeable; (3) of things: uncertain.
1991 O'Kane *You Don't Say* 18 *bruckle* = (1) changeable, not dependable, said of showery weather especially during hay-making; (2) easily broken; flaky or

brittle: 'That's very bruckle bread'.

2000 Fenton *Hamely Tongue* 27 = brittle, friable: *bruckle wather* = uncertain, changeable weather.

U.S.: **1804** (in **2004** Hartley *Lewis and Clark Lexicon* 52) this [cottonwood] timber is heavy ... Brickle & Soft.

1837 Sherwood *Georgia Provincialisms* 118 *brickly* = brittle.

1872 Schele de Vere *Americanisms* 586 We have had brickle weather of late.

1899 Green *Virginia Word-Book* 68 *brickly* = easily broken, brittle.

1930 Shoemaker *1300 Penn Words* 7 *brickle* = changeable, uncertain: 'Maids is brickle'.

1953 Randolph and Wilson *Down in Holler* 230 *brickle* = brittle, crisp: 'If cowcumber pickles ain't brickle, they ain't fit to eat'.

1969 Miller *Raising Tobacco* 33 However, in this condition leaves were *brickle* (brittle) and shattered easily.

1975 Jackson *Unusual Words* 158 Old timers are careful to point out that the *brickle* black birch is unsuitable; only the tough white birch is wanted.

brogan, brogan shoe *n* A coarse, heavy, leather work-shoe laced with thongs, usually homemade. Although no citation has been found from Ulster, the term is attested in Scotland and is undoubtedly derived from Irish, Scottish Gaelic, or both, even though the OED has citations only from the U.S. Same as **brogue**[1]. [diminutive of Irish *bróg* or Scottish Gaelic *bròg* 'shoe'; cf SND *brogue* n[1]; DARE *brogan* n 1 'a heavy work-shoe' widespread, but especially common in South, South Midland]

U.S.: **1835** Hoffman *Winter in West* 1.200 In another [corner of the room], a pair of Cinderella-like slippers would *chassez* cross with a brace of thick-soled broghans.

1908 Payne *Word-list East Alabama* 294 = a coarse, low shoe cut in Blucher style; formerly used of any shoe cut in this style, but now only of the coarse workman's shoe.

1939 Hall *Coll* Those brogans are weighing you down.

1943 Hannum *Mt People* 142 There were no rights and lefts to those homemade brogans, square cut from tanned hide ... Gradually they wore to shape.

1956 Hall *Coll* Back then when we didn't make our shoes, my dad would buy us one pair a year and it was a brogan shoe. [We] called 'em brogans, of course, heavy leather, and if we wore the shoe out, we went barefooted.

brogue[1], **brog** *n* A coarse, heavy, leather work shoe; a boot. In the U.S. this term as a noun was apparently replaced by **brogan** at an early period, but as a verb it came to mean 'to sole (a shoe, especially a moccasin) with leather; go about on foot, wander, especially to walk aimlessly'. See also **brogan**. [< Irish *bróg* or Scottish Gaelic *bròg* 'shoe'; OED *brogue* n[2] 1a 'a rude kind of shoe, generally made of untanned hide, worn by the inhabitants of the wilder parts of Ireland and the Scotch highlands' 1694→; SND *brogue* n[1] 'a rough Highland shoe of untanned hide, stitched with thongs of leather' 1738→; DARE *brogue* vb 'to walk, hike, trudge; to wander or go about aimlessly' chiefly southern Appalachians]

ULST.: **1804** Orr *Poems* 36 Owre braes, an' bogs, / The *patriots* seek their *sections*; / Arms, ammunition, bread-bags, brogues, / Lye skail'd in a' directions.

1880 Patterson *Antrim/Down Glossary* 13 *brogues* = a pair of common boots: 'As vulgar as a pair of brogues'.

1889 Hart *Derryreel* 12 By divesting myself of fishing-brogues and stockings, and taking the necessary jumps barefoot, I succeeded in reaching the flat rock though in a rather damaged condition with respect to my feet.

1891 Simmons *Armagh Words and Phrases* 4 = a strong boot sewed with thongs of leather.

c1910 Byers *Glossary* = a kind of rough shoe, made generally of untanned hide, and stitched with thongs of leather.

1953 Traynor *Donegal Glossary* 36-37 = (1) a boot; (2) the common name for a sort of high shoe; (3) a low strong boot half-way between a shoe and an ordinary boot.

2004 Smyth *Tartan in Ulster* The find consisted of a woollen jacket or jerkin, a small portion of a mantle or cloak, trews or trousers, and leather brogues. This was the style of clothing worn by men in those parts in the 16th and early 17th century.

U.S.: **c1765** Woodmason *Carolina Backcountry* 151 I don't know indeed whether He wore Brogues then, or not—I fancy they us'd Mockasins, as our Indians do.

1815 Brackenridge *Modern Chivalry* 104 I had to fly de kingdom, and brought nating wid me but my brogs, and ten guineas in my purse.

1859 Taliaferro *Fisher's River* 153 Instead of shoes, he wears hogskin moccasins brogued with sole-leather.

1883 Zeigler and Grosscup *Heart of Alleghanies* 51 I've brogued it through every briar patch an' laurel thicket, an' haint I bin with Guyot, Sandoz, Grand Pierre, and Clingman over every peak from hyar to the South Caroliny an' Georgy lines?

1913 Kephart *Our Sthn High* 203 I'm jest broguin' about.

1943 Justus *Bluebird* 44 I've got to brogue along home.

1959 Hall *Coll* That Indian was settin' there broguin' his moccasins. Broguin' [means] puttin' soles on.

1966 Medford *Ol' Starlin* 66 'Brogued it' (to travel in brogans) is another [expression not in the dictionary].

brogue² *n* A distinctive local accent or habit of pronunciation (in the U.S. the term does not necessarily imply real or perceived Irish or Scottish characteristics). Scholarly opinion is divided whether this sense derives from **brogue** 'a heavy shoe'. [OED *brogue* n¹ 'an Irish accent (from the idea of having a shoe in your mouth)'; cf **1998** Dolan *Dict Hiberno-Engl* 42 'There is a view that Irish people used to speak English unintelligibly (as a result of linguistic contamination from Irish syntax and vocabulary), and the effect was as if they had a shoe on their tongue'; but also see citation below from **1977** Braidwood *Brogue on Tongue*]

ULST.: **1893** Bullock *Awkward Squad* 128 For the lads it was a vast pleasure to hear his very human brogue rolling through the smoke.

1910 Joyce *English in Ireland* 225 = used also to designate the Irish accent in speaking English: for the old Irish thong-stitched brogue was considered so characteristically Irish that the word was applied to our accent.

1942 *Bangor Words* 12 = the accent of a Southern Irishman.

1977 Braidwood *Brogue on Tongue* 69 Before the 18th century *brogue* (Irish *bróg* a shoe) always refers to footwear. [The Oxford English Dictionary] queries whether *brogue* 'an accent' is the same word as *brogue*, 'a shoe'. But the Irish lexicographer Dinneen much more plausibly derives *brogue*, the accent, from an altogether different word, *barróg*, 'an embrace, a hold in wrestling, a tight grip; impediment or difficulty'; *barróg teangan* 'a lisp'. From the mid 18th century on the Irish of Boston talk, not just of the *brogue* but of *the brogue on the tongue*. The brogue, in fact, was originally the difficulty experienced by Irish speakers in getting their tongues round the alien English sounds.

U.S.: **1978** Montgomery *White Pine Coll* III-2 He's a Tennessean. I can tell by his brogue.

1996 Montgomery *File* He's just got an old mountain brogue.

bruckle See **brickle**

buddy See **body**

bumbee *n* A bumble-bee. [< *bum* 'to hum loudly' + *bee*; OED *bum-bee* n 'bumble-bee' 1653→, Scottish; SND *bum-bee* n 'the bumble-bee' 1718→]

ULST.: **1886** Lyttle *Ballycuddy* 23 As fur his reverence he wuz twirlin' the yin thoom roon the tither an' watchin' a bumbee that had cum in by the wundey.

c1910 Wier *Bab McKeen* Yin wee lad ... went happin' aboot through the hoose like a bum-bee.

1921 Irvine *Poor Folk* 136 Johnny had a big body, but his wee sowl would have had as much room in a thimble as a bumbee would in Lough Neagh.

1933 Foster *Tyrone among Bushes* 39 'There's not as much on [the chicken's] bones', sez I, 'as would make soup for a sick bum-bee.'

U.S.: **1950** Bradley *Word-list from SC* 17 = the bumblebee.

1982 Barrick *Coll* = bumblebee.

bunty *adj* Of an animal, especially a chicken: short-tailed or tail-less; of a person: short or small in stature, short-tempered, etc. Hence *n* Such an animal [SND (at *bunt*) 'a hen without a rump' 1721→; DARE *bunty* n 'a tailless fowl' chiefly Appalachians]

ULST.: **1891** Simmons *Armagh Words and Phrases* 3 = short, shorter than what it should naturally be.

1905 Marshall *Dial of Ulster* 68 = short-tailed, like a rabbit.

c1910 Byers *Glossary* = figuratively, short in the temper, as 'Whiles, he's a bit bunty'.

1920 Doyle *Ballygullion* 53 [The dog was] a low-set, crooked-legged baste, wi' a dirty brown coat, an' a wee bunty tail.

c1955 Montgomery *Heard in Ulster* 18 = undersized, short: 'He's very bunty lookin'.

U.S.: **1930** Shoemaker *1300 Penn Words* 5 = a rumpless, or tailless fowl, originally from the north of Ireland.

1956 McAtee *Some Dial NC* 7 My little bunty hen.

by times See **betimes**

by-word, bye-word *n* The favorite expression or proverb of an individual; a mild oath or exclamation used to avoid profanity. [OED *by-word* n 3 'a word or phrase of frequent occurrence in speech' obsolete; DARE *byword* n 'one's favorite expression, usually a mild oath' chiefly South Midland]

ULST.: **1863** Hume *Rabbin's Ollminick* 13 With that the bye-word riz—'Yer late, as Paddy Loughran sayd t' the ghost.'

1879 Lyttle *Paddy McQuillan* 55 'Sit up till the fire!' sez Paddy. That wuz a kind o' a bye-word wi' Paddy.

1880 Patterson *Antrim/Down Glossary* 15 *bye-word* = a saying.

1897 McIlroy *Lint in Bell* 138 'As wild as a Tumulty' became a bye-word in the neighborhood.

U.S.:   **1899** Green *Virginia Word-Book* 76 = a saying, a word used as a proverb: 'He knows all the by-words in the country'.

1953 Randolph and Wilson *Down in Holler* 232 *by-word* = one's favorite expression.

1975 Carter *Gospel Truth* When he really meant to cuss, he did it out by the barn or down by the granary. Around womenfolk he was usually more gentle. Restraint was part of the pride in him, but he often softened words as if he were a bit ashamed. He used 'by words' instead of cuss words. 'By damn' was acceptable.

1983 Pyle *CCC 50th Anniv* A:3:13-14 Mr. Scott says his by word was 'dog gone my cats'. He said, 'Dog gone my cats, the next time you get sick', he says, 'you're not a-going into the camp.'

1998 Ownby *Big Greenbrier* 12 We were never allowed to use any kind of a 'by-word' or accuse each other of telling a lie.

C

cabin *n* A traditional house-type having a single room, more prevalent in Ireland than Britain in the 18th century and brought to the U.S. from Ulster. See citations. [< Middle English *cabane*]

ULST.:   **1813** Porter *Poetical Attempts* [The light] came from a neighbouring cot, / Some called it the Cabin of Mourne: / A neat Irish cabin, snow-proof, / Well thatched, had a good earthern floor, / One chimney in midst of the roof, / One window, and one latched door.

U.S.:   **1965** Evans *Cultural Relics* 34 The single room averages about 17 by 21 ft. in internal dimensions: additions to the back of the house usually take the form of an 'ell' of light frame construction. The log-house normally has an unheated loft or bedroom in the roof space lit only by a small window in the gable and reached by steep stairs at the chimney end. The chimney, of brick or stone, is placed externally and the wide hearth is designed to take an open wood-fire. When one adds that there was often a back door opposite the front door and that half-doors were not uncommon it will be realised that the log-cabin faithfully reproduced in a novel medium the space-relations of the single-roomed gable chimney house of mud or stone that must have been the commonest house-type in eighteenth-century Ulster.

1984 Gailey *Migrant Culture* 25 Removed to pre-Revolutionary America, Scotch-Irish settlers initially built themselves what came to be known, from the middle of the eighteenth century, as 'log cabins'. The term 'cabin' was then in widespread use in Ireland for any small house, especially for the homes of the poor. Various writers have pointed to similarities of ground plan and internal arrangements between the Irish housing just described and these wilderness cabins, which were simple rectangles with opposed entrances in front and rear walls separating two spaces, at the gable end of one of which (sometimes both ends) there was a chimney.

caddow, cadda, cadder *n* A quilt or coverlet, usually a rough one. [origin uncertain; OED *caddow* 'a rough woollen covering' obsolete or dialect; DOST *caddow, cadday, cada* n 'a rough woollen covering or rug' 1576→]

ULST.:   c**1910** Byers *Glossary*, *cadda* = a quilt, coverlet; a cloak or cover, a small cloth which lies on a horse's back, underneath the 'straddle'.

U.S.:   **1843** *Our Cabin* 446 To make rag carpeting, such as sometimes covers kitchen floors now, and to sew two breadths of proper length together, was a good substitute for blankets ... These cadders (for so we called them,) were a great help in bed ... from their great ability to press a sheet or blanket close. **1899** Green *Virginia Word-Book* 76 = a quilt; a coverlet.

cadgy, cagey, caigey, caigy *adj* Spirited, sportive (in the U.S. also amorous, sexually aroused). [origin uncertain; OED *cadgy* adj 1 'sexually excited' c1724→, Scottish and northern dialect, 2 'cheerful, merry, glad' 1725→; SND *cadgy* 'cheerful, in good spirits; dotingly amorous; eagerly willing'; DARE *cadgy* adj 'lively, excited, spry; especially of stallions: sexually aroused' chiefly South Midland]

ULST.:   **1880** Patterson *Antrim/Down Glossary* 16 *caigey* = in very good spirits, lively, wanton, eager.

c1910 Byers *Glossary*, *cagey* = in good spirits, gay, cheerful, sportive: 'He's a cagey boy'.
1953 Traynor *Donegal Glossary* 42 *cadgy* = gay, cheerful, in good spirits.
2000 Fenton *Hamely Tongue* 31 *caigy* = lively; full of energy.
U.S.:   1917 Kephart *Word-list* 409 *caigy* = full of sexual desire.
1955 Parris *Roaming Mts* 177 The dogs are cagey. They are born to taunt rather than fight.
1993 Walker *Life History* 30 [A powder was] used to make the animals 'cagey' and reproduce.

ca-he See **cohee**

caigey, caigy See **cadgy**

canty, cantie *adj* Cheerful, lively. Hence **cantily** *adv* Cheerfully, with liveliness. [apparently from Low German/Dutch, cf modern Dutch *kant* 'neat, clever'; OED *canty* 'cheerful, lively, gladsome' 1724→, Scottish and northern dialect; SND *canty* 'lively, cheerful, pleasant' 1721→]
ULST.:   1734 *Northern Bard* 160 He'd cantily come o'er the Gate, / We' ane or two that was na bleat, / To tak their Mault.
1801 Bruce *Poems* 15 Fair fa' ye, canty Aqua Vitae, / Indeed, ye've gi'en's a dainty ditty.
1813 Porter *Poetical Attempts* A bottle o' the stoutest nappy, / That ever yet could boast the birth / O' either anger, wit, or mirth, / Cauldna hae made me half sae vauntie, / Or made me 'cock my crest' so cantie.
1920 McCallin *Ulster Plenishing* 62-63 It has faithfully done its duty to them that ... heartsome an' canty, saucered every drop of it, no matther what its brand might happen to be.
1953 Traynor *Donegal Glossary* 44 *canty* = (1) of persons: pleasant, cheerful, lively; (2) of things: small and tidy; 3) expert, skilful.
2000 Fenton *Hamely Tongue* 32 *cantie* = lively, small and neat, winsome: 'a cantie wee hizzy; a cantie powny'.
U.S.:   1930 Shoemaker *1300 Penn Words* 15 *canty* = merry, talkative.

caoine See **keen**.

cat and clay, catin clay *n* Clay or moss mixed with sticks or straw and used as a building material for chimneys or walls; a rude chimney made of such material. [SND *cat and clay* 'applied to the walls of a building formed of wicker-work plastered with clay inside and out', cf SND *ket* n 'matted wool in the fleece'; DARE *cat-and-clay* n 'a mixture of clay with sticks or straw used as a building or chinking material for chimneys' South Midland]
ULST.:   1891 Simmons *Armagh Words and Phrases* 5 *catin clay* = clay with rushes or straw, used in building the mud walls of cottages.
2000 Fenton *Hamely Tongue* 34 *cat* = fibrous material found in pieces or small clumps in peat.
U.S.:   1927 Woofter *Dialect West Virginia* 350 *cat and clay chimney* = a chimney built of sticks and daubed with mud.
1953 Randolph and Wilson *Down in Holler* 233 *cat-and-clay* = a rude chimney made of sticks and mud.

catch *n* A sudden, sharp pain, especially in the side. [OED *catch* II2 'a sharp pain'; SND *catch* n 2 'an acute pain, a "stitch"'; cf DARE *catch-pain* 'a sharp, sudden pain, usually in the side' chiefly South, South Midland]
> ULST.: 2004 Fenton *Notes* There's a wee catch there.
> U.S.: 1954 Harder *Coll* = a sudden muscular pain in the back.
> 1983 Broaddus and McAtee *Estill Co Word List* 34 = a sudden, sharp pain in the side.

chancy *adj* Lucky, auspicious. (Note: this sense was not found in Ulster, but note the citation below for **unchancy** 'unlucky', from which the existence of **chancy** can be inferred; the sense 'risky' is standard). Cf **wanchancy**. [OED *chancy* adj 1 'lucky ... auspicious' Scottish, obsolete; DOST *chancy* adj 'bringing or having good fortune, fortunate, lucky' 1513→]
> ULST.: 1937 Rowley *Tales of Mourne* 39 There'll not be a penny of Fairy money about this house. It's unchancy.
> U.S.: 1930 Shoemaker *1300 Penn Words* 12 = fortunate, good-natured.
> 1962 Thompson *Body & Britches* If you would like to know about the 'wanchancy' things that haunted our forests, you cannot do better than to read Jesse's *Legends of the Longhouse* (1938).
> 1971 Dwyer *Dict for Yankees* 24 = lucky: 'I know a chancy place to fish'.
> 1996 Montgomery *Coll* It's a chancy place to fish.

chay, **chegh**, **chey** *interj* (usually repeated) A call to cows, in order to calm them, bring them in to feed, etc. [perhaps < Irish *téigh-* 'to move, proceed'; see **1980/81** Adams citation]
> ULST.: 1880 Patterson *Antrim/Down Glossary* 18 *chay-chay* = said to cows to call them or quiet them.
> 1902 McIlroy *Druid's Island* 30 He kep' mutterin', 'Chay, now; chay, chay, chay, lady'.
> c1910 Byers *Glossary*, *chay-chay* = a word used in calling milch cows: 'Chay lady' = an exclamation used to quiet a cow.
> 1910 Russell *Language of Ulster* 37 What Australian or English tourist would understand the meaning of the word 'chay' although you will hear the word every day in the country? It is a word of endearment, and is only applied to a cow. As you approach, you say 'chay, lady' to calm or 'quaten' her.
> 1924 Logan *Ulster in X-Rays* 77 The word 'chay' is often uttered when a person approaches a cow to catch her.
> 1933 Foster *Tyrone among Bushes* 95 'Here give us the lantern till I tie her up again', and to the cow he entreated, 'Chay, cratur, chay.'
> c1955 Montgomery *Heard in Ulster* 23 *chey-chey* = a call to cows when bringing them from the field.
> 1980/81 Adams *Call-Words* 26 *chey* = commonly understood as being the Irish word *teigh*, 'go', and so spelt by those knowing Irish.
> 1997 Share *Slanguage* 49 *chegh* = call to herd or quieten a cow.
> 2000 Fenton *Hamely Tongue* 35 *chay!* = call to cows.
> U.S.: 1949 McDavid *Atlas Mill* 105 *Chay!* as a call to summon cows does not seem to occur elsewhere in the United States [other than in South Carolina].

check *n* A light meal, snack. [OED *chack* 'a "bite" (of food); a snack' 1818→,
Scottish; SND *chack* n³ 'a snack; a casual, slight, or hurried meal'; DARE
Appalachians; LAUSC West Virginia]
> ULST.:   **1880** Patterson *Antrim/Down Glossary* 18 = a slight meal.
> **1923** Lutton *Montiaghisms* 13 = a small quantity of food taken between meals,
> a lunch.
> U.S.:   **1774** Fithian *Journal* 2.6 This is an Irish settlement—They speak in a shrill,
> acute, Accent, & have many odd phrases ... 'Will you just take a Check?'—She
> meant a late dinner.
> **1872** Schele de Vere *Americanisms* 452 = the name of an impromptu meal of
> cold provisions.
> **1949** Kurath *Word Geog East US* 36 On the Kanawha [River of West Virginia]
> we find *check* ... beside the Southern *snack* for a bite between meals.

cheep *transitive vb* To reveal (a secret), betray (a confidence). Hence *n* A word,
hint, least mention. [originally 'to chirp'; DARE *cheep* vb 'to tell or reveal; to betray
a confidence' chiefly South Midland]
> ULST.:   **1942** *Bangor Words* 16 = chirp, sound, word: 'Not a cheep out of you now'.
> U.S.:   **1940** Haun *Hawk's Done* 22 I never did cheep it to Joe. I thought it best not
> to.

chegh, chey See **chay**

childer, childre *n* Children. [< Middle English *childer, childre* < late Old English
cildru, cildra; OED '*childer* was the regular northern and north midland form [in
England], and is still used in the dialects as far south as Leicester, Shropshire, and
Lincolnshire'; DOST *childer* n 1375→] (Note: the more common term in Ulster
today is *weans*.)
> ULST.:   **1738** Ray *Letter* I shall rejoyce exceedingly, to see you and her wee yer Childer.
> **1829** McSparran *Irish Legend* 84 There was a poor woman in ould times, as it
> might be, that had to luck for her bit through the world, dear, and moreover
> than that, she had six small childer.
> **1895** MacManus *Leadin' Road* 57 Wantin' sparin's ye are, is it, till the childre
> get out of the fever, an' ye're able to pull yerself together again?
> **1936** White *Mrs Murphy* 78 She had the house nice, and the childer lovely
> kept.
> **1942** *Bangor Words* 16 *childer* = the common plural of 'child'.
> **1981** Pepper *Ulster-English Dict* 18 Them childer wud drive ye astray so they
> wud.
> **2002** Reynolds *Granfeyther's Tunge* 13 Spare a thocht for the gallant boys, wha
> showed the wurl tha way, / That we micht hae oor freedom, tae leeve tha wye
> wae dae, / An that their childer's childer, wud alwyes hae their say.
> U.S.:   **1845** Thompson *Pineville* 162 His ready reply was, that he was ''bleeged' to do
> the best he could to get meat for her and the 'childer'.
> **1930** (in **1952** Mathes *Tall Tales* 167-68) They's too many women an' childer
> nowadays a-rippin' an' a-tearin', a-runnin' hither an' yon a-pleasurin'
> theirselves.

chimbley, chimley *n* A chimney. [OED *chimbley, chimley* n Scottish and dialect; DOST *chimlay* n 1540→; SND *chimbley, chimley* n; DARE *chimbley* n A chiefly South, Midland]

ULST.: 1829 McSparran *Irish Legend* 294 Out of the chimley she goes like a wild goose.
1880 Patterson *Antrim/Down Glossary* 18 *chimley* = a chimney.
1886 Lyttle *Ballycuddy* 43 They put anither big sod on the chimley so as nae licht cud get in.
1904 Byers *Sayings of Ulster* 31 I wonder are the Ulster children of the present age as well acquainted as their parents were with Johnny Nod, who came towards bedtime, not from 'the land of Nod, on the east of Eden', but right down the chimley (dialect form of chimney).
1928 McKay *Oul' Town* 64 His next move was to pelt stones down widow Rooney's 'chimbley', an' if he didn't break her teapot.
1981 Pepper *Ulster-English Dict* 18 That's the second time this week the chimley's went on fire.

U.S.: 1837 Sherwood *Georgia Provincialisms* 118 *chimbly* = chimney.
1939 Hall *Coll* Boys, you'uns [are] talkin' about rough country, but I'm gonna tell you one time the roughest country I was in. It was so steep the people had to look up the chimley to see if the cows was still in the pasture.
1969 *GSMNP*-38:62 They had it about all finished except the chimbley.

clabber, clabour, clobber *n* Mud, mire (hence *clabbers* clumps of mud); especially in the U.S., milk that has begun to sour and curdle (= **bonny clabber**); the term refers only to soured milk in the U.S., where **clabber milk, clabbered milk** are also known; see **1949** Kurath citation). Hence *vb* Of milk: to turn sour and thicken, curdle; of weather: to cloud up. Hence **clabbery** *adj* Curdled. [the sense 'soured, curdled milk' is usually taken as an extension from Irish *clábar* 'mud', but for an alternative etymology see **1960** Malone *Bonnyclabber*, which derives the term from *bonnyclabber* 'milk of the dasher (i.e. of a stage fit to be churned)' < Irish *bainne* 'milk' + *clabar* 'sour thick milk' < *clabaire* 'inverted cup through which the churndash passes'; OED attests *clabber* only from 1824; SND *clabber* n 'mud, clay, dirt, mire'; DARE *clabber* n[1] 1 'sour milk that has thickened or curdled' chiefly South, Midland, West]

ULST.: 1813 Porter *Poetical Attempts* Poor creature! he was doom'd to paddle / Thro' clabour since he quat the cradle.
1863 Hume *Rabbin's Ollminick* 6 The days is very short, an' mebby the groun's saft an' clabbery, but ye musn't min' that.
1880 Patterson *Antrim/Down Glossary* 19 *clabber* = mud: 'They clodded clabber at me'.
1910 Joyce *English in Ireland* 235 *clabber* = mud, thick milk.
1923 Lutton *Montiaghisms* 14 *clabber* = soft clay, sediment of drains, dirt of roads, puddle.
1942 *Bangor Words* 17 *clabbers* = fluid mud in the streets: 'You are all over clabbers'.
c1955 Montgomery *Heard in Ulster* 25 *clabber* = road muck of the color/consistency of wet cement, usually swept into piles by 'surface-men'.
1983 Marshall *Drumlister* 32 The deil a man in this townlan' / Wos claner raired nor me, / But I'm livin' in Drumlister / In clabber to the knee.

1991 O'Kane *You Don't Say* 26 *clabber* = thick, clinging mud such as might be found around a gate in winter where cattle have trampled the ground into an impassable broth.

U.S.:   **1784** *Lipscomb's Journal* 272 we made our Brackfast with the hens with a few slices of Bacon & half bushel of Clabber & Butter milk.

1908 Payne *Word-list East Alabama* 299 *clabber* = milk that is allowed to stand until it sours and thickens.

1949 Kurath *Word Geog East US* 36 Another South Midland expression is *clabber milk, clabbered milk*, which is here more common than the simple Southern *clabber*.

1953 Randolph and Wilson *Down in Holler* 235 *clabber* = cloudy, as when the sky clabbers up before a storm.

1997 Montgomery *Coll* This milk will clabber if you set it in a warm place.

1997 Nelson *Country Folklore* 62 Churning was a children's job. The milk had set by the kitchen stove in a crock jar, getting clabbered and ready to churn. Mama or Grandma placed it in the churn, and we pushed the dash up and down until we had butter and buttermilk.

1999 Nelson *Aroma and Memories* 16 We girls helped to churn the clabbered milk until it turned into butter and buttermilk.

clabbers See **clavers**

clart *n* Mire, a lump of mud; feces; an untidy woman, dirty housekeeper. Hence **clarty, clearty** *adj* Of soil: miry, sticking to the plow. [origin unknown; OED *clart* vb 'to smear or daub with dirt, bedirty' 13th century→, n a 'sticky or claggy dirt' Scottish and northern dialect; *clart* n 'sticky or claggy dirt, mud, filth; a daub of sticky dirt; a lump or clot of something disagreeable or distasteful' 1808→; SND *clart* n].

ULST.:   **1880** Patterson *Antrim/Down Glossary* 19 = a dirty, slovenly woman.

1904 Marshall *Dial of Ulster* 125 = a dirty housekeeper.

1928 McKay *Oul' Town* 82 There's many a swell of a girl has in her the makin' of a clart.

1981 Pepper *Ulster-English Dict* 19 You should see that house of hers. She's nathin but a clart.

1990 Todd *Words Apart* 46 Now, I'll not say she's an out 'n out clart but she could be a bit tidy of herself.

U.S.:   **1902** Clapin *Americanisms, clearty* = a Scotch word sometimes heard in sense of sticky, as of soil that sticks to the plow.

1944 Williams *Word-list Mts* 28 = feces.

clatter *n* A collection, large but indefinite number (in the U.S. attested only in the derivative *clatterment*, usually plural in form). [cf Scots *clatter-trap, clutterment*; see also OED *cladment* 'a garment, dress' obsolete, rare]

ULST.:   **1958** Gregg *Phonology* 401 = a large number.

1983 Pepper *Ulster Knowledge* 9 A herd of cattle will usually be described as, 'a clatter of bastes'.

1987 Porter and Cunningham *Mourne Dialect* 27 = indefinite number of things.

1990 McIntyre *Some Handlin'* 16 = a large number of something: 'Glenda's family owns a wild clatter of animals'.

2000 Fenton *Hamely Tongue* 38 = a large amount, a large number: 'It'll tak a clatter o money tae redd ye', 'a wile clatter o wains'.

U.S.: **1895** Edson and Fairchild *Tenn Mts* 371 *clatterments* = belongings, accoutrements: 'Sam, what did you do with all of the clatterments that belong to the mowin' scythes and the harness?'

clatty *adj* Dirty, muddy, slovenly. [< *clat* n[1] 'a clod, a clod of dirt, especially of cow-dung'; OED *clatty* b 'miry, dirty, nasty' 1619→, Scottish; DOST *clattie* adj 'muddy, dirty' 1629→]

ULST.: c1910 Byers *Glossary* = dirty, muddy, untidy, slovenly: 'You weren't both clatty and longsome at that' = Though you were quick about it, you did it badly and dirtily.

c1955 Montgomery *Heard in Ulster* 28 Isn't she sae clean to be sae clatty?

1983 Marshall *Drumlister* 32 An' if me shirt's a clatty shirt / The man to blame's me da.

U.S.: **1889** Farmer *Americanisms* = dishevelled, untidy. A similar meaning attaches to the word in Lowland Scotch.

clavers, clabbers, clayvers *n* An imaginary figure invoked to admonish children (perhaps based on John Graham of Claverhouse, authorized by Charles II to suppress Covenanters in Scotland in the 1680s. According to George Fraser Black in *Scotland's Mark on America* (1929, p. 12), 'The mountaineers of Tennessee and Kentucky are largely the descendants of these same Ulster people and their origin is conclusively shown by the phrase used by mothers to their unruly children "If you don't behave, Clavers [i.e. Claverhouse] will get you"'; in the U.S. the term is known only in such a phrase.)

ULST.: **1933** Foster *Tyrone among Bushes* 75 I've toul' it to you many's the time— Tillie's forebear, him an' his brother, crossed the say to Ireland in an open boat, with nothin' but the clothes on their back, fleein' from Bloody Clayvers.

U.S.: **1952** Wilson *Folk Speech NC* 527 *the Clavers will get you* = this would appear to be a threat, like *lay-overs to catch meddlers*.

1996 Landry *Coll* The Clabbers'll get you.

clearty See **clart**

clip *n* A mischievous child, especially a girl. [perhaps < Irish, Scottish Gaelic *cliobóg* 'a colt, a filly'; SND *clip* n 2 'a pert or mischievous girl']

ULST.: **1885** Lyttle *Robin Gordon* 15 He wuz the greatest yung clip A iver cum across.

1901 Savage-Armstrong *Ballads of Down* 67 She nivver cud axe fur a favour in vain— / A wheedlin' wee clippie is Betty MacBlaine.

1931 Anonymous *Holiday* 32 Lasses were different then from the clips and hairpins that gallant about nowadays in a way that would scunner ye.

2000 Fenton *Hamely Tongue* 40 = a pert or precocious girl (*a bowl wee clip*).

U.S.: **1930** Shoemaker *1300 Penn Words* 11 = a knowing, shrewd girl.

clobber See **clabber**

clout, cloot *n* A small piece of cloth (especially used for a diaper or nappy), a rag
or patch. [< Middle English *clut(e)* < Old English *clut*; OED *clout* n 1 'piece, patch,
flat piece, shred' 700→, n 4 'a piece of cloth (especially a small or worthless piece, a
"'rag")' 1225→; DOST *clout* n 'a piece of cloth, a patch, a rag' 1427→; DARE *clout* n[1]
1 'a piece of cloth; now especially a piece used for a baby's diaper' scattered, but
especially Midland]

    ULST.:   **1848** Herbison *Midnight Musings* 54-55 You were sae blanch'd and torn about,
    / I found you were na worth a clout, / To keep me dry.
    c1910 Byers *Glossary* = a rag, shred, fragment of cloth, an old piece of cloth; a
    cloth used for domestic purposes (e.g. 'dish-clout'); a garment: 'I haven't a
    clout to put on'.
    1932 Quinn *Collecting Rent* 123 I wuz able to see with the tail of my eye the
    rent man tied up on the sofa with a clout round his mouth.
    1942 *Bangor Words* 19 = a rag of cloth used for rough cleaning (dish-clout, etc.)
    1953 Traynor *Donegal Glossary* 54 = a patch; a patch on boots or shoes.
    1983 Marshall *Drumlister* 30 Alas! that was long ago, / The red coat's a clout.
    1991 O'Kane *You Don't Say* 29 = a piece of cloth used for patching.
    2000 Fenton *Hamely Tongue* 40-41 = a piece of cloth used as a bandage,
    duster, e.g. *face-cloot* = a face-cloth, *flure-cloot* = cloth used to wash the floor,
    table-cloot = a table-cloth.

    U.S.:   **1899** Green *Virginia Word-Book* 90 = any piece of cloth; as a baby's clout; or,
    one designed for a mean use; as a dish-clout, a rag.
    1899 Green *Virginia Word-Book* 47 *baby-clouts* = (1) pieces of stuff of different
    colors given to children to dress their dolls with; (2) the clothes used for
    swaddling babies.
    1940 Simms *Coll* = baby diaper.
    1953 Randolph and Wilson *Down in Holler* 235 = diaper.
    1995 Montgomery *Coll* = a rag for cleaning; a patch.

coagle See **coggle**

coagley See **coggly**

cog *n* A wooden vessel having a variety of uses. [origin uncertain; OED *cogue* n 1 'a
wooden vessel made with staves and hoops, used in milking cows or ewes, and for
other purposes' c1568→, 2 'a small drinking-vessel or cup, of wood' 1690→,
Scottish; DOST *cog* n[2] 'a wooden vessel made of hooped staves' 1546→]

    ULST.:   **1801** Bruce *Poems* [Glossary 3] *cogg* = a wooden vessel, out of which Scotch
    folk drink new ale.
    1895 (in **1898-1905** Wright *Engl Dial Dict*) = a vessel for carrying milk or
    holding water, made of hoops and staves, like a small barrel, with an open end.
    U.S.:   **1930** Shoemaker *1300 Penn Words* 10 = a small wooden vessel or dish.

coggle, coagle *vb* To shake, totter, be unsteady or rickety. Hence *n* The movement
of anything that should stand steady, or the propensity to be unsteady. [origin
uncertain, but possibly imitative; OED *coggle* vb[2] Scottish and dialect, possibly from
a root **kug-* with the sense 'rounded lump', cf German *Kugel*, Dutch *kōgel*; but this
is doubtful ; SND *coggle* vb[1] 1 'to rock, totter, shake']

    ULST.:   **1891** Simmons *Armagh Words and Phrases* 7 *coggle* = to shake, to be unsteady.

1904 Marshall *Dial of Ulster* 125 *coggle* = the movement of anything that should stand steadily.
1923 Lutton *Montiaghisms* 15 *coggle* = to stand unsteadily, so as to be at liberty to rock from side to side.
1942 *Bangor Words* 19 *coggle* = to rock, not being firmly placed on its base.
1980 McClean *Ulster Words II* 2 *coagle* = to balance unevenly.
2000 Fenton *Hamely Tongue* 41 *coagle* = to rock, wobble (e.g. of a chair with one leg slightly shorter than the others: 'That chire coagles'); to cause to rock, etc.: 'Daenae coagle the table'. *Ibid.* = a tendency to rock, wobble, etc.: 'haes a weethin o a coagle'.

U.S.:   1843 Hall *New Purchase* 142 Some carried and fixed tables, pushing and kicking and jambing at them till they consented to stay fixed and not coggle!

coggly, coagley, coggled, cogglety, cogly, coogley *adj* Rickety, unsteady, poorly or clumsily constructed; in the U.S. only **coggled up** is attested. [OED *coggly* adj 'shaky, unsteady, like anything resting on a rounded base' Scottish and dialect]

ULST.:   1880 Patterson *Antrim/Down Glossary* 22 *cogglety* = shaky, unsteady.
c1910 Wier *Bab McKeen* 19 For the sates we had twa' or three boords laid on turf sods roon the hoose, although they wur a big coogley.
1923 Lutton *Montiaghisms* 15 *cogly* = easily made to rock.
1942 *Bangor Words* 19 *coggly* = shaky, easily rocked.
c1955 Montgomery *Heard in Ulster* 24 The wheels on that cairt are a bit coggly.

U.S.:   1917 Kephart *Word-list* 409 *coggled up* = rickety, wobbly. 'That's the most coggled up far [= fire] I ever seed'.

cohee, ca-he, coohee, qua-he, quohe, quo-he, quo' he, qu'he (with parallel forms **quo' she**, etc.) *n* Originally a phrase used in oral narration in some parts of Ulster (apparently especially in Donegal), whereby a person reports another's speech by 'quo he', 'quo she', 'quo I', etc. (literally 'said he', etc.) In the 18th century this habit was brought to American colonies, where because of this mannerism the term was applied to rural, less cultivated persons in the backwoods from Virginia to the Carolinas who used it, becoming a nickname for them. In the U.S. the term has only this latter sense. [alteration of *quoth he*]

ULST.:   1753 *Scotch Poems* 373 Quo' he, does any ferly kythe / Dear neighbours, that ye're a' sae blythe?
1838 McIlwham *McIlwham Papers* iv Weel, then, quo' she, did ye no promise me a goon frae Glasgow for a new-year's gift.
1880 Patterson *Antrim/Down Glossary* 81 *quo' he* = said he (this with 'quo' she', 'quo' I' are in very general use).
c1910 Byers *Glossary, quo he* = pronounced as if spelled 'Ho, he'. In a murder case, a man said to a friend at Downpatrick Assizes, 'That's a *quo he* jury and I'll houl' (hold) they'll niver convict' = an uneducated one.
c1910 Wier *Bab McKeen* 19 Next mornin' he met the butler, an' quo' he, 'Well John, I hope the lairds temperature is nae higher the day.'
1920 McCallin *Ulster Plenishing* 62 'Ah, weel', quo she, lookin' first at me an' then at him, 'it's just no' like yersel' whiles when yer in the poo'pit.'
1942 *Bangor Words* 63 *quo* = said: 'Quo she'.
1953 Traynor *Donegal Glossary* 224 = an Inis Eoghain nickname for the Derry people across the Foyle ... From their frequent use of *quo' he, she*, hence phrase

the quohe side of the water, the Derry side of the Foyle.
c1955 Montgomery *Heard in Ulster* 25 Yer only a nuisance, ca-he (or qua-he).
1993 Montgomery *Barnish* 14 *co I* = said I; 42 *quo he* = said he.
1997 Robinson *Grammar* 72 Yiz see yous boys - qu' she - yiz ir aa daft.
2000 Fenton *Hamely Tongue* 160 *qu'* = quoth (only as in: *Sowl, qu'he, an ye daenae luck it. Och, awa or that! qu' she*).

U.S.:   **1789** May *Journal* 144 My little log hut was filled with two boats' crews of Yankees from Marietta, and a number of Kohees, belong to the [Wheeling, West Virginia] settlement.
1815 (in **1956** Eliason *Tarheel Talk* 126) The back country people [of Virginia] are called 'Co-hees' from some of the back country people using frequently the term 'quote he' or 'quote she' or as they usually speak it 'coo he' and 'coo she'.
1867 Lowell *Biglow Papers* lviii = applied to the people of certain settlements of western Pennsylvania, from their use of the archaic form *Quo' he*.
1899 Green *Virginia Word-Book* 96 *Coohees* = of Scotch origin 'Quo'he'.
Coohees was the nickname applied to people in western Virginia, while those in the east were called 'Tuckahoes'.

collogue, cologue, culloge *vb* To confer; conspire, gossip, collude, discuss or talk privately and confidentially, often implying a conspiring or being in league with one another. Hence *n* A private conversation, often of a confidential or colluding nature. [perhaps < French *colloque* 'conference, consultation'; OED *collogue* vb 4 'to have a private understanding with; to intrigue, collude, conspire' 1646→, now dialectal; SND *collogue* 2 vb 'to talk together, chat; to be in league'; DARE *collogue* vb 1 'to intrigue, to conspire' chiefly South Midland]

ULST.:   **1838** McIllwham *McIllwham Papers* 10 First, he says, ye hae been colloguein' wi' the enemies of the Kirk o' Scotlan'.
1880 Patterson *Antrim/Down Glossary* 23 *collogue* = confidential chat; to talk confidentially.
1899 MacManus *Chimney Corners* 178 Maybe sez he, if ye comed down an' had a collogue, ye might be able to raison him over.
c1910 Byers *Glossary* = (1) to conspire, talk or plot together for mischief, be in league with; to talk confidentially, with the suggestion of plotting; (2) a conversation between two or more people, of a private nature: 'They collogue with all kinds of people'.
1910 Joyce *English in Ireland* 237 = to talk and gossip in a familiar friendly way. An Irish form of the Latin or English 'colloquy'.
1923 Lutton *Montiaghisms* 15 *cologue-ing* = engaged in secret conversation on low and worthless subjects, or scheming.
1942 *Bangor Words* 20 = talk, gossip with the idea of conspiracy.
1964 Braidwood *Ulster/Elizabethan English* 98 In Ulster *to collogue* is 'to talk confidentially, take part in a colloquy, conspire, cooperate'. This is a good plantation-era word, dating from 1602, meaning originally 'to flatter, fawn, feign agreement, have a private understanding'.
1991 O'Kane *You Don't Say* 33 = to associate with; to conspire; to be friendly with in a slightly nefarious way: 'I wonder what those two are culloguin' about'.
2000 Fenton *Hamely Tongue* 42 = to talk confidentially; plot or conspire.

U.S.:   **1899** Green *Virginia Word-Book* 92 = to join together, in a bad sense, in league or in conversation: 'They were colloguing together for sometime'.

1908 Payne *Word-list East Alabama* 300 = to collude; to be on intimate terms with.

collyfox *vb* To mislead, avoid responsibility. [SND *collie-fox* 'to idle about, humbug']
ULST.: 1936 (in *Northern Whig*, as cited in 1931-76 Grant and Murison *SND*) With that Susie begins to ruffle his hair and loosen his tie, then her sister Annie, who has an eye after him, speaks up an' says to her: 'Can't you quit your collyfoxing?'
1953 Traynor *Donegal Glossary* 59 *collyfoxing* = humbugging, misleading, making a fool of one.
c1955 Montgomery *Heard in Ulster* 21 *colly-foxen* = fawning for favour.
2000 Fenton *Hamely Tongue* 42 = to skulk, move furtively, tease, act the smart alec.
U.S.: 1943 Kurath *LANE* Map 568 If a laborer or hired man is idle when he should be at work, he is said to be colly-foxing.

cologue See **collogue**

contrary, contrairy *adj*, *vb* (usually accented on second syllable: *con-TRAR-y*). [OED *contrary* adj 3b 'of antagonistic or untoward disposition, perverse, obstinately self-willed' colloquial and dialect, vb 2a 'to contradict, gainsay; to speak, write, or argue against (a person)'; DARE *contrary* vb 1 'to oppose; hence also to vex, annoy, anger' chiefly South Midland]
  1 *adj* Fractious, antagonistic, obstinate, self-willed; inconvenient, perverse.
ULST.: 1860 Patterson *Belfast Provincialisms* 11.
1880 Patterson *Antrim/Down Glossary* 23 *contrairy* = (1) obstinate, contradictory: 'Now, what's the good o' bein' so contrairy?'; (2) inconvenient: 'It happened at a most contrairy time'.
1889 Hart *Derryreel* 36 He had a habit of saying contrairy things, and uphowlding and arguing for the last word.
c1910 Byers *Glossary*, *contrairy* = cross-grained, obstinate, contradictory: 'He's as contrairy as a pig'.
1910 Joyce *English in Ireland* 239 *contrary* = cross, perverse, cranky, crotchety.
1920 McCallin *Fireside Tales* 69 When there's anything partickler you want him to do, try to get him to do the very contráry.
1990 Todd *Words Apart* 50 That'n is as conthrary as a bag o' wheezles.
U.S.: 1899 Green *Virginia Word-Book* 96 *contrary* = disagreeable, stubborn, cross-grained, contradictory: 'He is just as contrary as he can be'.
1930 Shoemaker *1300 Penn Words* 13 *contrairy* = wilful, unreliable.
1955 Dykeman *French Broad* 341 After you once get hogs broke to the road, you can't get them off, no matter how contrary they were at the start.
1982 De Armond *So High* 63 I guess that contrary mule brought out the worst in Robert.
  2 *vb* To contradict, provoke, oppose verbally.
ULST.: c1910 Byers *Glossary*, *cntrary* = to prove the contrary, to controvert, as 'I wouldn't contrairy that' = oppose waywardly, contradict.
1935 Megaw *Carragloon* 11 Contrary that if ye can, Robert Hugh.
1953 Traynor *Donegal Glossary* 60 *contrary* = to contradict, disapprove, refute, oppose: 'I'd contrairy ye if ye said that'.
2000 Fenton *Hamely Tongue* 44 *contrairy* = to oppose verbally, deny: 'Ye contrairy ivery word I say'.

U.S.: **1913** Kephart *Our Sthn High* 283 I didn't do nary thing to contrary her.
c1945 Haun *Hawk's Done* 300 But Ma was sick and I couldn't afford to contrary her too much.

coogley See **coggly**

coohee See **cohee**

crack, craic, crak *vb* Originally to boast, to engage in lively or entertaining conversation; gossip; tell jokes, etc. Hence *n* A boast; a quip; chat, entertaining talk or gossip (thus, fun); a person who is an entertaining talker. The spelling *craic*, now frequent in Ireland, erroneously suggests that the word is a derivation or borrowing from Irish, but this spelling arose only in the early 20th century. In English the term dates from as early as the 15th century. For the best historical commentary see the accounts below from **1964** Braidwood *Ulster/Elizabethan English* and **1998** Dolan *Dict Hiberno-English*. It is unattested in American English, but was presumably brought by Ulster emigrants in the sense of 'boast' and gave rise to **cracker** (q.v.). [OED *crack* vb 6(a) 'to talk big, boast, brag; sometimes, to talk scornfully (of others)' 1460→1855, now obsolete or dialectal; 7(a) 'to converse briskly and sociably, chat, talk of the news' c1450→, Scottish and northern dialect; DOST *crak(e)* n 3 'a loud boast or brag' early 16th century→, 7 'a talk or gossip' 1570→; SND *crack* n 5(2) 'a story, an entertaining or scandalous tale' 1721→; DARE chiefly South Atlantic]

ULST.: **1799** (in **1813** Porter *Poetical Attempts*) I could spen' monie a cheerfu' summer / To crack wi' Virgil, Pope, an' Homer.
1801 Bruce *Poems* 44 Gif ane maks transgression / On your gear or your person, / Ye aye can get mair mends in a crack.
1804 Orr *Poems* 135 Nybers, an' frien's, in boatful's pang'd, / Approach our larboard quarter; / Syne speel the side, an' down the hatch / To rest, an' crack.
1824 McHenry *Insurgent Chief* 24 Let this up-the-country frien' o' mine an' me, hae a jug o' punch in a room by ourels, for I hae some cracks for his ain ear.
1840 Boyce *Shandy Maguire* 27 'So, ye hae na news', he continued, 'sin I saw ye last—hah, changed times wi' ye, Nancy, ye ust to hae a crak in ye.'
1880 Patterson *Antrim/Down Glossary* 25 = (1) a chat; (2) to gossip or chat, to boast.
1884 McFadyen and Hepburn *Lays and Legends* 81 Tell it his honour here— shorten yer crack,— / For himself's in a tarrible fuss till get back.
1885 Lyttle *Robin Gordon* 8 Weel, we crackit awa.
1891 Simmons *Armagh Words and Phrases* 5 = a funny or jocular story, also fun of any kind; also, to tell jokes.
1904 Marshall *Dial of Ulster* 125 = (1) a conversation; (2) story or anecdote; as, 'That's the best crack I've heard in a long time'; 3) a person who is an entertaining talker.
1923 Lutton *Montiaghisms* 16 = enlivening conversation, merriment.
1935 Megaw *Carragloon* 86-87 Do ye know she's the quare crack when ye get her started and she toul me wee things about folk that ye wouldn't hear tell of by the roadside nor in the post office.
1939 Paterson *Country Cracks* 48 Many's the night be this very same fire he an' the neighbours cracked of the wee people.

1942 *Bangor Words* 21 = gossip, friendly talk: 'The crack was so good, that I forgot the time', 'I mind the time crack' (is a talk about old times).

1953 Traynor *Donegal Glossary* 64 = (1) to talk, gossip, chat; (2) a good story, gossip; (3) a good conversationalist, talker, especially one with a fund of amusing stories; 4) to chat, converse.

1964 Braidwood *Ulster/Elizabethan English* 99 Perhaps one of the most seemingly native Ulster words is *crack*, *good crack* 'lively talk, conversation'. In fact the word is of English and Scots origin. The noun is from the word *crack*, which originally meant, as in Shakespeare, 'to boast loudly or smartly', then simply 'to boast'. It is the same verb as *crack* 'to make a sharp noise'. From 1450 on it was used also in the sense 'to talk loudly about the news'. As a noun *crack* meant 'boast, loud talk' from 1450 on. In the sense 'brisk talk', and, especially in Scotland, 'news', it dates from 1725. Shakespeare, as we have seen, has it in the earlier sense of 'boast'. There is also a noun *cracker*, originally 'a boaster' (as in Shakespeare), then 'someone full of conversation' (Scotland). The present dialectal distribution of the noun *crack*, 'talk', outside Ireland is that it is in use all over Scotland and the north of England, getting just into Cheshire, but no further south. It has a variant *crake*, which, together with the northern distribution, suggests Norse origin.

1983 Marshall *Drumlister* 4 There'll be good crack when the lamp's lit, / And the fir flames in the fire.

1990 McIntyre *Some Handlin'* 18 = entertainment, conversation: 'We all have a good crack at the swimming pool'.

1991 O'Kane *You Don't Say* 33 = (1) general term for fun, an enjoyable, partying atmosphere; (2) talk or gossip, generally of a reprehensible character: 'That's terrible crack to come over in front of a child'; (3) to engage in enjoyable talk or banter: 'We cracked away all night'.

1997 Share *Slanguage* 61 = brisk talk, news, absorbing the idea of informal entertainment as represented by Irish neologism *craic*, as in cliche phrase *ceol agus craic*.

1998 Dolan *Dict Hiberno-English* 77 = entertaining conversation. Irish *craic* is the Modern English loanword *crack* < Middle English *crak*, loud conversation, bragging talk; recently re-introduced into Hiberno-English (usually in its Irish spelling) in the belief that it means high-spirited entertainment.

2000 Fenton *Hamely Tongue* 47 = (1) to chat, converse: 'A hae mair tae dae wae mae time nor sit here crakkin an takkin'; (2) = fun: 'Thon wuz great crak at the pairty'; entertainment: 'He's guid crak whun ye get him gan'; (3) conversation: 'Come on in an share yer crak'.

cracker *n* Originally a boaster or lively talker. The term became associated with the American backwoods by late colonial days (see 1766/1767 citations). Today it usually refers to a rural white person in the American South, especially from Georgia or Florida. For an account of its development in the U.S., see **1987** Otto *Cracker*.

ULST.:   **1880** Patterson *Antrim/Down Glossary* 25 = a boaster.

       1953 Traynor *Donegal Glossary* 64 = a boaster.

U.S.:   **1766** Cochrane *Letter* I should explain to your Lordship what is meant by Crackers; a name they have got from being great boasters; they are a lawless set of rascalls on the frontiers of Virginia, Maryland, the Carolinas, and Georgia, who often change their places of abode. They steal horses in the southern provinces and sell them in the northern and those in the Northern provinces they sell in the southern. They get Merchants by degrees to trust them with more and more goods to trade with the Indians and at first make returns till they have established some credit, then leave those that trusted them in the lurch, return no more but go to some other place to follow the same practice. Some of them stay in the Indian country and are perpetually endeavouring to stir up a war by propagating idle stories that they may join them and share in the plunder. They delight in cruelty which they often practice even to one another.

1767 (in 1921 *Cracker* 99) CharlesTown, August 7. Letters from Silver Bluff, on Savannah river, dated on tuesday last week, inform us, that a number of the people called Crackers, who live above Augusta, in the Province of Georgia, had gone in a hostile manner to the Indian town and settlement at Okenee, where, on their arrival finding only one old Indian man, all the others being out hunting, they plundered the village of everything of any value that they could carry off, and then burnt every house in it.

1854 (in 1956 Eliason *Tarheel Talk* 267) The townfolks are to have a barbecue ... They sent today [to invite] the 'country crackers'.

1908 Payne *Word-list East Alabama* 302 = a Georgian.

craic, crak See **crack**

crap *n* Crop. [Scottish form; DARE (at *crop* A) chiefly South, South Midland; for geographical spread in the eastern U.S. see 1961 Kurath and McDavid citation below]

　　ULST.:　　1860 Patterson *Belfast Provincialisms* 8 = crop.

　　　　　　　1885 Lyttle *Robin Gordon* 17 There wuz sich a sough throo the country aboot the Culleradoo Beetle that fowk said wud cleen destroy the pritta crap.

　　U.S.:　　　1834 Crockett *Narrative* 154 Having laid by my crap, I went home, which was a distance of about a hundred and fifty miles.

　　　　　　　1913 Kephart *Our Sthn High* 36 I can raise me two or three severe craps.

　　　　　　　1937 Haun *Cocke Co* 2 Folks still tote their turns of meal to mill in pokes and aim on raising a yieldy crap of corn next year.

　　　　　　　1961 Kurath and McDavid *Pron Engl Atl Sts* 143 The /æ/ of *cat* appears in *crop* in the folk speech of two areas: (1) the Atlantic coast from Chesapeake Bay to the Neuse River in North Carolina, and (2) the Appalachians south of the Kanawha River.

creep *vb* To move on all fours, crawl. [OED *creep* B1(a) 'to move with the body prone and close to the ground'; DARE *creep* vb B1 'to move on all fours, crawl' widespread, but chiefly Northeast, North Central]

　　ULST.:　　1845 Carleton *Irish Peasantry* (in 1978 McGuffin *Praise of Poteen*) 99 This was little Micky McQuade, a short-necked, squat little fellow with bow legs, who might be said rather to creep in his motion than to walk.

　　　　　　　1879 Lyttle *Paddy McQuillan* 30 A hae tae gang creepin' aboot wi' my han's spreed oot afore me.

　　　　　　　c1910 Byers *Glossary* A chile must creep afore it walks.

　　　　　　　1930 MacNeill *Told to Reverence* 87 When the door's closed ahind me I slip back and creep into the wee pig-house over thonder in the corner.

　　U.S.:　　　1971 Wood *Vocabulary Change* 41 A baby moving across the floor ordinarily *crawls*, though in a few instances outside of Louisiana he *creeps*.

crud(s) *n* Curds. [according to the OED, this is the original form in English, superseded except in northern dialects of Britain by *curd*; DOST *crud* n 14th century→; for distribution in the eastern U.S. see **1949** Kurath citation]

ULST.: **1880** Patterson *Antrim/Down Glossary* 26 = curds.

1928 McKay *Oul' Town* 24 I hear they put lemons intil it, and they call it Lemon 'cruds'.

1935 Megaw *Carragloon* 149 She could turn [sweet milk] like a clap of yer hand, and when ye put it intil yer tea, it would be nothin' but cruds.

1942 *Bangor Words* 22 = curds, renneted milk.

1949 Mac Airt *Tyrone Folktales* 43-44 So he took the grey mare with him and swam he through the milk, and with the stress of the milk when it thickened and was getting into cruds, she picked a foal.

U.S.: **1903** *Misc Word-list* 350 *crud* = curdled milk, as in 'cruds and whey'.

1949 Kurath *Word Geog East US* 36 Among the local words we may mention ... *cruds* for cottage cheese ... from the Alleghenies to the Ohio state line.

cruddle *vb* To curdle. Hence **cruddled milk** *n* Curdled or coagulated milk. [OED *cruddle* 'to make (milk) into curd' 1724→; SND *crudle* vb 'to curdle, coagulate' 1724→; for distribution in the eastern U.S. see **1949** Kurath citation]

ULST.: **1953** Traynor *Donegal Glossary* 69 = of milk: to thicken.

1991 O'Kane *You Don't Say* 34 = to curdle.

U.S.: **1901** *Contrib Cornell Univ* 138 = to curdle.

1949 Kurath *Word Geog East US* 36 Among the local words we may mention ... *crudded milk* for curdled milk (of Ulster Scot origin), from the Alleghenies to the Ohio state line. *Ibid.* 71 *Cruddled milk* (*crudded milk, cruddy milk*) in western Pennsylvania and to some extent also on the Susquehanna. *Cruddled milk* is also certainly of Scotch-Irish origin.

crumply, crumplety, crumpley *adj* Of horns: twisted, bent spirally. Hence *n* A cow with twisted horns. [cf OED *crumpled* adj 2 'bent spirally, curled' 15th century→; cf DARE *crumple-horned*]

ULST.: **1881** Hart *Mere Irish* 97 I had given ye notice of a crumplety-horned to be sold.

1953 Traynor *Donegal Glossary* 69 *crumpley* = of horns: crooked, bent spirally.

1959 Gregory *Ulster Ballads* 7 Plaze dinnae let him lift wee stones / Tae clod the gander or the goat, / ... Or dandher near the moylie cows, / Or roanies, wi' the crumpled horns.

U.S.: **1772** Hamilton *Inventory* To one Black Crumhorn cow £2/0/0.

1885 Murfree *Prophet* 70 In the corner of the rail fence was the 'crumply cow', chewing her cud.

1899 Green *Virginia Word-Book* 106 = crooked, twisted; as, a cow with *crumply* horns.

crusie *n* A small house-lamp. [perhaps from French *creuset* or earlier Old French *croiseul*; OED *crusie* n 1 'a small iron lamp or candle, burning oil or tallow; also a sort of triangular iron candlestick with one or more sockets for candles, having the edges turned up on the three sides'; DOST *crusie* n 'a form of lamp or candleholder' 1501→]

ULST.: **1957** Evans *Irish Folk-Ways* 89 The iron crusie or oil-lamp, its shape almost unchanged since classical times, was to be seen nearly everywhere around the coast until late in the last century ... but the paraffin lamp quickly swept it out of existence.

U.S.:   **1930** Shoemaker *1300 Penn Words* 14 = a small, oil burning lamp.

culloge See **collogue**

cutty *adj* Short. Hence *n* An object that is short, especially a pipe. [< *cut* + *-y*; OED *cutty* adj 1 'cut short'; SND *cuttie* adj 1 'short, stumpy, diminutive' 1721→]

ULST.:   **1880** Patterson *Antrim/Down Glossary* 27 = short: 'cutty pipe', 'cutty spoon'.
          1891 Simmons *Armagh Words and Phrases* 8 = short, much worn, as a cutty pipe, spade, etc.
          1920 McCallin *Ulster Plenishing* 51-52 She had just, that very minute, cleared the shank of her oul' cutty-pipe with a sprig o' me.
          2000 Fenton *Hamely Tongue* 51 = (1) a short clay pipe: 'A wee reek o the cutty's ill tae bate'; (2) a young, trim girl: 'as nait a wee cutty as ye iver lucked at'.

U.S.:   **1930** Shoemaker *1300 Penn Words* 15 = short.

D

daeless, daless See **doless**

dansy, dauncey, dauncy, dawney, dawny See **donsie**

dautie, dawtie *n* A sweetheart, dear or favorite one (in Ulster also **daut** *vb* To pat). Hence **dawted** *adj* Beloved. [< *daut* vb 'to pet, fondle, caress, make much of' Scottish, but origin unknown; OED *dautie* n 'a person caressed or indulged; a darling, pet, favourite'; DOST *dautie* n 'a pet, darling, special favourite' 1676→]
> ULST. 1811 Boyle *Poems* 5 But aiblins she'll return again, / An' wi' me dwell; / An' daut me like a sukin' wean; / Sae, frien', farewell.
> 1832 McKenzie *Masonic Chaplet* 25 I've seen thee by thy mither's knee, / Her gowden-hair'd – her dawted wean.
> U.S.: 1905 Miles *Spirit of Mts* 100 You little dawtie, little poppee-doll! Bless hits little angel-lookin' time!
> 1930 Shoemaker *1300 Penn Words* 19 *dautie* = a favorite child, or darling.

dayless See **doless**

deil, deel *n* The Devil. [Scottish form of *devil*]
> ULST.: 1753 *Scotch Poems* 370 But a fause critick's like the deel, / Slips, fau'ts, and failings, please them weel.
> c1800 Thomson (in 1992 Scott and Robinson *Samuel Thomson* 1) Some say thou'art sib kin to the sow, / But sibber to the deil, I trow.
> 1880 Patterson *Antrim/Down Glossary* 29 'The deil couldn't do it unless he was drunk' (said of something very difficult).
> 1920 McCallin *Fireside Tales* 224 They sorted bravely thegither, consitherin' they were both as crabbit as the deil.
> 1953 Traynor *Donegal Glossary* 78 *deil, deel*.
> U.S.: 1930 Shoemaker *1300 Penn Words* 17 *deil's own buckie* = one of the devil's kind.

dhruv See **druv**

diamond, diemon *n* A type of town square dating from the period of the Plantation of Ulster in the early 17th century. See citations.
> ULST.: 1840 Boyce *Shandy Maguire* 69 Then the riot became serious. The white ribbons rallied round the corner of the Diamond from every part of the fair, and aided, as they were, by friends and relations who had never joined, and others who had already abandoned the society, made a formidable force.
> c1910 Byers *Glossary, diamond* = a sort of rectangular space in the centre of towns like Raphoe, Carndonagh, Malin, Coleraine, Monaghan. In other towns called 'the Square'.
> 1975/76 Adams *Diamonds* 19–20 The Public Record Office of Northern Ireland states that on Francis Neville's map of Londonderry, published in 1693/95 to illustrate the siege, the central square is named as 'The Dymond or Market Place'. The date is over twenty years before Ulster emigration to America began and the spelling indicates a common Ulster pronunciation of the word ... The term may be English rather than Scottish in origin. Perhaps a search through the street-names in those areas whence the Plantation settlers came would reveal its ultimate source.

1978 *Ulster Folk Ways* 14 [At the turn of the century] as in Castlewellan, County Down, weekly markets and periodic animal fairs were normally held in the squares (or 'Diamonds' as they were usually called [in the west of the province]) at the centre of the small country towns.
1994 Robinson *Diamonds in Stone* 28 Plantation town planning was not restricted to the development of a regional urban plan, but involved the planned development of individual settlements too. Both Killyleagh and Moneymore were laid out on what essentially a cross-shaped pattern, focused on a central market. Other plantation towns such as Lisburn, Newtownards, and many others, developed more haphazardly along a 'Main Street' which was widened at one end into a market place or 'Diamond'.
2000 Fenton *Hamely Tongue* 56 *diemon* = (usually *the Diamond*) the market square in a village or town.
2001 Harvey *Diamonds in Rough* 108 Patrons of new or refounded towns [in the Ulster Plantation] were directed to make provision for market places ... This frequently resulted in a layout illustrated clearly in the two most obviously planned towns of Londonderry and Coleraine. The towns have slightly different ground plans, but share several features: a layout on rectilinear lines, with streets crossing at right angles on a grid plan and, in the center, a large open area, in the shape of either a square or rectangle, at which two or more main streets intersect. Public buildings—a town hall, prison, or market house—were sited on the square ... This square would acquire a uniquely Ulster name, 'the Diamond', and it would become a common name for central marketplaces in central and west Ulster; examples can be seen in the towns of Monaghan, Crossmaglen and Enniskillen, among others. *Ibid.* Harvey *Diamonds in Rough* 109 Numerous examples of 'diamonds' in Pennsylvania may be cited: in Elizabethtown in Lancaster County and Carlisle in Cumberland, both in the areas of earliest Scotch-Irish settlement; as well as one in Pittsburgh, reflecting the marked Scotch-Irish influence in western Pennsylvania. *Ibid.* 112 As settlement expanded, Springfield [Pennsylvania]'s commercial center moved in a westerly direction, toward the junction of the two stage routes in the central area—termed a square in Stroup's original town plan, but quickly called 'the Diamond' by its chiefly Scotch-Irish inhabitants.

U.S.:   **1829** Royall *Pennsylvania* 55 In all the towns of Pennsylvania, of any size, the public buildings and offices are built on squares, in the centre of their town ... These squares are uniformly called 'The Diamond'.
1969 Evans *Cultural Adaptation* 85 In ... Rehrersburg [Indiana], the street incorporates an elongated market place which is significantly known as 'the Diamond', a word which seems to be used elsewhere in this connection only in Ulster, though it is found in some American towns outside Pennsylvania, e.g. Cleveland, Ohio.

differ *n* (sometimes plural in form) A difference, matter. In the U.S. hence also *vb* To matter, make a difference. [OED *differ* n, shortening of *difference*, influenced by *differ* vb, 1627→, Scottish and dialect; DOST *differ* vb³ 'to be different, disagree' 1490→, n 'a difference of opinion, a dispute' 1566→, 'a difference in kind' 1617→; DARE *differ* n 'difference; difference of opinion, argument, quarrel' chiefly South, South Midland]
    ULST.:   **1799** (in **1813** Porter *Poetical Attempts*) Yet if the skin were aff us baith / There wad be little differ.

1840 Boyce *Shandy Maguire* 34 They say their childher have it on them, and that they can tell the differ' someway atween them an' ither people.
1880 Patterson *Antrim/Down Glossary* 30 *differ* = the difference.
1886 Lyttle *Ballycuddy* 29 The Enniskillen fowk wur aye playin' the music an' wudnae quat it, fur they seen nae differs in playin' it in a skulehoose an' playin' it in a meeting-hoose.
1893 Bullock *Awkward Squad* 77 'Well, when a woman gets it into her head that her man is doing something wrong', Shan went on, 'whether he is or not makes no differ.'
c1910 Byers *Glossary, differ* = difference, the quality distinguishing one thing from another: 'There's not a hair's differ atween them'.
1935 Megaw *Carragloon* 44 There's a differs between the man and the woman in the marryin'.
1936 White *Mrs Murphy* 251 There's hardly a hair of differ on her since I first laid eyes on her.
1948 Marshall *Planted by River* 19 Ye'll wipe your brogues in the yard for the time to come, or I'll know to the differ.
1953 Traynor *Donegal Glossary* 79–80 There's not much in the differ.
c1955 Montgomery *Heard in Ulster* 39 Well, I know to the differ, no matter what ye say.
1998 Daly *Pilgrim Journey* 28 A knot of bystanders would play the part of a Greek chorus, shouting words of encouragement and reproof to dealer and seller respectively. The 'middleman' would eventually urge them to 'split the differ'.
U.S.: **1913** Kephart *Our Sthn High* 94 They mean nigh about the same thing, only there's a differ.
1917 Kephart *Word-list* 410 It didn't differ what that cow [weighed].
1939 Hall *Coll* It might differ a little.
1987 Trent *Lore Yesteryear* 56 It doesn't differ which one goes.
1962 Dykeman *Tall Woman* 218 'Makes no differ to me', he mumbled, but he went to fetch another bucket of water.

dinge *n* A dent. Hence *vb* To dent. [origin uncertain, but possibly imitative or relating to **denge* from Old Norse *dngja* 'to hammer, bang, beat'; OED *dinge* vb 'to make a broadish hollow or depression in the surface (of anything), as by a knock; to dint, bruise, batter' 1611→; SND *dinge* 'to dent, bruise']
ULST.: **1895** MacManus *Leadin' Road* 35–36 Ye give him the neat, little bit of a dinge on the skull.
c1910 Byers *Glossary* = (1) to indent, dint, bruise: 'His hat is dinged in'; (2) an indentation, dint: 'There's a dinge in the can'.
1920 Gregory *Ulster Songs* 11 There! You've dinged your Daddy's hat.
1980 McClean *Ulster Words III* 3 = to dent.
1990 Todd *Words Apart* 60 Would ye look at me new car and it all dinged?
U.S.: **1978** *New Haven Register* Only Pittsburgh drivers know that when streets are 'slippy' they're likely to put a dinge or two in car fenders.
2004 *Pittsburghese* = a dent: 'That shopping cart put a dinge in my fender'.

discomfit *vb* To inconvenience, disconcert, throw into confusion. [OED *discomfit* vb 2b 'to throw into perplexity, confusion, or dejection; to disconcert'; DARE *discomfit* vb 'to inconvenience, bother' chiefly southern Appalachians]
ULST.: **1895** MacManus *Leadin' Road* 113 The sergeant retired discomfited, consoled by Mickey with the remark that though people usually called him Sargint

Well-done (Weldon), he would considher him Sargint Over-done from that time forward.

c1910 Byers *Glossary* = to put about, to put to inconvenience: 'You wouldn't discomfit the Club for that' = cause it to be disorganised.

1919 MacGill *Glenmornan* 161 'No, I wasn't doing anything', said the discomfitted Doalty.

U.S.:   **1939** Hall *Coll* I wouldn't want to discomfit you.

1995 Montgomery *Coll* I'd like to buy some corn from you if it won't discomfit you.

dish-clout See **clout**

disremember *vb* To forget, be unable to recall, pretend to forget, be unwilling or inclined not to remember. See 1910 citation. [OED *disremember* vb 'to fail to remember, to forget' chiefly dialect; DOST *disremember* vb 'to forget' c1651→; DARE *disremember* vb 'to be unable to remember; to forget; not to know' scattered, but chiefly South, South Midland]

ULST.:   **1889** Hart *Derryreel* 59 I disremember her name—if iver I knew it.

c1910 Byers *Glossary* = often implies a disinclination to remember. A witness in a court of law, unwilling to reply to any questions put, might say, 'I disremember' = it does not suit me to recollect ... As an explanation for why an old man left nothing to a relative with whom he had a quarrel, a friend said, 'When he had a row with anyone, he always disremembered him.'

1923 Lutton *Montiaghisms* 17 = to lose recollection of, to forget.

1953 Traynor *Donegal Glossary* 81 = to forget, often used when a person is unwilling to answer a particular question.

U.S.:   **1829** Dunglison *Virginia Museum* 105 = used in the Southern states for 'to forget; not remember'.

1829 Kirkham *English Grammar* 192 *disremember* = do not remember. Common ... in Pennsylvania.

1859 Bartlett *Americanisms* 122 = to forget. Used chiefly in the Southern states.

1913 Kephart *Our Sthn High* 78 I mind about that time, Doc; but I disremember which buryin'-ground they-all buried ye in.

1970 Foster *Walker Valley* 83 I disremember who told me that.

doless, daeless, dayless, doeless, dooless *adj* Lazy, dilatory, shiftless, doing little, inefficient. Hence *n* A person having these qualities, one who does little. In the U.S. only **doless** is attested. [OED *do-less* adj 'inactive, inefficient' 1785→, dialect and colloquial; SND *doless* adj 'lazy, lacking in energy, improvident'; DARE *do-less* adj 'lacking energy, inactive, lethargic; lazy, shiftless' chiefly South Midland]

ULST.:   **1804** Orr *Poems* 121 The tragedy o' doeless Dodd / Frae shame and free him if I cud.

1880 Patterson *Antrim/Down Glossary* 31 *dooless* = helpless, thriftless.

1902 McIlroy *Craig-Linnie Burn* 23 Ye'r a maist daeless, extravagant wumman.

1904 Marshall *Dial of Ulster* 70 *dooless* = an unhandy person, an ill-going or unsuccessful person; one who spoils his work, to whom the saying is applied, 'his fingers are all thumbs'.

1953 Traynor *Donegal Glossary* 83 *doless* = thriftless.

c1955 Montgomery *Heard in Ulster* 38 *dae-less* = a person unwilling to work: 'He's a dae-less bodey'.

1980 McClean *Ulster Words III* 3 *daeless* = idle, useless: 'He's a daeless bein".
2000 Fenton *Hamely Tongue* 52 *daeless* = incapable of firm decision or action; vague and incompetent; thriftless.

U.S.: 1859 Bartlett *Americanisms* 125 = inefficient. 'He's a doless sort of a fellow'.
1943 Justus *Bluebird* 133 The Tylers were everly doless folks.
1952 Wilson *Folk Speech NC* 534 = a person who does little; a lazy, worn-out person.
1953 Randolph and Wilson *Down in Holler* 240 *doless* = inactive, slothful, lazy: 'Sally's beau ain't a bad feller, he's just kinder doless'.
1958 Wood *Words from Tenn* 10 = lazy.
1974 Fink *Bits Mt Speech* 6 = lazy or trifling: 'I'm feeling plumb do-less this morning'.
1983 Broaddus and McAtee *Estill Co Word List* 38 = shiftless.

donnick, donock See **dornick**

donsie, dansy, dauncey, dauncy, dawney, dawny, doncey, doncy, donny, donsy
adj Sick, sick-looking; weak, frail, feeble, delicate; squeamish, fastidious about eating; stunted; dishonest, mean. [probably < Irish *donas* 'bad luck, misery' or Scottish Gaelic *donas/donais* 'mischief, harm; bad luck' + Scots *-ie*; OED *dauncy* adj 'sickly; delicate, not robust' U.S. and dialect; DARE *donsie* probably from Irish, Scottish Gaelic *donas* 'evil, harm' perhaps with influence from obsolete *daunch* 'fastidious, squeamish', *dunce*, and other words] (Note: no attempt is made to separate the many overlapping senses illustrated in citations below; for the range of senses on each side of the Atlantic see **1953** Traynor and **1976** Weals citations.)

ULST.: 1861 Hume *Rabbin's Ollminick* 17 People that's donsy like, or bad ov a decay, disn't last long about this time o' year.
1880 Patterson *Antrim/Down Glossary* 31 *donsy, dauncey* = sick, sick-looking.
1881 Hart *Mere Irish* 81–82 Immediately the door opened, and in walked a donsie looking wee fellow, not above a yard high.
1891 Simmons *Armagh Words and Phrases* 7 *donny* = sick, weak, in bad health.
c1910 Byers *Glossary, dawney* = in poor health, delicate, weak; *donsie* = neat, trim, affectedly neat.
1923 Lutton *Montiaghisms* 17 *donsy, donny* = feeble, weak, debilitated.
1924 Logan *Ulster in X-Rays* 69 A person who is delicate is said to be 'doncey'; at any rate, in Mid-Antrim this is applied to persons only, but once in North Antrim at a football match the opposing captain told me his boots were 'doncey', meaning, I suppose, that *they* were also 'delicate'.
1928 McKay *Oul' Town* 26 Many's the time he ploughed our field for us—my man is very 'dauncy' and sickly.
1930 McCurry *Ulster Village* 201 He ate nothin', an' was as dawny and worn as an oul' man.
1953 Traynor *Donegal Glossary* 84 *donsie* = (1) unfortunate, unlucky; (2) mean, miserly; (3) of persons: small, weak, stunted, diminutive; of things: defective; (4) uncertain, with difficulty; (5) frail, delicate, weakly; (6) ill, very ill; (7) dull, stupid.
1990 McIntyre *Some Handlin'* 22 *doncy* = (1) unwell, sick, dizzy: 'Frances was very well and she was feeling doncy'; (2) dishonest: 'I look after my money when that doncy boy is around'.
2000 Fenton *Hamely Tongue* 59 *donsie* = mean, petty, cheap: 'Wuzn't thon a donsie trick?'

U.S.:   **1805** (in **1912** Thornton *American Glossary* 1.261) Citizen Lafferty must have
            a 'doncy' opinion of the cause, when he is afraid to bet even.
            1872 Schele de Vere *Americanisms* 462 *dansy* = in Pennsylvania, of people who
            are failing of old age.
            1874 Eggleston *Circuit Rider* 'Sick, Mort? Goin' to have a chill? ... You look
            powerful dauncy', said the old man.
            1913 Kephart *Our Sthn High* 289 A remarkable word, common in the
            Smokies, is dauncy, defined for me as 'mincy about eating', which is to say
            fastidious, over-nice.
            1930 Shoemaker *1300 Penn Words* 16 *donsie* = light headed, not feeling up to
            the mark; giddy.
            1938 Hall *Coll* Dauncy about eatin' = don't feel good, don't feel like eatin'.
            1952 Justus *Children* 36 Herb tea is a mighty fine tonic when a body is feeling
            dauncy—and so is good company.
            1953 Randolph and Wilson *Down in Holler* 238 *dauncy* = lacking appetite,
            fastidious about food.
            1976 Weals *Words Stay Donsie* or *dauncy* is another vanishing mountain word
            that appears to have meanings that differ when it is applied to self and when it
            applies to another person. 'I feel donsie', might mean I feel dizzy, or slightly ill,
            or nauseated. When put on somebody else donsie can mean, at least in some
            localities, that the person is intoxicated, addled, silly, stupid, or, according to
            some local interpretations, quick-tempered, and even saucy and pert.

dooble See **double**

dooless See **doless**

doorstone, dorr-stane *n* A large, flat stone serving as a door-step or threshold.
ULST.:   **2004** Fenton *Notes*, *dorr-stane*.
U.S.:   **1935** Sheppard *Cabins in Laurel* 64 He had to hack him to pieces on the door
            stone to the house.
            1943 Hannum *Mt People* 93 White chickens war a-scratchin' on the
            doorstone, and la, we didn't have a white chicken on the place!

dornick, donnick, donock, dornack, dornig, dornog *n* A rock or stone, usually one
small enough to clasp in the hand and throw. [< Irish *dornóg/doirneog* or Scottish
Gaelic *doirneag* < *dorn/duirn* 'fist'; OED labels *dornick* 'U.S. dialect' in error; cf SND
dornack; DARE formerly more widespread, now especially North Central,
Pennsylvania]
ULST.:   **c1750** Craig *Diary* (in **1847** Davidson *Presby Church in Kentucky* 24) An
            anecdote is told of his having been sent by Hanover Presbytery to organize
            churches and ordain elders, among the settlements of New River and Holstein.
            On his return he reported a surprising number of elders whom he had ordained;
            and on being questioned how he found suitable materials for so many, he
            replied, in his rich brogue, 'Where I cudna get hewn stanes, I tuk dornacks'. A
            dornack is a rough mis-shapen stone, generally rejected by builders.
            1829 McSparran *Irish Legend* 41 Now, my brave fellows, bowl a halliagh,
            hannamondwowl knock out his brains with that dornig.
            1953 Traynor *Donegal Glossary* 83 *dornog* = a casting stone.
U.S.:   **1859** Bartlett *Americanisms* 127 *donock* = a stone, a term almost pecular to
            Arkansas, though used more or less throughout the South.

1930 Shoemaker *1300 Penn Words* 18 *dornick* = a round stone picked up in fields to throw at cattle.
1953 Randolph and Wilson *Down in Holler* 240 *donnick* = a stone, usually one small enough to be thrown or used as a weapon.
1975 Gainer *Speech Mtneer* 9 *dornick* = a stone small enough to be thrown: 'He hit him with a dornick'.

dorr-stane See **doortone**

double, dooble *vb* In making liquor: to strengthen poteen (or illicit whiskey in the U.S.) by putting the **singlings** from the first distillation **run** back through the **still**. The resulting liquor (**doublings**) has higher proof and is smoother; in the U.S. **double back, double still** are also known. [OED *double* n 1b; DARE *double* vb 4a 'to strengthen (whiskey) by redistillarion or use of a thump barrel; to redistill' southern Appalachians]

ULST.: 1840 Boyce *Shandy Maguire* 27 Why, ye might hae singled an' doobled it sin ye gaed oot, woman, but auld folks I see, maun ha their time.
1953 Traynor *Donegal Glossary* 86 = to have the second run of poteen through the still.

U.S.: 1800 Osborn *Diary* (28 Jul) I Doubled a run of Apple Brandy for uncle made 9 gallons.
1939 Hall *Coll* That's when you double back to start up again [i.e. when you run the liquor through the still the second time].
1959 Hall *Coll* You double it back and you run it again. Then you get your good whiskey, which the old people called 'corn squeezin's'.

doubletree *n* A crossbar or pair of crossbars on the front of a wagon or plow, to each end of which a **singletree** is attached when two horses or other draft animals are harnessed as a team. [probably formed by analogy with *singletree*, folk etymology for *swingletree*; OED labels *double-tree* 'U.S.' in error; DARE widespread except Northeast]

ULST.: 1904 Marshall *Dial of Ulster* 126 = a wooden bar for yoking horses to a plough or other implement of tillage.
2000 Fenton *Hamely Tongue* 61 = a wide 'tree' to which two singletrees (or swingle-trees) are attached.

U.S.: 1847 Webster *American Dictionary* 1034 A single-tree is fixed upon each end of the double-tree when two horses draw abreast.
1908 Payne *Word-list East Alabama* 306 = a pair of whiffletrees for a two-horse wagon; also the beam to which the single-trees are attached.
1930 Shoemaker *1300 Penn Words* 17 = the trace rod of a two horsed vehicle.
1966–68 *DARE Coll* = longer piece to which bars are tied.

doubling *vbl n* (usually plural in form) The second **run** through a **still** (in Ulster, of poteen, in the U.S. of illicit whiskey). Cf **singling**. See also **double**. [DARE *doublings* n 'in moonshining: redistilled liquor' chiefly South Midland]

ULST.: 1845 Carleton *Irish Peasantry* (in 1978 McGuffin *Praise of Poteen* 102) When the doubling was about half finished, he made his appearance, attended by a strong body of reluctant soldiers—for indeed it is due to the military to state that they never took delight in harassing the country people at the behest of a keg-hunter, as they generally nicknamed the gauger.

1956 Bell *Orange Lily* 54 That's right—[it's] the second run. The 'doublins' as some folks call it. This'll be the third run—the finished article as you might say.

U.S.:   **1867** *Congressional Globe* (21 Jan) 60 The singling tub is placed aside and the doubling tub put to the outlet of the worm.

1914 Arthur *Western NC* 273 When a sufficient quantity has been produced, the mash is removed from the still, and it is washed out, after which the 'singlings' are poured into the still and evaporated, passing through the worm a second time, thus becoming 'doublings', or high proof whiskey.

1992 Gabbard *Thunder Road* 150 The first time they run the mash, it was pretty poor. They called it 'singlin's', 50 or 60 proof, something like that. They'd pour it back in the mash or give it to young boys who worked the still because it was weak and they wouldn't get drunk as quick. When they ran it the second time, they was called 'doublin's'. That was the moonshine they sold.

dour *adj* Resolute, determined, sometimes to the point of disagreeableness. [probably ultimately < Latin *dūrus* 'hard'; OED *dour* adj originally Scottish, 1375→; SND *dour* adj 'determined, resolute, stern, obstinate']

ULST.:   **1880** Patterson *Antrim/Down Glossary* 31 = sulky, disagreeable.

1924 Logan *Ulster in X-Rays* 25 The Ulsterman has great will-power and determination. In fact, he is often classed as 'dour'.

1942 *Bangor Words* 26 = grim and difficult to deal with.

U.S.:   **1930** Shoemaker *1300 Penn Words* 18 = difficult, hard to manage.

down in under *phr* Underneath. See also **in under**.

ULST.:   **1889** Hart *Derryreel* 117 His head knocked again' the wall when we fell in, and he's down in under the water.

U.S.:   **1969** *GSMNP*-25:2:16 You've been through there I guess and saw, well, right in under from the bridge right down in under the bridge sort of in that house.

1969 *GSMNP*-46:16 Smith's home was down in under there.

drabble *vb* To trail or drag through liquid mud. Hence **drabbled** *adj* Messy and wet, especially with mud. [< Middle English *drabelen*; OED *drabble* vb 1 'to become wet and dirty by dabbling in, or trailing through, water or mire' 15th century→, 2 'to make wet and dirty by contact with muddy water or mire. Also in extended use'; SND *drabble* 'to dirty, to besmear']

ULST.:   **1884** McFadyen and Hepburn *Lays and Legends* 74 Till jist wan fine mornin' the Priest saw him trackin' / His road through the gutters as daylight wis brackin', / All drookilt an' drabbl'd, with clay on his hide.

1923 Lutton *Montiaghisms* 17 = to bespatter the lower part of the dress in walking, to draggle.

U.S.:   **1949** McDavid *Atlas Mill* 108 *drabbled* = water-soaked: 'Like a drabbled rat'.

drap *vb* To drop. Hence *n* A drop. [OED (at *drop*) Scottish dialect form; SND Scottish form of English *drop*; DARE *drop* A chiefly South, South Midland]

ULST.:   **1813** Porter *Glossary Poetical Attempts* = drop.

1932 Quinn *McConaghy's Money* 23 Aggie, stir yerself, an' put the kettle on to make them a drap o' tay.

2000 Fenton *Hamely Tongue* 2 On accoont o wha ye ir, A'll let it drap.

U.S.:   **1837** Sherwood *Georgia Provincialisms* 119 *drap*, for drop.

1904–07 Kephart *Notebooks* 4:859 I got the drap on him.
1924 (in **1952** Mathes *Tall Tales* 35) We're pore folks an' hain't got nothin'
much, but if ye ever git out in them mountings yander we'd be real proud fer
ye to drap in.
1942 Hall *Phonetics* 28 [dræp].

drewth See **drouth**

drib *n* Especially of a liquid: a small amount, drop, dreg (often in figurative phrase
in dribs and drabs = little by little, in small increments). Hence *vb* To draw the last
drop of milk from a cow. [apparently an imitative formation based on *drip* or *drop*;
OED *drib* n 'a drop, a petty or inconsiderable quantity' Scottish and dialect, vb 1 'to
fall in drops, figuratively to go on little by little', 1523→; SND *drib* n 1 'a drop, a
small quantity of liquid or semi-liquid' 1721→; DARE *drib* n 'a drop; a small
quantity', probably back formation from *dribble*, chiefly Midland]
> ULST.: **1880** Patterson *Antrim/Down Glossary* 32 = small amounts: 'He pays it in dribs
> and drabs'.
> **1923** Lutton *Montiaghisms* 18 = (1) a very small sum of money, a small
> installment of a debt; (2) to drain the last milk from a cow.
> **1953** Traynor *Donegal Glossary* 88 = a small quantity of liquid; 2) = to draw
> the last drop of milk from a cow.
> **1981** Pepper *Ulster-English Dict* 26 I onny want a wee drib of sugar.
> **1991** O'Kane *You Don't Say* 41 = a small amount or piece, as in 'dribs and drabs'.
> **1993** Montgomery *Barnish* 63 'It came out in dribs and drabs' = it came out
> in small amounts.
> U.S.: **1908** Payne *Word-list East Alabama* 307 = a drop, a small quantity: 'He paid
> him in dribs'.
> **1996** Montgomery *Coll* He just drank a drib of shine.

drouth, drewth, drooth, druth *n* Dryness (especially a period of dry weather after
rain); thirst. [< Old English *druȝað* 'dryness'; DOST *drouth* n 1 'prolonged or
extreme dry weather, drought, or a spell of this' 2 'thirst'; DARE especially western
Pennsylvania; LAUSC Pennsylvania]
> ULST.: **1813** Porter *Poetical Attempts* Yet, water, for to tell the truth / Is famous aye for
> quenchin' drouth.
> **1881** Hart *Mere Irish* 155 There's nothing like an angry heart for bringing on
> the drouth, so the long and the short of it was that Ferigal took far more nor
> was good for him of Shan Dhu's whiskey.
> **1891** Simmons *Armagh Words and Phrases* 8 *druth, drewth* = thirst, drought,
> dryness.
> **c1910** Byers *Glossary* = (1) a spell of fine, dry weather, applied to absence of
> rain for a long time; (2) thirst: 'I have a druth on me I wouldn't sell for 5/-'.
> **1948** Marshall *Planted by River* 96 Indeed we were glad of the drooth while it
> lasted, for it brought its own blessing. The hay was saved without heartbreak.
> **c1955** Montgomery *Heard in Ulster* 35 I hae an awful drooth on me.
> **1990** McIntyre *Some Handlin'* 22 = drying: 'You wouldn't hang clothes out on
> a wet day because there would be no drooth'.
> **1991** O'Kane *You Don't Say* 42 = (1) thirst: 'There was a terrible drooth on
> me'; (2) drying weather conditions, a period of drought: 'There's not much
> drooth today'.

U.S.:   **1899** Green *Virginia Word-Book* 124 = dry weather, want of rain; thirst, want of drink.
1961 Kurath and McDavid *Pron Engl Atl Sts* 167 The type of /druθ/ was confined to Scotland and Northern Ireland, whence it was brought to Pennsylvania.

drouthy *adj* Thirsty; dry, causing thirst. [OED *drouthy* adj 1 'dry, without moisture; arid' 1603→, 2 'characterized by drought; deficient in rainfall', 1605→, 3 'thirsty; often = addicted to drinking' 1626→; DOST *drouthy* adj 'dry, rainless' c1590→]
    Ulst.:   **1880** Patterson *Antrim/Down Glossary* 33 = thirsty: 'Talkin's drouthy work'.
1937 Rowley *Tales of Mourne* 179 In drouthy weather he'd leave a jug of buttermilk where [the Wee Folk] could help themselves.
1990 McIntyre *Some Handlin'* 22 = thirsty.
    U.S.:   **1899** Green *Virginia Word-Book* 124 = dry; thirsty, requiring drink; thirsty from heat or fever.

drown the miller *vb phr* To dilute liquor with too much water. [OED (at *miller* n 10b(c) 'to add too much water to spirits, tea, dough, etc.']
    Ulst.:   **1880** Patterson *Antrim/Down Glossary* 33 = this is said to be done when too much water is added to a glass of grog.
    U.S.:   **1899** Green *Virginia Word-Book* 124 = to pour too much water into the spirit when mixing grog.
1975 Gould *Maine Lingo* 82 'Don't drownd the miller!' It is almost always heard in this negative imperative, because it means to over-water the rum or whiskey, which is never taken to kindly.

druth See **drouth**

druv, dhruv, druve *vb* Drove, driven.
    Ulst.:   **c1910** Byers *Glossary* A've dhruv this horse these five years.
1920 McCallin *Fireside Tales* 137 Two important, as well as urgent causes spurred her on and, sometimes in spite of herself, almost druve her frantic.
1921 Irvine *Poor Folk* 54 Afther cavortin' around for a while, they got into their cyart, and sittin' purty close tigither they druv home.
1921 O'Neill *More Songs of Glens* 26 At the latter end of all I dhruv the heifer home.
    U.S.:   **1845** Thompson *Pineville* 65 'And how fast they druv', observed one.
1956 Hall *Coll* A witch doctor drawed a picture of the witch and nailed it back of the door, druv a nail in her heart, and then she died.
1970 Broome *Earth Man* 62 Once we druv a cyar through a creek and wet its shassy and then came a big freeze and froze it to the ground.

E

egg, agg *vb* (usually with *on* or *up*) To provoke, incite (to mischief), urge on. [<
Old Norse *eggja*, cognate with English *edge*; OED *egg* vb[1] 'to incite, encourage, urge
on; to provoke, tempt' c1200→]

> ULST.: **1892** *Ballymena Observer* (in **1898–1905** Wright *Engl Dial Dict*) He egged the
> boys on.
> **c1910** Byers *Glossary* = to incite, especially to mischief or wrong-doing, to urge
> on: 'He egged on the boys to fight'.
> **1920** Doyle *Ballygullion* 42 An' eggin' a man on till it's near as bad as the thing
> itself, if the law tuk it that way.
> **1923** Lutton *Montiaghisms* 9 *agg* = to incite, to stir up, to encourage to do
> mischief: 'Agg him up'.
> **1938** McCallin *Killywhapple* 80 But her man's egged on by his sisthers to have
> [the child named] Sophia Elizabeth, afther one of their last generation that was
> bred up as quality.
>
> U.S.: **1917** Kephart *Word-list* 407 Both sides agged it up.
> **c1940** Aswell *Glossary Tenn Idiom* 1 *agg* = stir up trouble.
> **1983** Broaddus and McAtee *Estill Co Word List* 38 *egg it up* = to egg on a fight.

evening *n* The afternoon, the time between the middle of the day (usually marked
by a meal) and dusk. [OED *evening* 2c 'afternoon' dialect and U.S. local; DARE
evening n B 'afternoon; the time of day between noon and twilight' chiefly South,
South Midland]

> ULST.: **1919** MacGill *Glenmornan* 311 Evening with them starts at noon and finishes
> at dusk.
> **1969** Braidwood *Ulster Dial Lex* 4 I have not come before you this
> afternoon—or, as I should say, evening, since Ulster English accords no
> recognition to 'afternoon'.
> **1983** Pepper *Ulster Knowledge* 8 Whereas elsewhere [afternoon] is usually
> taken to mean the period between two and six o'clock p.m., this is generally
> referred to as evening in Ulster.
> **1990** McIntyre *Some Handlin'* 24 = afternoon: 'The breadman usually comes
> at three o'clock in the evening'.
> **1990** Todd *Words Apart* 68 Come round this evening, any time afther two.
>
> U.S.: **1859** Bartlett *Americanisms* 138 In the South and West there is no afternoon.
> From noon till dark is evening. It is strange to an unaccustomed ear to be
> accosted with 'Good evening' at two or three o'clock in the day. Where this
> usage prevails, immediately after sunset is 'night'.
> **1899** Green *Virginia Word-Book* 133 = time between noon and dark, including
> afternoon and twilight.
> **1939** Hall *Coll* The middle of the evenin' is about three o'clock.
> **1943** Hannum *Mt People* 131 [F]or southern mountain people 'evening'
> begins at twelve o'clock noon. For them the morning and the evening are the
> day, as it is recounted in Genesis of a world still in the making.
> **1973** *GSMNP*-78:21 At twelve we would arrange our benches and have a
> spelling bee all Friday evening.

everly *adv* Always, constantly. [< *ever* 'always' + *-ly*; OED *everly* adv 'always, continually' 1314→, obsolete or Scottish; SND *everly* adv 'constant, without interruption'; DARE *everly* adv 'always' chiefly southern Appalachians, Ozarks]

ULST.:   c1910 Byers *Glossary* He's always and everly complaining.

        1920 McCallin *Fireside Tales* 239 They still stick to the oul' habit o' rakin' the fire at bedtime; so that now as everly it's ready to be brisked up at an early hour when there's always somebody afoot an' at the work.

U.S.:   1916 Combs *Old Early English* 288 It has everly been the custom.

        1953 Randolph and Wilson *Down in Holler* 65 *Everly* means always, or at least usually: 'It's everly been Pap's way to holler a little when he gets to drinkin''.

        1995 Montgomery *Coll* He was everly going down to the store.

ewe See **yo**

F

face-clout, face-cloot See **clout**

fail *vb* To decline in health. [DOST *fail* vb 1 'to lose strength or vigour']
    ULST.:   **1953** Traynor *Donegal Glossary* 96 = to grow weak, decline in health.
    U.S.:   **1914** England *Rural Locutions* 72 = to fail in health: 'The old jedge is failin' up pow'ful fast'.

fair *vb*, **fair up** *vb phr* (in the U.S. also **fair off**) *vb* Of the weather: to clear up, become less cloudy. [OED *fair* vb 1b 'of the weather: to clear (especially with *away*, *off*, or *up*)' dialect and U.S.; SND *fair* IV vb 'of weather: to clear up after rain or snow, to become fine' 1820→; DARE *fair up* (at *fair off*) vb phr 'of the weather: to become clearer' chiefly South, South Midland]
    ULST.:   **c1910** Byers *Glossary* 'The day's going to fair (or fair up)' = to clear, leave off raining, become fine.
        1948 Marshall *Planted by River* 111 The rain had faired, but, on account of the long spell of wet, it was not likely that any of our people would be busied far from the house.
        1953 Traynor *Donegal Glossary* 96 *fair* = of weather: to clear up, stop raining.
        1991 O'Kane *You Don't Say* 47 *fair* = to become fair (mostly used in the sense of stop raining): 'It rained all night and only faired at eleven o'clock today'.
        2000 Fenton *Hamely Tongue* 71 *fair up* = (of the weather) to stop raining.
    U.S.:   **1899** Green *Virginia Word-Book* 135 = to clear up, cease raining; as, 'It will fair up toward night'.
        1917 Kephart *Word-list* 411 It may fair up and be a pretty week.
        1953 Randolph and Wilson *Down in Holler* 243 *fair up* = to become bright or clear, often used in speaking of the weather: 'I reckon it'll fair up, come Sunday'.
        1979 *GSMNP*-112:6 I went back to school when it did fair up.
        1983 Broaddus and McAtee *Estill Co Word List* 39 *fairing off* = becoming less cloudy.

falt See **fault**

far piece, ferr piece, fur piece *n phr* A substantial distance. See also **piece 1**. [DARE *far piece* n 1 scattered, but chiefly South, South Midland, North Central]
    ULST.:   **1981** Pepper *Ulster-English Dict* 30 Ye'd better get yir skates on for it's a ferr piece down the road.
    U.S.:   **1940** Haun *Hawk's Done* 34 It seemed like it was a right far piece to the cave.
        1975 Chalmers *Better* 65 A short road is a piece ways, or, if the road is longer, it may be a fur piece.

fash *vb* To annoy, trouble or vex (oneself), become impatient. [< French *facher*; OED *fash* vb 1 To afflict, annoy, trouble, vex' 1533→, 2 'to weary, be annoyed; to bother or trouble oneself; to take trouble' 1535→, chiefly Scottish and northern dialect; DOST *fasch* vb 'to trouble, bother, annoy' 1540→]
    ULST.   **1734** *Northern Bard* 160 I guess your Meaning by your Wink, / Ne'er fash your Heed.

1813 Porter *Glossary Poetical Attempts* = to trouble, to care for.
1840 Boyce *Shandy Maguire* 39 Niver fash yourself—it's no harm, I tell ye.
1880 Patterson *Antrim/Down Glossary* 36 = to trouble oneself: 'Don't fash your lug' = pay no heed, never mind.
c1910 Byers *Glossary* = to trouble; to have too much of, as 'I am fashed with it'.
1920 McCallin *Fireside Tales* 148 Most o' ye must a-noticed that, as a rule, people soon got fashed listenin' till a man when he starts bletherin' about them that have shown a fondness for him.
2005 Wright *No Sae Bad* 17 But A'm no that fashed whun A think wae a grin / O aa tha airts ma get up hae bin.

U.S.:　　**1870** Stewardson *Nesh Neb Butty* 249 *to fash oneself* = to worry.
　　　　　1956 Settle *Beulah Land* 280 Don't fash yourselves.

fault, falt *vb* To find fault with, blame, criticize. [OED *fault* vb 7 'to blame or censure'; DARE *fault* vb B 'to criticize, blame, scold' chiefly South Midland]

ULST.:　**1880** Patterson *Antrim/Down Glossary* 37 *fault* = to blame.
　　　　1915 MacGill *Rat Pit* 17 You shouldn't fault me for my sin, said the beanscho.
　　　　1934 Cavanagh *Dunleary Legend* 88 Thim same cakes was well mashed up wid the hurry of his ride, but sure the childer never faulted thim for that.
　　　　1953 Traynor *Donegal Glossary* 99 *fault* = to blame, to find fault with.
　　　　2000 Fenton *Hamely Tongue* 221 In troth A cannae falt him for daein whut he did.

U.S.:　　**1896** *Word-list* 416 = blame: 'I didn't *fault* him for that'.
　　　　1913 Kephart *Our Sthn High* 282 In mountain vernacular many words that serve as verbs are only nouns of action, or adjectives, or even adverbs ... 'Granny kept faultin' us all day'.
　　　　1928 (in **1952** Mathes *Tall Tales* 65) They ain't no use faultin' the boy fer somethin' he ain't to blame fer.
　　　　c1959 Weals *Hillbilly Dict* 4 *fault* = blame: 'I don't fault you fer the cow gittin' out'.
　　　　1962 Dykeman *Tall Woman* 166 'She's always faulting herself for her cooking', Paul teased.

favor, favour *vb* To resemble (especially in countenance) a member or side of one's family. [OED *favour* vb 8 'to resemble in face or features' 1609→; SND *favour* II v 'to resemble'; DARE widespread, but chiefly South, South Midland]

ULST.:　**1880** Patterson *Antrim/Down Glossary* 37 = to resemble, as regards family likeness: 'That chile favours his father'.
　　　　1991 O'Kane *You Don't Say* 49 = to resemble: 'That child favours his mother'.
U.S.:　　**1908** Payne *Word-list East Alabama* 310 *favor* = to resemble.
　　　　1930 Shoemaker *1300 Penn Words* 23 *favor* = to resemble.

feard, feared, feart, feerd, feered, feert *predicate adj* Afraid, frightened. Same as **afeard.**

ULST.:　**1879** Lyttle *Paddy McQuillan* 25 A wuz heart feerd o' my ma, fur she haes a terble bad tongue.
　　　　1885 Lyttle *Robin Gordon* 34 A'm feered A'll no be able tae mak ye mony comfortable denners withoot a bit o' meat o' some sort.
　　　　1933 *North Antrim* 38 I'm no' sae feart o' fairies—shure they widna touch a maid / That was seekin' for a treasure wi' a footy kin' o' spade.

1934 Cavanagh *Dunleary Legend* 88 Herself met the Riverence at the door, wid the small wans hidin' behind her, they was so feared whin they see his Riverence's black looks.

c1955 Montgomery *Heard in Ulster* 48 I'm no feart o' ye.

1975 Murphy *You're Talking* 63 I never got to bed. I was that feert I meant to sit up till you would come.

1983 Pepper *Ulster Knowledge* 25 I'm still feared he mightn't recognise you for he's still randerin.

2000 Fenton *Hamely Tongue* 239 There's naw a yin o them A'm feart o.

U.S.: **1834** Downing *Life Andrew Jackson* 208 This, gineral, was leavin an example which I'm feart your successors wont imitate.

1899 Green *Virginia Word-Book* 38 Are you feard to go?

fergenst See **forgainst**

fernenst, fernent, fernenth, ferninst, fernint See **fornent**

ferr piece See **far piece**

fetch *n* An apparition of death. [origin obscure; OED *fetch* n 1 'the apparition, wraith, or double of a living person']

ULST.: **1953** Traynor *Donegal Glossary* 101 = a spectre, spirit, the apparition of one alive: 'Saw the reflection of a wraith, the fetch of a future husband'.

U.S.: **1930** Shoemaker *1300 Penn Words* 23 = a spirit that foretells death, a 'token'.

fireboard, fireboord *n* A horizontal shelf or ledge over a fireplace, mantelpiece. [DARE *fireboard* n 1 'a mantel over a fireplace' chiefly South, South Midland]

ULST.: **1936** White *Mrs Murphy* 22 I clean forgot I had them. Set them up on the fireboard, Rachel, woman.

1953 Traynor *Donegal Glossary* 103 = the mantel-piece.

c1955 Montgomery *Heard in Ulster* 49 = wooden mantel shelf above old hearths, on which were found the 'Tay caddy', a coloured tin box for knick-knacks, China dogs, box of matches, and maybe coffee.

2000 Fenton *Hamely Tongue* 75 *fireboord.*

U.S.: **1886** Smith *Southern Dialect* 350 = mantle-piece.

1949 Kurath *Word Geog East US* 36 *Fire board* for the mantel shelf [is found] not only in the Southern Appalachians (from the Kanawha [River] to South Carolina) but also in the corridor from the Cape Fear to the Peedee [River].

1962 Dykeman *Tall Woman* 148 Lydia set her clock on it proudly and said, 'A fireboard needs a clock'.

1975 Purkey *Madison Co* 6–7 The mantel or fireboard was like a museum, a catchall for all the odds and ends.

first foot *vb phr* Of a person: to be the first to step into a house on New Year's morning. Hence **first footer** *n.* The first person to enter a house on New Year's morning. Good fortune for the coming year was most often thought to accompany a first footer who was a dark-haired man bearing something to drink or eat. [SND *first fit* n 2 'the first person to enter a house on New Year's morning, considered as the bringer of good (or bad) luck for the year' 1792→; cf DARE *first footer*]

ULST.: **c1910** Byers *Glossary, first footer* = the first person to enter a house on New Year's Day.

1971 St Clair *Folklore Ulster* 33 The tradition of 'first-footing' is a happy blend of [Scottish and Irish] tradition, and after midnight, one visits one's friends with a bottle, a loaf of bread and a lump of coal, and if you happen to be a dark-haired man, then you're thrice welcome.
1983 Pepper *Ulster Knowledge* 29 To allow a red-haired person to first-foot you on New Year's morning also invites calamity.
1990 McBride *Our Past* 80 New Year's Day was a time for preserving the luck of the household. There was a belief that happiness and prosperity depended on the first person to enter the house on New Year's Day. A dark haired man was thought to be lucky as a first footer. Women were thought to be unlucky, especially if they had red hair.
2000 Fenton *Hamely Tongue* 75 *first-fittin* = a visit (usu. planned) by the first person to come through the door as the new year begins (traditionally being dark-haired and bringing a piece of coal to ensure a lucky year).

U.S.: **1961** Sackett and Koch *Kansas Folklore* 187 A New Year's Day custom called 'first-footing', which consisted of taking a basket of wine and fruitcake and calling on all your friends early in the morning New Year's Day and having a drink of wine and a piece of fruitcake at each house.
1984 *DARE Coll* Dad used to do what they always called first-footing. On New Year's he'd be the first one to come in the door—[what] they'd call the first-footer. He would go out and come in with a bottle of wine and some pennies or some biscuits or something ... in his hand, and then he'd give everybody a penny; that was supposed to be luck ... They wanted somebody lucky to be the first-footer. Dad was pretty lucky about winning things, and so he was usually the one that did the first footing.

first shot *n* Poteen or illicit whiskey from the first distillation **run** back through the **still**. Same as **singling(s)**. [DARE South, South Midland].

ULST.: **1845** Carleton *Irish Peasantry* (in **1978** McGuffin *Praise of Poteen* 102) Even this running was going on to their satisfaction, and the singlings had been thrown again in to the still, from the worm of which projects the strong medicinal first-shot as the doubling commenced—the last term meaning in its pure and finished state.
1910 Joyce *English in Ireland* 323 = the weak pottheen whiskey that comes off at the first distillation, agreeable to drink but terribly sickening.
c**1910** Wier *Bab McKeen* 55 It was first shot and a toucher at that, an' am sure he hes niver got onythin' tae equal it since.
1922 McKay *Mts of Mourne* 104 The fiddler had a bottle snugly hidden in his pocket as well, a portion of which was given to 'Granda' (Mr Larkin). It proved to be 'First Shot', and before all was over, poor Larkin was 'shot' right enough.

U.S.: **1840** *New Orleans Picayune* (30 Aug) 2 O, it's illigant, Mrs. Mahoney, and as strong as fust shot (strong whiskey) says Mrs. Casey
1939 Hall *Coll* I was drinking first shot of singlings, you know, and it made me drunk.
1949 Maurer *Argot of Moonshiner* 9 = the initial distillate which emerges from the flake stand as the stilling process begins.

flake stand *n* In the distillation of poteen or illicit whiskey, a container having cold, flowing water in which the condenser of a **still** is set. [possibly < Old Norse *flake, fleke* 'hurdle, wicker shield'; OED *flake* n[1] 1 'a waddled hurdle' c1330→; DOST *flake* n 2 'a frame on which meat, cheese, etc. are displayed' 1598→; DARE southern Appalachians]

ULST.: 1953 Traynor *Donegal Glossary* 104 = poteen-making term: the barrel in which the worm is cooled.

1978 McGuffin *Praise of Poteen* 14 A lateral tube was then luted into the worm, which was a copper tube of an inch and a half bore, coiled in a barrel for a flakestand (a worm tube).

U.S.: 1967 Williams *Moonshining in Mts* 14 In higher altitudes, the worm is stretched like a coil spring and fixed rigidly in the open air, but in the most of the mountain country the coil is immersed in a barrel of cold water (called the 'flake' stand) and projected about three inches from the bottom of the barrel, which is placed on a platform high enough to permit vessels to be set with ease under the end of the worm.

flannel *adj* Of a baked good: rough in outer texture. In Ulster *flannel bread* is made of maize (American corn); in the U.S. *flannel cake* (a type of pancake) is made of flour. [variant of *flannen*, possibly from Welsh *gwlân* 'wool'; OED *flannel* n 6 suggesting the object's rough texture; cf SND *flannen bannock, flannen biscuit*; DARE *flannel cake* n 'a pancake' chiefly Appalachians]

ULST.: 1903 MacManus *Lad of O'Friels* 117 All three of us enjoyed a hearty meal, with flannel-bread and oat bread well buttered.

1953 Traynor *Donegal Glossary* 104 = bread made of maize.

U.S.: 1847 Briggs *Tom Pepper* 112 A very delicate species of food, which I tasted then for the first time, called flannel cakes.

1949 Kurath *Word Geog East US* 34 *Flannel cake* for a griddle cake made of wheat flour is ... in common use beyond the Alleghenies on the Youghiogheny in southwestern Pennsylvania, and scattered instances of it have been noted even farther west.

flannen, flanen, flanin, flannin, flennin *n* Flannel, a woolen fabric used to make garments, wash-cloths, etc. [OED *flannen* 'an open woollen stuff, of various degrees of fineness' 1503→; DARE *flannen* n 'flannel' chiefly South, South Midland]

ULST.: 1804 Orr *Poems* 62 When claughlin' wives, wi' heads in flannin', / Forgather'd on a Sabbath e'enin', / Pit spoonfu's twa a piece o' green in.

c1910 Byers *Glossary* = correct form for flannel, from Welsh *gwlanen* = woollen material.

c1955 Montgomery *Heard in Ulster* 45 Rid (red) flanen nixt yer skin is the thing fer the rheumatiz.

1964 Braidwood *Ulster/Elizabethan English* 101 *Flannen* for *flannel* (cited by Patterson) ... is actually the historically correct, and the normal Elizabethan form.

1978 Pepper *See Me* 58 There's a flannin in the jawbox if you want to wash your face.

1981 Pepper *Ulster-English Dict* 30 There, son. Give yer face a wee rub with the flannin.

1990 Todd *Words Apart* 73 That child could be doin wi' a flannen roller to keep her stomach in.

2004 Nuhan *Memories* 69 He had aboot a yerd o' flennin roon the hen, an' had her feet tied thegither.

U.S.: 1805 (in 2004 Hartley *Lewis and Clark Lexicon* 107) The weather being warm

I had left my leather over shirt and had woarn only a yellow flannin one.
1899 Green *Virginia Word-Book* 143 *flannen* = a warm, loosely woven woolen stuff, used especially for undergarments, bed covering, etc.
1987 Trent *Lore Yesteryear* 5 Flannel cloth was referred to as flannen.

fleech, fleetch *vb* To coax by flattery, cajole, entreat. Hence *n* A wheedling or fawning person. [origin uncertain; OED *fleech* vb 2 'to beguile, cajole, coax, wheedle; to entice' 1375→, Scottish and northern dialect; DOST *fleche* vb 1 'to coax, cajole' c1400→; DARE *fleech* vb 'to coax, wheedle, flatter' South Atlantic]

ULST.:   **1753** *Scotch Poems* 369 Some think themsel's ayont your reach, / And fae will neither fear nor fleetch.
c1800 Thomson (in **1992** Scott and Robinson *Samuel Thomson* 105) When fleechin winna do, ye'll even / Attempt to frighten them to heaven!
1880 Patterson *Antrim/Down Glossary* 38 *fleech* = to coax or supplicate in a fawning way.
c1910 Byers *Glossary*, *fleech* = to entice by flattery, to beseech, entreat, importune; to cajole or persuade by words: 'A fleeched at him tae A wus tired'.
1923 Lutton *Montiaghisms* 20 *fleech* = to flatter, wheedle, fawn; a person who does so.
1953 Traynor *Donegal Glossary* 105 *fleech* = to entreat, coax, supplicate: implies flattery: 'I fleeched him not to touch it'.

U.S.:   **1910** Cobb *Early English* 7 'She scooped me', meaning she had got the better of him, run away from him, scampered off at the last moment. 'And', he said, 'she could fleech you, young man.'
1938 FWP *Ocean Highway* 189 'Fleech' means to flatter, not a complimentary term since the native is sparing with his praise.
1952 Wilson *Folk Speech NC* 540 *fleech* = to flatter.

flennin See **flannen**

flit *vb* To move house. Hence *n* A move to a new house. [< Old Norse *flytja* 'to transport, migrate'; OED *flit* vb 6 'to remove from one habitation to another, change one's residence, "move"' 1504→, Scottish, northern English; DOST *flit* vb 2b 'to leave one's place of residence or occupation' c1500→]

ULST.:   **1880** Patterson *Antrim/Down Glossary* 38 = to change house: 'Do you flit this week or next?'
c1910 Byers *Glossary* = to change house, migrate; to remove from one house to another; to remove things from one house to another. 'Saturday's flit a short sit' (servants say) or 'will never sit'. Hence they reluctantly enter on service on that day, owing to this superstitious prediction.
1953 Traynor *Donegal Glossary* 105 = to change one's habitation, move to a new residence.
1983 Pepper *Ulster Knowledge* 29–30 When visiting a friend who has moved house a present of salt should be brought and a few grains sprinkled in every room. This ensures 'a happy flit'.

U.S.:   **1843** Hall *New Purchase* 264 A *nice* young gentleman engaged to be married ... is meditating 'to flit' to a bran new settlement.
1930 Shoemaker *1300 Penn Words* 22 *flitting* = moving to a new abode.
1939 Aurand *Idioms and Expressions* 24 We want you and the entire family to come and help us with the FLITTIN' (moving) on April 1st.
1982 Barrick *Coll* = moving; load of furniture: 'There goes a flittin'.

flure-cloot See **clout**

folk, fouk, fowk *n* People; the members of a family. [OED *folk* n 3a 'people, indefinitely' c1000→; DOST *folk* n 1 'in collective sense: people, persons' 1375→]

ULST.:   1733 *North Country Description* 25 I ged doon a great Place that a' the Floor was cover'd we bread Stens, and a Warld o' Foke gaing up and doon thro' yen another.
1838 McIlwham *McIlwham Papers* 8 My auld freen', McNeight, is nane o' thae folk wha 'are given to change.
1879 Lyttle *Paddy McQuillan* 43 Jennie Broon an' Susanna Todd wull help ye to lay the table an' attend tae the fowk.
c1910 Byers *Glossary* = men, people. The men- or the women-folk of a house = the sexes.
c1910 Wier *Bab McKeen* 52 Mony a time I hae wonnered there wasna mair fouk was catched.
1935 Megaw *Carragloon* 86–87 She toul me wee things about folk that ye wouldn't hear tell of by the roadside nor in the post office.

U.S.:   1978 Montgomery *White Pine Coll* VI–1 There were a lot of folk that they wouldn't dream of letting their children play cards when we were growing up.
1986 Ogle *My Valley* 39 Here we mountain folk used to fish for the now rare native brook trout; hunting in the shallows for what we called stick bait.

fool *adj* Foolish, silly. [OED *fool* B 'foolish' 1225→; DOST *fule/fuil* adj 'foolish' 1400→; DARE *fool* adj formerly widespread, now especially South, South Midland]

ULST.:   1885 Lyttle *Robin Gordon* 31 A forgot a' aboot Sally Kirk an' her fool talk.
1903 MacManus *Lad of O'Friels* 221 It's only fool questions without rhyme or raison he puts on me.
1930 McCurry *Ulster Village* 201 If ye asked him a question he wud give ye a fool answer, an' mebby commence writin' in the middle of it.
1932 Quinn *McConaghy's Money* 31 Ye wur never married yerself Rosie, an' had no trouble of yer own—that's why you go in for such fool nonsense.
2000 Fenton *Hamely Tongue* 78 = foolish: 'a fool eedyit'; 'a fool thing tae dae'.

U.S.:   1854 Holmes *Tempest and Sunshine* 12 Tempest ... can hardly wais till I'm dead till she spends money in fool fixin's.
1935 Enslow *Schoolhouse* 78 What sorter fool notion is that, Sammy?
1953 Hall *Coll* The horse give out. We lifted the horse over the log—four or five of us. We carried that fool horse up the mountain.
1977 Hamilton *Mt Memories* 14 Aunt Lela caught me by the arm and led me outside and said, 'Don't ask your Mama any more fool questions.'

footer *n* A clumsy, bungling person; a task performed in a clumsy, bungling manner. Hence *vb* To work in a clumsy, bungling manner. Hence **footer/footory/foutory** *n* The work of such an individual. [< Old French *foutre* < Latin *futuere* 'to copulate with'; SND *fouter* n 1 'a term, orig. of gross abuse or contempt, for a hateful, objectionable person' 1714→]

ULST.:   1860 Patterson *Belfast Provincialisms* 23 = to bungle; a bungler.
1920 Ervine *Mrs Martin's Man* 74 What does she want with a man when she has two childer, an' me with no childer at all but an ould footer of a man, spittin' and cursin' in the corner!
1923 Lutton *Montiaghisms* 22 *foother* = to do any work or business in a

bungling, unskilful manner; a clumsy, awkward workman; an ill-done job. **1931** Anonymous *Holiday* 32 I've been called a foother for linking the kettle off the crane when it came to a boil and setting it with it stroop in the reek. **1958** Gregg *Phonology* 399 = a clumsy person.
2000 Fenton *Hamely Tongue* 78 = (1) a clumsy, ineffectual worker; (2) to work or handle in an ineffectual, lazy or absent-minded way: 'footerin an workin an daein very little'; 'footerin at this owl injin this oors'.

U.S.:   **1930** Shoemaker *1300 Penn Words* 22 *foutory* = flimsy, insignificant, contemptible.

for See **be for**

forenenst See **fornent**

forgainst, fergenst, forgans *prep* Next to, beside. [DOST *forgainst, forgane* prep 'exhausted with going']
ULST.:   **1646** Latimer *Templepatrick Session Book* 164 The qlk day John Cowan, being sumoned, compeered and confessed his breach of sabbath in beating his wyfe one the Lord's day. And Yerefor the Session ordains him next Lord's day to stand leigh forgans the pulpit, and being called by the minister to confesse in ye face of ye congregation his offence.
           1953 Traynor *Donegal Glossary* 109 *forgainst* = beside, next to.
U.S.:   **1919** Combs *Word-list South* 33 Over fergenst the mountain.

fornent, fernenst, fernent, fernenth, ferninst, fernint, forenenst, forenent, fornense, forninst, furnentz *prep* Alongside, near, against; opposite, in front of, facing. [*fore* adv + *anent*; OED *fornent, fornenst* prep 1 'right opposite to, over against, facing' Scottish and northern; DOST *fornent* prep 1 'in front of, over against, opposite' 1429→; DARE *fornent* prep 1 'opposite to, in front of, against, near; in front, opposite' chiefly Midland]
ULST.:   **1880** Patterson *Antrim/Down Glossary* 40 *fornenst* = opposite to, in exchange for.
           1891 Simmons *Armagh Words and Phrases* 8 *fornent, fornenst* = opposite to, in front of.
           c1910 Byers *Glossary, fornenst* = opposite to, facing, over against, in exchange for: 'There it's joost (just) forninst you' or 'It's straight forninst ye'.
           1910 Joyce *English in Ireland* 258 *fornent* = opposite: 'He and I sat fornenst each other in the carriage'.
           1920 Gregory *Ulster Songs* 42 They sentenced him tae be hung, at dawn, / Furnenst his own house in Islandmagee.
           1923 Lutton *Montiaghisms* 21 *for-nent* = opposite to, face to face, in the presence of.
           1935 Megaw *Carragloon* 46 They started cloddin' [each] other forninst our gate and ye never heard the names they were callin' [each] other.
           1936 White *Mrs Murphy* 110 The first thing that I see is that oul eyesore there fornenst me.
           1942 *Bangor Words* 32 *fornenst* = opposite: 'They were sitting fornenst one another'.
           1953 Traynor *Donegal Glossary* 109 *forenent* = (1) opposite, directly in front of; (2) in opposition to; (3) corresponding to, for.

1981 Pepper *Ulster-English Dict* 30 Ye cudn't miss it. It's fernenst the Post Office.
1990 McIntyre *Some Handlin'* 25 *forenenst* = opposite: 'The church is forenenst the school'.
1993 Montgomery *Barnish* 21 *fornenst* = opposite, in front of.
1998 Dolan *Dict Hiberno-English* 112 Things will aye be some way, if they shouldnae be fornenst ither.
2000 Fenton *Hamely Tongue* 79–80 *fornenst* = facing, directly opposite; in lieu of, in payment of: 'That's fornenst the things A got last week'.

U.S.:   **1829** Kirkham *English Grammar* 192 *furnentz* = opposite. Common ... in Pennsylvania.
1835 Crockett *Account* 153 I walked with them to a room nearly fornent the old state-house.
1859 Bartlett *Americanisms* 160 *fornent* = opposite to. This Scottish word is much used in Pennsylvania and the Western States.
1904–07 Kephart *Notebooks* 4:749 Just afore it got quite fernent me, I shot.
1930 Shoemaker *1300 Penn Words* 22 *ferninst* = against, in contact with anything.
1939 Hall *Coll* He lived over fernint the store.
1943 Bewley *Picturesque Speech* 4 The word fernent should, I believe, be spelt 'ferninst'. A good old Irish word meaning 'alongside', though some say it means 'opposite'.
1967 *DARE Coll* = opposite to; very close, only a short distance away.
c1975 Lunsford *It Used To Be* 174 'Fernenth' means beyond and opposite, as 'Look yonder fernenth that sassafras and find my mattock'.

for to, for tae, for till *infinitive phr* To (usually = 'in order to'). [OED (at *for* prep 11a) now dialect or vulgar]

ULST.:   **1813** Porter *Poetical Attempts* Yet, water, for to tell the truth / Is famous aye for quenchin' drouth.
1861 Hume *Rabbin's Ollminick* 9 Whin they hev only a wee bit o' lan'[,] thats not enough for to keep two horses.
1886 Lyttle *Ballycuddy* 21 If A micht ventur to gie ye a wurd o' advice A wud say fur till hae a wheen o' these yins pit oot.
1900 Given *Poems* 210 I want for tae ken is there truth in the story / That auld Cullybackey will soon hae a hall, / Whar its Masons may meet in their ancient-day glory, / 'Thoot breakin' the law though policemen may call.
1903 Gwynn *Highways and Byways* 10 Ah'm not goin' for to brag till yer honor, but their chara'kter was just noble, that's what it was.
1942 *Bangor Words* 32 *for to* = used frequently before the infinitive: 'Why did you go for to do that?'
1975 Murphy *You're Talking* 42 The wife was pleading with the husband for to give the old man a chance but he wouldn't listen.
1982 Glassie *Folk History* 85 Then there was agents appointed then for to collect the rents.
2000 Fenton *Hamely Tongue* 79 A'll need the key for tae lock in the hens.

U.S.:   **1800** Osborn *Diary* (1 Jan) I began again for to run my still but but I am not very fit for hard Leabour.
1834 Crockett *Narrative* 62 It was about two weeks after this that I was sent for to engage in a wolf hunt.
1851 (in **1983** Heap *Bucks Co Word List* 33) Elizabeth Seabrook come for to spend the day with them.

1871 Eggleston *Hoosier Schoolmaster* 40 I was goin fer to say that when Squaire Hawkins married Virginny Gray he got a heap of money.
1908 Payne *Word-list East Alabama* 312 *for to* = in order to: 'What did you come here for to do?'
1931 Maxfield *Speech SW Penn* 19 Sarah never like for to have Jane wear mourning.
1939 Hall *Coll* I had to pick sang and pick up chestnuts for to buy what we had to wear.

for why *adv phr/conj phr* Why, for what reason, the reason why. [OED *for why* adv/conj A2 'for what reason, why' c1175→1710, obsolete; SND (at *why* 1); DARE *for why* adv 'why' chiefly South Midland]
> ULST.:   **1893** O'Neill *Glens and Speech* 369 It was long enough before I realised why two young men in our neighbourhood were known respectively as the Duck and the Daisy. For why?
> **c1910** Byers *Glossary* An' for why will ye be away two days?
> **1934** Cavanagh *Dunleary Legend* 83 I'll tell you for why, an' what I'm telling you now is no lie.
> **1975** Murphy *You're Talking* 31 He asked for why she was afeared of him.
> **2000** Fenton *Hamely Tongue* 79 A'll shane tell ye for why.
> **2004** Robinson *Prugh* 127 She sez tha catter's changeit me, / A cannae think for-why.
> U.S.:   **1800** Osborn *Diary* (16 May) I cent tell you for why but I have not eat nothing this day.
> **1913** Kephart *Our Sthn High* 297 The speech of the southern highlanders is alive with quaint idioms: 'I swapped horses, and I'll tell you fer why'.
> **1944** Laughlin *Word-list Buncombe Co* 25 He went downtown. I don't know for why.

fouk See **folk**

founder *vb* To fail or falter from exhaustion or cold, become bloated or incapacitated. [apparently from Old French *fondrer* ' to plunge to the bottom, submerge; to collapse, fall in ruins' < Latin *fundus* 'bottom'; OED *founder* vb 5 'to cause to break down or go lame; especially to cause (a horse) to have the founder, thus disabling him' 1593→; DOST *founder* vb 4 'of persons: collapse, break down, sink helpless, with drink, exhaustion, or illness, esp. a chill']
> ULST.:   **1880** Patterson *Antrim/Down Glossary* 40 *foundered* = exhausted or lamed with wet and cold: 'The horse was foundered in one of his forelegs'.
> **1904** Byers *Sayings of Ulster* 60 The doctor may, however, be informed that the person he is going to see had, as the result of a severe wetting, 'got a founder'. (The use of this old word, as applied to a horse, is well known, but as used in the case of human beings it is common in Ulster.)
> **1953** Traynor *Donegal Glossary* 110 = (1) to perish with cold; (2) of a horse: to break down through exhaustion, cold or wet.
> U.S.:   **1942** Chase *Jack Tales* 5 Well, Jack eat about all the dinner he could hold, but the King's old woman kept on pilin' up his plate till he was plumb foundered.
> **1975** *GSMNP*-59:10 He'd get in the corn or something like that and eat too much and founder him, make him sick and possibly kill him ... A mule you can't founder them by eating.

1990 Fisher *Preacher Stories* 25 An animal such as a cow or hog or horse is said to be foundered if it eats too much. At times the term is applied humorously to human beings.

foutory See **footer**

fowk See **folk**

furnentz See **fornent**

fur piece See **far piece**

G

gab *n* The mouth. Cf **gob**. [variant of *gob*; OED *gab* n³ 'the mouth' 1724→, Scottish; SND *gab* 2(1) 'the mouth' 1721→; DARE now especially Great Lakes, Upper Midwest]
    ULST.:   **1801** Bruce *Poems* [Glossary 3] = to vex, to trouble.
                1880 Patterson *Antrim/Down Glossary* 41 = the mouth; hence talk: 'Gie us none of your gab'.
                1892 *Ballymena Observer* (in **1898–1905** Wright *Engl Dial Dict*) All gab and guts like a young crow.
    U.S.:   **1908** Payne *Word-list East Alabama* 313 = the mouth: 'Shut up your gab'.

gad *n* A twisted coil or rope. [< Irish, Scottish Gaelic *gad*; OED *gad* 'A band or rope made of twisted fibres of tough twigs' 1728→, Anglo-Irish and military; DOST *gad* n⁴ 2 'a goad' 1662→]
    ULST.:   **1829** McSparran *Irish Legend* 16 He was overcome and bound with gads or withes twisted from the shoots of a sapling oak. *Ibid.* 247 He mounted his capul bawn, accoutred in a straw saddle, or what the Irish call a sugan, with stirrups of gads or withes and a pair of branks.
                1953 Traynor *Donegal Glossary* 113 = a coil of twisted straw or rushes.
    U.S.:   **1930** Shoemaker *1300 Penn Words* 24 = a whip for driving cattle, or punishing children.

gaily, gayly *adj* Of a person: in good health or spirits. [cf SND *geylies* adv 2 (1) used predicatively 'well enough, middling, tolerably well' 1721→; DARE *gaily* adj 2 'of a person: well, in good health' South Midland]
    ULST.:   c**1910** Byers *Glossary* = in good health and spirits, very well, satisfactorily.
                1953 Traynor *Donegal Glossary* 113 = cheerful, healthy, in good form.
    U.S.:   **1899** Green *Virginia Word-Book* 156 *gayly* = spirited, as a *gayly* horse.
                1939 Hall *Coll* Do you feel gaily tonight?
                1972 Cooper *NC Mt Folklore* 92 = well; recovering from illness.
                1975 Chalmers *Better* 66 'I feel gaily', said Aunt Charity, 'stout with health and religion, but last week I wasn't much.'

gallivant, galavant, gallavant, gillivant *vb* To gad about in an obstentacious way, especially with members of the opposite sex. [OED *gallivant* vb 'to gad about in a showy fashion, especially with persons of the other sex', perhaps a humorous perversion of *gallant* (verb)]
    ULST.:   **1902** McIlroy *Druid's Island* 17 Auld Mr. McIntyre never gaed awa gillivantin' an' holiday-makin'.
                c**1910** Byers *Glossary, gallivant* = to flirt, philander, 'keep company': He goes gallivantin' about his work instead of coming home to his supper'.
                1959 Gregory *Ulster Ballads* 31 Jist you wait a wee while; / Let thon foolish pair go galavantin'.
                1991 O'Kane *You Don't Say* 56 *gallivant* = to range around the country in search of pleasure and diversion. Mostly said by parents of young people who, instead of being sensible and staying in at night, insist on traipsing to dances and bars: 'She's out gallivantin' every night of the week'.

U.S.:   **1899** Green *Virginia Word-Book* 154 *gallivant* = to spend time in pleasure-seeking, especially with the opposite sex.
1908 Payne *Word-list East Alabama* 313 *gallavant* = to go about as a gallant, go courting, run about: 'He's gallavantin around among the gals'.
1930 Shoemaker *1300 Penn Words* 25 *gallivant* = to move about from place to place, in search of a good time.

gallows, gallus *n* (usually plural in form: *galluses, gallises, gallowses*) A suspender to hold up a man's trousers. [obsolete form of *gallows* (ultimately < Old English *galga*), construed as a collective noun perhaps by analogy with *pants, trousers*, etc.; OED *gallows* n 6 now dialect and U.S.; CSD *galluses* 'trouser braces' (at *gallows* n) 'trouser braces']

ULST.:   **1880** Patterson *Antrim/Down Glossary* 42 *gallowses* = suspenders.
1891 Simmons *Armagh Words and Phrases* 9 *gallows* = braces, or suspenders, for keeping up trousers.
1958 Gregg *Phonology* 398 *galluses* = braces.
1991 O'Kane *You Don't Say* 56 *galluses* = braces worn by men to hold up their trousers and useful for sticking their thumbs through when holding forth.
2005 McDonald *Wullie's New Claes* 26 'Ach, you an yer galluses!' said Maggie, 'Naeboadie his thaim nooadays.'

U.S.:   **1883** Zeigler and Grosscup *Heart of Alleghanies* 249 An unbleached, linen shirt, crossed by 'galluses' which held his homespun pantaloons in place, covered his body.
1973 *GSMNP*-14:4 He didn't have a thing on but his galluses and his shoes.
1982 De Armond *So High* 10 Mama bent to button the top button of Papa's one and only, best shirt, then fastened the galluses to the bib of his overalls.
1991 Haynes *Haywood Home* 35 I realize galluses are supposed to be called suspenders, but we called them galluses.

galoot *n* A man, usually an older, foolish one (a term of contempt). [possibly *ga-* variant of *ker-* + *loot*, Scots variant of *lout*; OED *galoot* n 2 'awkward or uncouth fellow']

ULST.:   **c1910** Byers *Glossary* = a man (generally in contempt); a worthless fellow; a fool; a big, awkward creature; clownish, a foolish person; a long, lanky, useless person.
1921 Irvine *Poor Folk* 59 'Ye civil galoot', says he, 'for why do ye be lettin' a dacint man be makin' a fool of himself.'
1929 O'Donnell *Adrigoole* 144 Brigid didn't want her name up with any of the neighbours. Most likely she had some galoot on her tail down at home.
1990 McIntyre *Some Handlin'* 26 = a silly person.

U.S.:   **1908** Payne *Word-list East Alabama* 314 = a fool, a simpleton.
1976 Garber *Mountain-ese* 33 = old fool: 'The Salvation Army gave the old galoot food and a pallet to sleep on'.
1998 Montgomery *Coll* He's as crazy as any old galoot.

gar *vb* To compel to, cause to. [< Middle English *gere, ger* < Old Norse *gera* 'to make, to do'; OED *gar* vb 2 'to make, to cause' chiefly Scottish and northern dialect; DOST *gar* vb 'to make, cause; to force, compel, especially to make a person do (something)' 1386→]

ULST.:   **1734** *Northern Bard* 160 He'd garr them Peg another Cask, / Their Hant o mend.
1799 (in **1813** Porter *Poetical Attempts*) But aiblins time might gar you feel / I hae nae thought o' flatt'rin'.

1885 Lyttle *Robin Gordon* 14 A wud gar him stan' up on my knee, an' A wud
tell him, 'Say da, Wully.'
c1910 Byers *Glossary* = to make or cause, to compel: 'If you don't do so and so,
A'll gar ye'.
1942 *Bangor Words* 34 = dare or force: 'I'll gar ye do it'.
2000 Fenton *Hamely Tongue* 83 Gar him dae what he's towl.

U.S.:   **1928** Chapman *Happy Mt* 312 = to make, force, compel: 'I garred him to get a
haircut'.

gayly See **gaily**

gear *n* Household belongings and goods; worldly possessions. [OED *gear* n 1
'possessions in general' 1711→; DOST *geir* n 2 'articles or personal possessions of any
kind, goods or property' 1488→]

ULST.:   **1801** Bruce *Poems* [Glossary 4] = wordly goods, riches.
1824 McHenry *Insurgent Chief* 120 Ye seem to care naething o' the warld's
gear.
1920 McCallin *Ulster Plenishing* 6 They were as well-matched a pair, not only
in war'ly gear, but in style an' figure, as it was possible to be.
c1982 Clifford *Poems* 29 We leeve in hourly dread an' fear / That maybe at the
next half-year / He'll land us oot wi' a' oor gear – / Bereft o' hoose an' hame.

U.S.:   **1944** Wilson *Word-list* 43 = property, belongings: 'And after the infare at her
father's, they went to their li'l house, where there wa'n't much *gear*'.
1965 Glassie *Old Barns* 22 The rectangular log construction unit still used in
Europe as a granary was easily adapted to the storage of maize and became the
corn crib found throughout the Southern Mountains. Frequently the corn crib
has a shed for the storage of farm equipment—'gear' or 'plunder'.

gillie, gilly *n* A foolish or gullible person. [< Irish, Scottish Gaelic *gille* 'lad, youth';
OED *gillie* n 1 'an attendant of a Highland chief'; DOST *gillie* n 'a lad, a youth'; SND
gillie n[1] 1 'an attendant on a Highland chief' 2 'a young lad']

ULST.:   **2000** Fenton *Hamely Tongue* 85 *gillie* = a fool.
U.S.:   **1930** Shoemaker *1300 Penn Words* 24 *gilly* = an easily led, or quickly corrupted
person.

gillivant See **gallivant**

gin[1] *conj, prep* Of time: against, before, by the time. See **again**.

gin[2] *conj* If, whether. [perhaps from *gien*, variant of *given*, past participle of *give*;
OED *gin* conj 'if, whether' Scottish and dialect; SND conj 2 'if' 1622→; DARE *gin*
conj[1] 'if, whether' chiefly Appalachians]

ULST.:   **1737** Murray *Letter* I will come to Ereland gin the Lord spare me about Twa
Years after this.
1840 Boyce *Shandy Maguire* 10 But gin a body gets his share of what's goin' he
shudna grumble.
1897 McIlroy *Lint in Bell* 54 Ye'll ken best the velue o' money gin ye earn it.
1953 Traynor *Donegal Glossary* 119 Ye tak' th' ane side (of the road) an' Ah'll
tak' th' ither, and gin ye dee't Ah'll gar ye dee't.

U.S.:   **1904–07** Kephart *Notebooks* 4:723 Ask the woman gin you can git a bite.
1944 Wilson *Word-list* 43 = if.

gipe See **gype**

glaikit, glaiket, glaikid, glakit *adj* Foolish, thoughtless, careless, giddy. Hence
glakedness *n* Carelessness, stupidity. [< Old Scots *glaik* 'senseless, foolish' c1470→;
cf SND *glaikit* 1 'stupid, careless, foolish', *glaikitness* 'ineptitude, stupidity,
carelessness, levity']

ULST.:   1817 Orr *Posthumous Works* An' now an' then divert awa their care, / By tellin'
tales to please some glaiket wean.
1923 Lutton *Montiaghisms* 22 *glakit* = giddy, thoughtless, inattentive.
1936 White *Mrs Murphy* 88 If your father happen to lift anything (and it's the
world's wonder if he does, he's that glaikit) he's sure to lift it wrong.
1953 Traynor *Donegal Glossary* 120 = (1) foolish, stupid, of little sense; easy-
going; (2) thoughtless, inattentive, careless.
1980/81 McClean *Ulster Words IV* 5 *glaiket* = dull, without initiative.

U.S.   1889 Farmer *Americanisms* 266 *Glaikid—Glaikit*, in Lowland Scotch is given
by Jamieson as unsteady; giddy; stupid; and with the last of these meanings
glakid is used in Pennsylvania.
1928 (in 1952 Mathes *Tall Tales* 65) I've a notion to bust ye open jes' fer yer
glakedness!
1952 Wilson *Folk Speech NC* 545 *glaiket* = lazy, careless, foolish.

glede, gleed *n* A red-hot coal used to start a new fire. [< Old English *glæd, gled*;
OED *gleed* n 'a live coal, an ember' c950→, now only archaic and dialect; DOST *glede*
n 'a live coal, an ember' late 14th century→]

ULST.:   1811 Boyle *Poems* Let every matron wish guid speed, / That boils a pot, or
harns her bread, / Or hings a kettle ower a gleed, / At close o' day.
1829 McSparran *Irish Legend* 84 Arrah, good marrow marnen to yes, says she,
and the luck and the blessing be in your store, will ye help the poor woman?
and dwowl a gleed was on the hearth more than on my nose.
1900 Given *Poems* 170 There watchin' she sat till her gleed o' a fire, / Past
faces familiar its embers did take.
1953 Traynor *Donegal Glossary* 121 *gleed* = a spark, a red-hot coal, a flame.
1980/81 McClean *Ulster Words IV* 5 *glede* = a red ember.
2000 Fenton *Hamely Tongue* 86 *gleed* = a glowing ember: 'sittin stairvin
withoot a gleed o fire'.

U.S.:   1930 Shoemaker *1300 Penn Words* 27 *glede* = a red hot coal carried on a small
tongs from one pioneer cabin to another to start fires.

gob, gub *n* The mouth. Cf **gab**. [of obscure origin, possibly from Irish *gob* or
Scottish Gaelic *gob/guib* 'beak, bill of a bird; mouth'; OED *gob* n² 'the mouth'
c1550→, northern dialect; DOST *gob* n 'the mouth; the beak of a bird', early 16th
century→]

ULST.:   1904 Byers *Sayings of Ulster* 32 'Gob' is used in two senses, first as meaning
the mouth (we have also the dialect 'gab' derived from the Gaelic 'gob' = the
beak or bill of a bird, the mouth, this is the Irish 'gob', 'gab', 'cab' = the beak,
snout, mouth, and with these may be compared the Welsh 'gwp' = the head
and neck of a bird. Hence, instead of saying, 'hold your tongue', or 'shut your
mouth', the phrase in Ulster often is 'shut up your gub' (another variant of
'gob'). It is said by some that 'gab' (derived from the old English 'gabben') = to
talk idly, is connected with the Celtic 'gob' (a good talker has the 'gift of the

gab') and 'give me none of yer (your) gab' (variants, 'back-chat', 'lip', 'jaw'),
heard sometimes in County Down and County Antrim, means, 'give me no
impudence'. Probably 'gabble' and 'jabber' are connected with 'gab'. 'Gab' is
also used in the North of England and in Scotland as meaning the mouth, and
hence the old proverb: 'Ye take mair (more) in your gab than your cheeks can
had' (hold), which has been modernised by our Transatlantic cousins into the
well-known saying: 'You have bitten off more tobacco than you can well chew'.
'Gob' has also a second meaning, which is a 'mouthful'.
    1932 Quinn *McConaghy's Money* 45 He hit a detective with a snowball—aye,
    fair in the gub.
    1939 Paterson *Country Cracks* 90 Divil the blade wud they let in their gubs.
    1953 Traynor *Donegal Glossary* 124 = the mouth, a beak, snout.
    c1955 Montgomery *Heard in Ulster* 52 Close yer gob.
U.S.:   1912 White *Word-list Cent NY* 567 Open your gob!
            1967 Cerello *Dakota Co* 61 He had a gob full of feed and nevertheless he kept
            right on talking.

good liver *n* One who is prosperous or has a comfortable living. [OED (at *live* n[2]
1c(b)) 'a well-to-do person' dialect; cf OED *liver* n[2] 1b 'one who lives in a specified
way']
ULST.:   1953 Traynor *Donegal Glossary* 125 = one who lives well in material sense.
U.S.:   1962 Dykeman *Tall Woman* 221 The Thurstons were fine people, 'good livers',
            as folks said, with their busy sawmills and fat livestock and plentiful tables of
            food.
            1988 Landry *Coll* Well, he was a good liver in here, but he never did work
            nowhere. He just farmed.

good man *n* God, Jesus, the deity (often a child's term). [OED *the guid man* n 2 (at
guid) 'God' chiefly child's term; DARE *good man* n 'God; Jesus' chiefly Midland,
especially South Midland]
ULST.:   1953 Traynor *Donegal Glossary* 179 = God.
U.S.:   1917 Kephart *Word-list* 412 = God; child's term.
            1943 Justus *Bluebird* 121 'The Good Man'll look atter us, I reckon', she would
            say.
            1952 Wilson *Folk Speech NC* 546 = God; Jesus Christ.

graip, graipe *n* A pitchfork. [cf Old Norse *greip* 'the space between the thumb and
the fingers'; OED *graip* n 1459→, Scottish and northern dialect; DOST *graip* n 'an
iron fork with three or four prongs, fitted to a handle like that of a spade, used for
lifting dung, etc., or for digging' 1494→; SND *graip* n]
ULST.:   1906 MacDermott *Foughilotra* 59 He had seen at one place a spade, rake, and
            what is called a 'graip', resting against a wall, just as they had been left by
            whoever had owned them.
            1953 Traynor *Donegal Glossary* 127 *graip* = a three- or four-pronged fork, used
            for agricultural purposes; a dung fork.
            1959 Gregg *Phonology* 413 *graip* = pitch-fork.
            1976 Murphy *Mountainy Crack* 34 This [winnowing cloth] he draped as a
            wind-shield around a fresh 'priddy-pat' by hanging it loosely on their spades
            and graips after they had stripped the earth off.
            2002 Gillen *Wizard's Quill* 49 The clerk may get on wae his pencil, / An his

sterch't collar cuttin his throat, / Me, I'll stick tae the graipe an the borra, /
Aye, maybe I hae join't tae date.

U.S.: **1930** Shoemaker *1300 Penn Words* 24 *graip* = a trident pitchfork.

granny *n* A midwife. [OED (at *granny* n 2) calls this usage 'U.S. local'; DARE chiefly
South, South Midland]

ULST.: **1969** Braidwood *Ulster Dial Lex* 32 *Granny*, 'midwife', [is] recorded in Ulster
from Drumahoe in Derry.

U.S.: (more commonly *granny woman*; also *vb* To serve as midwife for).
1812 (in **1956** Eliason *Tarheel Talk* 274) Paid Granny Judy.
1868 Carpenter *Diary* 149 Pegey Wise a[ge] 75 dide oc[t] 15 1868 she wars
granny womin for contry.
1956 Hall *Coll* The old people done the doctorin', made their own teas. My
mammy Nancy Hicks and Aunt Mary grannied me.
1959 Pearsall *Little Smoky* 130 The only major differentiation of roles is
between 'man' and 'woman', although some may in addition be 'preacher',
'grannywoman' (midwife), or 'conjure doctor' by virtue of possessing more of
folk knowledge than their fellows.
1975 Chalmers *Better* 52 Etta Brown is the last of these 'granny-women'
trained by Miss Phyllis.
1995 Montgomery *Coll* When someone asked where our Grandma was,
Grandpa would say, 'Oh, she's off a-grannying.'

green *vb* To deceive, cheat. [OED *green* vb 3 'to make to appear "green", simple, or
gullible; to hoax, take in, humbug'; DARE *green out* (at *green* vb 2) 'to outwit (in a
transaction); swindle' southern Appalachians]

ULST.: **1953** Traynor *Donegal Glossary* 128 = to cheat, entrap, impose upon, to deceive
and ensnare with lies: 'I greened him properly'.

U.S.: (only in phrase *green out*)
1904–07 Kephart *Notebooks* 2:459 I got a good one on him—greened him out
bodaciously.
1952 Wilson *Folk Speech NC* 547–48 *green out* = to outwit, make a fool of:
'The merchants used to *green out* their customers quite a bit'.

gub See **gob**

gumption, gumtion, gunktion *n* Common sense, good judgment, practical
understanding; shrewdness, initiative, resourcefulness. [OED *gumption* originally
Scottish (cf *rum-, rumble-gumption*) n 1 'common sense, mother wit, shrewdness,
also initiative, enterprise' 1719→, colloquial; SND *gumption* n 'common sense,
"horse sense", shrewdness, mother wit, savoir faire' 1711→; DARE *gumption* n 1
'common sense, good judgment' especially South, South Midland, 2 'ambition,
initiative; tenacity'] [Note: The two senses of this word, both of which have long
existed, overlap and in some cases cannot be distinguished in citations.]

ULST.: **1880** Patterson *Antrim/Down Glossary* 47 = quickness of understanding,
common sense, tact.
1903 MacManus *Lad of O'Friels* 150 Nuala Gildea, have a little gumption and
stan' out of our roads.
c1910 Byers *Glossary* = tact, judgment, common sense, quickness of
understanding, shrewdness, capacity.

1923 Lutton *Montiaghisms* 23 = rationality, common sense (also *gunktion*).
1942 *Bangor Words* 38 = courage associated with common sense: 'Ah, for goodness sake have a wee bit of gumption'.
1948 Marshall *Planted by River* 154 Glasgow College can make Doctors of Divinity, but gumption is the gift of God.
c1955 Montgomery *Heard in Ulster* 51 = good sense or judgment: 'He hes plenty o' guid Ulster gumption'.
1991 O'Kane *You Don't Say* 63 = shrewd commonsense, with the added implication of doing your duty; the quality of being trustworthy and reliable: 'Sure if he had any gumption he would have fixed up the house and paid off the old man's debts'.

U.S.:   **1815** Humphreys *Yankey in England* 105 *gumtion* = sense, understanding, intellect.
1899 Green *Virginia Word-Book* 172 = acuteness of practical understanding; clear, practical common sense; quick perception of the right thing to do under ususual circumstances.
1908 Payne *Word-list East Alabama* 318 = sense: 'He's got plenty of gumption'.
1940 Haun *Hawk's Done* 156 Wilbur didn't have any more gumption than to let Nick beg him into going.
1974–75 McCracken *Logging* 11:81 If a fellow had enough gumption, why, it was worth something to him.
1989 Landry *Smoky Mt Interviews* 191 They called that teaching you gumption, you know. Now they call it common sense.
1994 Montgomery *Coll* He didn't have enough gumption to come in out of the rain.

gype, gipe *n* A fool. [< Old Norse *geip* 'nonsense'; SND *gype* 2 'a foolish, awkward person' 1826→]

ULST.:   **1980/81** McClean *Ulster Words IV* 5 *gipe* = one deficient in mental capacity.
2000 Fenton *Hamely Tongue* 93 *gype* = a fool.

U.S.:   **1930** Shoemaker *1300 Penn Words* 24 *gype* = a silly easily fooled person.

H

haet, hait See **hate**

handwrite *n* Handwriting, style of penmanship. [OED *handwrite* n 'handwriting' 1483→, Scottish, Irish and U.S.; DOST *handwrit* n 1 'the writing of a particular hand or person' late 15th century→; cf SND *hand of write* (at *hand* 8 (18)); DARE *handwrite* n 'handwriting' chiefly South, South Midland]

ULST.:   c1910 Byers *Glossary* = handwriting.
             1942 *Bangor Words* 39 = writing: 'I don't know that hand write'.
U.S.:   1908 Payne *Word-list East Alabama* 318 = handwriting.
             1973 *GSMNP*-83:26 They was sixty words wrote, and they was two handwrites.
             1995 Montgomery *Coll* He had a good handwrite.

hantle *n* A large amount or number. [perhaps modification of *handful*; OED *hantle* n 'a (considerable) number or quantity; a good many, a good deal' 1692→, Scottish and northern dialect; DOST *hantle* n 'a considerable quantity (of things), a large number (of persons)' 16th century→; DARE *hantle* n 1 'a handful; a small number', 2 'a large number, a crowd' chiefly southern Appalachians]

ULST.:   1733 *North Country Description* 26 The Cheel we a hantle o' Keys in his Hand cam, and tuke it intill the middle o' the Kirk, and laid a Buke upon it.
             1801 Bruce *Poems* 17 But I've a hantle mair to say, / Which I may tell anither day. *Ibid.* [Glossary 4] = a great deal.
             1824 McHenry *Insurgent Chief* 118 He lets me besides hae a hantel o' siller every week.
U.S.:   1928 Chapman *Happy Mt* 63 The inside of the schoolhouse was scarcely to be seen for the hantle of people.
             1940 Berrey *Sthn Mt Dialect* 46 = a great many.
             1995 Montgomery *Coll* = a handful; a great plenty.

hap *n* A covering, especially bedclothes (in the U.S. a coverlet or quilt). Hence *vb* To tuck in bed, wrap up in; to put on a covering, as a cloak or blanket for warmth; surround. [OED *hap* vb 'to cover up or over; to cover for warmth, as for extra clothing or bed-clothes, to wrap' 14th century→, now only Scottish and dialect, n 'a covering of any kind' northern dialect, 1724→; DOST *hap* n² 'a covering' 1593→; DARE chiefly western Pennsylvania; LAUSC Pennsylvania]

ULST.:   1722 Starrat *Epistle* 71 Right tozylie was set to ease my Stumps, / Well hap'd with Bountith-hose and twa soll'd Pumps.
             1880 Patterson *Antrim/Down Glossary* 49 = (1) a covering, as a cloak or a blanket; (2) to cover, to wrap up in muffling or bed-clothes.
             1881 Hart *Mere Irish* 157 He was happed up in his coat to keep the cowld out, and snoring like mad.
             c1910 Byers *Glossary* = to cover, enwrap, wrap up in muffling or in bed clothes; to envelop, surround: 'hap up a child' = to tuck in the bedclothes round a child; *bed-happin's* = bedclothes.
             1920 McCallin *Ulster Plenishing* 56 The oul' man o' the house was snugly happed-up in the Meetin'-House Green.
             1921 Doyle *Ulster Childhood* 154 Tell him that I'll not go out this night, but

will lie here warm and well happed till the morning.

1937 Rowley *Tales of Mourne* 110–11 The little house looked snug and gay, tucked comfortably under the shoulder of the hill, and happed in all the green bravery of the young larch and birch.

1942 *Bangor Words* 39 = a cover, or to cover up: 'That rug will make a fine hap for the car'; 'It's a very cold night, see and hap yourself up well' (put on a heavy coat and muffler, and use a rug if going in a car or other conveyance).

1991 O'Kane *You Don't Say* 67 = to cover with clothes, to wrap up; to tuck around with blankets: 'You're well happed up today'. (When potatoes were stored outside in pits or clamps they used to be covered with straw or rushes, then happed with soil to keep out frost.)

2000 Fenton *Hamely Tongue* 96 = to swaddle, cover with bedclothes; *happed up* = comfortably tucked in, buried.

2000 McBride *Ulster Scots* 32 = wrap up warmly.

U.S.:   **1916** Heydrick *Pennsylvania* 338 = a bed 'comforter': 'There are two blankets and a hap on the bed'.

1930 Shoemaker *1300 Penn Words* 28 = bed covering of woolen material.

1949 Kurath *Word Geog East US* 61 In the mountains of central Pennsylvania *hap*, one of the few Scotch-Irish words, is in common use beside *comfort*.

1982 McCool *Pittsburghese* 15 = a comforter or quilt, as in 'I need my hap to take a nap'.

hard-favored *adj* Of a person: having coarse or unattractive features, stern-faced, not handsome. [OED *hard-favoured* adj 'having a hard or unpleasant ... appearance' →1852, archaic; DARE *hard-favored* adj 'coarse-featured, unattractive' South, South Midland]

ULST.:   **1942** *Bangor Words* 40 = rugged or grim-featured.

U.S.:   **1835** Longstreet *Georgia Scenes* 16 She hadn't seen *me* then, or she never would have loved such a hard favoured man as you are.

1946 *Shore Sign* 4 I knowed when she got old and hard-favored, he'd start runnin' round with some young hussy.

1975 Gainer *Speech Mtneer* 11 He's a hard-favored man.

hate, haet, hait *n* (usually in negative contexts) A whit, the smallest thing or quantity. [OED *hate, haet* n[2] 'orig. The words *hae't* in the phrase *Deil hae't* ... 'Devil have it!' This deprecatory expression became a strong negative, and thus equivalent to 'Devil a bit', i.e. not a bit, not a whit. Hence *haet*, with an ordinary negative, as *not a haet*, came sometimes to be understood as equivalent to 'whit, atom', or 'anything, the smallest thing that can be conceived' (Jamieson)'; SND *haet* n 1 '"ha(v)e it", used in imprecative sentences with negative force = not a grain or particle, "damn all", in such phrases as *deil, fi(e)nt, foundit, fule, plague, sorra, sorry, sorrow*, etc. *haet*, also used as an exclamation of impatience, annoyance or disgust ... originally an exclamatory phrase *deil hae't* = devil have it! from imperative of *hae* = to have, used as a strong negative. It became synonymous with *devil a bit*, etc. not a whit, and the indefinite article was introduced into the phrase'; CUD (*the*) *deil haet, deil hae it* (at *have*), 'lit. the devil have it = devil a bit, not a bit'; DARE *hate* n 'a whit, a jot, the smallest thing' chiefly Appalachians, Ohio Valley]

ULST.:   **1880** Patterson *Antrim/Down Glossary* 48 *hait* = anything; 'deil a hait' = anything at all.

1891 Simmons *Armagh Words and Phrases* 11 *hate* = half-penny worth, a small quantity: 'not worth a hate'.
1902 McIlroy *Druid's Island* 111 A didna daur tak' them aff, an' no' a haet could a dae wi' them on.
1904 Marshall *Dial of Ulster* 127 *hate* = the smallest portion, nothing; as, 'not a hate'.
1939 Paterson *Country Cracks* 41 That has devil a hate to do with the wee people, exceptin' that it wus after they come that they first wanted till leave.
1953 Traynor *Donegal Glossary* 131 *haet* = a whit, the smallest thing that can be conceived.
1981 Pepper *Ulster-English Dict* 38 I don't know a hate about it.
2000 Fenton *Hamely Tongue* 93 *haet* = jot, whit, scrap: 'A haenae a haet in the hoose'; 'dae a haet wae'; 'mak a haet o' = do or make anything of (by way of improvement or reform); 'deil the haet'; 'feen a haet'; 'shame a haet' = not a jot, nothing at all.

U.S.: **1826** Royall *Grison Republic* 90 Their favorite word of all, is *hate*, by which they mean, the word thing; for instance, *nothing* 'not a hate—not waun hate will ye's do'. What did you buy at the stores, ledies? 'Not a hate—well you hav'nt a hate here to eat.'
1859 Bartlett *Americanisms* 191 *hate* = a bit, as 'I don't care a hate'; 'I didn't eat a hate' ... It is the Scotch *haet*, as in the phrase 'fient a hate', i.e. the devil a bit.
1930 Shoemaker *1300 Penn Words* 28 *hait* = a matter of no consequence.
1971 Dwyer *Dict for Yankees* 27 Hate, haet, hait = a bit, small amount.
1975 Gainer *Speech Mtneer* 11 'I don't give a hate' means 'I don't care'. 'I don't give a hate what you do.'

heap *n* (often in plural) A large quantity. [OED *heap* n 4a; DOST *hepe* n 1 c1400→; SND *heap* n 'a large number or quantity, a great deal'; DARE *heap* n 1 'a large number, great deal' chiefly South, South Midland]

ULST.: **1893** O'Neill *Glens and Speech* 371 Sure, she can get heaps and heaps of men.
c1910 Wier *Bab McKeen* 58 There's nae sayin' but sometimes this'll mak' a heap o' difference.
1921 O'Neill *More Songs of Glens* 25 I larned a thrick to watch it out an' still to hould me tongue, / An' sure enough it saved a heap o' bother.
2000 Fenton *Hamely Tongue* 98 = a lot (very common in *a heap o money*, *a heap o yins*, etc.) 'It's a heap o odds!' = (sarcastically) It matters a lot!; 'think a heap o' = be very fond of; think highly of.

U.S.: **1824** Knight *Letters* 107 Some words are used, even by genteel people ... in a new sense; and ... pronounced very uncouthly, as ... heap of times.
1924 Spring *Lydia Whaley* 3 I've seed a heap of ups and downs and had a world of trouble the whole world through and I hope I get to a better one some day.
1939 Hall *Coll* [I] caught a heap of fish in them mountain streams.
1957 Parris *My Mts* 7 A heap of folks borrow trouble just because they don't read nature's signs and don't listen to their elders.

hear tell (of) *vb phr* To be informed of, learn of by word of mouth. [OED *hear* vb c1220→]

ULST.: **1880** Patterson *Antrim/Down Glossary* 51 = to hear: 'Did ye ever hear tell o' the like?'

1902 McIlroy *Druid's Island* 93 A think a niver hear'd tell o' a greater fool or a mair evil-disposed youth.
1933 MacNeill *Reverence Listens* 23 I'm certain sure you never heard of anything like this trouble of mine.
1942 *Bangor Words* 40 = hear the story of: 'I heard tell you were going away'.
1982 Glassie *Folk History* 35 I used to hear tell of the Red Meadow before I knew what it meant, do you see.
2005 Robinson *Alang Shore* 73 A heerd tell the growed-up men uised tae play [marbles] fur money.

U.S.:   **1939** Hall *Coll* He never was heared tell of no more.
1973 *GSMNP*-5:27 She was the illest-tempered youngun I've ever heard tell of in my life.
1973 *GSMNP*-76:9 His brother left his daddy and mother, and they never heard tell of him from that day to this.

heir *vb* To inherit (from). [OED *heir* vb 1 'to inherit' c1330→; SND *heir* vb II2 'to become heir to, inherit' 1753→; DARE chiefly South Midland]
ULST.:   **1880** Patterson *Antrim/Down Glossary* 51 To heir a person is to inherit his property.
U.S.:   **1899** Green *Virginia Word-Book* 183 = to inherit: 'He heired that land from his mother'.
1953 Randolph and Wilson *Down in Holler* 251 Henry must have heired some money off'n his pappy's folks.

hillbilly *n* In the U.S., a native of the Appalachian or Ozark mountains. The term is usually derogatory when used by outsiders and therefore is generally avoided by mountain people, though they may use it for themselves in a jocular, self-deprecating way, to express pride, or to contrast more rustic mountaineers from less rustic ones. In Ulster in recent years it has sometimes been supposed that it was coined to refer to followers of King William III and brought to America by early Ulster emigrants (for whom *billie* was known to mean 'fellow, comrade'; see **1801** Bruce citation), but this derivation is almost certainly incorrect, and no attestation of *billie* has been found in America other than from Bruce, who was an emigrant from Ulster. In America *hillbilly* was first attested only in 1898, which suggests a later, independent development. [cf EDD *billy* substantive[2] 2 'a comrade, friend' Scottish and northern English]
ULST.:   [**1801** Bruce *Poems* 45 But hark ye now, billies! / (Howe'er guid your will is) / The weakest, ye ken, maun fa' back.]
[**1844** Huddleston *Poems and Songs* An' see how many blackguard rogues, / An' strappin' billies listenin'; / Wi' courage bauld charm'd ower their sads, / An' cagy shillin's fistin', / Wha'll rue't some day.]
1981 Adamson *Identity of Ulster* 44 Although the Scotch-Irish were merging quickly now into the American Nation, the Ulster speech itself was to stay alive in the hill-country of Appalachia and beyond, where Scotch-Irish traditional music may still be heard. Among the earliest songs were ballads of King William of Orange, so those who sung them became known as Billy-boys of the hill-country or 'hillbillies'.
U.S.:   **1917** Kephart *Word-list* 413 = a mountaineer: humorous or depreciative.
1941 Hall *Coll* 'Hillbilly' [is] not much used by mountain people because of

its unfavorable effect. Apparently used occasionally of mountain people of low class or uneducated types or by way of contrast with such types: for example, 'She's no hillbilly', said of a person known for her fine qualities. *Ibid.* = people who live back in the hills; ... 'I've got an old hill-billy up here—got him to spend all his money on the piccolo [= nickelodeon]'.

1957 *GSMNP*-23:2:7 I'm really not a hillbilly, but I'm a native, a mountaineer. I've been here all my life, and I'm proud of it, certainly am proud of it. They just got that name up there, the hillbilly there. They call lots of those folks hillbillies because they was raised up here.

1973 *GSMNP*-79:3 I have been borned just about as high in the mountains here as anyone, so I guess you can really tell I'm a hillbilly from my talk, or as some people says we're mountaineers, said we're not hillbillies to start with.

hippin, hippen *n* A diaper, nappy. [< *hip* + *-ing*; OED variant of *hipping*² 'a napkin wrapt about the hips of an infant' 1768→, Scottish and northern dialect; SND *hippin* 'a baby's napkin' 1731→; DARE *hippen* n 'a baby's diaper' chiefly South, South Midland]

ULST.: **1906** Marshall *Dial of Ulster* 19 *hippins* = baby clothes.
1928 MacGill *Black Bonar* 173 I saw her in hippens.
1953 Traynor *Donegal Glossary* 142 *hippens* = swaddling clothes.
2000 Fenton *Hamely Tongue* 103 *hippin* = a child's nappy.

U.S.: **1917** Kephart *Word-list* 413 = a diaper, breech clout.
1953 Randolph and Wilson *Down in Holler* 252 *hippin's* = diapers.
1975 Chalmers *Better* 40 She had a few left over from the last baby, but could use a gown or two and some more hippens.
c1975 Lunsford *It Used To Be* 174 'Didies' and 'Hippins' are expressions used for diapers.

hire *intransitive vb* To take a specific job, hire oneself out. [OED *hire* vb 2b 'to engage oneself as a servant for payment'; DOST *hire* vb 3b 'to engage oneself as an employee' c1776→]

ULST.: **1840** Boyce *Shandy Maguire* 15 If you hire[,] keep the other shilling.
1953 Traynor *Donegal Glossary* 142 = to engage as servant.
c1982 Clifford *Poems* 4 He sidels up 'I s'pose says he' / 'Yer hirin'' 'Aye, I am' says she. / They bargain, argue, chap, divide, / Till lang at last the erls is paid.

U.S.: **1871** (in **1983** Heap *Bucks Co Word List* 38) A boy came to hire eat supper here—But we do not want him.
1942 Chase *Jack Tales* 147 'Do you want to hire to do my cookin' and washin' for me?' 'Yes', she says, 'I'll hire'.
1974 *GSMNP*-50:1:23 I just hire out, you know, where they would need a girl ... We was poor folks and hired out [to] get enough money to buy cloth to make me a dress.

hit *pron* It, especially as the initial element in a clause and in other stressed positions, most often as a subject. [this was the usual Middle English form and was prevalent into the 16th century in English generally < Old English *hit*; after the 16th century the form was found mainly in Scotland and northern England; DOST *hit/hyt* pron c1400→; SND *hit* pron 1 (emphatic); DARE (at *it* pron A1) chiefly South, South Midland]

ULST.: **1861** Sproule *Letters* (4 June) Hit is not noan what he is a douing.

1936 Marshall *Ulster Speaks* 13–14 We hardly ever misuse the letter 'h' as they do so commonly in many parts of England, but when we want to emphasise the word 'us' we call it 'huz' or 'hus', and an emphatic 'it' is 'hit'.
1953 Traynor *Donegal Glossary* 150 = it.
1997 Robinson *Grammar* 72 *Hit* is still used in the east Donegal dialect of Ulster-Scots.

U.S.:   **1836** *Pawpaw Hollow Minutes* 78 The Church wish Brother Lammon Jones to attend them twelve months longer & Br Jones agrees to hit.
1875 King *Great South* 788 Some of the mountaineers speak of 'hit', instead of 'it', and emphasize the word as in this case, 'I meant to have brought my gun, but I forgot hit'.
1913 Kephart *Our Sthn High* 36 By that time the land will be so poor hit wouldn't raise a cuss-fight.
1942 Hall *Phonetics* 86 Even unstressed *hit* often occurs without initial loss, as in the sentence ... 'I don't know how long hit's been'. But unstressed *hit*, like *he, him, her,* etc. usually occurs without [h] ... 'I guess it's been ten or fifteen years ago'.
1973 *GSMNP*-84:26 I know positive that hit wasn't all true.
1996 *GSMNPOHP* 1:5 They had to raise the young one and take care of hit.

hives *n* Red, itchy spots on the skin, especially on a child. [origin uncertain, but possibly related to *heave*; OED *hives* n plural '"any eruption on the skin, when the disruption is supposed to proceed from an internal cause" (Jamieson), applied to red-gum or *Strophulus*, chicken-pox, nettle-rash; also inflammation of the bowels or *Enteritis* (*bowel hives*), and inflammation of the larynx, croup, or *Laryngitis*' c1500→; DOST *hyvis* n 'any children's skin complaint, applied especially to red-gum or *stitupolus*' c1500→; SND n 1 'any childish skin eruption', 2 'inflammation of the bowel']

ULST.:   **1880** Patterson *Antrim/Down Glossary* 52 = red, itchy, raised spots on the skin.
1891 Simmons *Armagh Words and Phrases* 11 = a small swelling, usually very itchy.
1942 *Bangor Words* 41 = heat spots in children, nettlerash.
1953 Traynor *Donegal Glossary* 142 = any rash or red, itching cutaneous disorder such as eczema.
1990 Todd *Words Apart* 93 This good weather has brought the chile out in hives.
2000 McBride *Ulster Scots* 32 = large itchy spots on the skin.

U.S.:   **1939** Hall *Coll* Blacksnake root, that's one of the best remedies I ever saw used for hives ... Ground ivy is a good tea for hives for babies.
1982 Powers and Hannah *Cataloochee* 258 There was a vine she called 'ground ivy' ... she boiled it to make a tea to give small babies to break them out with the hives.

honey *n* A term of endearment, especially for a woman or child. [OED *honey* n 5a 'a term of endearment; sweet one, sweetheart, darling' formerly chiefly Irish; SND *hinnie* n 1 'a term of endearment, sweetheart, darling']

ULST.:   **1831** McWilliams *Songs* 16 By taking me you might do weel, / My dearest, sweetest honey.
1880 Patterson *Antrim/Down Glossary* 53 = a term of endearment.

> **1902** McIlroy *Druid's Island* 45 Oh no, honey. What wud an oul' weeda wumman like me luck like, wearin' floors?
> **c1910** Byers *Glossary* = a pet, sweetheart; a form of endearment, generally addressed to women and children, as 'Betty, me honey, take care of the money'.

U.S.:   **c1765** Woodmason *Carolina Backcountry* 150 Dear Honeys, its long Time since You sent me any Gift to the Waxaws and you know Honeys, that you promis'd me a good Subscription would I come here.
> **1815** Brackenridge *Modern Chivalry* 53 If I had not given him a twitch by the nose, and bid him lie over, dear honey, he would have ravished her virginity, and murdered her.
> **1899** Green *Virginia Word-Book* 190 = sweet one, darling, a word of endearment.
> **1908** Payne *Word-list East Alabama* 321 = darling, sweetheart.

hooder See **hudder**

hove up *vb phr* To inflate, swell. Hence **hoved up** *adj phr* Inflated, swollen. [SND *hove* vb 3 'to cause to swell, to distend; to become swollen or distended']

ULST.:   **1880** Patterson *Antrim/Down Glossary* 53 = swollen, inflated.
> **c1910** Byers *Glossary* = distended, swollen: 'Her body is hoved up'.
> **1993** Montgomery *Barnish* 27 = swollen.

U.S: **2000** Lowry *Folk Medical Term* My side hoved up three days ago.

hudder, hooder *n* The sheaf (or sheaves) placed on top of a stack of grain, usually two bundles laid crosswise. [< *hood* vb + *-er*; cf OED *hooder* 'hood-sheaf' local; DARE *hudder* n 'the sheaf (or sheaves) placed at the top of a shock of grain' especially southern Appalachians]

ULST.:   **c1955** Montgomery *Heard in Ulster* 64 *hudder* = the finishing sheaf of grain on a 'hut'.
> **1957** Evans *Irish Folk-Ways* 162 Stooks with their 'hudders' (hooding sheaves) also take on human forms, and I have known various names for these large stooks applied as nicknames to broad-based country women.
> **1993** Montgomery *Barnish* 28 *hudder* = top sheaf.
> **2000** Fenton *Hamely Tongue* 105 *hooder* = the top, coping or 'hooding' sheaf in a *hut* of corn.

U.S.:   **1907** Heydrick *Provincialisms of SE Penn* 379 *hudder* = cap sheaf: 'the cap of wheat will get wet unless it has a hudder on it'.
> **1953** Randolph and Wilson *Down in Holler* 255 *hudder* = the cap on a stack of wheat; it usually consists of two bundles put on crosswise.

hunker *n, vb* [origin obscure, but cf modern German *hocken* 'to sit on the hams or heels, to squat'; OED *hunker* vb a 'to squat, with the haunches, knees, and ankles acutely bent; so as to bring the hams near the heels, and throw the whole weight upon the fore part of the feet' 1720→, originally Scottish; SND *hunker* 1 'to squat with thighs, knees, and ankles acutely bent, to seat oneself in a crouching position or on one's haunches' 1720→; DARE *hunker* n 1 'the haunch or buttock' especially South Midland]

1 *n* (usually plural) The haunches or buttocks.

ULST.:   **1861** Hume *Rabbin's Ollminick* 38 It's asy for you to be talkin', / Jist sittin' at home on yer hunkers, / An' burnin' yer shins at the greeshaugh.

1886 Lyttle *Ballycuddy* 19 Sit doon on yer hunkers if yer tired, or else awa hame.

1923 Lutton *Montiaghisms* 26 'Sitting on your hunkers' is to sit in a squatting position.

1990 Todd *Words Apart* 96 When we were in school we had to sit on our hunkers in the corner if we couldn't spell right.

2000 Fenton *Hamely Tongue* 107 = the haunches; 'slide on yer hunkers' = travel down a slide while squatting on one's haunches.

U.S.:   **1859** Taliaferro *Fisher's River* 152 He was ever busy ... sitting on his 'hunkers' cutting out millstones in the lonely mountains.

1939 Hall *Coll* We started along on our hunkers.

1974 Fink *Bits Mt Speech* 12 I sat back on my hunkers.

2 *vb* To crouch, squat on one's haunches so as to bend one's knees and ankles.

ULST.:   **1824** McHenry *Insurgent Chief* 33 I heard yin of them say something aboot Mr Middleton; so I just hunkered doon to hear what it was.

1880 Patterson *Antrim/Down Glossary* 54 = to crouch on the ground with the heels under the hams.

1891 Simmons *Armagh Words and Phrases* 11 = to sit by bending the legs without resting on a seat.

1903 MacManus *Lad of O'Friels* 215 He stood her upon a hassog and hunkered low himself.

1937 Rowley *Tales of Mourne* 14 'Hunker down behin' yon boulder', whispers Phelim, an' the farmer hid himself, scarcely knowin' why he done all he was bid.

1953 Traynor *Donegal Glossary* 148 = to squat with the haunches, knees and ankles acutely bent so as to bring the hams near the heels.

1991 O'Kane *You Don't Say* 74 = to squat on one's calves, with heels firmly on the ground, particularly when sliding on a frozen pond or down a hill.

U.S.:   (also in figurative phrase *hunker down* = to get down to work; in phrase *hunker up* = to squat or bend over, as to avoid discomfort or keep warm)

1944 Wilson *Word-list* 44 = to squat on the haunches; to be humped up or bent over awkwardly: 'It was so cold he hunkered up in the wagon'.

1969 *GSMNP*-27:12 But you see he even seed us hunkered down at the house.

1975 Gainer *Speech Mtneer* 12 = to squat or to sit on haunches: 'I hunkered down behind a bush and waited for him'.

1990 Bailey *Draw Up Chair* 12 He may have to 'hunker down' and rest on one heel just as his Scottish ancestors did.

1997 Montgomery *Coll* = always used figuratively in reference to work, as in 'Let's hunker down and get this done'.

I

ill *adj* Of a person or an animal: angry, vicious, intractible, harsh. [OED (at *ill* adj 2a (of humans), 2b (of animals)), but apparently Scots dialect in reference to humans; cf SND *ill* adj I.4; DARE *ill* adj 1 'vicious, bad-tempered, cross, fretful' chiefly South, South Midland]

ULST.: **1920** McCallin *Ulster Plenishing* 17 He was hard to thole and ill to please, and a weary to himself as well as to them that had to live at the same hearth as him.

1933 Foster *Tyrone among Bushes* 87 Peter, dacent man, had an ill-word of nobody.

1936 White *Mrs Murphy* 61 It's ill to tell how much or how little them that's gone knows about their childer.

c1955 Montgomery *Heard in Ulster* 68 = difficult or hard: 'He's very ill to please'.

1991 O'Kane *You Don't Say* 75 = often used in a sense of difficult or awkward: 'He's ill to handle when he gets a drink or two'.

U.S.: **1857** Olmsted *Journey Texas* 78 'Ill' for 'vicious'. 'Is your dog ill?'

1917 Kephart *Word-list* 413 = ill-natured, vicious: 'That feller's ill as h[ell]'.

1939 Hall *Coll* We understand your ill way of talking.

1946 Woodard *Word-list Virg/NC* 18 = cross, in a bad humor. Said of children.

ill able *adj phr* Unable. [SND *ill-able* 'unable, unfit']

ULST.: **1953** Traynor *Donegal Glossary* 149 = hardly able.

U.S.: **1922** Dyer *Tenn Civil War Ques* 1387 But Ime now olde illabel to do enything looseing my reclection.

ill convenient *adj phr* Inconvenient, not suiting. Hence **ill-convenience, ill-convaynience** *n* Inconvenience.

ULST.: **1889** Hart *Derryreel* 74 'Thank ye, Mem', said Father Bryan, 'ye needn't put yerself to any illconvaynience on my account.'

c1910 Byers *Glossary* = inconvenient.

U.S.: **1837** Sherwood *Georgia Provincialisms* 119 *illconvenient* = inconvenient.

1899 Green *Virginia Word-Book* 198 = inconvenient, not to be done conveniently.

1965 *Dict Queen's English* 6 He got sick at an *ill-convenient* time.

in *prep* Used as initial element in compound prepositions (especially **in under**, q.v.), but adding little meaning. [OED *in* prep 15 with advs and preps; SND *in* adv 1(9) before preps, *in aboot ... in at ... in* has little more than intensive force; in Scotland *in under* has merged with *anunder* prep/adv 'under, underneath'; it is unclear whether the latter derives from *on* + *under* or *in* + *under*]

ULST.: **1902** McIlroy *Druid's Island* 34 He's in alow the h'y.

c1910 Byers *Glossary, in under* (or *onder*) = under, underneath.

1931 Bratton *Turf Fire* 60 Sure enough out rouled the pea from inunder the [shell] he lifted.

1939 Paterson *Country Cracks* 18 In a day or two he was lyin' in under the grass in oul' Killavey.

1975 Murphy *You're Talking* 56 He puts the satchel of sovereigns in in-under the saddle and hangs the sack of coppers on the saddle.

U.S.:   1939 Hall *Coll* Very near everybody made it. An uncle of mine and a cousin [were] making liquor in above my home. *Ibid.* He's laying right on the right in under the Smokies, the head of the left hand fork of Deep Creek.

1953 Hall *Coll* Later on, in a few weeks or months after that, they found a dead pant'er in across at the river bluffs down to the end of the Smoky Mountain in there.

1969 *GSMNP*-46:20 Bradburn had a stack [of wheat] just in behind the schoolhouse out here at Shoal Creek, and they wouldn't go up there and thrash it.

1974–75 McCracken *Logging* 5:49 About the first skidder I helped move after we left Elkmont set right about where we're at, right back in against the hill there. *Ibid.* 10:38 We had a big garden right down in under yonder. *Ibid.* 23:32 We started wooding there, along not far from Polls Gap and a-going back in on toward Heintoga, behind the timber cutting.

in course *adv phr* Of course. [OED *in course* (at *course* 35c) 'naturally, as might be expected' now only in vulgar use; SND *in coorse* (at *in* B4.4(a)); DARE (at *in* prep B2) 'of course' chiefly South, South Midland, somewhat old-fashioned]
    ULST.:   c1910 Byers *Glossary* Why, in course, he will.
              1953 Traynor *Donegal Glossary* 149 = of course: 'Sartinly in coorse I will. Why wouldn't I?'
    U.S.:   1911 Shute *Plupy* 22 Why, in course, in course, sonny, come right over.

infare, infair *n* The home-coming of the bride after the wedding ceremony; a dinner or feast following a wedding, often at the home of the groom's parents, with much merry-making and dancing, replaced in more recent times by the wedding reception. [ultimately < Old English *infær* 'an entrance' < *in* + *fær* 'journey'; OED *infare* n 2 'a feast or entertainment given on entering a new house, especially the reception of a bride in her new home' Scottish, northern dialect and U.S.; DOST *infair* n 2 'the feast in the bridegroom's house after the wedding' late 16th→19th century; DARE chiefly South, South Midland]
    ULST.:   1880 Patterson *Antrim/Down Glossary* 56 *infair* = the bringing home of a bride.
              c1910 Byers *Glossary* = the home-coming for the bride, the entertainment given for the reception of a bride in the bridegroom's home; the reception after the wedding: 'Shots are fired at the infair, or bringing home of the bride'.
              1953 Traynor *Donegal Glossary* 150 = (1) the bringing home of the bride to her new abode; shots are fired and cheers given along the road as the happy couple pass; (2) a feast held on the home-coming of the bride and groom.
    U.S.:   1834 Crockett *Narrative* 64 At our next meeting he set the day for our wedding; and I went to my father's, and made arrangements for an infair; and returned to ask her parents for her.
              1908 Payne *Word-list East Alabama* 323 = a feast given by the groom's parents in honor of the bride's coming to her new home.
              1939 Hall *Coll* When one would start from where they was married to go to their husband's home, that was called the infare.

1981 Whitener *Folk-Ways* 72 For the uninitiated, the infare was a bit of frolicking at the home of the groom, usually in the afternoon after a morning wedding. At this occasion the groom furnished the whiskey, food, and sweets (usually candy for the ladies) for a proper celebration. The celebration itself usually included folk dancing, singing, games, and occasionally a certain amount of horseplay during which bride and groom were made to suffer certain indignities of a minor nature.

1991 Haynes *Haywood Home* 61–62 Infares were put on by the groom's parents and were wedding feasts (suppers). They started at least a week ahead to get everything ready. The best cooks on Fines Creek or Crabtree were invited to make sure everything was all right. After the couple was married in church, the wedding party went to the groom's parents house for the infare ... After supper, there'd be music and square dancing with local musicians playing ... Then about nine or ten p.m., all the guests would escort the bride and groom to their assigned sleeping quarters and inspect the room before they said goodnight.

in under, innundher, inunder, inundher *prep* Beneath, below, underneath (in the U.S. only **in under**). See also **in**. [OED (at *anunder* prep 1) 'under'; probably variant of earlier *anunder* (<*an* 'on' + *under* or *in* + *under*)]

ULST.:   **1880** Patterson *Antrim/Down Glossary* 56 *innundher* = underneath.

c**1910** Byers *Glossary*, *in under* (or *onder*) = under, underneath.

1912 Gregory *Ulster Folk* 35 Padric sits in the garden / Inundher the bright new moon.

1931 Bratton *Turf Fire* 60 Sure enough out rouled the pea from inunder the [shell] he lifted.

1937 Rowley *Tales of Mourne* 147 Then down would come the brown fiddle from the chimney-jamb, and he would tuck it inunder his chin, and try over the old rants and reels.

1939 Paterson *Country Cracks* 18 In a day or two he was lyin' in under the grass in oul' Killavey.

1955 Murphy *Culprit of Shadows* 16 Go out and find something to do. Hens not let out, pigs to be fed an' cleaned inunder, the sow needs a ring.

2000 Fenton *Hamely Tongue* 109 = underneath (and usually out of sight: 'lyin inunther the dresser'; under: 'Inunther Provydence, whut ir ye tellin me?'

U.S.:   **1930** Shoemaker *1300 Penn Words* 32 *in-under* = underneath, below.

1939 Hall *Coll* When I got out to the Bear Pen Gap, why the dogs was a-fighting the bear right in under the top of Smoky, pretty close up to the top.

1969 *GSMNP*-37:2:12 I told my brother, I says, 'We'll have to go right around this, in under these big pines.'

iz yins See **us'uns**

J

jag *vb* To prick, pierce with a point. [probably imitative; OED *jag* vb 1b 'to prick with something sharp, as with a spur or thorn' 1700→, Scottish, northern English, and U.S. dialect, 1c 'to pierce, thrust, prick' obsolete, *jag* vb 3 ' a protruding bristle, hair, or fibre; a hairy, bristly, or thread-like outgrowth or projection' 1519→; DOST *jag* n² 'a prick' 1672→; DARE especially Pennsylvania]

    ULST.:   **1831** Carson *Poems* 31 You may be taught, without delay, / To 'stitch the louse and jag the flea'.

              1866 Flecher *Poems* 240 = to pierce with a sharp point.

              1901 Savage-Armstrong *Ballads of Down* 208 A rising ripple jagged the water's line; / And down I sat to steer, with shortening breath.

              1953 Traynor *Donegal Glossary* 15 = to prick or pierce with a sharp instrument.

              2004 McIlhatton *Whin Bush* Its wonderful this old whin ... growing green and high. / With jags worse than barbed wire and I'm not joking now I say, / The jags would deter both man and beast and send them on their way. / Oh the jaggiest you ever seen indeed everyone will say.

    U.S.:   **1883** Smith *Southernisms* 50 = 'to prick or pierce with a thorn or any sharp-pointed thing'. Common in various parts of the South. So in South Carolina, a man in swimming is said to have been 'jagged by a snag'.

jaggedy, jaggety *adj* Of metal, wood, etc.: having a sharp, jagged edge; of cloth: having a torn or ragged edge. [DARE *jaggedy* adj 1 'having a jagged edge' South, South Midland]

    ULST.:   **1953** Traynor *Donegal Glossary* 15 *jaggedy* = rough or torn at the edges.

              1997 Share *Slanguage* 149 *jaggety* = having rough or torn edges.

    U.S.:   **1967** Williams *Subtlety Mt Speech* 16 He could see the jaggedy aidge of a great big rock poked aout away up high above him.

jeuk See **jouk**

jokey *adj* Playful, amusing. [OED *joky* 'inclined to joke, jocular'; DARE especially South, South Midland]

    ULST.:   **1925** McKay *Mourne Folk* 72 He wus a gintleman, if ever there wus wan; he wus very jokey too, an' the best company.

              1928 McKay *Oul' Town* 92 Right enough, there was the height of good luck followed his visits. He was jokey, too.

              1931 Bratton *Turf Fire* 88 Tam was a jokey kind of playboy, and he used to say that he wouldn't a bothered his head about her at the dance only he had a brave wee sup on him at the time.

    U.S.:   **1953** Randolph and Wilson *Down in Holler* 257 *joky fellow* = a clown.

              1955 Ritchie *Singing Family* 155 He's allus a right jokey kind of feller. Going across the Duane Mountain he got to showing off what a good rider he was.

jouk, jeuk, jook, juke *vb* To duck down or crouch, dodge, elude, evade by cunning, hide. Hence *n* A dodge, evasive or furtive movement or maneuver. [origin uncertain; OED *jouk/jook* vb² 1 'to bend or turn the body with a quick, adroit movement downward or to one side, in order to avoid a missile or blow; to dodge; to duck' 1513→, 2 'to dart or spring with an adroit elusive movement out of the way or out of sight' c1510→, Scottish; DOST *jouk* vb 1 'to move the body quickly downward', 2 'to duck down out of the way or out of sight' 1513→, 3 'to bob downward by bending the knees'; SND *jouk* 1(1) 'to duck, to stoop or (one's head) away quickly to avoid a missile or blow, to dodge', 2 'to dodge, evade, elude, give the slip to (someone or something) by a quick sideways movement'; DARE especially Pennsylvania]

ULST.:
1860 Patterson *Belfast Provincialisms* 23 *jeuk* = to elude by shifting; to dodge.
1880 Patterson *Antrim/Down Glossary* 57 *juke* = to stoop the head suddenly, so as to avoid a blow, to turn off quickly when running away, to hide round a corner.
1893 Bullock *Awkward Squad* 27 Whisht, boys, whisht! but there's three men joukin' up the hill be the hedge.
1920 McCallin *Ulster Plenishing* 69 It was acknowledged by all, especially by them that didn't let the noggin' juke past them at the house-weemin'.
1942 *Bangor Words* 45 *jouk* = to dodge or elude: 'Look at him jouking round the corner'.
1945 Murphy *Gullion's Foot* 96 [In the game the ball-in-the-hat] the boy whose hat the ball went into had to run and grab and then try to hit one of the fleeing or jooking (hiding) competitors.
1953 Traynor *Donegal Glossary* 154 *jouk* = (1) to duck or stoop to avoid a blow or to keep out of sight; (2) to deceive, evade by cunning.
c1955 Montgomery *Heard in Ulster* 70 *juke* = to lower the head or act in a suspicious manner in order to avoid notice: 'What er ye juken aboot?'
1990 McIntyre *Some Handlin'* 35 *jeuk* = duck down, avoid: 'Nicola jeuked when her da was going to clash her'.
1990 Todd *Words Apart* 100 He was jukin and keekin and lookin could he see what was goin on.
1991 O'Kane *You Don't Say* 77 *jook* = any furtive or evasive movement: 'You should have seen the jooks of him along the hedge'.
2000 Fenton *Hamely Tongue* 112 = dodge; duck; advance in a crouching, surreptitious way (to avoid observation): 'He spens a' his time jookin an watchin'.
2000 Fenton *Thonner and Thon* 5 Whar micht he rin, what scot-hole tak, / Whar jook, the wain?

U.S.:
1834 Downing *Life Andrew Jackson* 230 They say three hundred thousand dollars was drawn from the Nashvil Bank tu aid your election, that there is positive proof of this, and that there isn't any way to jouk it.
1890 *Various Contrib* 1.74 *jook* = to avoid a blow by dodging.
1896 *Word-list* 419 *juke* = to hide quickly.
1989 Landry *Smoky Mt Interviews* 181 He said when [the bear] saw the panther a-layin' on this big log by the river, it just jooked down like a cat about to leap on something.

juke See **jouk**

K

kase See **bekase**

keen, caoine, keeny *vb* To wail, cry in lamentation, especially over a corpse. Hence *n* A wail or cry of lamentation. [< Irish, Scottish Gaelic *caoin* 'to lament, weep']
ULST.:   1829 McSparran *Irish Legend* 142 During the time of interment the bards on both sides, as if in emulation, performed in melancholy tone the Irish caoine, accompanying their mournful harps with their voice.
1880 Patterson *Antrim/Down Glossary* 58 = (1) a cry in lamentation over a corpse; (2) to wail or cry over a corpse.
1900 Irvine *Lady Chimney Corner* 83 She sat on th' wall wid her head in her han's keenin' an' moanin'.
1945 Murphy *Gullion's Foot* 76 She was said to be always combing her hair, and lamenting in a keen, like the old keeners at wakes.
1949 Mac Airt *Tyrone Folktales* 39 He [went] to the keeneying and roaring through the house and couldn't be pacified.
1990 Todd *Words Apart* 101 That chile'll keeny somebody out o' the house.
U.S.:   1935 Sheppard *Cabins in Laurel* 218 If the preacher harrows the sorrowing kinfolks with the promise of Judgement and Wrath-to-come until they break into wild keening that sends shivers through the listeners, it is only what might be expected in bereavement, and likely to bring some sinner to his senses.
1971 Dwyer *Dict for Yankees* 28 = to wail, cry: 'His daughter went to keening at the funeral'.

kilt *vb* Killed (as both past-tense and past-participle forms) Hurt, badly injured, overcome. [SND; DARE (at *kill* vb B) South, South Midland]
ULST.:   1845 Carleton *Irish Peasantry* 413 Och ... but I'm kilt wit you.
1936 White *Mrs Murphy* 32 When he come in I thought at first he'd been kilt dead, and it was his ghost walkin'.
1983 Pepper *Ulster Knowledge* 17 D'ye want to get yerself kilt like they advertise on TV?
1993 Montgomery *Barnish* 30 = killed.
2000 Fenton *Hamely Tongue* 116 = killed (especially figurative in *kilt workin*; *kilt wae the teethache*; *kilt wae wun*, etc.): A'm kilt! (following a fall or a blow).
U.S.:   1815 Brackenridge *Modern Chivalry* 252 By de holy apostles, I shall be kilt and murdered into de bargain!
1937 Thornborough *Great Smoky Mts* 93 A party of hunters came up from Knoxville and kilt 'em a load o'bear.
1974 Fink *Bits Mt Speech* 14 Who kilt that dog?

kin *n* An individual blood relation. [OED *kin* n¹ 3c 'used of a single person: Kinsman, relative' →1790, archaic; DOST *kin* n 3 'a kinsman or -woman' 1375→]
ULST.:   1934 Cavanagh *Dunleary Legend* 50 Two hundred pound fortin in her fisht, an' more to come when her uncle, who have no kin but her be dead.
1953 Traynor *Donegal Glossary* 159 = a relative.
U.S.:   1937 Hall *Coll* A kin of mine.
1976 *GSMNP*-114:4 They was some kin.
1989 Landry *Smoky Mt Interviews* 194 We're a little bit of kin, not much.

1991 Haynes *Haywood Home* 70 He was not really our uncle. He was no kin to us that I know of. But the young of my time were taught to address older people as uncle or aunt whether they were any kin or not. It was respectful.

kirtle *n* A woman's petticoat. [cf Old Norse *kyrtill* 'tunic'; OED *kirtle* 2 'a woman's gown, a skirt or outer petticoat' c995→]

ULST.: **1953** Traynor *Donegal Glossary* 160 = a woman's outer petticoat or short skirt.
1959 Gregory *Ulster Ballads* 78 O she worked an' made her kirtle dark / An' a bodice o' virgin sheen.
U.S.: **1930** Shoemaker *1300 Penn Words* 35 = a petticoat, a woman's undergarment.

kist *n* A chest, large wooden box. [< Middle English *kist* < Old Norse *kista*]
ULST.: **1880** Patterson *Antrim/Down Glossary* 59 = the chest.
1942 *Bangor Words* 46 = chest or box.
c1955 Montgomery *Heard in Ulster* 73 = large wooden trunk or chest.
1990 Todd *Words Apart* 103 Kists was always kep' in homes in the counthry until people started to bring in newfangled furniture.
2000 Fenton *Hamely Tongue* 116 *tay-kist* = tea box; *kist o drars* = chest of drawers; *kist o whussles* = a church organ (scornful description, by those opposed to its use, of).
U.S.: **1930** Shoemaker *1300 Penn Words* 36 = a chest or locker.

knab See **nob**

L

lang-headed, lang-heided See **long-headed**

lash, lashing(s) *n* (especially in phrases *lashings and lavings, lashins and lavins*) A
great number, large quantity, especially of food. [< *lash* vb 'to rain heavily; to dash,
pour, rush'; SND *lash* n¹ 'a heavy fall of rain; a large or abundant quantity of things
or persons'; DARE *lashings* n 'an abundance, a great plenty' especially South, South
Midland]

ULST.:   **1880** Patterson *Antrim/Down Glossary* 61 = a large amount: 'The master
bought a lash o' things from them'; *lashing* = plenty: 'lashins and lavins' = more
than plenty.
1895 MacManus *Leadin' Road* 163 It was a lee long time ago when ould
Ireland was happy and contented, with lavin's and lashin's—plenty to ait and
little to do.
1920 McCallin *Fireside Tales* 11 I don't think that it would be far wrong to say
that she helped him through a lash o' bothers, an' that for her he mightn't a-
got on as fast as he did.
1931 Bratton *Turf Fire* 34 When the tay was brought in iverybody started on
that, and there was lashin's and lavin's of good strong tay and curran' bread.
1953 Traynor *Donegal Glossary* 165 = (1) a heavy fall of rain; (2) a great
number, abundance: 'There's a whole lash more of them in the stable'; *lashing*
= abundance, great quantities.
1991 O'Kane *You Don't Say* 84 *lashings* = more than enough, an abundance of
food or drink: 'Come to the party, there'll be lashin's of drink'.
2000 Fenton *Hamely Tongue* 120 = to rain heavily (hence *lashin*).

U.S.:   **1939** FWP *Guide Tenn* 458 'Lashings' or 'slathers' (liberal quantities) of
sorghum, served with yellow butter on brown biscuits, battercakes, or
flapjacks, is the 'best eatin' ever intended to man'.
1953 Randolph and Wilson *Down in Holler* 259 *lashins and lavins* = 'Them
Hawkins boys has all got money, lashins an' lavins of it'.
1984 Wilder *You All Spoken* 71 *lashin's an' lavin's* = an abundance, plenty and
some to spare, more than you can shake a stick at in a whole week.

lasty *adj* Long-lasting, durable. [*last* n + -*y* adj-forming suffix; SND (at *lest* vb, n I);
DARE *lasty* adj 'durable; long lasting, enduring' chiefly southern Appalachians,
South Midland]

ULST.:   **1935** Megaw *Carragloon* 171 Says I to myself, if this isn't a lasty bottle, I'm
bate.
2000 Fenton *Hamely Tongue* 120 = long-lasting; durable: 'dear at the time, but
lasty'.

U.S.:   **1886** Smith *Southernisms* 50 I heard myself last summer a 'foot-washing'
Baptist preacher in Craddock's Great Smoky Mountains say, 'Stone is the most
lastiest, the most endurablest material there is.'
1939 Aurand *Idioms and Expressions* 24 That's a WERY (very) LASTY
(durable) basket.
1943 Justus *Bluebird* 19 There's good heat in red cedar, and it's mighty lasty,
too.
1974 Fink *Bits Mt Speech* 15 Them was lasty britches.

lavins *n* (lit. 'leavings') See **lashings**

leader *n* (usually in plural) A tendon or ligament. [OED *leader* n¹ 10 'a tendon' 1708→; SND *leader* 6 'a tendon, sinew'; DARE *leader* n 1 'a tendon, ligament' South, South Midland]

ULST.:　1923 Lutton *Montiaghisms* 28 *leaders* = the tendons of the hands and feet; it often signifies the muscles generally.
1942 *Bangor Words* 48 *leaders* = tendons, sinews.
2000 Fenton *Hamely Tongue* 121 = a tendon.

U.S.:　1805 (in 2004 Hartley *Lewis and Clark Lexicon* 147) the twitching of the fingers and leaders of the arm.
1899 Green *Virginia Word-Book* 217 = a tendon, a sinew.
1990 Cavender *Folk Medical Lex* 26 *leaders* = tendons or ligaments, most frequently used in reference to the ligaments in the neck and ankle.

leave *vb* To allow (to), permit to, let; to hand (only in Ulster). [OED vb¹ 3e 'to allow, permit, let'; SND vb² 1 'to give leave to, permit, allow' late 14th century→]

ULST.:　1919 MacGill *Glenmornan* 203 'Leave go iv me, Doalty Gallagher', she said.
1936 White *Mrs Murphy* 206 The minute I leave anything down out of my hand you would think somebody come and whipped it away.
1948 Marshall *Planted by River* 93 Leave aff [the sword], ye ondacent vagabone, an' see if ye can bate a man with only one arm an' a bit o' cowl iron.
1975 Murphy *You're Talking* 29 The ones carrying it thought they heerd or felt a rattling in the coffin and they left it down.

U.S.:　1865 (in 1983 Heap *Bucks Co Word List* 70) Were ordered ... to proceed on our march, which we did but not without blessing the officers that would not leave us worn out soldiers rest.
1956 Hall *Coll* Just leave it sit there and in a few weeks it'll become kraut.
c1959 Weals *Hillbilly Dict* 5 = let: 'Leave me do that'.
1976 Carter *Little Tree* 2 'Leave him be', he had said. And so they left me be.
1982 McCool *Pittsburghese* 23 = let or allow, as in 'If you clean your room, Mom will leave you go to the movies'.
1995 Adams *Come Go Home* 42 We're just going to leave him lay; he'll never know the difference.

leave, leeve *adv* See **lief**

leg-bail *n* (in phr *give leg bail* = to abscond, fail to appear in court). OED *give leg-bail* (at *bail* 5c) 'to be beholden to one's own legs for escape, to run away']

ULST.:　1845 Carleton *Irish Peasantry* 30 'So, Jack', says he, 'you're going to give us leg bail, I see.'
1910 Joyce *English in Ireland* 283 A person gives (or takes) *leg bail* when he runs away, absconds.
1923 Lutton *Montiaghisms* 28 'To give leg bail' is to fly from arrest, in case of debt or misdemeanour.

U.S.:　1917 Kephart *Word-list* 414 *give leg bail* = to abscond: 'He give 'em leg-bail and lit out for home'.

lenth *n* Length.

ULST.:　c1614 McClellan *Assignment* Quhilk sall be and begin presentlie at the dait heirof And sua furth therefter to continew to the saids lands and uthers foresaids with the pertinents to be peaceablie bruiked joyssit occupied labored manured sett ussed and disponnitt upon be the said Gawand Kelso and his foresaids dureing the said space as the samyne lyis in lenth and breid.

1860 Patterson *Belfast Provincialisms* 10 = length.

1920 McCallin *Ulster Plenishing* 29 It was no odds to him how it could be spun-out by the big guns o' the colleges that were able to crack with each other in Latin, and reckon-up the len'th of the road to the moon an' back.

1936 White *Mrs Murphy* 111 I can walk no lenth now without lossin' me breath.

1959 Gregory *Ulster Ballads* 41 Ivery girl I've named is saucey, / (God grant them their len'th o' days.)

1997 Robinson *Grammar* 62 The 'length', 'breadth' and 'depth' of anything is the *lenth(t)*, *brenth(t)* and *depth(t)*.

U.S.:　　　**1798** (in **1956** Eliason *Tarheel Talk* 313) *lenth*.

1829 Kirkham *English Grammar* 192 *lenth* = length. Common ... in Pennsylvania.

1878 Burt *Dialects* 413 The Pennsylvanian says *strenth* and *lenth* for *strength* and *length*.

1905 Pound *Speech in Nebraska* 58 Sometimes [n] appears for [ŋ] in *strenth*, *lenth*, especially among those of Irish descent.

let on *vb*

1 To pretend, feign. [OED (at *let* vb[1] 36b) labels this sense 'originally dialect and U.S.' apparently in error; SND (at *lat* vb B.2.11a); DARE widespread except New England]

ULST.:　　**1804** Orr *Poems* 35 Some lettin' on their burn to mak', / The rear-guard, goadin', hasten'd.

1881 Hart *Mere Irish* 140 When Shan left Scarraway, he let on to Ferigal that he was going home.

1923 Lutton *Montiaghisms* 28 = to feign.

c**1955** Montgomery *Heard in Ulster* 79 He's only lettin on that he's hurt.

1981 Pepper *Ulster-English Dict* 47 I knew rightly she didn't mean what she said. I knew she was onny lettin on.

2000 Fenton *Hamely Tongue* 122 Sure A wuz only lettin on.

U.S.:　　　**1826** Royall *Grison Republic* 89 When they would say *pretence*, they say *lettinon*, which is a word of very extensive use amongst them. It signifies a jest, and used to express disapprobation and disguise; 'you are just lettinon to rub them spoons—Polly is not mad; she is only lettinon'.

1953 Randolph and Wilson *Down in Holler* 260 I just let on like I didn't care nothin' about it.

1978 Montgomery *White Pine Coll* VIII-2 I don't think White Pine has grown near as much because of the interstate that this article let on like it had.

2 To divulge, disclose, mention. [OED (at *let* vb[1] 36a) labels this sense 'to reveal, divulge' 'originally dialect and U.S.' apparently in error; SND (at *lat* vb B.2.11b)]

ULST.:　　**1879** Lyttle *Paddy McQuillan* 26 Ye mauna let on what A'm tellin' ye.

1880 Patterson *Antrim/Down Glossary* 62 = to show knowledge of a thing: 'I never let on like I seen him'.

1895 MacManus *Leadin' Road* 157 I nivir let on I heard them.

1921 O'Neill *More Songs of Glens* 26 I was lookin' after Nancy, but of course I'd not let on, / An' she was lettin' on she didn't care.

1923 Lutton *Montiaghisms* 28 = to divulge a secret, to give intimation of.
1942 *Bangor Words* 49 = to tell: 'Don't let on I told you'; 'He never let on he knew anything about it'.
1993 Montgomery *Barnish* 60 'Don't be letting on' = Keep it under your hat, please keep it secret.
2000 Fenton *Hamely Tongue* 122 = disclose, give sign of: 'Niver let on ye' = Don't show that you know, notice, etc.

U.S.: **1939** Hall *Coll* I passed on up, and the last one I was aiming to trot on and not let on like I saw them.
1940 Haun *Hawk's Done* 120 Burt didn't let on like he heard.
1956 McAtee *Some Dial NC* 27 They were talking about me but I never let on that I heard them.
1976 Garber *Mountain-ese* 53 He's purty sick but he's too proud to let on.

lick *n* A sharp blow or stroke with the hand or a heavy instrument. Hence *vb* To strike, beat severely; **licking** *vbl n* A severe beating, whipping. [OED *lick* n[1] 4a 'a smart blow'; SND *lick* n I(3) 'a hard blow, smack, wallop' 1746→, vb III(3) 'to wallop, thrash; to beat, surpass, overcome'; DARE *lick* n 1 'a sharp blow or stroke, as with the fist, a weapon, or a tool' chiefly South, South Midland, Texas, Oklahoma]

ULST.: **1879** Lyttle *Paddy McQuillan* 32 Wait till I get aff my coat, fur A can lick the best man amang ye!
1880 Patterson *Antrim/Down Glossary* 62 = (1) a blow; (2) to beat; *licking* = a beating.
1885 Lyttle *Robin Gordon* 15 Nae metter what he din we niver had the heart tae gie him a lickin'.
1942 *Bangor Words* 49 = to beat: 'Tom licked Bill at the exam' = Tom did better than Bill; 'His mother gave Bill a good licking, for stealing the sugar'.
1955 Murphy *Culprit of Shadows* 17–18 If I know his breed he'd only be too glad to get a lick after all the talk that was about his marriage.

U.S.: **1871** Eggleston *Hoosier Schoolmaster* 119 I'd lick you till your hide wouldn't hold shucks.
1939 Hall *Coll* I knocked [the bear] in the head ever so many licks before I could get it to roll over and hush hollerin'.
1993 Walker *Life History* 75 The first lick he throwed he hit that wildcat and knocked it out.

lief, leave/leeve, liefer, live *adv* Gladly, willingly, likely, rather (especially in such phrases as *as lief, just as lief, just as leave* + verb). [originally *would lief/liefer* 'would gladly', but the auxiliary has been contracted and usually lost completely; *lief* is now confused with *leave* 'permission, liberty'; OED *lief* adv B 'dearly, gladly, willingly' c1250→; SND *lief* II adv 'gladly, willingly' 1724→; DARE *lief* adv 'willingly, soon' chiefly Northeast, Midland]

ULST.: **1910** Joyce *English in Ireland* 286 = willing: 'I had as lief be working as not'; 'I had liefer' (I had rather).
1935 MacManus *Bold Blades* 1 Uncle Donal, I'd liefer stay at home with you, all the time.
1937 Rowley *Tales of Mourne* 49 'Here's a companion I'd liefer have nor any woman', and he pulled a flute out of his hip-pocket.
1942 *Bangor Words* 49 = willingly, rather: 'I had a lief not go'.
1953 Traynor *Donegal Glossary* 169 *liefer* = more willingly, rather.

1964 Braidwood *Ulster/Elizabethan English* 102 *Lief* (Old English *leof* 'dear', cf German *lieb*) still survives in Ulster ... in the adverb phrase *I had as lief*, e.g. 'I'd as lief go without'. This is common Elizabethan and Jacobean English, probably best-known from Hamlet's advice to the players: 'I had as *lief* the town-crier spoke my lines' (3.2.4).

1991 O'Kane *You Don't Say* 85 = to be willing to, to prefer: 'I'd as lief be working today as sitting here lookin' at the sea'.

U.S.:   **1835** Longstreet *Georgia Scenes* 29 He just as live go agin the house with you.

1899 Green *Virginia Word-Book* 218 *leeve* = willingly, a word of indifference: 'I'd as leeve go as stay'.

1904–07 Kephart *Notebooks* 2:642 Liefer as not, that's not so.

1994 Montgomery *Coll* I'd just as lief hear a sow rub her ass as to hear a pianner.

like *vb*

1 (+ *prep* or *adv*) with elliptical infinitive, as in *like in, like off* = like (to come/get /go) in, off, etc.

ULST.:   **2005** Fenton *Notes* The cat lakes in.

U.S.:   **1916** Pound *Wordlist Nebraska* 282 Would you like in? Would you like out?

1982 Barrick *Coll* The dog likes out.

2 (+ *past participle*) with elliptical infinitive, as in *likes fed*, etc.

ULST.:   **2005** Fenton *Notes* The hens is lakin fed; The hens lakes fed in the moarnin.

U.S.:   **2002** Murray and Simon *Intersection of Dialects* 33 She really likes cuddled.

Ibid. 41 [That dog] sure does like petter.

lipping (full), lippin-laggin' *adj* Full to capacity. [OED *lip* vb 3 'of water, etc.: to rise to, cover, or flow over the lip or brim of a vessel' 1703→; cf SND *lip* vb 3(2) 'to be full to the brim, or overflowing']

ULST.:   **c1910** Byers *Glossary* = of a container: full to the brim.

1981 McClean *Ulster Words V* 2 *lippin*=*laggin'* = brimming full.

2000 Fenton *Thonner and Thon* 1 The watter, glancin ower its dark, babs lippin, whusperin by.

U.S.:   **1856** Reid *Scalp Hunters* 142 The first little rivulet that trickled forth from their lipping fulness would be the signal of their destruction.

c1978 Trout and Watson *Piece of Smokies* 39 By November, the corn crib, apple house, and smokehouse were 'lippin' full'.

little piece See **piece 1**

live See **lief**

loaf bread *n* Bread made from wheat flour and yeast, in contrast to that made from oats (in Ulster) or corn (in the U.S.). [OED *loaf bread* 'bread made in the form of loaves' now dialect; SND (at *loaf* n 1) 'wheaten-flour bread' (in contrast to oatbread/oatcakes); DARE *loaf bread* n 'yeast-leavened bread, especially made with wheat flour, that is shaped into a loaf' chiefly South, South Midland]

ULST.:   **1931** Bratton *Turf Fire* 120 A noggin of sowans would keep out the coul', / but loaf-bread and tay would just starve ye, in sowl.

U.S.:   1775 (in 1921 Kilpatrick *Journal William Calk* 366) we Start early and git to foart chissel whear We git some good loaf Bread & good Whiskey. 1949 Kurath *Word Geog East US* 67 In the South and the South Midland [wheat] bread is commonly known as *light-bread*, in the coastal area also as *loaf-bread*, as distinct from *pone bread* for corn bread. 1967 *DARE Coll* = bread made with wheat flour.

lone *n* Alone; (one's) own self (especially in phr *one's lone* = alone, by oneself). [shortening of *alone*; OED *lone* adj 6b 'by myself, itself (etc.)' 1613→, Scottish and northern; DOST *lane* adj 1557→]

ULST.:   1880 Patterson *Antrim/Down Glossary* 2 *all my lone* = alone.
1889 Hart *Derryreel* 44 Father Bryan had the habit of spakin' out what he would be thinkin' on, even when he was his lone.
c1910 Byers *Glossary*, *its lone* = by itself: 'Can the child go its lone?'
1919 MacGill *Glenmornan* 206 [He's] goin' away without a word and leavin' me here me lone.
1928 McKay *Oul' Town* 91 Many a time I think, when I'm all 'me lone', how little satisfies a wean.
1931 Bratton *Turf Fire* 89 Nancy would be sittin' her lone down in the big kitchen.
1934 Cavanagh *Dunleary Legend* 70 The sounds is like a mighty storm an' it tormentin' a tree that's been left all be its lone on the hillside.
1934 White *Gape Row* 12 And then I left her, for I knew she had a mind to be by her lone.
1942 *Bangor Words* 51 = alone, sole: 'Has he anybody living with him? No, he's just his lone'; 'He is away off by his lone'.
1975 Murphy *You're Talking* 43 He was an old farmer and a miser living his lone only for the servant girl, Brigid, and she'd been a lifetime with him.
1990 McIntyre *Some Handlin'* 64 'I'm sitting here on me lone' (alone).
1991 O'Kane *You Don't Say* 88 = by oneself (or themselves): 'The old couple are livin' their lone now'.
1997 Share *Slanguage* 171 *its lone, my lone*, etc. = alone.

U.S.:   (usually *by one's lone* (*self*) = by oneself)
1917 (in 1944 Wentworth *Amer Dial Dict* 15) I was here all my lone.
1973 *GSMNP*-6:24 He knew where I had gone on top of Bullhead by my lone self.
1997 Montgomery *Coll*, I guess I'll have to do it by my lone; He lived by his lone self for two years after his wife died.

long-headed, lang-headed, lang-heided *adj* Determined, calculating, stubborn. [cf OED *long-headed* 2 'discerning'; SND (at *lang* I.6(22)); DARE *long-headed* adj 2 'stubborn, obstinate, pig headed' South, South Midland]

ULST.:   1886 Lyttle *Ballycuddy* 1 Wully wuz a different boy a'thegither. My, he was terble lang-heided, an he jist drunk in the lernin as fast as the master gied it.
1902 McIlroy *Druid's Island* 52 Dan was a gey, lang-heided yin, hooiver, an' no' a wurd wud he say, one w'y or anither.
1942 *Bangor Words* 51 *long-headed* = wise and cautious, given to thinking things out before acting.
c1955 Montgomery *Heard in Ulster* 79 *long-headed* = shrewd, far-seeing: 'He's a lang-headed boy that'.

1981 McClean *Ulster Words V* 2 *lang-headed* = clever, clear thinking.
1991 O'Kane *You Don't Say* 88 *long-headed* = knowing, calculating, cautious (a long-headed person makes provision for the future and thinks things through).

U.S.: **1883** Harris *Nights with Remus* 254 Dish yer youngster gittin' too long-headed fer me; dat he is.
1938 Hall *Coll* = stubborn; with one's head set on something; can't get it changed.
1939 Hall *Coll* You're so long-headed [I] can't tell you anything.

look *vb* To inspect, search (for). [OED *look* vb 40h 'to find by looking, choose out by looking'; DOST *luke* vb 6 'to look at, inspect, examine' late 14th century→]

ULST.: **1880** Patterson *Antrim/Down Glossary* 64 = to search: 'Away an' look the child's head'.
c**1910** Wier *Bab McKeen* 45 I tell't hir I wus ower busy makin' the breakfast tae luck the clock.
1975 Murphy *You're Talking* 35 When the man come looking his money she was to tell him that her own man was down by the shore, three miles away gathering wrack.

U.S.: **1899** Green *Virginia Word-Book* 268 To look someone's head for lice there.
1982 Slone *How We Talked* 62 Some of the greens we used were not cooked, but eaten raw. They were 'looked' (checked for bugs and rotting spots), washed, sprinkled with salt and wilted or 'killed' by pouring real hot grease over them.
1993 Ison and Ison *Whole Nother Lg* 40 *look the beans* = to inspect dried beans or other food for foreign objects.

loss *vb* To lose. [probably back-formation from past-tense form *lost*; SND *loss* vb 'to lose, in all senses' 1701→]

ULST.: **1860** Patterson *Belfast Provincialisms* 23 = to lose.
1884 McFadyen and Hepburn *Lays and Legends* 77 Yer playin' a game, lad, at which ye'll be lossin', / An' findin' the Priest, troth, is proof av yer tossin'.
1906 MacDermott *Foughilotra* 14 Thon mon that questioned me wasn't a-lossin' his time wi' me.
1936 White *Mrs Murphy* 111 I can walk no lenth now without lossin' me breath.

U.S.: **1829** Kirkham *English Grammar* 207 Where did you loss it?
1837 Sherwood *Georgia Provincialisms* 119 = lose.
1907 Heydrick *Provincialisms of SE Penn* 381 Be careful of that or you'll loss it.

M

man *n* One's husband (used often by a woman in reference to her mate). Cf
woman. [OED *man* n[1] 8 now only Scottish and dialect, except in phr *man and
wife*; DOST *man* n 2 'a woman's husband' late 14th century→; SND *man* 3 'a
husband']

ULST.: 1920 Ervine *Mrs Martin's Man* 54 It's my man that's comin' back.
        1975 Murphy *You're Talking* 63 After a while he knowed it wasn't her own
        man. This man had on a sleeve-waistcoat and he knew it wasn't her husband.
        1983 Marshall *Drumlister* 33 So I swithered back an' forrit, / Till Margit got a
        man.
        1983 Pepper *Ulster Knowledge* 55 My man wouldn't go content to his work or
        his darts without the pan.

U.S.:   1895 Edson and Fairchild *Tenn Mts* 374 I studied about her hair to my man
        when I got home.
        1930 Shoemaker *1300 Penn Words* 40 = name used for husband.
        1956 Hall *Coll* I was married in eighteen eighty-six. My man was seventy-three
        year old when he died.

many's the, mony's the, monies a *phr* Many a. [OED *many* adj/pron A1c 'in
predicative use, usually with inversion of subject, now chiefly in *many's the time*'
13006→, now regional or colloquial]

ULST.: 1838 McIlwham *McIlwham Papers* 8 Mony's the time I counted on yer bein'
        far abune an Elder.
        1880 Patterson *Antrim/Down Glossary* 66 *many's the time* = many a time.
        1920 McCallin *Fireside Tales* 12 There's manys the one among ye, with a
        bigger reputation than his for smartness, not able to claim great brags in that
        direction.
        1920 McCallin *Ulster Plenishing* 6 I've witnessed manys the scene o' grief in
        my time, but never any like when that crather lifted up his han' an' gave out a
        cry from the depths o' despair.
        1925 McKay *Mourne Folk* 55 Many's the thorn I took out of his wee fut, an'
        many's the time I put him in my bed til I would patch his bits of breeks.
        c1982 Clifford *Poems* 1 And then when at last comes the night o' the Churn' /
        There'll be singin' and dancin' and many's a turn.
        2000 Fenton *Hamely Tongue* 134 Mony's the yin wud'a put it in their poaket
        an niver let on.

U.S.:   1976 Carter *Little Tree* 29 Granpa said he had many's the time seen that same
        kind of thing, feelings taking over sense, make as big a fools out of people as it
        had ol' Rippitt.

massacre *n* (final syllable pronounced *-cree* [kri]) A massacre, killing. Hence *vb* To
massacre, kill. [DARE (at *massacre* n, vb) chiefly South, South Midland, old-
fashioned]

ULST.: 1860 Patterson *Belfast Provincialisms* 13.
        1881 Hart *Mere Irish* 79 It was about the time of the massacreeing in
        Cromwell's day that the best part of them went away from Ireland.
        1893 Bullock *Awkward Squad* 98 He said he trimbled where he stud to think
        o' the shockin' massacree that was intended.

1933 Foster *Tyrone among Bushes* 51 'Mother, for God's sake leave that book alone', she screamed. 'He'll massacree us if anythin' happens t'it.'
1936 White *Mrs Murphy* 84 Why, there's parties would have been massacreein' [one] another, day in, day out if it wasn't for me.

U.S.:   1899 Green *Virginia Word-Book* 233 If you do that he will massacree you.
1942 Hall *Phonetics* 79.

meach See **miche**

meeting *vbl n* A gathering of people for religious worship; a service of divine worship (in Ulster in the Presbyterian tradition; in the U.S. more generally applied in earlier times). See also **meeting house, Sunday-go-to-meeting.** [originally applied to services of Dissenters (as opposed to those of the Established Church) in the British Isles; OED *meeting* vbl n 3b, 1593→; DARE *meeting* n 1 'a religious service; an assembly for worship' chiefly Northeast, South Midland]

ULST.:   1886 Lyttle *Ballycuddy* 14 Whun the meetin' was ower the elders an' the committee men a' met in the seshin-room an' we had a terble scene.
1897 MacManus *Dhroll Donegal* 18 Sure where anondher the sun is the good of me goin' to prayer or meetin'.
c1910 Byers *Glossary* Presbyterian Churches are usually called 'Meeting-houses' and 'going to meetin'' means going to church.
1930 McCurry *Ulster Village* 141 He was tarrible fond of her, but all unknownst for she was 'meetin'', and wudn't cross a church doore to save her life.
1936 White *Mrs Murphy* 159 They tell me they find the farmers very hard to lift, but the farm-hands go to the meeting regler, both boys and girls.
1942 *Bangor Words* 53 = Presbyterian church or its service: 'I'm going to meeting'.
1953 Traynor *Donegal Glossary* 183 = the service in a Presbyterian church; hence a Presbyterian church.
c1955 Montgomery *Heard in Ulster* 83 = Presbyterian church or kirk service: 'Are ye goin' tae the meetin' the nicht?'; 'I haven't seen ye oot at the meetin' this while back'.

U.S.:   1789 *Big Pigeon Minutes* 3–4 if any Member shall Neglect theare attendance Two Church Meetings togeather shall be liable to the Churches Censher without rendering a reasonable satisfaction for the same.
1856 *Elijoy Minutes* 89 the Church met at Elijoy meting house & after Sermont they put the sacrement of till the next meting and all other business on the account of Sickness.
1859 Bartlett *Americanisms* 267 = a religious assembly, congregation. Among Methodists, Baptists, and Quakers, it is usual to say, 'we are going to meeting', when speaking of going to their church or place of worship.
1909 Payne *Word-list East Alabama* 348 = divine service, specifically, protracted services: 'When are you goin to have your meetin?'
1913 Kephart *Our Sthn High* 239 She actually changed her eyes to jet black whenever she went to 'meetin'' or other public gatherings.
1956 Hall *Coll* He got a preacher from over in Tennessee to come up there and hold a meeting.
1982 Ginns *Snowbird Gravy* 146 They would dress up to go to meeting.

meeting house, meeting hoose *n* A house of worship, in Ulster in the Presbyterian tradition, in the U.S. more generally applied historically but now confined mainly to Quaker houses of worship. [OED *meeting house* n 2a, 1632→]

ULST.:   **1737** Murray *Letter* I hea 20 Pund a Year for being a Clark to York Meeting-House.

1825 Bowden *Portaferry Congregation* 8 Mr. Sinclair came and poled the Congregation and alowed that Mr. Moreland was fearly elected and allowed him to be our constant suply untill ordaind. Mr. Galaway to prevent that locked the Meeting house and carried away the key—on the prinsaple that his father and Mr. Armstrong took out the joint lease and trust and his father wass the survivor.

1886 Lyttle *Ballycuddy* 7 A think it wuz a wheen big men aboot the Presbytery that passed the law that ye shudnae play ony sort o' instrayments in the meetin'-hooses.

1902 McIlroy *Druid's Island* 96 Why, she nae sooner got her heid inside the meetin'-hoose do'r than she set aff up the aisle, an' a ragiment o' sojers wouldnae hae kep' her back.

c1910 Byers *Glossary* = a non-Episcopal place of worship: 'Does he go to Church?' 'No, he goes to the meetin''.

c1955 Montgomery *Heard in Ulster* 83 = a Presbyterian church: 'I'll see ye at the meetin-hoose the morra'.

1983 Marshall *Drumlister* 124 Here is their meeting-house, the place / Where Sabbath prayer is made.

2000 Fenton *Hamely Tongue* 131 = usually a Presbyterian church.

U.S.:   **1755** McCullough *Journal* (12 July) y^e fort at y^e meting hous Was begun July y^e 30.

1794 *Big Pigeon Minutes* 16 the Members appointed to look out a place for a meeting house.

1801 Osborn *Diary* (14 Jun) I went with Mr. Aikens & his family to their Mathodist meeting house it was a sasiety meeting.

1856 *Elijoy Minutes* 89 the Church met at Elijoy meting house & after Sermont they put the sacrement of till the next meting and all other business on the account of Sickness.

1859 Bartlett *Americanisms* 267 = a place of worship of Methodists, Quakers, etc.

1883 Zeigler and Grosscup *Heart of Alleghanies* 263 The fields and meadows were vacant; and the mountaineers, observant of the Sabbath, were all within their homely dwellings, or assembled at the meeting-house.

1899 Green *Virginia Word-Book* 235 = any house of worship.

1961 Medford *History Haywood Co* 30 Within a few years after the first settlements had been made in this county, two or three little log 'meetin' houses' had been built by the Baptist denomination.

mend *vb*, **mend up** *vb phr* To make better; improve in health, recover one's health after illness, regain weight. [OED *mend* 5a 'to restore to health, cure, heal' now archaic and regional, 'to regain health, recover from sickness'; DOST *mend* vb 7 'to restore to health, cure, heal; to be restored to health, be cured, to recover' late 14th century→; DARE *mend* vb 1 'to improve in health; to recover from illness' chiefly South, South Midland]

ULST.:   **1817** Orr *Posthumous Works* Deceiv'd by hope, they thought till now to mend, / But he thought lang in death's embrace to sleep.

1920 Doyle *Ballygullion* 77 I'll dhrop over to the widow's in the mornin' an'
tell her you're mendin' fast.
1923 Lutton *Montiaghisms* 29 = to recover from sickness, to heal.
1933 MacNeill *Reverence Listens* 43 I put him to his bed, and gi'en him gruel
and slops, and he mended bravely.
1953 Traynor *Donegal Glossary* 183 = (1) to cure, heal; to make better,
improve; (2) to improve in health.
1981 Pepper *Ulster-English Dict* 50 Our bootmaker's awful well mended for he
was at death's dure.

U.S.:   1834 Crockett *Narrative* 130 At the end of two weeks I began to mend
without the help of a doctor, or of any doctor's means.
1909 Payne *Word-list East Alabama* 348 = to improve in health; also in the
phrase 'on the mend'.
1974 Fink *Bits Mt Speech* 16 = improve physically: 'He's mending slowly'.

miche, meach, mich, mitch, mitche *vb* To play truant from school. [< Old French
muchier 'to hide; skulk, lurk'; OED *miche* vb 1a 'to play truant' 1580→, now
dialectal]

ULST.:   1880 Patterson *Antrim/Down Glossary* 68 = to play truant.
1921 Doyle *Ulster Childhood* 99 I loved the Spring ploughing, and 'mitched'
from school many a Spring day to follow the plough.
c1955 Montgomery *Heard in Ulster* 82 = being absent from school without
permission: 'He was caught mitchin. He's in for it'.
1964 Braidwood *Ulster/Elizabethan English* 103 All over Ireland schoolboys
still *mich*. The original meaning of the word seems to be 'to skulk, to lurk
stealthily', and explains the long-puzzling phrase in Hamlet, *miching Malicho*,
'sneaking, skulking mischief'.
1983 Marshall *Drumlister* 105 Up in heaven do kiddies play, / Or go to
school, or mitch, or run away?

U.S.:   1870 *Notes* 56 Genuine English of Shakespeare's time ... is the participle
applied to the boy who played truant and good Scotch, we suppose, is the
'scutching' he received for his 'miching' ... 'Recess' as we say now the young
'micher' of fifty years ago called 'little noon'.
1944 Wilson *Word-list* 46 = to get around stealthily, to slink, to appear
dishonest or shifty: 'I seed a fellow *meachin'* round up the cove like he might 'a'
been a revenuer'.

might can, might could *auxiliary vb phr* These and similar combinations of
auxiliary verbs express tentativeness and indirectness. In the U.S. many more
combinations are found than in Ulster. Cf **will can**. [cf SND *can* vb[1] III.2; DARE (at
may B) chiefly South, South Midland]

ULST.:   1988 Braidwood *Notes, might could*.
1997 Montgomery *Ulster File* I might could do something for her, but you
maybe should take her home.
2000 Fenton *Hamely Tongue* 132 *micht could* = may/might be able to.

U.S.:   1909 Payne *Word-list East Alabama* 349 Go to see Mr. Smith. He might can
tell you.
1970 Foster *Walker Valley* 62 One of them might could tell a man where her
grave is at.
1974–75 McCracken *Logging* 9:3 If I think about it, I might could tell you.

1995 Montgomery *Coll* I might can go with you tomorrow.
1999 *GSMNPOHP* 1:5 If you folks don't have a cow barn, you might ought to build one.

mind, mine

1 *n* Attention, heed, thought. [DARE *mind* B2 'attention, heed' chiefly South, South Midland]
ULST.:   **1942** *Bangor Words* 54 = thought: 'I gave no mind to it'.
U.S.:   **1923** Taylor *Snake Co Talk* 214 = attention: 'He wouldn't give no mind to me'.
    1974 Fink *Bits Mt Speech* 19 Don't pay them no mind.
    1982 Ginns *Snowbird Gravy* 136 Nobody paid it no mind.

2 *vb* To remember, recall. [OED *mind* vb 2 'to remember, have in one's memory' 1382→, now archaic and dialect; DOST *mind* vb 2 'to remember, have in mind' 1661→; SND *mind* vb 1 'to remember, recollect, call to mind'; DARE *mind* C2 'to remember' especially South, South Midland]
ULST.:   **1880** Patterson *Antrim/Down Glossary* 68 = to remember: 'I don't mind much about my father bein' killed'.
    1897 McIlroy *Lint in Bell* Wur rooted an' grundet in the faith—har'ly minin' a time whun we were outside the fold.
    1942 *Bangor Words* 54 Oh, I mind you rightly now, you used to live across the street.
    1953 Traynor *Donegal Glossary* 185 = to remember, recollect, bear in mind; recall: 'I don't mind when I was at the pictures'.
    1981 Pepper *Ulster-English Dict* 50 D'ye mine the day we all went up the Cavehill fir a picnic and it poured?
    1983 Marshall *Drumlister* 30 I mind them in the moonlight / Shearing at the corn.
    1990 McIntyre *Some Handlin'* 40 We all mind the day we went to the Folk Museum.
U.S.:   **c1765** Woodmason *Carolina Backcountry* 154 If any of You should fall out about Your Calves and Your Kine, You be sure to mind and think upon Abraham.
    1860 *Week* 122 I mind I was powerful sick then, and I do believe, Mister, I should 'a' died but for some truck the Gineral gave me, God bless him!
    1923 (in **1952** Mathes *Tall Tales* 8) I mind it jest like hit was yisterday.
    1974 Fink *Bits Mt Speech* 16 Don't you mind the day he came?

3 *vb* To remind, bring to the mind or notice. [OED *mind* vb 1a 1340→, now rare; DOST *mind* vb 1 'to put (one) in mind of (something), to remind' 1524→; SND *mind* vb 4 'to remind, to bring to one's notice, to jog one's memory'; DARE *mind* C1 'to remind' chiefly South, South Midland]
ULST.:   **1880** Patterson *Antrim/Down Glossary* 68 = to remind: 'Now mind me of that to-morrow'.
    1893 Bullock *Awkward Squad* 96 I wus minded to pass around the word to stale up to the walls an' have a peep.
    1953 Traynor *Donegal Glossary* 185 Mind me of that another time.
U.S.:   **1899** Green *Virginia Word-Book* 282 = remind: 'He minded me of my purpose'.
    1942 Hall *Phonetics* 53 He minds me of you.

1963 Edwards *Gravel* 122 I'm minded of the time when I was a strip of a boy and Pap was alive.

4 *vb* To watch, be aware of, give heed to. [OED *mind* vb 6 'to admonish, recall to, bethink oneself, ponder'; DOST *mind* vb 2b 'to direct the attention to, give heed to']

ULST.:   **1880** Patterson *Antrim/Down Glossary* 68 = to observe: 'See, d'ye mind the way she's walkin'?'
1885 Lyttle *Robin Gordon* 27 Na, A'll no min' it this mornin'.
1934 Cavanagh *Dunleary Legend* 13 Them wee weans takes a dale of minding.
1942 *Bangor Words* 54 = attend: 'Mind the baby for me'.
1953 Traynor *Donegal Glossary* 185 Do you mind the way he's talking?
1983 Pepper *Ulster Knowledge* 37 Today's variants of this involve heeding injunctions to 'Mind the dog' and 'Mind the tar'.
1993 Montgomery *Barnish* 60 'Mind yoursel'' = Look after yourself.

U.S.:   **1834** Crockett *Narrative* 39 I reported to Col. Coffee the news. He didn't seem to mind my report a bit, and this raised my dander higher than ever.
1939 Hall *Coll* I heard him a-hollerin'. He called for me to come up there and mind the coons up the tree.

miscall, misca *vb* To abuse verbally, malign, call names. [OED *miscall* 1 'to call by a bad name, to call (a person) names; to revile, abuse, malign' 1449→, now archaic and regional; DOST *miscall* vb 1 'to call by a bad name, to call (a person) names, revile, abuse verbally' 1598→]

ULST.:   **1753** *Scotch Poems* 369 Why do the POETS, ane and a', / Sae fiercely on the criticks fa': / Misca' them fae, that nane can pass, / Without his share of goose and ass.
1921 O'Neill *More Songs of Glens* 11 Never think I'm wantin' to miscall the race o' men, / There' not a taste o' harm in them, the cratures!
1935 Megaw *Carragloon* 86 I promised ye I would make it up with Sophie for miscallin' me.
2000 Fenton *Hamely Tongue* 132 *misca* = call names: 'misca'd hir for a' the trails an tramps in the country'.

U.S.:   **1899** Green *Virginia Word-Book* 240 = to give an unworthy name or character to, berate, revile.

misdoubt, misdoot *vb* To have doubts about, distrust, fear (that something is true), suspect (the veracity of), disbelieve. [cf Middle French *mesdoubter* 'to doubt, suspect'; OED *misdoubt* vb 1a 'to have doubts as to the existence, truth, or reality of (a thing)', 1b 'to doubt (that something will happen, will be done, etc.)' now chiefly U.S. regional 1640→, 2a 'to fear or suspect the existence or occurrence of (something undesirable or evil' 1550→, obsolete, 2b 'to fear or suspect (that something is or will be the case)' now chiefly British regional 1596→, 2c 'to suspect (a person or thing) of doing or being something' 1599→, obsolete, 3a 'to have misgivings, suspicions, or forebodings in regard to (something)' 1570→, 4b 'to have doubts about the character, honesty, etc., of, to be mistrustful or suspicious of' 1592→, now chiefly Scottish and northern Irish English; DOST *misdoubt* vb 1605→; SND *misdoubt* 1 'to doubt, disbelieve, suspect the veracity of, distrust' 1818→, 2 'to anticipate as a likelihood, to be afraid that, to suspect (that a thing is so)' 1818→;

DARE *misdoubt* vb 'to doubt; to fear, suspect, feel sure; to distrust, be suspicious of' especially South, South Midland]

ULST.:   1880 Patterson *Antrim/Down Glossary* 69 *misdoubt* = to doubt, to suspect.
1895 MacManus *Leadin' Road* 106 Betwixt ourselves, I'm much misdoubtin' that statement.
1920 Doyle *Ballygullion* 76 There was a desperate lot av springs an' joints about the things, an' I misdoubted but that Pether would do it little good.
1939 Paterson *Country Cracks* 28 He died on Carnagore in sight of his burial, an' I misdoubt me if that wusn't the greatest funeral that iver was.
1953 Traynor *Donegal Glossary* 186 = (1) to disbelieve, regard with suspicion; (2) to suspect, fear, apprehend; (3) to be mistaken: 'If I dinna misdoot ...'
1991 O'Kane *You Don't Say* 94 = to doubt, to think otherwise: 'I hear John was drunk again last night and I wouldn't misdoubt it'.

U.S.:   1909 Payne *Word-list East Alabama* 349 = to suspect, doubt.
1979 Carpenter *Walton War* 170 I misdoubt I could ever draw a free breath if I had to stay shut up in a town.
1994 Montgomery *Coll* I misdoubt that she could do that.

mitch, mitche See **miche**

mizzle

1 *n* (also **mizzling**) A fine, mist-like rain. [< perhaps from Dutch *misel, mysel* 'drizzling rain'; OED *mizzle* n[1] 1483→; DARE *mizzle* n 'a very fine misty rain' chiefly South, South Midland]

ULST.:   1880 Patterson *Antrim/Down Glossary* 69 = (1) a drizzle; (2) to drizzle, to run away, to disappear.
1959 Gregory *Ulster Ballads* 21 I mind, when I was a slip o' a wean, / A-waddlin' tae school, in the sun an' rain / (An' mitchin', odd whiles, 'gainst the master's rules).
1981 Pepper *Ulster-English Dict* 51 I'd left my umbrella in to be restrung, and there I was, caught in the mizzle.
1981 McClean *Ulster Words V* 2 *mizzle* = light rain.
1990 Todd *Words Apart* 116 Sure that's not rain. It's not even a mizzle.

U.S.:   1899 Green *Virginia Word-Book* 285 = fine rain.
1953 Randolph and Wilson *Down in Holler* 265 = a very light shower.
1976 Garber *Mountain-ese* 58 It ain't raining much, jist a mizzlin' uv fallin' weather.

2 *vb* To rain in fine, mist-like drops. [OED *mizzle* vb[1] 'to rain in very fine drops; drizzle' dialect; DARE *mizzle* vb[1] 'to rain in very fine drops' chiefly South, South Midland]

ULST.:   1953 Traynor *Donegal Glossary* 187 = to rain in very fine drops, drizzle.
c1955 Montgomery *Heard in Ulster* 83 There's a mizzlin' rain ootside.
1990 McIntyre *Some Handlin'* 40 = raining lightly: 'You would soon be drookit the more it's only mizzlin', so put on your coat'.
1991 O'Kane *You Don't Say* 95 = to rain lightly: 'It was mizzlin' when I came in'.

U.S.:   1843 Hall *New Purchase* 123 The rain kept mizzling away.
1952 Wilson *Folk Speech NC* 565–66 = to rain in fine or foglike drops.
1973 Davis *'Pon My Honor* 99 = drizzle, rain with small drops.
1974 Fink *Bits Mt Speech* 16 They was a mizzling sort of rain.

moiley, moily, moulleen, moyley, moylie (all only in Ulster), **mooley, muley** (both only in the U.S.) *n* A hornless cow, goat or ox. [of Celtic origin (cf Irish *maolaí* or Scottish Gaelic *maolag/maolán* (from *maol* 'bald, hornless'); OED *moiley* adj 1 Scottish and Anglo-Irish, *muley* now chiefly U.S.; SND *moyley*; DARE *muley* adj widespread except Atlantic Coast; the form *muley* is probably U.S. folk etymology from similarity of headshape to a mule]

ULST.:   **1880** Patterson *Antrim/Down Glossary* 69 *moily* = a hornless cow.
1904 Byers *Sayings of Ulster* 39 Of a constant talker some one may allege 'He'd talk the horns off a moily cow'.
1937 Rowley *Tales of Mourne* 216 My mother was a widow; she had a nice bit of a farm up in Moneydarragh, an' she had a wee moiley cow was the apple of her eye.
1942 *Bangor Words* 55 = bare head, no horns (a moyley goat or a moyley cow is hornless).
c1955 Montgomery *Heard in Ulster* 82 *moily* = a cow naturally without horns, or a moily goat.
1959 Gregory *Ulster Ballads* 7 Plaze dinnae let him lift wee stones / Tae clod the gander or the goat, / ... Or dandher near the moylie cows, ; Or roanies, / wi' the crumpled horns.
1969 Braidwood *Ulster Dial Lex* 31–32 The word is derived from Irish *moilin*, 'a hornless cow', from *maoile* 'baldness, bareness'. I am informed by Dr. W. N. Scott, Assistant Librarian in the University, that the term 'moiley' is applied to a specific breed of cattle, the 'Irish moiled', formerly wide-spread in Ireland. It was a coarse-framed, deep-bodied, short-legged, naturally hornless type, coloured red, red and white, or red roan, and was capable of producing a high yield of milk.
2000 Fenton *Hamely Tongue* 134 *moily* = a hornless cow (originally of a special breed, but used generally).

U.S.:   (also **muley cow**)
1909 Payne *Word-list East Alabama* 351 *muley*(-*cow*) = a hornless cow.
1930 Shoemaker *1300 Penn Words* 40 *muley* = a hornless, or dehorned cow.
1962 Dykeman *Tall Woman* 48 Come on, Robert, let's get our little muley-cow to work again.
1968 Vincent *Best Stories* 44 This cow ain't got no horns. She's a muley.
1970 Justus *Tales* Missy, the muley cow, was a great pet of Mammy's.

monie's a, mony's the See **many's the**

mooley See **moiley**

mortial, mortyal *adj/adv* Mortal(ly); extreme(ly). [OED *mortial* (at *mortal*) 18th century→; DARE especially southern Appalachians, New England]

ULST.:   **1840** Boyce *Shandy Maguire* 10 I'll niver open my lips to mortial brathin about it.
1880 Patterson *Antrim/Down Glossary* 70 = very, or very great: 'mortial cold.'
1920 Doyle *Ballygullion* 12 'It was', sez I, 'mortial bad'. *Ibid.* 23 It seemed such a mortial pity to let the poor man walk into such a man-thrap wi' his eyes shut.
1928 McKay *Oul' Town* 50 It's a 'mortial' cowld morning, said Paddy, 'draw up yer chair t' the fire an' take a hate (heat).'

1983 Marshall *Drumlister* 22 There's wans in other parts, I've heered, / That mortyal big that you're afeerd.

U.S.:   **1914** England *Rural Locutions* 76 *mortial* = very.

moss *n* A bog or swamp. [< Middle English *mosse* < Old English *mos*; OED *moss* n[1] 1a 'a bog, swamp ... especially a peatbog' c1000→, now chiefly Scottish, English regional (northern) and Irish English; DOST *moss* n 1 'a marsh, bog, a tract of soft, wet land' 1710→, 2 'a bog from which peats are dug' 1714→]

ULST.:   **c1614** McClellan *Assignment* [Be] it kend till all men be thir present Letters Me Sir Robert Macclelland of Bombie Knyght To haiff sett [and] in tak and assedatioun lettin Lyke as I be thir presents settsSVC and in tak and assedatioun for the dewtie efterspecifyit ... to my weill beloved Gawin Kelso in Holywood in Irland his air assignayes and subtennents all and haill fyve scoir of aikers of land of gud plewadge and pasturage without ether boge or moss of my land of the Haberdashors thair proportioun.

1825 McHenry *Hearts of Steel* 81 Their way lay through the turf-ground, or *moss* as it is called in that country, for about a mile and a half, in traversing which their journey was greatly lengthened by the frequent windings they had to make to keep clear of the swamps.

1880 Patterson *Antrim/Down Glossary* 70 = a peat bog.

1900 Given *Poems* 150 How soople we did run, / Jamie lad, / Tae jump binks in the moss, / Whar we got both coup an' soss, / An' oor claes shun lost their gloss.

1931 Anonymous *Holiday* 31 I've sailed in a cart to the moss, and seen peats cut from the bink and footed it and fir hagged.

U.S.:   **1930** Shoemaker *1300 Penn Words* 41 = a swamp or bog.

moulleen See **moiley**

mountain dew *n* Home-made, illict poteen or illicit whiskey. [OED dates term only from 1816 and has no citations from Ireland; SND (at *mountain* n 1(4)) 'Highland whisky, esp. that prepared in an illicit still'; DARE scattered, but more frequent South, South Midland]

ULST.:   **1824** Moore *Captain Rock* (in **1997** Share *Slanguage* 191) On the third evening of my stay, however, the influence of the genial 'mountain dew', which my Reverend host rather bountifully dispensed, so far prevailed over my fears and my prudence, that I sallied forth, alone.

1895 MacManus *Leadin' Road* 182 The inmates, all unconscious of the impending danger, are commemmorating the successful brewing of the last 'run' of mountain dew.

1897 McIlroy *Lint in Bell* 141 Wonderful courage is born of a few glasses of 'Mountain Dew'.

1910 Joyce *English in Ireland* 296 = a fanciful and sort of pet name for pottheen whiskey. Usually made in the *mountains*.

1930 Shiels *Mt Dew* 96 I've all the money I want—I made it, thousands of pounds, and lost thousands—in Mountain Dew.

1942 *Bangor Words* 55 = name for poteen (because it is usually made in the mountains).

1956 Bell *Orange Lily* 50–51 In a society where the cottier farming six to ten acres of indifferent soil was as likely as not to open a bare cupboard in the morning, the liquor he made on the mountain was made to be sold. The purchasers were strong farmers and agents buying for the gentry 'who had a fancy, a sort of pride in saying to their guests, "I can give you a drop of the mountain dew."'

c1982 Clifford *Poems* 9 The drink had been his special care; / His guidin' motto – 'Drink tae spare', / Sweet mountain dew frae Alec's hill / A barrel frae his ain wee still.

U.S.:   **1913** Morley *Carolina Mts* 66 For corn is not only the principal food of the mountaineer, but supplies as well that important beverage, variously known as 'corn-juice', 'moonshine', 'mountain-dew', 'blockade', 'brush whiskey', and in the outer world, 'corn-whiskey', which is extracted from the grain and surreptitiously distributed.

1962 Williams *Metaphor Mt Speech* 12 Good 'mountain dew', the kind made by expert hands and aged in a charred white oak keg, will make 'a preacher lay his Bible down', 'a man wink at his mother-in-law', and 'the lamb and the lion lay down together'.

1982 Maples *Memories* 72 When the moonshiner heard the shotgun beller somewhere on a mountainside or in a holler, he knew it was time to get his running legs, or to try to hide some of his mountain dew or some of his still before the sheriff got there.

moyley, moylie, muley See **moiley**

N

narvish See **nervish**

nary *adj, pron* Not a (one), none, any. [< *ne'er a*, reduction of *never a*; OED *nary* A adj 1 'neither; not a, not a single; no' B adv 'not, not at all, in no way; neither; not even' chiefly U.S., English regional (south-west) and Irish English]

ULST.:   **1934** MacGill *Glen of Carra* 37 Nary a one knows.
1953 Traynor *Donegal Glossary* 194 = not a one; no one.

U.S.:   **1837** Sherwood *Georgia Provincialisms* 120 *nary one* = neither.
1895 Edson and Fairchild *Tenn Mts* 376 I never seen nary 'thout that wasn't one.
1939 Hall *Coll* We hunted all night, till ten o'clock the next morning, [but] never struck nary track.
1978 Montgomery *White Pine Coll* X-2 I never was mistreated not nary a minute by nobody.

near cut *n* A short cut. [OED (at *cut* n II 1614→, still common in Scotland; SND (at *near* II 1(4)) 'a short cut, a quick or more direct way'; DARE *near cut* n 'a shortcut' chiefly South Midland]

ULST.:   **c1890** Lyttle *Daft Eddie* 4 Late wayfarers, passing it as they crossed the country for a 'near-cut', had spoken frequently of flitting lights and weird forms seen moving to and fro.
1945 Murphy *Gullion's Foot* 71 A ghost can walk with one anywhere, but cannot cross a running stream. They say it is a bad thing to take near-cuts, pad (paths) across fields after the Big Hour, that is, midnight.
1948 Marshall *Planted by River* 111 Run to the house as fast as your feet can carry you. Take the near cut over the field, and make sure you're not seen.
1953 Traynor *Donegal Glossary* 194 = a short cut in journey or method.
1975 Murphy *You're Talking* 65 Never go the near-cut while you have the hard, level road going round.

U.S.:   **1805** (in **2004** Hartley *Lewis and Clark Lexicon* 170) I took a near cut and at night came out ahead of the party.
1956 Hall *Coll* [My grandfather] thought he'd take a near cut through this laurel thicket, and he didn't know what he was getting into.
1973 *GSMNP*-4:1:5 Now a lot of times we would take what we called near cuts, you know, through the woods rather than walking all the way around the highway road.

nearder, neardest *adj/adv* Nearer, nearest. [OED *nearder/neardest* (at *near* adv²); DARE (at *near* adj/adv B) chiefly South, South Midland]

ULST.:   **1861** Hume *Rabbin's Ollminick* 8 Ye wud think the fire's up there when its neardther home.
1906 MacDermott *Foughilotra* 67–68 It would be nearder truth till say that he, bein' sick an' not able till work, died of starvation an' wan' of care.
1935 Megaw *Carragloon* 78 'It's this way', says the beggar body, 'the cure lies nearder the disease nor folks thinks.'
2004 Fenton *Slaimish* Here A stan, / Back luckin noo tae nearder hichts, / Tae this waitin lan aroon me.

U.S.:   1871 Eggleston *Hoosier Schoolmaster* 76 I'd help stretch him to the neardest
            tree.
            1975 Gainer *Speech Mtneer* 14 You're nearer to the door than I am.

neb *n* The beak of a bird; the nose. Hence *vb* To be nosy. [< Middle English *nebbe*
< Old English *nebb*; OED *neb* n 1 'the beak or bill of a bird' c1000→, 2 'a person's
nose' c1000→, now chiefly Scottish, northern Irish English, and northern English;
SND *neb* n 1 'the beak or bill of a bird ... the nose(tip) of a person']
   ULST.:   1733 *North Country Grace* 29 Bless us free aw Witches and Warlocks, and aw
            lang nebbed Things that creeps intill Heather; but fre that exhorbitant Power
            of France, oh, deliver us!
            c1800 Thomson (in 1992 Scott and Robinson *Samuel Thomson* 96) An wifes,
            forsooth, wi' nebs like snipes, / Stan' out frae cheeks, like scrapit tripes.
            1880 Patterson *Antrim/Down Glossary* 72 = the nose, a bird's bill.
            1891 Simmons *Armagh Words and Phrases* 13 = the nose, or beak, or a point.
            1932 Quinn *McConaghy's Money* 21 Will ye stop pushin' yer neb in where it's
            not wanted?
            1953 Traynor *Donegal Glossary* 195 = (1) a bird's beak; (2) the tip or point of
            anything.
            c1955 Montgomery *Heard in Ulster* 89 = human nose: 'Keep yer neb oot o'
            my affairs'.
            1991 O'Kane *You Don't Say* 97 = the nose, the face generally: 'She has a right
            neb on her today' (i.e. she is looking none too pleased).
            2000 Fenton *Hamely Tongue* 138 *pit yer neb in* = interfere in (a conversation,
            verbal dispute, etc.)
   U.S.:   1834 Downing *Life Andrew Jackson* 70 Hit him in the pudding bag, make a
            pen of his neb, lush his muzzle with pokeberry juice.
            1930 Shoemaker *1300 Penn Words* 43 = the nose, the beak of a bird.
            1950 Dalton *Wordlist* 23 Keep your neb out of things that don't consarn you.

nebby *adj* Inquisitive, impertinent, nosy. [OED *nebby* adj 'interfering, inquisitive,
nosy' chiefly Scottish, Irish English (northern) and English regional (northern);
SND *nebbie* adj 2b 'cheeky, impertinent ... inquisitive, nosey'; DARE chiefly
Pennsylvania]
   ULST.:   1891 Simmons *Armagh Words and Phrases* 13 = interfering, impudent.
            1929 O'Donnell *Adrigoole* 150 It's that nebby Betty that's behind it all.
            1953 Traynor *Donegal Glossary* 195 = impertinent, ill-natured.
            c1955 Montgomery *Heard in Ulster* 89 = nosey, prying into other people's
            business.
            1981 Pepper *Ulster-English Dict* 52 She's terrible nebby.
            1991 O'Kane *You Don't Say* 97 = cross-looking, possessed of a threatening
            countenance.
   U.S.:   1930 Shoemaker *1300 Penn Words* 42 = curious, inquisitive.
            1931 Maxfield *Speech SW Penn* 20 = to be nosey, or inquisitive.
            1953 Ashcom *Lg Bedford Penn* 251 = inquisitive.
            1982 McCool *Pittsburghese* 25 = nosey, as in 'Aunt Edie is so nebby nobody
            can stand her'.

need *vb* (followed by the past-participle form of a verb rather than by a verbal noun or infinitive, i.e. with elliptical *to be*). [cf SND *need* vb I 4; DARE *need* vb 2 followed by a past participle without *to be*, chiefly Midland, especially Pennsylvania]

ULST.:   **1997** Robinson *Grammar* 129 It is sometimes observed that a typical 'Ulsterism' is to say *thon fluir needs cleaned,* rather than 'that floor needs cleaning'. However, in Ulster-Scots the more usual expression of this would be *thon fluir cud dae wi a clean.*
2000 Graham *Bread and Butter* In addition Mr Mallon pointed to a number of urgent questions which he believes need addressed.
2003 Erwin *Pressure Grows* 11 The Human Rights Commission is broken. It needs fixed.
2003 *Tourist Board* The street needed swept and the leisure centre needed decoration and a good clean.

U.S.:   **1954** Harder *Coll* Does my hair need combed?
1978 Montgomery *White Pine Coll* IV-4 They started before sunup and worked to after sundown, if you had a job that needed finished.
1982 McCool *Pittsburghese* 26 *needs* = used for 'needs to be', as in 'The car needs washed'.
1986 Huskey *Sugarlands* 5 There were men and women living in the Sugarlands with talent and the ability to do most anything needed done in the community.

needcessity *n* Necessity. [OED *needcessity* n 1 'necessity, need, an instance of this' 1562→, 2 (in plural) 'needs, necessities, indispensable things' originally Scottish, now chiefly Irish English (regional); SND *needcessity* n 1 'necessity, need' 1706→, 2 'necessities'; DARE *needcessity* n Scots folk etymology for *necessity*, chiefly South Midland]

ULST.:   **1825** McHenry *Hearts of Steel* 87 He was sorry to part us, but *needcessity* gar'd him do it again' his wull.
1861 Hume *Rabbin's Ollminick* 4 If there's any needcessity to, Ah'll go up in a Balloon, an' look roun' me in the sky;—there's noan o' the flyin' machines can houl' the ken'le t' that.
1880 Patterson *Antrim/Down Glossary* 72 = necessity.
1895 MacManus *Leadin' Road* 112 There'll be a'most no needcessity for givin' ye the stick any more.
1953 Traynor *Donegal Glossary* 195 = the necessary things.

U.S.:   **1795** Brown *Journal* 307 He was then Riduced to the needcessity of take his shelter on a high Stump where he stood and wated his fate.
1871 Eggleston *Hoosier Schoolmaster* 101 I find myself under the necessity— need-cessity the Rev. Mr. Bosaw would call it—of rising to explain.
1924 (in **1952** Mathes *Tall Tales* 32) They wouldn't be no needcessity of that, Mister.
1943 Erskine *Adventures* 203 When they made up their stock they peddled it from door to door and traded what they could at the store for tobacco, snuff, salt, cloth, and other 'needcessities'.

nervish, narvish *adj* Nervous. [OED *nervish* adj 'nervous, anxious, agitated' 1760→; SND *nervish* adj, 1825→; DARE *nervish* chiefly South Midland]

ULST.:   **1879** Lyttle *Paddy McQuillan* 17 When we went tae the coort, A felt mysel' a bit nervish an' floostered like.

1884 McFadyen and Hepburn *Lays and Legends* 22 'Lord pardon ye, Barney!' groaned Shelah in fright, / As trimblin' an' narvish she gripped at the pillion / An' Barney, who acted in front as postillion.
1902 McIlroy *Druid's Island* 77 He was a thocht nervish at the beginnin', a'though he made a winnerful han' o' his discoorse.
1920 McCallin *Fireside Tales* 48–49 She fell into one narvish dwam afther another, an' cut all the capers o' what they call the high-sthrikes.
1953 Traynor *Donegal Glossary* 195 *nervish, narvish.*

U.S.: **1904–07** Kephart *Notebooks* 2:475 Of course, I'm weak yit and right nervish. Old Uncle Bobbie Tuttle's got a pone come up on his side; looks like he might drap off, him bein' weak and right narvish and sick with a head swimmin'.
1919 Combs *Word-list South* 34 *narvish, nervish.*

nicker, nicher, nigher *vb* Of a horse: to neigh, whinny, especially at feeding time; of a person: to laugh, snigger. Hence *n* Such a sound. [*nick*, variant of *neigh* + -*er* frequentative suffix; OED *nicker* vb 1 'of a horse, donkey, etc.: to neigh' 1618→, 2 'to laugh loudly or shrilly; to snicker' chiefly Scottish and northern dialect; SND *nicher*; DARE widespread except Northeast, Great Lakes, less frequent South Atlantic; LAUSC Midland]

ULST.: **1804** Orr *Poems* 79 The roof re-echoes ev'ry nicher, / An' ev'ry chorus.
1880 Patterson *Antrim/Down Glossary* 72 *nicker* = to neigh.
1884 McFadyen and Hepburn *Lays and Legends* 21 Jist then they heard such a wil' nicherin' an' neighin', / They knew that some horse was convaynient at hand.
1923 Lutton *Montiaghisms* 30 *nicker* = to neigh; also a loud laugh.
1942 *Bangor Words* 57 *nicher, nigher* = a short sharp laugh, to whinney like a horse: 'He let a nicher out of him'.
1953 Traynor *Donegal Glossary* 196 *nicker* = (1) of persons: neigh, whinny; (2) to snigger, laugh in a suppressed way.
c1955 Montgomery *Heard in Ulster* 90 'What er ye nickerin' at?' is sometimes sarcastically said to anyone who is laughing.
2000 Fenton *Hamely Tongue* 139 *nicher* = (of a horse) whinny, snicker: 'It's a poor horse'll no nicher whun it sees coarn' = said in defence of a roving eye.

U.S.: **1899** Green *Virginia Word-Book* 298 = to make the sound of a horse, to neigh.
1924 (in **1952** Mathes *Tall Tales* 47) Sure enough in a few minutes four lank horsemen were dismounting at the gate amid much nickering of horses and yapping of hounds.
1949 Kurath *Word Geog East US* 42 From the Virginia Piedmont *nicker* has spread westward all the way to the Ohio Valley ... and southward in the Blue Ridge and the Appalachians to Georgia. *Nicker* now dominates this vast area.

nob, knab *n* A person of wealth or social standing, or a pretense to these. [origin uncertain, but possibly influenced by a shortening of *noble* or *nobleman*; OED *nob* n[3] 'a person of some wealth or social distinction' 1676→]

ULST.: **1801** Bruce *Poems* [Glossary 5] *knab* = a rich man.
2000 Fenton *Hamely Tongue* 140 *nob* = a person of wealth or high social standing.

U.S.: **1930** Shoemaker *1300 Penn Words* 42 *nob* = fine, showy, swell looking.

nor *conj* Than. [OED *nor* conj² 1479→, chiefly Scottish, Irish English, U.S. regional, and English regional; DOST *nor* conj² 'than' 16th century→; SND *nor* conj² 'used after comparisons and words with similar constructions']

ULST.: **1630** Haldane *Letter* 137 The worst of it will be to trail a pick a few yeirs untill ye be able, and your body is abler for that nor it was.

1737 Murray *Letter* they wad get mere Money in ane Year for teechin a Letin Skulle, nor ye yer sell wad get for Three Years Preeching whar ye are.

1861 Hume *Rabbin's Ollminick* 14 Betther late thrive nor nivver do well.

1895 MacManus *Leadin' Road* 3 The divil—for it was no other—tempted them to agree one night that they could do worse nor buy a slip of a pig.

1900 Irvine *Lady Chimney Corner* 81 That's harder nor ye think.

1942 *Bangor Words* 57 = used in comparisons for 'than': 'It's mair nor middlin'; 'Mine's bigger nor yours'.

1953 Traynor *Donegal Glossary* 198 Not more nor a week ago.

1983 Marshall *Drumlister* 32 The deil a man in this townlan' / Wos claner raired nor me, / But I'm livin' in Drumlister / In clabber to the knee.

2000 Fenton *Hamely Tongue* 140 A wud rether nor oanythin A hadnae went.

U.S.: **1823** Cooper *Pioneers* 17 I have yarbs that will heal the wound quicker nor all his foreign 'intments.

1871 Eggleston *Hoosier Schoolmaster* 39 Don't I remember when he was poarer nor Job's turkey?

1872 Schele de Vere *Americanisms* 511 = in New England frequently substituted for the proper word *than*: 'Better nor a thousand of them were killed'.

1878 Burt *Dialects* 413 The Pennsylvanian often uses *nor* for *than* after a comparative adjective: 'One thing is more *nor* another'.

1975 Gainer *Speech Mtneer* 14 He's a better fiddler nor me.

not at oneself See **at oneself**

notion *n* A fancy or inclination, especially one for a person of the opposite sex. [OED *notion* n 8b 'a liking or affection for someone, esp. one of a romantic or sexual nature' 1789→, British regional (chiefly Scottish) and U.S. regional; cf SND *notion* n 1 'a liking or affection']

ULST.: **1840** Boyce *Shandy Maguire* 14 Sure, we thought ye hadn't the leaste notion at all of her, after all the abuse they give ye about her at the Lammas market!

1905 Marshall *Dial of Ulster* 125 = a fancy; a liking or inclination for.

1920 Doyle *Ballygullion* 78 Michael has a terrible notion av her now.

1953 Traynor *Donegal Glossary* 198 'to have or take a notion of or at' = to fall, to be in love with.

1991 O'Kane *You Don't Say* 99 = an amorous attraction, a hankering after someone of the opposite sex: 'I think he has a notion of the new nurse'.

2000 Fenton *Hamely Tongue* 141 (with *o*) fondness for; attraction towards: 'He haes a wile notion o that wee hizzy'; inclination.

U.S.: **1899** Green *Virginia Word-Book* 257 = a desire, inclination, intention, or sentiment, generally not very deep or rational; a caprice; a whim.

1902 *Pioneer Dial* 140 = liking or fancy: 'I've tuck a powerful notion to you'.

O

old Christmas *n* An alternative observance of Christmas, reflecting the date of the holiday as calculated according to the Julian (or Old Style) calendar, which was replaced by the more precise Gregorian (New Style) calendar in Britain and Ireland in 1752, at which time the date was moved ahead by eleven days. In some places the populace continued to observe Christmas according to the older calendar and associated the day with such miraculous events as the kneeling of livestock in the direction of Bethlehem at the stroke of midnight and the sudden blooming of flowers. The day was recognized in Ulster, but whether such signs were known there is unclear, and belief in them and observance of the holiday was brought by early settlers to the North American colonies. In some places in southern Appalachia the belief that the day was the true, sacred Christmas persisted well into the twentieth century. The observance has no connection, as its date of occurrence has suggested to some, with Twelfth Night or Epiphany. (For discussion see Chester Raymond Young, 'The Observance of Old Christmas in Southern Appalachia' in *An Appalachian Symposium*, ed. J. W. Williamson. Boone, N.C.: Appalachian State University, 1977). [DARE chiefly Mid Atlantic, South Midland]

ULST.:   **1863** Hume *Rabbin's Ollminick* 6 [Mon. Jennewerry 5] Oul' Chrissimis Day: They say it's more luckier nor the new one; but most o' the young ones knows nothin' about the oul' times afore the stile wos changed, an' the people lost their eleven days.

        1953 Traynor *Donegal Glossary* 201 *Old Christmas day* = January 6th.

U.S.:   **1895** Edson and Fairchild *Tenn Mts* 373 = January 6th. (The day is remembered by those who never heard of Twelfth Night or Epiphany.)

        1905 Miles *Spirit of Mts* 107 But he and Arth do not disagree about certain weather signs their mother had taught them when they were shirt-tail boys', signs about Groundhog Day, for example, and the Ruling Days, the twelve days from the twenty-fifth of December to Old Christmas, each of which rules the weather of a month of the coming year.

        1942 Thomas *Blue Ridge* 158–59 There are people who may never have heard of the Gregorian or Julian calendar, yet in keeping Old Christmas as they do on January 6th, they cling unwittingly to the Julian calendar of 46 B.C., introduced in this country in the earliest years. To them December 25th is New Christmas, according to the Gregorian calendar adopted in 1752. They celebrate the two occasions in a very different way. The old with prayer and carol-singing, the new with gaiety and feasting.

        1970 Adams *Appal Revisit* 46 One of the most beautiful superstitions was in connection with the celebration of Old Christmas, which occurs on January 6, the date on which Christmas occurred in early England before the calendar change in the 18th century to December 25. The folk believed that on the eve of Old Christmas, the elderberry bushes shot out their blossoms and that at midnight the cattle would kneel down in their stalls to pay homage to the Baby Jesus who had been born in a stable.

        1974 Betts and Walser *NC Folklore* 4 In 1752 England officially adopted the Gregorian calendar. Some people continued to celebrate Christmas according to the old Julian calendar, making their Ule holiday January 5. The tradition of Old

Christmas came to North Carolina with its English settlers. And although Old Christmas is no longer widely celebrated, the people of Rodanthe on the Outer Banks still have an observance of the original holiday. One feature of their celebration is the appearance of Old Buck, a fierce bull-like creature (really two men in a costure). Every year he cavorts about, trying to frighten the children.

on *prep* Used after a verb to express an occurrence that is unfortunate, harmful, disadvantageous, or beyond one's control (especially in phrase *die on*).

ULST.: **1930** McCurry *Ulster Village* 102 Well, sir, he niver done any good afther it. The cattle died on him one afther the other, an' that very day year the horse he was on missed his fut, an' he fell off it, an' broke his neck.
1953 Traynor *Donegal Glossary* 202 = against, to the disadvantage of.
1983 Marshall *Drumlister* 75 Calves died on me, too, in the springtime.
2000 Fenton *Hamely Tongue* 143 Somebody stole it on me; The car broke doon on me.

U.S.: **1931** Maxfield *Speech SW Penn* 20 His wife died on him.
1960 Campbell *Birth Natl Park* 60 Asked later about the health of 'Mrs. Henry Ford [= Wiley Oakley's daughter]', Wiley sadly announced, 'She died out on me.'
1979 Carpenter *Walton War* 172 When my cow up and died on me, hit wuz a main blow.

on- *prefix* Un-. (Note: some forms in *on-/un-* correspond to standard ones in *in-/im-*, e.g. *ondecent/undecent* = indecent, *onpossible/unpossible* = impossible). [OED *on-* prefix[4] frequent Middle English, early Modern English, and dialect variant of *un-*[1]; SND *on-* prefix[2] a formal variant of *un-*, now obsolete, with negative force, sometimes also corresponding to English reversive or privative prefixes *dis-* or *in-*, and chiefly used before adjectives or adverbs]

ULST.: **1860** Patterson *Belfast Provincialisms* 8 *oneasy, oninjured, onopened ...* = uneasy, uninjured, unopened.
1895 MacManus *Leadin' Road* He lived, an ondependent private gintleman, himself and his mother, for the rest of their days.
1978 Pepper *See Me* 16 And to emphasise how *on*-ward the people are, mention might be made of their insistence in substituting 'on' for 'in' at every opportunity.

U.S.: **1867** Lowell *Biglow Papers*, *U* [in the Yankee dialect] always becomes *o* in the prefix *un* (except *unto*).
1899 Green *Virginia Word-Book* 260 = a prefix, is *un*; as *ondo* (undo), *ondress* (undress), *ontie*: 'Don't you see your shoe is ontied?'
1909 Payne *Word-list East Alabama* 354 = un-. Common in such words as *onnatural, onlucky, oncivil*, etc.
1916 Combs *Old Early English* 294 *In, im,* and *un* are often used interchangeably ... *ingrateful*.

on account of *prep phr* Because (of); taking into consideration.

ULST.: **1879** Lyttle *Paddy McQuillan* 3 'Weel', sez he, 'on account o' the femily ye belang till, A'll trust ye.'
2000 Fenton *Hamely Tongue* 2 On accoont o wha ye ir, A'll let it drap.

U.S.: **1938** Rawlings *Yearling* 31 He ain't full weight right now, on account of his stomach bein' shrunk up.

onaisey, onaisy See **oneasy**

onbeknownst See **unbeknownst**

oncertain *adj* Uncertain.

ULST.:   **1893** Bullock *Awkward Squad* 16 'I've an ould blunderbuss in the corner yonder', said a voice in the back, 'that'll kill dead if she carries straight; but she's oncertain.'

U.S.:   **1999** Spencer *Memory Lane* I:10 Grandma was amused at how upset and oncertain he got one time about one applicant who had given him a note. This oncertain feeling probably lay in the fact that this fellow lived several miles away.

oncommon *adj/adv* Unusual(ly), remarkable(y).

ULST.:   **1895** MacManus *Leadin' Road* 4 Thady had the self-same, uncommon, wondherful dhraim about the lap-boord and the goose.

U.S.:   **1978** Massey *Bittersweet Country* 207 It was on-common good.

ondecent, ondacent, ondaicent See **undecent**

one, ane, wan, yin *pron* (following adjectives and pronouns. In Ulster *yin* predominates in Ulster-Scots areas, *wan* in Mid-Ulster ones. In the U.S. the only form known is *one*, which is sometimes reduced to *'un* or *'n*.) See also **them'uns, us'uns, we'uns, yous'uns.** [OED *'un* (at *one* pron) late 17th century→; cf SND *yin* pron/adj 3]

ULST.:   **1804** Orr *Poems* 34 Peace, peace be wi' ye – ah! return / Ere lang and lea the daft anes.

1861 Hume *Rabbin's Ollminick* [Mon. Jennewerry 5] Oul' Chrissimis Day: They say it's more luckier nor the new one; but most o' the young ones knows nothin' about the oul' times afore the stile wos changed, an' the people lost their eleven days.

c1910 Byers *Glossary* 'He's a rale bad'un' (= undesirable).

c1910 Wier *Bab McKeen* 18 We went at the work like a pair o' guid yins.

1959 Gregory *Ulster Ballads* 86 All o' a suddint, I met a maid— / The wee-est wee ane that I've ever seen.

1981 Pepper *Ulster-English Dict* 85 She's a funny yin, that new woman next door.

1983 Marshall *Drumlister* 61 It's sartin to turn out a bad 'un, / The baste that ye buy from McFadden.

1990 Todd *Words Apart* 50 That'n is as conthrary as a bag o' wheezles. *Ibid.* 131 Them'ns is all powerful smart.

1997 Robinson *Grammar* 60 In Mid-Ulster, 'one' is pronounced *wan* and is so written by dialect writers. The pronunciation (and spelling) of 'one' as *yin* is shared between east Ulster and South-West Scotland, although in Older Scots it was always written as *ane*.

2000 Fenton *Hamely Tongue* 240 *iz yins* = we, us; *oor yins* = our family; *them yins* = those people, that crowd; *yer ain yins* = your family; *yous/yuz yins* = you people, you lot.

U.S.:   **1939** Hall *Notebook* 9:25 [The community] finally got so that the old'uns and bad'uns died out.

1942 Hall *Phonetics* 86 *which'un, that'un, next'un, big'un, another'un.*

1967 Hall *Coll* This here'un is made out of metal.
1969 *GSMNP*-37:2:15 I don't recollect any of his young'uns.
1974–75 McCracken *Logging* 6:98 I had an old coat just like that un's in your coat down there. *Ibid.* 10:4 They's all sizes from little'uns to big'uns.
2004 *Pittsburgh Dictionary* When a Pittsburgher is asked, 'Which apples do you want?' they reply 'Those ones', instead of simply saying 'Those'.

oneasy, onaisey, onaisy *adj* Uneasy, worried.
>   ULST.:   **1860** Patterson *Belfast Provincialisms* 8 *oneasy* = uneasy.
>   **1925** McKay *Mourne Folk* 92 It's meself that's gettin' oneasy, for he ought to be home by now.
>   **1930** McCurry *Ulster Village* 106 The docthor says there's nothin' to be onaisy about.
>   **1936** White *Mrs Murphy* 247 Jacob says you needn't be onaisy about the thatch takin' fire. He says there's no danger at all and he bid me sleep in peace.
>   **1965** Braidwood *Ulster Dial Dict* 13 Och, she's like a layin' hen, more onaisey than seek (more hippish than ill).
>   U.S.:   **1929** (in **1952** Mathes *Tall Tales* 132) I'm oneasy they'll git Davy's feet in the miry clay.

onless *conj* Unless. [DOST (at *unless* conj) late 16th century→; SND (at *unless*)]
>   ULST.:   **1860** Patterson *Belfast Provincialisms* 8 *onless* = unless.
>   **1879** Lyttle *Paddy McQuillan* 56 They'll no bother their heid attendin' ye onless yer dressed in yer very best.
>   **1895** MacManus *Leadin' Road* 5 It saims he can't take a hint onless ye impriss it on him with a stout stick.
>   U.S.:   **1861** (in **1938** Taliaferro *Carolina Humor* 15) They ... made preachers, who won't be satisfied onless they are on the backs o' the peepul ridin inter popularity and great wealth.
>   **1939** Burnett *Gap o' Mts* 12 I warn you that onless we gyard the ballot in whuch our manhood and freedom air wropped—we will all be slaves.

onpossible See **unpossible**

ontil *conj* Until. [DOST (at *unto*) late 15th century→; SND (at *until*)]
>   ULST.:   **1884** McFadyen and Hepburn *Lays and Legends* 7 An' ontil you repent an' are doin' right well / It'll be your murther an' ruin!
>   U.S.:   **1938** Bowman *High Horizons* 42 Nigh sundown she up an' died, but her body stayed limp as a rag ontil her baby, 'twar a leetle gal, died 'bout midnight— hit's a shore sign I reckon.
>   **1953** Hall *Coll* [When] the spring of the year come, why he went to plowing and planting his corn and beans, potatoes and things ... cultivating that stuff at home. He'd take care of that ontil he got through and got his crop laid by.

outlander *n* An outsider to a district or community. [< *outland* n 'a foreign land' + *-er*; OED *outlander* 1 'a person from outside one's own town, area, or region, a foreigner, stranger, outsider' 1598→; DOST *outlander* n 'a person from outside the town' 1634→; DARE chiefly east of Mississippi River]
>   ULST.:   **1928** MacGill *Black Bonar* 246 On the Brown Knowe, a mile and a half from Knockagar, ... for the convenience of the Outlanders, the mountaineers.
>   **1953** Traynor *Donegal Glossary* 204 = one who lives outside one's own district.

U.S.:   **1940** Simms *Coll* A mountain man wanted to know, Who and what give the
             outlanders the idee (idea) that we'uns (the mountain people) air a lot ov hell-
             goin' trouble-raisers?
             1957 Justus *Other Side* 71 As for me, I am not willing for an outlander woman
             to take up her abode in our house.

own *vb* To acknowledge or claim as one's own. [OED *own* vb 3 'to acknowledge as
one's own; to acknowledge or recognize as an acquaintance; to claim for one's own',
5a 'to acknowledge (something) in relation to oneself, to confess to be valid, true,
or actual' 1610→; DOST *own* vb 'to acknowledge or to claim' 1667→; SND *own* vb
'to acknowledge as a relation or acquaintance, to give recognition to ... to lay claim
to']
ULST.:   **1953** Traynor *Donegal Glossary* 205 = to recognise, acknowledge acquaintance.
U.S.:   **1974** Fink *Bits Mt Speech* 18 He wouldn't own it as his'n.
             1981 Whitener *Folk-Ways* 29 When he finally pushed back his plate with a
             sigh of satisfaction, he owned that 'that was the best stew I've every tasted in
             my life'.

P

paling, palin *n* A stake or slat of split wood, usually riven from a block of wood and sharpened at the top, driven upright in the ground in a row and secured by horizontal rails, wire, etc.; hence *n* A fence or palisade of these stakes. Hence *vb* To construct a fence of pales around a garden to keep animals out; to fence with such an enclosure. [< French *pal* < Latin *pālus*; OED *paling* n[1] 3b 'a fence made of pales' < *pale* vb[1] + *-ing*, *pale* n 1a 'originally a stake; a pointed piece of wood intended to be driven into the ground, especially as used with others to form a fence, now usually one of the upright bars or strips of wood nailed vertically to a horizontal rail or rails to form a paling' 1347→; DARE *paling fence* n 1 'a fence made of vertical bars or slats; a picket fence' chiefly South, South Midland; LAUSC Midland, South]

ULST   **1990** Todd *Words Apart* 125 It's the loveliest wee place now with a palin all the way round.
2000 Fenton *Hamely Tongue* 147 *palin-stab* = a pointed fencing-stake.

U.S.   **1839** G.M.M. *Bachelor Beset* 5.751 Before the door was a ... row of trees ... fenced in by a white paling, around the top of which ran a comice.
1867 Harris *Sut Lovingood* 143 I jis' tore off a palin frum the fence, an' tuck hit in bof hans.
1899 Green *Virginia Word-Book* 265 The yard was enclosed with oak palings.
1909 Payne *Word-list East Alabama* 355 = a picket, a fence stave. *Paling* is practically the only term in use in the South.
1937 Hall *Coll* They paled in the garden.
1949 Kurath *Word Geog East US* 55 Fences with pointed or blunt upright slats which commonly surround the dwelling and the garden are known ... as *paling fences, paled fences*, or simply as *palings* in the Midland and the Southern area.
1973 *GSMNP*-1:15 That's what the mountain people called them, palin's. They're split out just like boards.
1989 Oliver *Hazel Creek* 15 Chickens and hogs, of course, could come through a rail fence and to keep them out of the garden it was enclosed with a fence made of palings, which were strips of wood split with a froe or broadaxe and set as close together as possible.

pea, pee *interj* A call (usually repeated) to guinea fowl (in Ulster) or turkeys (in the U.S.) to come to feed. In the U.S. the word has been incorporated into the figurative phrase *not say pea turkey* (= not say anything at all), expressing one's displeasure or disgust with another person's lack of manners or breach of etiquette. [DARE *pea-turkey* n 1 (in phrases *not to say* (or *hear*) *pea-turkey* 'not to say (or hear) a single word' chiefly South, South Midland]

ULST.:   **1880** Patterson *Antrim/Down Glossary* 77 *pee-pee* = the call for pea-fowl.
1942 *Bangor Words* 60 *pee pee* = farmers' call to turkeys to come and be fed.
1997 Share *Slanguage* 211 *pee! pee!* = call to peafowl, turkeys.
2000 Fenton *Hamely Tongue* 149 *pee!pee!* = call to turkeys.

U.S.:   **1899** Green *Virginia Word-Book* 270 = call for turkeys.
1909 Payne *Word-list East Alabama* 356 = anything: 'She never said pea-turkey to me about it'.
1940 Haun *Hawk's Done* 63 All that bunch of starved chickens and turkeys started after me. I seed I might as well go back and feed them ... I was

shucking away and calling the chickens at the same time, 'Chickie, chickie—
pea, turks, pea, pea, pea, pea' when all at once I took note that I had a red ear.
1984 Wilder *You All Spoken* 152 *never said pea turkey* = failed to give
information, or to invite one to some function, as 'She lef' heah, I tell you, an'
nevah said pea-turkey'.
1997 Montgomery *Coll* He got up and left without saying pea turkey.

pernickety, persnickety *adj* Hard to please, fussy, crotchety (especially about food);
challenging, ticklish. [origin obscure, but possibly influenced by *particular*; OED
pernickety 'of persons, their attributes, or actions: precise or particular about
minutiae or trifles, fastidious, punctilious; of things: requiring precise or particular
handling or care, ticklish' 1808→ originally Scottish and perhaps northern English
dialect, but in common use in U.S., and more recently introduced in literary
English by writers of Scottish nationality; SND *perneketie* adj 1, 1826→; DARE
persnickety adj 'fussy, meticulous; crotchety' scattered, but chiefly North]
  ULST.:   **1880** Patterson *Antrim/Down Glossary* 77 = particular, hard to please.
        1904 Marshall *Dial of Ulster* 128 = ill-tempered, hard to please.
        1942 *Bangor Words* 60 = hard to please: 'He's a pernickety kind of body that'.
        1953 Traynor *Donegal Glossary* 210 = (1) particular, fastidious, precise about
        trifles; (2) troublesome, hard to please.
        2000 Fenton *Hamely Tongue* 149 = extremely fastidious and hard to please
        (especially in the matter of food).
  U.S.:   **1834** Downing *Life Andrew Jackson* 232 Sich fellers are troubled with a vertigo
        in their consciences, and are never very pernikety how they steer if it leads
        them tu profit.
        1905 Pound *Speech in Nebraska* 63 *persnickety, pernickety* = disagreeable, or
        snippy: 'They acted mighty persnickety'.
        1914 England *Rural Locutions* 77 *pernickety* = fussy, particular, crotchety.
        1956 McAtee *Some Dial NC* 33 *pernickety* = meticulous.

peruse *vb* To wander about. [OED *peruse* vb 2d 'to travel or journey through
observingly or scrutinizingly' obsolete except dialect; SND *peruse* vb 'prowl around,
stroll about'; DARE *peruse* vb 'to wander, saunter, prowl; to make one's way'
especially South Carolina, Georgia]
  ULST.:   **1903** Gwynn *Highways and Byways* 9 In answer to the objection that it was
        bare of herbage, he replied, 'It's not for what they'd get off it, but they'll just
        peruse over it' (pronounced 'pereuse').
  U.S.:   **1853** Baldwin *Flush Times* 89 I asked Nash, what he was doin perusin about
        the country, and Nash said he was just perusin about the country to see the
        climit.
        1940 Haun *Hawk's Done* 102 [How are you all getting along?] We are perusing
        about.

piece *n*
  1 A distance or period of time, usually a short or indefinite one; hence *little piece*
= a relatively short distance; *far piece* = a relatively great distance. [OED *piece* n
15a 'a portion of the space or distance between two points, a short distance'
1612→, now dialectal; DOST *pece* n 12 'a distance, especially a short distance'
15th century→, chiefly dialect; SND *piece* n^1 2(3) 'an indefinite space or distance,

short for *piece of gate, ground,* etc.'; DARE *piece* n 7 'an indefinite (often short)
distance of travel' widespread, but more frequent South, Midland, Texas]

ULST.:   **1933** Foster *Tyrone among Bushes* 80 Aloud he said, 'Aye, it's not a great piece
from here'.

1948 Marshall *Planted by River* 56 The good woman gave me a tearful
farewell, and her busband convoyed me a piece along the road.

1953 Traynor *Donegal Glossary* 211 = (1) an indefinite space or distance: 'I'll
go a piece along the road with you'; (2) a short period of time: 'Wait a piece
and I'll be with you'.

1955 Murphy *Culprit of Shadows* 17 I'm going up the road apiece for a lock of
minutes ... to lose a quid or two.

1969 Braidwood *Ulster Dial Lex* 32 *To put someone a piece of the road* in Ulster
is 'to accompany or convoy him part of the way'.

U.S.:   **1800** Osborn *Diary* (16 Jan) I rode a peace with her this evening.

1858 (in **1983** Heap *Bucks Co Word List* 45–46) We left the cars and stepped
into an omnibus ... and rode quite a good piece.

1872 Schele de Vere *Americanisms* 518 = in the sense of a while, a small
distance, is provincial in the north of England and, with us, in Pennsylvania:
'Go a piece with me' and 'Won't you go along a piece farther?' are common
expressions.

1909 Payne *Word-list East Alabama* 357 = distance.

1939 Hall *Coll* I run [a raccoon] a little piece and catched it.

1973 *GSMNP*-76:3 They was a big hollow run down here. They call it the
Groundhog Hollow, and he went up it [a] little piece.

1983 Broaddus and McAtee *Estill Co Word List* 29 *little piece* = a short
distance.

2 A snack or small packed lunch, as for a school child, most often a piece of
bread with butter or another spread. [OED *piece* n 15b 'short for "piece of bread"
(with or without butter, etc.), specifically such a piece eaten by itself, not as part
of a regular meal' →1787, Scottish and English dialect; DARE *piece* n 8 'a slice of
bread, usually with some topping; a snack or light meal'; LAUSC North Midland]

ULST.:   **1853** Herbison *My Ain Native Toun* Whan wandering wi' ither sculeboys to
the scule, / Wi' piece in my satchel and rule, / Nae pride was amang us, nae
boastin' o' gear.

1880 Patterson *Antrim/Down Glossary* 77 = what a child gets for lunch; it is
generally a piece of bread.

1886 Lyttle *Sons of Sod* 30 We hae jist din eatin a peece breid an' butter.

1905 Marshall *Dial of Ulster* 125 = luncheon: 'Is it near piece time?'

1939 Gallagher *My Story* 16 We ate what we had left over of our pieces and
started.

1942 *Bangor Words* 60 = a lunch which is wrapped up in paper, and is taken
by a child to be eaten in school at the lunch hour, or by the adult to be eaten
on the premises, at the lunch interval.

1953 Traynor *Donegal Glossary* 211 = (1) a part or portion of anything, a little
(often with omission of *of*): 'a piece bread and butter'; (2) a slice of bread and
butter, especially a school child's lunch.

1983 Pepper *Ulster Knowledge* 15 The oul lad has a wee plastic bax for his
piece.

1991 O'Kane *You Don't Say* 105 = (1) a slice of bread spread with butter and

jam or similar relish: 'Would you like some syrup on your piece?'; (2) the food
eaten at lunch-breaks by workmen on building sites and which they bring in a
'piece-box', i.e. a square biscuit tin or similar box.
2000 Fenton *Hamely Tongue* 149 = a slice of bread with butter, jam, etc.; a
packed lunch: 'Whut wud ye lake in yer piece?'; *piece-box* = lunch-box.
2003 Dodds *Newry Nyuck* = sandwich (in packed lunch).

U.S.:   **1859** Bartlett *Americanisms* 320 = a piece of bread and butter, a snack: 'Have
you had your 11 o'clock piece?'
1870 *Notes* 56 'It's time to get piece' was [in Pennsylvania] the way of saying it
was time to prepare luncheon, 'piece' being still the term for a child's lunch in
the north of Ireland.
1930 Shoemaker *1300 Penn Words* 47 = a large slice of bread spread with apple
butter or jelly.
1949 Kurath *Word Geog East US* 72 *Piece* is in general use in all of
Pennsylvania (except for Philadelphia and its immediate vicinity), in northern
West Virginia, and in the Ohio Valley. It is less common in the Shenandoah
Valley and rather rare on the Kanawha [River], where the Southern *snack* has
become established.

piggin *n* A small wooden basin or tub with one stave extending above the rim to
serve as a handle, used to carry liquids such as fresh milk. [origin uncertain; OED
piggin n 'a small pail or cylindrical vessel, esp. a wooden one with one stave longer
than the rest serving as a handle; a milking pail; a vessel to drink out of' 1554→,
chiefly dialect; SND *piggin* n 1789→; DARE *piggin* n 1 'a wooden bucket or dipper
with one stave extended as a handle' chiefly New England, South, South Midland]

ULST.:   **1880** Patterson *Antrim/Down Glossary* 77 = a small wooden vessel, made of
hoops and staves, with one stave prolonged so as to form a handle, used for
milking in, &c.
1889 Hart *Derryreel* 5 Some of the cold water, which the woman brought to
us in a wooden 'piggin', we mixed with sherry from my glass.
1935 Megaw *Carragloon* 101 He would be as hard to trail off the books as a
sow out of a full piggin.
1942 *Bangor Words* 61 = a wooden basin made of staves, and hooped like a
barrel. One stave, much longer than the other, was used as a handle. Used
either for milking into, or eating porridge out of.
2000 Fenton *Hamely Tongue* 150 = a wooden vessel with an extended curved
handle, used for ladling, carrying, etc. milk.

U.S.:   **1839** (in **1863** Kemble *Journal Georgian* 52) A very small cedar pail—a piggin,
as they termed it.
1927 Mason *Lure of Smokies* 124 The 'piggin', as old as Chaucer himself, was
an odd pail, of red cedar usually, with the handle on one side made of an
extended stave with a 'hand holt' cut in it.
1937 Hall *Coll* Piggins [were] wooden vessels used in the old days, cedar
buckets. Coopers [made] the vessels. Piggins were a half-gallon and one gallon,
the outside white and the inside red.

pinkie, pinky *n* The little finger. [ultimately < Dutch *pinje* diminutive of *pink*
'little finger'; OED *pinkie* n[2] 2 'small, diminutive, tiny', chiefly Scottish; SND (at
pink n[2] 2 'the little finger'; this term was brought to the U.S. not only from Ulster
and Scotland but also directly from the Netherlands; its usage in the U.S. has been

reinforced by Dutch settlements in New York]

ULST.: 1965 Adams *File* = the little finger.

U.S.: 1859 Bartlett *Americanisms* 322 = the little finger. A very common term in New York, especially among small children, who, when making a bargain with each other, are accustomed to confirm it by interlocking the little finger of each other's right hands, and repeating the following doggerel: *Pinky, pinky, bow-bell, / Whoever tells a lie / Will sink down to the bad place, / And never rise up again.*

1999 Montgomery *Coll* He's crying but he only hurt his pinkie.

pismire, pishmire, pismither, piss meyer *n* A small black ant. [*piss* + *mire* 'ant' (of Scandinavian origin); OED *pismire* n 'an ant' c1386→, obsolete except dialect; SND *piss-ant* (at *pish* III(2)) 'from the smell of the ant-heap'; DARE *pismire* n 1 'an ant' chiefly Northeast]

ULST.: 1880 Patterson *Antrim/Down Glossary* 78 *pismire, pismither* = an ant.

1919 MacGill *Glenmornan* 109 He was a thran man, busy as a pismire and hasty as a brier.

1997 Share *Slanguage* 216 *pishmire* = irritable individual.

1998 Dolan *Dict Hiberno-English* 199 Watch out for the pismires with that child.

U.S.: 1863 Anonymous *Flatback's Plantation* 37 It is a fine thing ... to sit under these noble trees ... until a caravan of gigantic black or red pismires begin a pilgrimage up your backbone.

1930 Shoemaker *1300 Penn Words* 47 *piss meyer* = a winged ant, commonly supposed to be the male of the species.

poke *n* A small paper container, a bag or sack; a pouch or small bundle; in Ulster also a cone-shaped bag for sweets. [< Middle English *poke*, probably < Norman French *poke, poque*, of Germanic origin, akin to Old English *pokka* 'bag, pocket', but cf Old Norse *poki* 'a bag'; OED *poke* n 1 'a bag; a small sack' 1300→, now chiefly dialect; DOST *poke* n 1 'a bag or small sack' 1328→; DARE *poke* n[1] 1a 'a bag or sack, especially a small one; now usually a paper bag' chiefly Midland, especially Appalachians; LAUSC Midland]

ULST.: 1753 *Scotch Poems* 375 He munts the stage, and 'neath his cloak, / He brought a pig stow'd in a poke.

1834 Beggs *Minstrel's Offering* 7 An' now the poke an' the staff I maun tak' / An' wander awa', an *awmous* to beg.

1880 Patterson *Antrim/Down Glossary* 79 = a bag.

1889 Hart *Derryreel* 86–87 Wan day the wandering craythur of a man that was earning his living by sthreeling about the country, with his pail and pokes, and begging, came limping up to the doore of the house.

1953 Traynor *Donegal Glossary* 215 = a bag, sack; a wallet, pocket; a small paper bag for sweets, tea, etc.

1997 Share *Slanguage* 219 = bag, sack, wallet, pocket

1998 Daly *Pilgrim Journey* 32–33 Greedy appetite was whetted when we watched Miss McKillen weigh a handful of sweets on her weighing machine, adding a couple of extra sweets for good measure, then deftly fold a piece of yesterday's newspaper into a cone-shaped packet or 'poke' and hand it over in exchange for the coin.

U.S.:   **1816** Pickering *American Vocabulary* 152 = a bag. I have heard this old word
           used by some persons here in the compound term *cream-poke*; that is, a small
           bag, through which cream is strained.
           1860 (in **1938** Taliaferro *Carolina Humor* 10) He has a 'poke' on his back, full
           of dried beef and venison, and corn bread.
           1895 Edson and Fairchild *Tenn Mts* 373 He had a poke of peanuts.
           1930 Shoemaker *1300 Penn Words* 46 = a sack or bag.
           1949 Kurath *Word Geog East US* 56 *Poke* is current, often by the side of *bag* or
           sack, in a large area extending from central Pennsylvania westward, and
           southward to the Carolinas. In Virginia the Blue Ridge forms the eastern
           boundary of the *poke* area, in North Carolina the Yadkin [River].
           1986 Ogle *Lucinda* 56 [At Christmas] pokes were filled with one apple,
           orange, maybe a banana and two sticks of candy and some grocer mixed kind
           of candy.

poorly *predicate adj* In poor health, unwell. [OED *poorly* adj/adv 'in a poor state of
health, somewhat ill, unwell, indisposed' chiefly colloquial; DARE *poorly* adj 'ill;
weak; depressed' chiefly South, South Midland]
   ULST.:   **1893** Bullock *Awkward Squad* 48 Father's poorly, an' the childer have a power
             o' coulds.
             1919 MacGill *Glenmornan* 228 Maura was out, having gone to see Breed
             Dermot, who was still poorly.
             1933 MacNeill *Reverence Listens* 50 The next mornin', though he pushed out,
             he was ter'ble poorly, I could see.
             1993 Montgomery *Barnish* 40 = sick.
   U.S.:   **1815** Humphreys *Yankey in England* 107 = miserable, ill.
             1871 (in **1983** Heap *Bucks Co Word List* 46) Uncle is very poorly ... is
             doctoring with Rowland in Jersey.
             1930 Shoemaker *1300 Penn Words* 47 = failing in health, 'going down hill'.
             1959 Pearsall *Little Smoky* 88 He must provide for his family, but on days he
             feels 'too poorly' to work no one is likely to press him.
             1974 Fink *Bits Mt Speech* 20 I'm feeling purty poorly.

poor mouth *n phr* A person who pleads poverty or seeks pity for his/her
misfortune. Hence *vb phr* (also **make a poor mouth**, **talk poor mouth**, etc. *vb phr*)
To complain or seek pity for one's misfortune, usually in an affected or exaggerated
way; to plead poverty. [< Irish *béal bocht* 'continual complaint of poverty' or
Scottish Gaelic *beul-bochd* 'pleading of poverty'; OED *to make a poor mouth* (at
mouth n 20k) 'to plead poverty, to complain' regional (Scotland and U.S.) and Irish
English; DARE *poor mouth* n phr in vb phr *to make poor mouth*, etc. 'to complain
(usually in an exaggerated way) of poverty or other misfortune' chiefly Midland,
South]
   ULST.:   **1880** Patterson *Antrim/Down Glossary* 79 *make a poor mouth* = to complain of
             troubles or poverty, and to make the most of these, for the purpose of exciting
             pity.
             1991 O'Kane *You Don't Say* 107–08 = a person who proclaims poverty as his
             lot and makes out that times are bad with him. Can be applied to anyone who
             is stingy or avoids paying their share on the ground that money is tight, too
             many commitments, fallen on hard times, and so on.

U.S.:   1892 Fruit *Kentucky Words* 231 *to put up a po' mouth* = to plead poverty.
          1930 Shoemaker *1300 Penn Words* 46 *poor-mouth* = to discant on one's
          poverty.
          1952 Wilson *Folk Speech NC* 578 *talk poor mouth* = to plead poverty.

power *n* A great deal, large quantity or amount. [OED *power* n[1] B.II.10a 'a large
number, a multitude, a "host" of persons' 1662→, 10b 'a large number, quantity, or
amount of things; an abundance, a great deal, "a lot"' 1680→, now dialect or
colloquial; SND *pooer* n 2 'a large number (of persons or things), a great quantity,
many, much' 1786→; DARE *power* n 1 'a large number or quantity; a great deal, lot'
chiefly South, South Midland]
     ULST.:   c1910 Byers *Glossary* = a great deal: 'He has a power o' money'.
               1936 White *Mrs Murphy* 131 It has been a faithful day's rain if ever I seen one.
               It will do a power of good.
               1942 *Bangor Words* 62 = many, or very many: 'There was a power of people at
               the meeting'.
               1953 Traynor *Donegal Glossary* 218 = a large number or quantity.
               1991 O'Kane *You Don't Say* 108 = a great deal: 'That medicine did me a
               power of good'.
               2000 Fenton *Hamely Tongue* 155 = a large amount: 'a power o money'.
     U.S.:   1837 Sherwood *Georgia Provincialisms* 120 = much or many.
               1860 *Week* 123 I clarified some of [the sugar] and you can't think what a
               power of nastiness I got out of it.
               1952 Wilson *Folk Speech NC* 578 = a great deal, very much; a great many, a
               crowd: 'She's got a *power* of hair'.

preaching *n* A religious service having a sermon, or one consisting only of a
sermon. In the U.S. in former times, many small rural congregations had only one
service a month at which a sermon was preached because they did not have or
could not afford a full-time pastor. Church members would often gather on other
Sundays of the month for singing, fellowship or Sunday School. [DOST *preching* vbl
n 3 'that part of a service ... given over to a sermon; a service ... which contained a
sermon' 1562→; SND *preachin* 'a sermon'; DARE *preaching* n chiefly South, South
Midland]
     ULST.:   1861 Hume *Rabbin's Ollminick* 28 Ye wud hear nothin' else talked ov, at a fair,
               or a preachin, or a cant, or a cock-fight, or the like o' sich getherin'.
               1886 Lyttle *Ballycuddy* 6 The furst Sunday that my brither Wully wuz at hame
               I tuk him tae the preachin' wi' me.
               1930 McCurry *Ulster Village* 94 A believe some of them were playboys at the
               prachin'.
     U.S.:   1826 Flint *Recollections* 62 The bell of the court-house ... would, on a half
               hour's previous notice, generally assemble a full audience, to what is here
               technically called 'a preaching'.
               1903 Crumb *Dialect SE Missouri* 325 = meeting, service: 'We all went to
               preaching last Sunday'.
               1962 Dykeman *Tall Woman* 154 'We'll have the ceremony the next preaching
               Brother Gudger holds', Kate said.
               2000 Spencer *Memory Lane* III:7 I would toddle along with John and Elzora
               to Sunday school or to both that and preaching.

press *n* A large, shelved cabinet or walled cupboard, as in the kitchen; a walled
storage cabinet for clothes, a wardrobe. [OED *press* n¹ 15 'a large (usually shelved)
cupboard, especially one placed in a recess in the wall, for holding clothes, books,
etc.; in Scotland, also for provisions, victuals, plates, dishes, and other table
requisites' 1386→; SND *press* n 2 'a large cupboard, generally one built into a recess
in the wall but also applied to free-standing cupboards of all kinds' 1741→; DARE
press n 1 'any of various kinds of furniture for the storage of clothes and other
household items: a wardrobe, cabinet, buffet, chest of drawers' chiefly South,
South Midland]
    ULST.:   **1851** Sproule *Letters* (21 Sept) for his press he woud got 12 S and only 7 S 6 d
          for his ful bedsted.
          1919 MacGill *Glenmornan* 206 The sugar is in a press and the tay is in a box
          somewhere.
          1925 McKay *Mourne Folk* 80 Finally Janice went to the press and took out of
          a jug (her cash-box) the price of the cloth.
          1955 Murphy *Culprit of Shadows* 13 Butter the bread. There's jam in the press.
          1991 O'Kane *You Don't Say* 109 = a cupboard or wardrobe used for storing
          clean clothes, an airing cupboard.
          2000 Fenton *Hamely Tongue* 156 = especially a wardrobe; a large cupboard.
    U.S.:   **1899** Green *Virginia Word-Book* 287 = an upright case or cupboard in which
          clothes, books, china, or other articles are kept.
          1977 Hamilton *Mt Memories* 9 Sometimes I would stand for a long while in
          front of the 'press', whose upper shelves held lovely old plates, pitchers, etc.
          The press was handmade from choice cherry wood and I loved the elegant
          doors, with the panes of glass so expertly and intricately placed.

prideful *adj* Proud, haughty. [OED *prideful* adj 1450→; SND (at *pride* n¹ 1)]
    ULST.:   **1801** Bruce *Poems* [Glossary 4] = goods of any kind, riches.
          1933 Foster *Tyrone among Bushes* 21 And even in her hardened mood Ellen
          could not resist Maggie's prideful plea.
          1953 Traynor *Donegal Glossary* 219 = full of pride.
    U.S.:   **1997** Montgomery *Coll.*

Q

qua-he See **cohee**

quern *n* A non-mechanized mill for grinding grain, usually consisting of two circular stones, the upper one turned by hand. [< Old English *cweorn*; OED *quern*[1] 'a simple apparatus for grinding corn, usually consisting of two circular stones, the upper of which is turned by hand' c950→; SND *quern* n 1 'a primitive type of hand-mill for grinding corn, etc.' 1734→]

ULST.:   **1880** Patterson *Antrim/Down Glossary* 81 = the old hand-mill, consisting of two stones.

1945 Murphy *Gullion's Foot* 36 Corn was ground on hand-querns, of which pieces remain.

1953 Traynor *Donegal Glossary* 223 = a small stone hand-mill for grinding corn (obsolete).

1988 Bell and Watson *Farming in Ulster* 54 Querns of several types have a very long history in Ireland. By the mid-nineteenth century, most areas had a corn mill, often built by the local landlord, where grain could be ground on a large scale. Small hand querns survived in use, however, when small amounts of flour were required, or when oats were being crushed to feed to livestock such as poultry.

U.S.:   **1913** Kephart *Our Sthn High* 291 In some places to-day we still find the ancient quern or hand-mill, jocularly called an armstrong machine.

c1950 Wilburn *Quern* Another photograph in our series shows a Kentucky mountaineer grinding corn with a quern or handmill such as was used in ancient Britain. The nether stone is set in a hollow log similar to a bee-gum. The upper one has a hole through the center, where the grain is fed by hand, and is turned round and round by a driving-stick, the upper end of which is held in position by a right-angled arm ... It cannot be said that querns were in actual use in the Great Smoky Mountains National Park in 1926–1930. However, several of the old settlers were familiar with them and had seen them in use in earlier times.

quo-he, qu'he, quo' he, quo-she, quo' she See **cohee**

R

race *n* A rush, dash, quick journey. [OED *race* n I 1 'a journey at speed, the act of rushing'; SND *race* n¹ 1 'a run, a journey at speed' 1768→; WEB3 (at *race*) 'the act of rushing onward' Scotland]

ULST.:   **1895** MacManus *Leadin' Road* 66 For a man who was ready to 'dhrop dead' Jemmy made a very respectable race.

      1920 Doyle *Ballygullion* 104 Thin the Head takes the shovel in his hand, gathers himself together, makes a race at the clock, an' has it in the bucket in a twinklin'.

      1936 White *Mrs Murphy* 33 Maybe I'll take a race down and see that poor girl for a minute or two.

      1991 O'Kane *You Don't Say* 113 = a quick, brief visit or journey: 'I'm just going down to the shop a wee race'.

U.S.:   (in phrase *granny race*)

      1982 Slone *How We Talked* 24 = the rush of a midwife to a home to deliver a baby.

      1984 Wilder *You All Spoken* 36 = the hurryment of granny women— midwives—to help in childbirthing. Southern Appalachian granny women tried to outrace the baby and the doctor, if there was one on call, and have hot water on the stove and a chicken ready for frying after the main event.

rare, rair, rear *vb* (usually with *up*) To become angry, rage, cry out, berate. [cf OED *rear* vb¹ 13c 'to make the voice heard'; DOST *rar* vb 1 'to shout aloud or cry, as in pain, anger, grief or fear'; SND *rair* vb 6 'to weep, cry loudly'; DARE *rare* 5a 'to become violently angry or excited' chiefly South, South Midland]

ULST.:   **1953** Traynor *Donegal Glossary* 228 *rear up on* = to become angry with, abuse verbally.

      1991 O'Kane *You Don't Say* 114 *rare-up* = to get angry, to scold or upbraid: 'He rared up on us this morning for being late'.

      2000 Fenton *Hamely Tongue* 161 *rair up* = object vociferously; fly into a rage: 'If ye dae, he'll rair up'.

U.S.:   **1930** Shoemaker *1300 Penn Words* 51 *rairing* = to be terribly angry or excited.

      1931 Goodrich *Mt Homespun* 50 She'll be a rarin' and a ragin'.

      1981 GSMNP-117:19 Well, they cussed and rared around. That boy cussed.

redd, red, rid *vb* (usually with *up*, sometimes *off* or *out/oot*) To clean or tidy (a room or table), set in order, clear debris from, arrange. [< Middle English *redden*, probably < Middle Low German/Middle Dutch *reden* 'to put in order'; OED *redd* vb² 6a 'to put in order, to make neat or trim' obsolete except dialect; DOST *red* vb² 1 'to clear (a space, or a passage) by removal of debris, undergrowth or other encumbrances' 2 'to clear a place, a piece of ground, a passage, waterway, etc.) (of encumbrances, as rubbish, debris, etc.) 1446→, 3 'to clear away or remove (debris, rubbish, etc.) 1517→; SND *redd* vb 7(1) 'of a room, building: to tidy (up)' and *rid up* (at *rid* vb 6); CUD *redd*¹ vb 2 'clear, tidy up', *rid* vb 1 'set in order'; DARE *redd* vb 3a 'to clear off a table' chiefly North Midland, especially Pennsylvania, Ohio, Appalachians]

ULST.:   **1823** Atkinson *Ireland Exhibited* 359–60 The hostler apologised for its disorder by saying, that they had 'bin so basy gatin in oats, (that is, busy getting in) that they hadn't time to *redd* it (that is, to make it ready, or to cleanse it)'.

1880 Patterson *Antrim/Down Glossary* 82 red = (1) done work: 'What time will you get red?'; (2) to put in order, to separate fighters.

1881 Hart *Mere Irish* 93 At last, when the whole place was redd up and put to rights, he sat down at the fire again, and joined the potatoes that were waiting for him.

c1910 Byers *Glossary* 'I was reddin' up the room a bit and I went about it as mum as a mouse' = tidying up or arranging.

1910 Joyce *English in Ireland* 311 = clear, clear out, clear away: 'redd the road' (clear the way).

1923 Lutton *Montiaghisms* 33 *redd up* = to adjust and put in order things that are in confusion.

1942 *Bangor Words* 64 *redd up* = tidy or clean up: 'I haven't redd up yet'; clear up and finish: 'When will you be redd up this evening?'

1953 Traynor *Donegal Glossary* 228 red(*d*) = to set in order; to tidy, clean up (generally with *up*): 'Redd up the furniture'; 'Redd up the fire'. *Ibid.* 232 rid = to clear.

1990 McIntyre *Some Handlin'* 46 *redd up* = clean or tidy up: 'We have to redd up our classroom before we go home'.

1991 O'Kane *You Don't Say* 115 red = to clean up, to clear out, to make a clearance: 'Will you help me to red out the garage?'

2000 Fenton *Hamely Tongue* 164 (often with *oot*) = empty, clear out: 'A took an redd oot the shade'; *redd the road* = clear the way; *redd up* = clear up, tidy up.

U.S.   **1869** Gibbons *Pennsylvania Dutch* 24.477 When a death occurs, our Dutch neighbors enter the house ... Some 'redd up' the house.

1913 Kephart *Our Sthn High* 83 Then that tidal wave of air swept by. The roof settled again with only a few shingles missing. We went to 'redding up'.

1938 Justus *No-End Hollow* 130 I mean to wash and redd up the house before I do any special cooking.

1974 Fink *Bits Mt Speech* 22 red up = arrange, make tidy: 'Set here while I red up the room'.

1982 Barrick *Coll, redd out* = clean out 'I got to redd out my cupboards'.

1982 McCool *Pittsburghese* 29 *redd* = clean or tidy an area, as in 'Quick, redd up the house, Mom is coming'.

reek *n* Smoke. Hence *vb* To emit smoke. [< Old English *rec* 'smoke'; OED *reek* vb 'to emit smoke; to emit hot vapour or steam, to smoke with heat' c1000→; DOST *reik* vb 'to emit smoke' 1375→]

ULST.:   **1825** McHenry *Hearts of Steel* 116 There's guid day-licht get's into it, an' a guid stane chimney is noo built to let oot the reek.

1920 McCallin *Ulster Plenishing* 14 The reek that often fumes roun' me, instead o' peacefully meandtherin' up the chimley, merely helps to deepen the hue that age has bestowed on me.

1931 Anonymous *Holiday* 32 I've been called a foother for linking the kettle off the crane when it came to a boil and setting it with it stroop in the reek.

2000 Fenton *Hamely Tongue* 164 = smoke: 'wudnae gie ye the reek o his fart' (of a very stingy person); 'Yer dung'll niver reek on it' = You'll never be there.

U.S.:   **1930** Shoemaker *1300 Penn Words* 51 = smoke, fumes from cooking.

reel foot, reel fit *n* A club foot, deformed foot. Hence **reel-footed, reel-fitted** *adj*
Club-footed. [OED *reel-foot* n 'a club foot' Scottish; SND *reel-fit* (at *reel* n¹) II 5 'a
foot so deformed or turned inwards that it causes a walk with a rolling or
staggering motion, a club-foot' 1825→]
>   ULST.:   **1880** Patterson *Antrim/Down Glossary* 82 *reel-fitted*.
>   **1910** Joyce *English in Ireland* 311 *reel foot* = a club foot, a deformed foot.
>   **1942** *Bangor Words* 64 = club foot.
>   **1953** Traynor *Donegal Glossary* 230 *reel-footed* = club-footed, having deformed
>   or thick feet.
>   U.S.:   **1913** Kephart *Our Sthn High* 108 [The bear 'Old Reelfoot'] got his name
>   from the fact that he 'reeled' or twisted his hind feet in walking, as some
>   horses do, leaving a peculiar track.
>   **1984** Wilder *You All Spoken* 154 *reel-footed* = club-footed.

rench See **rinch**

residenter *n* An older inhabitant of an area who has been long associated with it
(or whose family has), early settler, old-timer. [OED *residenter* n 2 'a resident,
inhabitant' Scottish and U.S.; DOST *residenter* n 'a resident or inhabitant' 1664→;
SND (at *resident* vb) 'a resident, inhabitant, generally one of long standing']
>   ULST.:   **1880** Patterson *Antrim/Down Glossary* 82 = an old inhabitant.
>   **c1910** Byers *Glossary* = a resident, one who has resided a long time in a
>   locality: 'A wheen o' auld freens, neibours, an' raysidenturs'.
>   **1939** Paterson *Country Cracks* 92 The Moores, oul' residenters in the district, are
>   said to have been friendly with the wee people an' to have visited them at times.
>   **1953** Traynor *Donegal Glossary* 231 = (generally with *old*) a resident, especially
>   one a long time in a place.
>   **1959** Gregory *Ulster Ballads* 62 The ould residenters thro' the town, / For
>   years, had watched him trake up an' down, / Cud swear that, whiles, he wud
>   laugh; whiles, frown.
>   **1991** O'Kane *You Don't Say* 115 = someone with a long association with the
>   town or district they live in.
>   U.S.:   **1788** *Petitions French Broad* 3 a land office shall be opened for that purpose of
>   entering such lands, that is to each settler or residenter a survey of six Hundred
>   and forty Acres att al low Rates as possible.
>   **1939** Hall *Coll* This here's the old residenter bear hunter.
>   **1970** Foster *Walker Valley* 59 The old man John Huskey was the oldest
>   residenter that I knew that lived up here.

rid See **redd**

rift *vb* To belch. [< Old Norse *rypta*; OED *rift* vb² 1 'to belch out (wind, etc.)'
c1300→, now Scottish and northern; DOST *rift* n 'a belch' 1420→, vb 'to belch'
1456→; DARE *rift* vb 'to belch' especially Pennsylvania]
>   ULST.:   **1733** *Sawney Sinkler* Their Harts mun be as hard as Stean,/ That wonnot rift
>   and greet and grean.
>   **1953** Traynor *Donegal Glossary* 232 = to belch.
>   **1959** Gregg *Phonology* 405 = belch.
>   **2000** Fenton *Hamely Tongue* 167 = to belch: 'Them scallions haes kep me
>   riftin a' day'.

U.S.: **1930** Shoemaker *1300 Penn Words* 50 = to belch.

rin See **run**

rinch, rench, rensh *vb* To rinse. [DARE *rench* (at *rinse* vb 1) chiefly South, South Midland, *rinch* (at *rinse* vb 4) chiefly South, South Midland]

ULST.: **1860** Patterson *Belfast Provincialisms* 7 *rensh* = *rinse*.

1953 Traynor *Donegal Glossary* 230 *rench* = to rinse.

1981 Pepper *Ulster-English Dict* 62 He wuddent even help me to rench the dishes.

1990 McIntyre *Some Handlin'* 46 *rench*.

U.S.: **1904–07** Kephart *Notebooks* 2:429 Rinch that out.

1930 Shoemaker *1300 Penn Words* 50 *rinch* = to rinse or lightly wash the hands without soap.

1974 Fink *Bits Mt Speech* 22 Be sure to rench the clothes good.

rippet, rippit *n* A quarrel, uproar, row, noisy disturbance or party. [OED *rippet* (at *rippit* n) perhaps of imitative origin, Scottish and U.S. dialect; DOST *repet* n 'noisy cheer or outcry; uproar; tumult' 1508→; SND *rippet* n 1 'a noisy disturbance, an uproar, an excited clamour, the sound of boisterous revelry'; DARE *rippet* n 'a noisy disturbance, dispute, or fight' chiefly South Midland]

ULST.: **1861** Hume *Rabbin's Ollminick* 37 If ye offer to stir up a rippet, / An' thinks that yer imperance cows me, / All the veins in yer heart ye shall rue it.

1880 Patterson *Antrim/Down Glossary* 83 *rippet* = a row, or disturbance.

1990 McIntyre *Some Handlin'* 48 *rippit* = a row.

2000 Fenton *Hamely Tongue* 168 *rippit* = a furious quarrel.

U.S.: **1890** Fruit *Kentucky Words/Phrases* 66 *rippit* = a great noise.

1913 Kephart *Our Sthn High* 294 If they quarrel, it is a ruction, a rippit, a jower, or an upscuddle—so be it there are no fatalities which would amount to a real fray.

roarer *n* A broken-winded horse. [cf OED *roar* n 3 'a disease of horses, causing them to make a loud noise when breathing under exertion']

ULST.: **1953** Traynor *Donegal Glossary* 234 = a broken-winded horse.

U.S.: **1930** Shoemaker *1300 Penn Words* 50 = a broken-winded horse.

ruction, ruck-sty *n* A loud, often violent quarrel, contentious disagreement. [OED *ruction* n of obscure origin ... associated with *insurrection* ... dialect or colloquial; DHE n originally Irish alteration of *insurrection*]

ULST.: **1880** Patterson *Antrim/Down Glossary* 84 = a row, or disturbance.

1895 MacManus *Leadin' Road* 43 The waiters raised the divil of a ruction, and sent for the owner of the hotel himself.

1910 Joyce *English in Ireland* 315 = fighting, squabbling, fight, a row.

1923 Lutton *Montiaghisms* 33 = a riot, uproar, tumult, quarrel (also *ruck-sty*).

1953 Traynor *Donegal Glossary* 237 = a disturbance, 'row'.

1990 Todd *Words Apart* 139 There'll be ructions when my Ma sees that you have the windy broke.

U.S.: **1899** Green *Virginia Word-Book* 310 = a vexation or annoyance, a disturbance, a row or rumpus.

1913 Kephart *Our Sthn High* 284 If they quarrel, it is a ruction, a rippit, a jower, or an upscuddle—so be it there are no fatalities which would amount to a real fray.

1974 Fink *Bits Mt Speech* 22 They was a turrible ruction at camp meeting.

rue *vb*, **rue back** *vb phr* To renege, back out of a trade or agreement, or to repent and attempt to back out of one. [OED *rue* vb 10 'to be repentant, or full of regret or dissatisfaction, in respect of some act ... especially in regard of a bargain or promise, and frequently with implication of consequent withdrawing from it' Scottish; DOST *rue* II vb 2 'to break or withdraw from a bargain or contract'; DARE *rue* vb 'to back out of an agreement or bargain' chiefly South, South Midland]

ULST.:   1880 Patterson *Antrim/Down Glossary* 84 = to change one's mind, to draw back ('to take the rue' = to repent of an engagement, or promise).

1953 Traynor *Donegal Glossary* 237 = to change one's mind, go back upon one's word.

2000 Fenton *Hamely Tongue* 171 = renege, change one's mind: 'a quare price, as lang as he daesnae rue'; (attempt to) reverse a move at draughts.

U.S.:   1891 Brown *Dial in Tenn* 174 To *rue back* is to *back out*, and is used in such examples as 'he cheated me and I want to rue back'.

1953 Randolph and Wilson *Down in Holler* 279 *rue back* = to trade back, to reverse a bargain: 'We done swapped horses, fair an' square, an' now Ed he's a-tryin' to rue back on me'.

1982 Slone *How We Talked* 39 = to back out of a trade, not accept an agreement already made.

ruinate *vb* To destroy or reduce (especially one's morals or reputation) to ruin. See also **ruination**. [< medieval Latin *ruinere*; OED *ruinate* vb 1a 'to reduce to ruins' 1548→, now rare; DARE *ruinate* vb chiefly South, South Midland]

ULST.:   1880 Patterson *Antrim/Down Glossary* 84 = to destroy.

1898 MacManus *Bend of Road* 61 It's ruinated ye desarve to be.

U.S.:   1844 Thompson *Major Jones' Courtship* 81 [He] come out here a tryin to ruinate some poor innocent gal.

1899 Green *Virginia Word-Book* 311 = to bring to ruin, overthrow, undo.

ruination *n* Especially of the morals: ruin, destruction. See also **ruinate**. [< medieval Latin; OED *ruination* n 'the action of ruining; the fact or state of being ruined' 1664→]

ULST.:   1880 Patterson *Antrim/Down Glossary* 84 = ruin.

1893 O'Neill *Glens and Speech* 374 His wife was lamenting one day over some improvident marriage in the Glen and prophesying speedy 'ruination' and repentance for the couple.

1920 McCallin *Fireside Tales* 33 Now, ye all know as well as I do that that has been the ruination of manys the shop-keeper.

1937 Rowley *Tales of Mourne* 73 Dan went out to the yard, an' looked at the destruction had fallen on his thrivin' farm. It was fair ruination till him, for in those days no small farmer ever thought of insurance.

2000 Fenton *Hamely Tongue* 171 Fa'in in wae thon pak o ranygates wuz the ruination o him.

U.S.:   1940 Haun *Hawk's Done* 47 [I] told her it was going to be the ruination of him.

1994 Montgomery *Coll* This moonshine's going to be the ruination of my family.

run, rin

1 *vb* (also **run off** *vb phr*) To distill liquor (poteen in Ulster, illicit whiskey in the U.S.); in the U.S. also to make sorghum, syrup, etc. Hence *n* A single cycle of distilled liquor (or the liquor produced in this cycle), a production of sorghum, syrup, etc. [OED *run* vb 7(2); SND *rin* 7(2) 'to draw (liquor), to distill (whisky)' 1721→]

ULST.:   **1895** MacManus *Leadin' Road* 182 The inmates, all unconscious of the impending danger, are commemmorating the successful brewing of the last 'run' of mountain dew. *Ibid.* 198 Tell me where's the poteen ye run last night. **1978** McGuffin *Praise of Poteen* 60 The first run would come out and be caught in half of a large plastic fruit container. We normally always drank the singlings rather than give it a second run. This meant that although we got drunk we got a shocking hangover because the fusel oil hadn't been eliminated. **1990** Todd *Words Apart* 139 = to distill poteen: 'Was that poteen well run?'

U.S.:   **1800** Osborn *Diary* (1 Jan) I began again for to run my still but I am not very fit for hard Leabour. **1939** Hall *Coll* We used fifty pounds of sugar to a bushel of meal and ran it off a dozen times or so. **1978** Montgomery *White Pine Coll* I–3 A lot of areas still have a lot [of moonshine] being passed between individuals who know someone who is still running a still and still running it off.

2 *n* A small stream, creek. [OED *run* n^1 II.9 'a small stream, brook, rivulet, or watercourse' chiefly U.S. and northern dialect; DOST *rin* n 1 'the overflow from an enclosed body of water; a stream having its source in such an overflow; a channel to carry away such a flow' 1581→; SND *rin* n 1; DARE *run* n 1a 'a small stream' scattered but chiefly western Pennsylvania, Ohio, West Virginia, Maryland]

ULST.:   **c1910** Byers *Glossary* = a small stream: 'Severals told me about it'.

U.S.:   [**1816** Pickering *American Vocabulary* 167 This is sometimes conversation; but not in writing. The English dictionaries do not give this sense of the word.] **1930** Shoemaker *1300 Penn Words* 50 = a mountain torrent. **1960** Hall *Smoky Mt Folks* 59 = a marshy place or small stream, as in Tight Run, near Ravensford. **1968** Powell *NC Gazetteer* 427 [Occasionally used for small watercourses]: Rough Run (Jackson Co, flowing into West Fork Tuckasegee River).

S

saft *adj* Soft. [OED Scottish form of *soft*; DARE *soft* adj chiefly South, Midland]

ULST.:   1861 Hume *Rabbin's Ollminick* 9 Sometimes there's a long set o' saft weather, spittin' an' rainin' an' smurrin' even on.
1910 Russell *Language of Ulster* 40 You may hear incidentally that 'it is a saft day', meaning that the day is soft; i.e. inclined to be damp or wet: German 'saft', meaning juicy.
c1912 Byers *Characteristics of Ulsterman* 16 Saft words butter no parsnips.
1921 Irvine *Poor Folk* 148 'Yer words are too saft, Anna', he said, 'th' spulpan needs a man t' read th' riot act.'
1932 Quinn *McConaghy's Money* 23 A can't help squeezin' ye, Aggie; ye're saft an' fresh, lack good creamery butter.

U.S.:   1837 Sherwood *Georgia Provincialisms* 121 = soft.
1871 Eggleston *Hoosier Schoolmaster* 12 We a'n't none of your saft sort in these diggins.
1930 Shoemaker *1300 Penn Words* 60 = weak, silly, characterless.
1961 Medford *History Haywood Co* 89 Then, when 'saft soap' making time arrived (in the fall or spring), the ashes would be uncovered and water poured over them.

scape, skep *n* A bee-hive (made of straw in Ulster). Hence *n* To put a swarm of bees into a hive. [< Old Norse *skeppa* 'basket, bushel'; OED *skep* n 3 'a bee-hive' 1494→; DOST *skepp* n 'a bee-hive' 1585→; SND *skep* n 2 'a straw bee-hive'; DARE *skep* n[1] chiefly Northeast]

ULST.:   1880 Patterson *Antrim/Down Glossary* 91 = a straw bee-hive.
1957 Evans *Irish Folk-Ways* 205 Coiled basketry is best represented in the once universal bee-skep, the seat-baskets of the south, the seats and armchairs of the west, and in the food-carrying baskets of the Aran Islands.
2000 Fenton *Hamely Tongue* 186 *skep* = (1) a beehive (specifically, a straw beehive); (2) to put (a swarm of bees) into a hive.

U.S.:   1930 Shoemaker *1300 Penn Words* 54 *scape* = a bee-hive.

scatterment *n* A noisy dispersal or disruption of objects or people. [OED *scatterment* (at *scatter* vb II.2) 'a scattering, dispersal, rout']

ULST.:   1895 MacManus *Leadin' Road* 152 Be the hokey, I'll soon make a scattherment on the nest.
1920 McCallin *Fireside Tales* 195 The very night before he died he was in crackin' wi' me about it an' lamantin' about his brother Bab ... an' bemoanin' the scattherment that would be sure to take place when he'd be gone.

U.S.:   1942 Thomas *Blue Ridge* 53 The pack fell from his back and there was a scattermint of tinware from top to bottom of that hill.

scholar *adj* A schoolchild; a person who can read and write. [OED *scholar* n 1a 'one who is taught in a school, esp. a boy or girl attending an elementary school' c1055→, now somewhat archaic; DARE *scholar* n 'one who attends school, a student, pupil' chiefly Atlantic, North Central]

ULST.:   1880 Patterson *Antrim/Down Glossary* 86 = one who can read and write: 'It's a

sore thing not to be a scholar'.
1920 McCallin *Fireside Tales* 107 But that was no easy matter, for he was but a poor scholar, an' not much use at the pen.
1945 Murphy *Gullion's Foot* 129 This schoolground contest had a more profound and productive result. It started an early attitude of rivalry and competition between the two boys. They began to develop such jumping ability that the rest of the scholars became spectators.

U.S.:   **1834** Crockett *Narrative* 29 I had an unfortunate falling out with one of the scholars,—a boy much larger and older than myself.
1871 Eggleston *Hoosier Schoolmaster* 20 Ralph looked round on the faces of the scholars—the little faces full of mischief and curiosity, the big faces full of an expression which was not further removed from second cousin from contempt.
1956 Hall *Coll* [At a subscription school the] county would pay half and the scholars would pay the other half.
1973 *GSMNP*-74:41 [Daddy] just went to the third grade, but my mother was a pretty good scholar.
1997 Nelson *Country Folklore* 29 After meeting the scholars, I realized there'd probably not be too much time for playing. I had some students in each grade.

scope *n* A tract of land, timber, etc., especially an extensive one. [OED *scope* n[2] 10 'a tract of land' Anglo-Irish; DARE *scope* n 'a tract, expanse, patch (of land, woods, etc.)' South, South Midland]

ULST.:   **1880** Patterson *Antrim/Down Glossary* 86 = an extent of land: 'He owns a large scope of mountain'.
2000 Fenton *Hamely Tongue* 176 = an expanse: 'a big scope o grun'.

U.S.:   **1784** *Petitions French Broad* 2 it leaves them in possession of a narrow scope of country, between the above mentiond river, and the mountains.
1895 Edson and Fairchild *Tenn Mts* 374 My brother has a big scope of land.
1953 Randolph and Wilson *Down in Holler* 281 They got a big scope of road to grade up this winter.
1960 Hall *Smoky Mt Folks* 21 There used to be a good big scope of seng on the mountain.

scriffin See **striffin**

scrunt *n* A runt. Hence **scrunty** *adj* Stunted. [OED *scrunt* n 'anything stunted or worn out, especially the stump of a tree' Scottish; SND *scrunt* n 'anything shrunken, stunted or worn down by usage, age, etc.'; DARE *scrunt* n especially Pennsylvania]

ULST.:   **1974** Braidwood *Crowls and Runts* 81 *Scrunty* appears as both substantive and adjective. As a substantive it means 'a small, worthless fruit, a dwarfish animal' Armagh (Montiaghs), 'a very worthless small article' Armagh (Portadown), a 'niggard' (Belfast). As an adjective it signifies 'small' Belfast, Armagh, 'dwarfish' Armagh (Portadown), 'parsimonious, niggardly' mid Ulster and Belfast.

U.S.:   **1889** Thompson *Ben and Judas* 897 How I gwine fin' out 'bout what mek your watermillions so runty and so scrunty?
1967 *DARE Coll* I don't want that little scrunty potato.

scunner *vb* To cause disgust, revulsion, or a sickened feeling. Hence *n* A dislike, aversion, repugnance. [origin obscure, but possibly related to *shun*; OED *scunner* vb

1 'to be affected with violent disgust, to feel sick' 1375→, Scottish and northern, 2 'to disgust, sicken'; DOST *scunner* vb 1 'to feel disgust, revulsion or discouragement' late 14th century→; SND *scunner* vb 1 'to get a feeling of disgust, revulsion or loathing, to feel surfeited or nauseated']

ULST.:　　1886 Lyttle *Sons of Sod* 33 Ye'll no grup me bein' sich a fool again. A'm jest skunnered wi' coortin', so a 'em!

　　　　　1904 Byers *Sayings of Ulster* 62 There is said to be a 'kick-up' between them, and sometimes the quarrel cannot be 'patched up', because one of the parties has taken a dislike to the other; if this is the case, it may be said: 'she took a lasting scunner against him', or he was 'clean scunnered of her'.

　　　　　1920 McCallin *Ulster Plenishing* 75 If at that moment I hadn't been that skundthered wi' the sight an' the sounds o' the tins that, rattlin' as if jeerin' at me, made me ready to smash them all into smithereens.

　　　　　1931 Anonymous *Holiday* 32 Lasses were different then from the clips and hairpins that gallant about nowadays in a way that would scunner ye.

　　　　　c1955 Montgomery *Heard in Ulster* 121 I have taken a scunner at eggs; The sight o' it scunnered me.

　　　　　2002 Gillen *Wizard's Quill* 49 Aye monies a time I get scunner't, / But sure that's the nature o' man / An it gars ye think more o' the guid times, / I'll aloo that's al' pert o' the plan.

U.S.:　　　1868 White *Words and Uses* 499 But cultivated and well-meaning people sometimes take a scunner against some particular word or phrase.

　　　　　1910 Cobb *Early English* 7 I inadvertently mentioned the young man's name to the lady's mother, who said, 'Oh, he scunners me', meaning 'He disgusts me', which would seem to be a causative use of what meant 'to loathe'.

　　　　　1947 Hutson *Gaelic Loan-Words* 21 = an instinctive dislike.

severals *n* Several.

ULST:　　1861 Hume *Rabbin's Ollminick* 7 I know'd people, severals o' them, that sayd they had seen fallen stars, an' bits o' them on the groun'.

　　　　　c1910 Byers *Glossary* = several people or things: 'Severals told me about it'.

U.S.:　　　c1765 Woodmason *Carolina Backcountry* 244 This has been the Case, and Ruin of severals.

　　　　　1859 Bartlett *Americanisms* 395 = for several, used in Pennsylvania: 'How many hats have you?', 'I used to have severals, but now have got only one'.

　　　　　1867 Sherwood *Georgia Provincialisms* 71 *Severals*, for several.

shank's mare *n* One's own legs (as a means of transportation), in phrases *go by shank's mare, ride shank's mare* = to walk.

ULST.:　　1880 Patterson *Antrim/Down Glossary* 89 *shank's mare* = on foot: 'We went there on shank's mare'.

　　　　　1910 Russell *Language of Ulster* 40 To 'travel' always means locomotion by 'shank's mare' (that is, by walking) in Ulster.

　　　　　1942 *Bangor Words* 69 = the legs and feet: 'How did he get here? He came on Shank's mare'.

U.S.:　　　1831 (in 1940 Motte *Charleston to Harvard* 30) It appeared more convenient to ride out, notwithstanding my general preference to *shanks-mare*.

　　　　　1909 Payne *Word-list East Alabama* 363 *ride shank's mare* = to walk, go on one's own shanks.

　　　　　1930 Shoemaker *1300 Penn Words* 53 *to ride on shank's mare* = to walk.

　　　　　1967 *DARE Coll, ride shank's mare* = go on foot.

1992 Bush *Dorie* 154 Fred and Pa showed no interest in the car and still went by Shank's Mare (walking) or in the jolt wagon.

sich *pron/adj* Such.

ULST.:   **1861** Hume *Rabbin's Ollminick* 28 Ye wud hear nothin' else talked ov, at a fair, or a preachin, or a cant, or a cock-fight, or the like o' sich getherin'.
1885 Lyttle *Robin Gordon* 17 There wuz sich a sough throo the country aboot the Culleradoo Beetle that fowk said wud cleen destroy the pritta crap.
1983 Marshall *Drumlister* 18 His specs are sich as the Yankees wear, / an' his chat comes down to his nose.

U.S.:   **1849** Lanham *Allegheny Mts* 89 Now, the way the thing happened was this, and I reckon you never heard sich like afore.
1859 Taliaferro *Fisher's River* 57 But he kep' sich a movin' about and sich a splutteration that I couldn't git a bead at his head.
1871 Eggleston *Hoosier Schoolmaster* 116 I 'low God don't no ways keer to be remembered by sich as him.
1923 (in **1952** Mathes *Tall Tales* 17) An' nobody hain't never heared sich a preachin' as Preacher Ike give that day.
1984 *GSMNP*-153 She cooked for all of his work hands. There was no sich a thing as me carrying my lunch basket or anything.

singletree *n* The movable horizontal bar to the ends of which the traces of a horse or other draft animal are hitched to pull a wagon, plow, or other object. [alteration of *swingletree*, formed by analogy with *doubletree*; DARE *singletree* n 'a bar attached at the ends to the traces of a horse harness and having a flexible coupling in the center by which the draft is transmitted to the vehicle or other load' widespread except Northeast and Michigan; LAUSC South, South Midland]

ULST.:   **1904** Marshall *Dial of Ulster* 129 = a wooden bar used in yoking horses to a plough or other agricultural implement.
1942 *Bangor Words* 70 = swingle tree.
1953 Traynor *Donegal Glossary* 259 = swingle-tree: 'He attempted to strike him with a single-tree'.
1976 Murphy *Mountainy Crack* 45 Phelim held his own mare by the head, her backrope and harness on, with a single-tree hanging from the collar hemes.

U.S.:   **1847** Webster *American Dictionary* 1034 A single-tree is fixed upon each end of the double-tree when two horses draw abreast.
1899 Green *Virginia Word-Book* 337 = a bar of wood with a hook in the middle, and a cuff at each end to which traces may be fastened for hauling.
1949 Kurath *Word Geog East US* 58 In the South and the Southern Appalachians *singletree* and *swingletree* stand side by side, but *singletree*, a counter-term to *doubletree* (shortened from *double swingletree*), is gaining ground and already predominates decidedly in the Virginia Piedmont.
1974–75 McCracken *Logging* 1:10 That horse on his side broke that singletree and here he come, just swinging around, and hit him right on the leg, broke his leg.

singling *vbl n* (usually plural in form) The low-proof liquor (poteen in Ireland, illicit whiskey in the U.S.) produced by the first distillation **run** through a **still**. Cf **doubling**. [< *single* vb 'to separate from others'; OED *singling* vbl n 3; SND (at *single* vb 3) 'the first distillation in the making of whisky' 1796→; DARE *singlings* n chiefly southern Appalachians]

ULST.:   **1845** Carleton *Irish Peasantry* (in **1978** McGuffin *Praise of Poteen* 102) Even this running was going on to their satisfaction, and the singlings had been thrown again in to the still, from the worm of which project the strong medicinal first-shot as the doubling commenced—the last term meaning in its pure and finished state.
1891 Simmons *Armagh Words and Phrases* 15 *singlings* = weak poteen of first or single distillation.
1910 Joyce *English in Ireland* 323 *singlings* = the weak pottheen whiskey that comes off at the first distillation, agreeable to drink but terribly sickening. Also called 'first shot'.
1956 Bell *Orange Lily* 55 I've seen men drink the singlings—the first run. They did it out of greed not ignorance.
1978 McGuffin *Praise of Poteen* 14 Water in the worm tube was cooled by throwing buckets of cold water into the lower levels to force the warmer water at the top to overflow. Singlings were produced after about two hours and four such distillations made up a charge for producing poitín in a further distillation. *Ibid.* 60 The first run would come out and be caught in half of a large plastic fruit container. We normally always drank the singlings rather than give it a second run. This meant that although we got drunk we got a shocking hangover because the fusel oil hadn't been eliminated ... The practice had been common for years of selling off 'singlings' ... to people suffering from sprains, hacks and cuts. 'Just rub the singlings on and the pain will disappear like magic', it was widely believed.

U.S.:   **1800** Osborn *Diary* (1 Jan) since the 13 of November I run one still full of singlings then Masht a run for myself.
1867 *Congressional Globe* 60 The singling tub is placed aside and the doubling tub put to the outlet of the worm.
1913 Kephart *Our Sthn High* 135 The product of this first distillation (the 'low wines' of the trade, the 'singlings' of the blockader) is a weak and impure liquid, which must be distilled at a lower temperature to rid it of water and rank oils.
1992 Gabbard *Thunder Road* 150 The first time they run the mash, it was pretty poor. They called it 'singlin's', 50 or 60 proof, something like that. They'd pour it back in the mash or give it to young boys who worked the still because it was weak and they wouldn't get drunk as quick. When they ran it the second time, they was called 'doublin's'. That was the moonshine they sold.

skep See **scape**

skiff, skiffle, skift *n* A small amount (in Ulster usually of rain); a thin layer (in the U.S. usually of snow). Hence *vb* (apparently only in Ulster) To rain or snow lightly. [perhaps < *skiff* vb 'to move lightly and quickly, esp. so as to barely touch a surface; to glide, run, etc., in this manner'; OED *skiff* n² 2 'a slight sketch, trace, touch, etc.' chiefly Scottish; SND *skiff* II n 2 'a slight or flying shower of rain or snow, a drizzle' 1817→; DARE *skift* n² 1 'a light fall of snow (or, rarely, rain); a thin

layer of snow or frost on the ground, or of ice on water' widespread except
Northeast, South, Southwest]
ULST.: (also *vb* To rain lightly)
1880 Patterson *Antrim/Down Glossary* 91 *skiff* = a slight shower.
1923 Lutton *Montiaghisms* 37 *skiffle* = a light shower of rain.
1942 *Bangor Words* 70 = slight shower of rain of short duration: 'It's only a
skiff of a shower, it will be over in a wee minute'.
1953 Traynor *Donegal Glossary* 260 *skift* = (1) a slight shower; (2) to rain or
shower lightly.
c1955 Montgomery *Heard in Ulster* 131 = a passing shower.
1991 O'Kane *You Don't Say* 129 *skiff* = a short, light shower of rain.
1993 Montgomery *Barnish* 57 'There's a wee skiff of a shooer' = there's a light
shower.
U.S.: 1834 (in 1956 Eliason *Tarheel Talk* 294) last night we had a little skift of snow.
1930 Shoemaker *1300 Penn Words* 52 *skift* = a passing fall of snow.
1939 Hall *Coll* We just got out on the top and there was a little skift of snow
a-fallin'.

skite, skyt *vb* To move quickly, dart. Hence *n* A sudden move or dart. [< Old
Norse *skyt-*, the stem of *skyota* 'to shoot, propel, dart'; OED *skite* 1 'to shoot or dart
swiftly, especially in an oblique direction, to run lightly and rapidly, to make off
hastily' Scottish and dialect; SND *skite* vb[1] 1 'to dart, to shoot, fly through the air
suddenly and forcibly and frequently in an oblique direction, to fly off at a
tangent' 1720→; DARE *skite* vb 'to go or leave quickly; to hurry; to run about'
especially North, North Midland]
ULST.: 1885 Lyttle *Robin Gordon* 7 Wi' that she threw a lump o' fir in the fire, an'
gied the hearth a bit skite wi' the beesom.
1932 Quinn *McConaghy's Money* 39 Somebody has got to be terrible in this
house, with yer Da wanderin' the streets demented, an' you skitin' about from
dance-hall to picture-palace.
1976 Murphy *Mountainy Crack* 24 They take a flyin' skite an' then let go their
hoults of other an' kick out their legs till you can damn near see the floor-bag
petticoats.
1991 O'Kane *You Don't Say* 129 *skite* = (1) a sudden slap or blow; (2) a
frivolous, light-headed, giddy person, one who talks emptily or too much; (3)
a great rush or informal visit: 'Take a skite down and visit us sometime'.
U.S.: 1859 Bartlett *Americanisms* 410 To skite about is to go running about.
1896 *Word-list* 424 'Skite out' = get out, run away quickly.
1930 Shoemaker *1300 Penn Words* 52 *skyt* = be off, 'go'.
1931 Bratton *Turf Fire* 61 I made another spring to get a skite at one of them.

skitters, skitter, squitters *n* Diarrhea. [c1440→; from *skit*, of Scandinavian origin;
OED *skit* vb[1] 'to void thin excrement' Scottish; SND *skitter* n 'diarrhea, excrement';
DARE *skitters* n 'diarrhea' chiefly Pennsylvania, Maryland, West Virginia, Ohio]
ULST.: 1953 Traynor *Donegal Glossary* 280 They have the squitters.
2000 Fenton *Hamely Tongue* 187 *skitters*.
2004 Cromie *Byre* 116 Weel the bullock got stuck here an it musta got a bit
scared for the next thing the skitter flew oot o it an ivver the stairs.
U.S.: 1899 Green *Virginia Word-Book* 339 *skitters* = diarrhoea.

1930 Shoemaker *1300 Penn Words* 56 *skitters* = diarrhea.
1973 Davis *'Pon My Honor* 101 *skitters*.

sleight, slight *n* A mental or manual skill, dexterity, knack of doing something sell.
[OED *sleight* n[1] 3 'skill, skilfulness, cleverness, or dexterity in doing or making
something' 1318→, now rare.]
>   ULST.:   **1953** Traynor *Donegal Glossary* 264 *sleight* = the plan, skill, knack of doing a
>   thing.
>   U.S.:   **1896** *Word-list* 424 She had a good slight at hoein'.
>   **1924** Raine *Saddlebags* 98 The mountain mother refers to her daughter's skill
>   as 'Sally's *sleight* at buttermaking', a use of the word found in Chaucer and
>   identical with Spenser's 'y-carved with curious sleights'.

slew *n* (sometimes plural in form) A great many, large quantity. [probably < Irish
slua(gh); the OED calls this form 'originally U.S.' and this may in fact be true; it
appears to be rare in Ulster and its history is imperfectly known; see **1947** Hutson
citation]
>   ULST.:   **1953** Traynor *Donegal Glossary* 264 *slews* = great numbers.
>   **1998** Dolan *Dict Hiberno-English* 244 = a large number or amount of
>   something.
>   U.S.:   **1930** Shoemaker *1300 Penn Words* 55 = a whole lot of anything, a crowd.
>   **1947** Hutson *Gaelic Loan-Words* 20 *Slew* ... has kept a close approximation to
>   its Irish pronunciation and meaning. It means in America a great deal, or a
>   great number; the parallel Gaelic word is *sluagh*, meaning a host or multitude.
>   The first use of *slew* in the meaning cited by the [*Dictionary of American
>   English*] is in 1840. Though it is in general use throughout the United States, I
>   have seen no mention of it by the [*Oxford English Dictionary*], Farmer,
>   Thornton, or Mencken. And it does not seem to be known to Joyce [i.e.
>   Patrick Joyce, author of *English as We Speak It in Ireland*].
>   **1968** *DARE Coll* = a large number: 'She has a whole slew of cousins'.

slight See **sleight**

slip *n* (especially in phr *slip of a girl*) A young, growing girl. [OED *slip* n 2a 'a young
person of either sex, esp. one of small or slender build' 1596→]
>   ULST.:   **1880** Patterson *Antrim/Down Glossary* 93 = a young, growing girl.
>   **1881** Hart *Mere Irish* 122 The eldest—that was Nelly—was a slip of a colleen
>   about sixteen.
>   **1921** Doyle *Ulster Childhood* 155 If it's a handsome slip of a girl comes to you
>   what will she be looking but to get married, and what would you tell her but
>   that she will?
>   **1928** McKay *Oul' Town* 71 When I was but a 'slip' of a girl, I went with a
>   wheen of lasses to get my fortune 'speyed'.
>   **1942** *Bangor Words* 71 = small or young girl: 'She is just a slip of a girl'.
>   **1959** Gregory *Ulster Ballads* 21 I mind, when I was a slip o' a wean, / A-
>   waddlin' tae school, in the sun an' rain / (An' mitchin', odd whiles, 'gainst the
>   master's rules).
>   **1990** McIntyre *Some Handlin'* 51 = slim young girl.
>   U.S.:   **1913** Kephart *Our Sthn High* 111 Within the hut I found only a slip of a girl,
>   rocking a baby almost as big as herself, and trying to knit a sock at the same time.

slippy, slippey *adj* Slippery. [OED *slippy* adj 'slippery' 1548→; SND *slippy* adj 'slippery' 1772→]

ULST.:   **1892** *Ballymena Observer* (in **1898–1905** Wright *Engl Dial Dict*) 'as slippy as an ell' = said of a person.

1904 Byers *Sayings of Ulster* 51 A man may be ... 'as hard as Derry's walls', or 'as slippy (slippery) as a Bann eel' (at Toomebridge).

c1955 Montgomery *Heard in Ulster* 134 *slippy tit* = very hard to hold: 'He's a slippy tit, that gent' (= untrustworthy in his dealings).

1983 Pepper *Ulster Knowledge* 46 He's a slippy tit—even comes into the house like a drop of soot.

2000 Fenton *Hamely Tongue* 199 'There's a slippy stane ootside iverraboady's dorr' = a cautionary reminder that any family may experience a 'fall' of one or more of its members.

U.S.:   **1801** Osborn *Diary* (18 Feb) But the morning being wet made the roads slippy so that he did not Like for to go but would lay it over till tomorrow.

1931 Maxfield *Speech SW Penn* 20 The walks are slippey today.

1982 McCool *Pittsburghese* 32 *slippy* = slippery, as in 'Watch your step, the sidewalk's slippy'.

slut *n* A primitive lamp or candle, consisting of a string or strip of cloth dipped in resin or oil. [origin obscure; OED *slut* n 4a 'a piece of rag dipped in lard or fat and used as a light' 1609→]

ULST.:   **1891** Simmons *Armagh Words and Phrases* 16 = a candle made of resin.

1923 Lutton *Montiaghisms* 38 = a poor substitute for a candle, made by dipping and rolling a tow-string or strip of cloth in melted black resin.

1945 Murphy *Gullion's Foot* 38 The resin was melted in the water, and then the water poured off to cleanse. The 'sluts' were slips of calico or cotton about half an inch wide, and these were drawn through the boiling resin a few times from end to end of the cahm.

1953 Traynor *Donegal Glossary* 266 = a home-made candle formed of tow dipped in oil or tallow.

U.S.:   **1953** Randolph and Wilson *Down in Holler* 285 = a primitive lamp, made by attaching a rag wick to a pebble and setting it in a vessel of grease.

1966 Frome *Strangers* 76 She made her own soap from a boiled mixture of the lye of hickory ashes and grease, and her own candles or else used a 'slut', a saucer filled with fat around a string of cotton cloth that served as a wick.

smidge, smidgen, smidgeon, smitch *n* A small but indefinite bit or amount, as of meal, powder, grain, etc. [origin unknown; OED *smidgen* 'a tiny amount, a trace' originally and chiefly U.S.; WEB3 probably alteration of *smitch* 'a very small piece or portion, a little bit', perhaps related to *smit* 'a particle, bit' Scottish and U.S.; cf SND *smitch* n 'a very small amount, a speck, jot, tittle, touch, trace']

ULST.:   **1906** Marshall *Dial of Ulster* 19 *smitch* = a touch or slight trace, a small portion.

1990 Todd *Words Apart* 148 Could ye just put a wee smidgeon of butther on the bread, like a good girl.

U.S.:   **1909** Payne *Word-list East Alabama* 372 *smidgen* = a very small piece.

1917 Garland *Son of Border* 56 Two bites laid a leg of chicken as bare as a slate pencil. To us, waiting our turn, it seemed that every 'smitch' of the dinner was in danger.

1917 Kephart *Word-list* 417 *at a smidge* = next or near to.
1939 Hall *Coll* Go over an' borry a smidgen of salt.
1940 Haun *Hawk's Done* 28 But the Old Man, he set right there without moving a smidgin.

smirr, smur, smurr *n* A fine rain, slight shower. Hence *vb* To drizzle. [origin obscure; OED *smur* n 'fine rain; a drizzle of rain' 1808→, dialect and Scottish; SND *smirr* n¹ 'a fine rain, drizzle, occasionally also of sleet or snow' 1818→]

ULST.:   **1861** Hume *Rabbin's Ollminick* 9 Sometimes there's a long set o' saft weather, spittin' an' rainin' an' smurrin' even on.
1880 Patterson *Antrim/Down Glossary* 94 'a smurr of rain' = a slight shower.
1891 Simmons *Armagh Words and Phrases* 16 *smur* = fine, thick rain.
1942 *Bangor Words* 72 *smirr* = a slight shower of rain; to cover with a slight haze.
1983 Marshall *Drumlister* 52 The tree-tops shivered in a breeze grown cold, / And, in a smur of rain, the Night drew nigh.
1990 McIntyre *Some Handlin'* 70 = a thick drizzle or rain.
2000 Fenton *Hamely Tongue* 191 = to drizzle: 'smurrin rain'.

U.S.:   **1916** Smith *Cape Cod Notes* 264 A similarly interesting term is employed by the weather-wise when a slight haze begins to dull a clear sky or dim a bright sun: 'Guess we're in for a bit o' rain; it's smurrin' up to the eas'ard; and when it gets smurry with the wind this way, it's sure to rain'.
1928 Chapman *Happy Mt* 313 *smirr* = Scotch mist, fine misty rain.

snurl, snirl *n* A knot, tangle, twist. Hence **snirly, snurly** *adj* Of wood: knotty, gnarly, twisted. [probably a variant of *snarl*; cf OED *snurl* vb 1 'to ruffle or disturb' dialect; SND *snirl* n 1 'a snigger, snarl']

ULST.:   **1953** Traynor *Donegal Glossary* 269 *snirl* = a knot, tangle, loop: 'When a twisted hay-rope is allowed to go slack, it goes into a snirl'.
2000 Fenton *Hamely Tongue* 192 *snurly* = of carrots, roots, branches, etc.: gnarled or twisted.

U.S.:   **1925** Dargan *Highland Annals* 21 It had lost so many limbs when it was young and pushin' up, that it was jest the snirliest tree I ever saw.
1941 Hall *Coll* I hit a snurly place in the wood [when sawing it].

soogan See **suggan**

sook, suck *vb* To suck. Hence **sook! sook!, suck! suck!, sucky!** *interj* In Ulster a feeding call to calves, lambs, or piglets; in the U.S. usually to cows. In the U.S. many derivative forms have developed (e.g. *soo calfy, soo cow, sook boss, sook bossie, sook buck, sook cow, sookee, sook heifer, soo sookee, swoo cow,* etc.). [OED *sook* n/interj 'a call used to summon or drive away cattle (in Scotland generally calves)' Scottish and U.S. dialect; SND *sook* interj 'a call (usu. repeated) to an animal, most often a calf, but occasionally a lamb or pig'; WEB3 alteration of *suck*; *soo cow* perhaps alteration of *sook cow*; LAUSC Midland]

ULST.:   **1880** Patterson *Antrim/Down Glossary* 101 *suck! suck!* = a call to a calf.
c**1955** Montgomery *Heard in Ulster* 130 = a call to cows.
1969 Braidwood *Ulster Dial Lex* 32 *sook/sookie* 'a call to calves', [is] current in Scots, it being the Scots form of *suck*.

U.S.:   **2000** Fenton *Hamely Tongue* 193 = to suck; *sook! sook!* = feeding call to calves.
1899 Green *Virginia Word-Book* 349 = a call for hogs, used when they are called to their food.
1942 Chase *Jack Tales* 25 'Sook buck!' says the old lady. 'Sook here! Sook buck! Stand still now!'
1949 Kurath *Word Geog East US* 38 The Midland call *sook!* has been carried rather farther into the piedmont of Virginia and North Carolina than most Midland expressions, perhaps as the result of the introduction of stock raising from the western parts of these states into the plantation country.
1966–68 *DARE Coll, sook sookee, swoo cow, soo cow, sook cow* = calls to get the cows to come in from the pasture.
1977 Hamilton *Mt Memories* 60 I would look and look and call them, 'Sook Jersey, Sook Bonnie' till old Jersey would shake her head at the flies, and the bell would tinkle.
1994 Parton *Dolly* 13 I caught the first glimpse of the kerosene lantern Mama was holding as she called Bessie, 'Sook, sook!'

spang In Ulster usually a noun (= a bound or leap) or verb (= to bound or leap); in the U.S. the term is apparently only an adverb (= directly, absolutely, completely). [OED *spang* vb 1 'to spring, leap, bound; to move rapidly' 1513→, originally and chiefly Scottish and northern, adv 'with a sudden spring or impetus; slap, smack. entirely, quite; exactly, fair' 1843→, originally and chiefly U.S.; DOST *spang* n 'a sharp, powerful, jerky movement; the noise accompanying this' 16th century→; SND *spang* n[2] 'a pace, stride, long vigorous step, a bound, leap']

ULST.:   **1829** McSparran *Irish Legend* 12 Thrusting my hat down on my head that it might not fly off, I was with him in two or three spangs.
1880 Patterson *Antrim/Down Glossary* 97 = a bound or spring.
1904 Byers *Sayings of Ulster* 42 He may be one of those undesirable men who give you a 'back-spang', that is, fair to your face but treacherous behind your back (the word spang = a violent blow, a variant of spank, is met with in provincial English and Scotch, but in its Ulster use it conveys the idea of want of straightness or treachery).
1923 Lutton *Montiaghisms* 39 = a sudden spring, leap or bound.
1931 Bratton *Turf Fire* 22 I made a spang for the door, thinkin' all the time that Huedy's ghost was at my heels.
1953 Traynor *Donegal Glossary* 274–75 = (1) to walk quickly, to walk with long quick strides; (2) a leap, bound, spring, a long stride.
c1955 Montgomery *Heard in Ulster* 121 = long stride: 'He tuk a coupla spangs and made a buck lep ower the dyke'.

U.S.:   **1909** Payne *Word-list East Alabama* 373 = exactly, squarely, completely.
1917 Kephart *Word-list* 417 = exactly, directly: 'He was right spang on the spot'.
1943 Hannum *Mt People* 100 His hair rose straight up on his head, and his chin whiskers like to pulled spang out.
1974 Fink *Bits Mt Speech* 24 That dog jumped right spang into the creek.

spark *vb*, **spark with** *vb phr* Especially of a man: to woo. Hence **sparking** *vbl n* Courting. [OED *spark* vb 4(4) 'to court, woo']
ULST.:   **c1910** Byers *Glossary* = to court (a girl), flirt with (a person of the opposite sex).

1953 Traynor *Donegal Glossary* 275 = to court.

U.S.:   **1935** Sheppard *Cabins in Laurel* 172 When he comes and takes her to the church-house and calls on her with presents of candy and Victrola records, they have advanced to the sparkin' stage.

1974 *GSMNP*-51:13 If I could just get to read that letter, why I'd know how to start. We called it sparking then.

split(s) *n* A strip of wood usually cut from a log, in Ulster used as kindling or a light, in the U.S. usually to weave baskets, chair bottoms, etc. [SND *split* n 2 'a small piece of split reed or cane']

ULST.:   **1929** Morrison *Modern Ulster* 217 From the fir also were made the splits with which in days not so long ago the house and offices were lighted in the winter. Two old hooks or sickles—the instruments with which in olden times they shored the oats—were stuck into a beam over the fire, with what had been the cutting edge up; the splits were kept lying in these hooks and were dry and ready to burn. A piece of iron with an opening in which to stick the end of the split was driven into the fireplace, and by this light many a bright Ulster boy prepared his lessons. A lighted split was carried about as it was required, and when visitors came in a piece of the fir was thrown on the fire and burned brightly and slowly for a long time, and quite illuminated the room.

2000 Fenton *Hamely Tongue* 196 = a kindling spill.

U.S.:   **1899** Green *Virginia Word-Book* 354 = a thin strip of green white-oak used in basket-making.

1937 Eaton *Handicrafts* 37 It has been interesting to trace the shaving horse, used by the mountain basket and chairmakers of North Carolina, Tennessee, Kentucky, and West Virginia to cut out their splints, or 'splits', as they are commonly called in the Southern Highlands, and rungs, back to Shropshire County, England, where in its original form it is still used, or was until recently, to make 'spelks' and 'trugs' for local baskets.

splutter *n* A hurry, bustle, commotion. Hence *vb* To hurry, bustle. [of imitative origin; OED *splutter* n 1a 'a noise or fuss' 1677→, 1b 'violent and confused declamation, discourse, or talk; an instance of this']

ULST.:   **1879** Lyttle *Paddy McQuillan* 50 He wuz in the biggest splutter that iver ye seen tryin' till get aff his horse.

1891 Simmons *Armagh Words and Phrases* 18 = a hurry.

1925 Hayward *Ulster Songs* 113 Bob jumped, humphed, and started, and got in a splutter, / And threw his ould flute in the blest Holy Water.

1931 Bratton *Turf Fire* 84 When Lanty seen the crowd, he got intil a great splutter, and threatened to do wild things if they didn't clear out.

1956 Bell *Orange Lily* 61 So at last it goes on till buyer and seller are brought together in a splutter of flattery and denigration, hand is slapped in hand and split-the-differs gets his reward.

1975 Murphy *You're Talking* 63 The man and wife made a splutter and he got under the straw in the corner and hid himself.

U.S.:   (also **splutteration, splutterment**)

1859 Taliaferro *Fisher's River* 57 But he kep' sich a movin' about and sich a splutteration that I couldn't git a bead at his head.

1899 Green *Virginia Word-Book* 408 = bustle, stir, commotion.

1913 Johnson *Highways and Byways* 276 He was always gettin' into a splutter, with his mouth runnin' like a bell clapper.

1961 Williams *Content Mt Speech* 15 They's the biggest spluttermint in that house ever I hearn tell of, I reckon.
1992 Jones and Miller *Sthn Mt Speech* 109 *splutterment* = commotion.

spreckled, sprickled *adj* Spotted, speckled. [cf Norwegian dialect *sprekla* 'a fleck', Middle High German *spreckel* 'a speckle'; OED *spreckle* n 'a speck or speckle' Scottish and northern; CSD *sprekle, spraickle* 1752→]
ULST.:   **2000** Fenton *Hamely Tongue* 197 *sprickled* = speckled, as *sprickled bun* (having currants or raisins), *sprickled breed.*
U.S.:   **1930** Shoemaker *1300 Penn Words* 54 *spreckled* = a spotted, or more latterly a dominique fowl.

squitters See **skitters**

stab See **stob**

stave *vb* To act recklessly or heedlessly, drive, dash, smash, etc.; to sprain, wrench. [OED *stave* vb 12 'to sprain' Scottish; SND *stave* vb II 3 'to sprain, bruise or contuse a joint of the body' 1825→]
ULST.:   **1932** Quinn *Quiet Twelfth* 96 She says a man was found dead on the road with his skull stove in.
          2000 Fenton *Hamely Tongue* 200 = to injure the joints of (a finger or thumb) by stubbing.
U.S.:   **1939** Hall *Coll* All the dogs was right with us. They just stove right out at [the bear].
          1960 Hall *Smoky Mt Folks* 12 He 'stove' the [knife] into the animal's stomach and cut a hole five or six inches across.
          1967 Hall *Coll* He come stavin' off the hill. The revenue law was in up there.

stay *vb* To reside, lodge. [OED *stay* vb[1] 8b Scottish and U.S.; SND *stey* vb 'to dwell, reside (permanently or usually), make one's home' 1730→]
ULST.:   c**1910** Byers *Glossary* = to lodge: 'He stays on the Lisburn Road'.
U.S.:   **1953** Hall *Coll* I lived at the lower end of this county—was born and raised there—and stayed there up till nineteen forty-five.
          1973 *GSMNP-78:23* The old mill that stayed here first practically went into dirt before they got a chance to build it back.

still [shortening of *distill*]
1 *n* In making liquor, the metal pot or container into which liquor (poteen in Ireland, illicit whiskey in the U.S.) is distilled. [OED dates term from 1582→ but has no citations from Ireland]
ULST.:   **1861** Hume *Rabbin's Ollminick* 15 There wuz a man woncet kep' a private still, an' when word come that the gaugers wos on him, he give the grains t' the cow afore the whiskey was clane out o' them.
          1881 Hart *Mere Irish* 140 What'll you give for information of a still, and more nor one bag of malt that's hid not far off?
          1920 Doyle *Ballygullion* 161 Yez know there's some wicked men does be keepin' a bit of a still up in the hills beyont.
          c**1982** Clifford *Poems* 9 The drink had been his special care; / His guidin'

motto – 'Drink tae spare', / Sweet mountain dew frae Alec's hill / A barrel frae his ain wee still.

U.S.:   **1800** Osborn *Diary* (1 Jan) I began again for to run my still but I am not very fit for hard Leabour.

1897 Pederson *Mtneers Madison Co* 824 Breaking one's oath in court is nothing, but the betrayal of a secret still is a heinous crime.

1912 Mason *Raiding Moonshiners* 197 This man was to pilot us forty miles that night to two 'moonshiner stills' in the 'old tenth' district, one of the most notorious localities for illicit distilling in the foothills of the Smoky Mountains.

1939 Hall *Coll* We went over and put us up a still, and we was a-makin' some awful good [liquor]. It was so good you could taste the girl's feet in it that hoed the corn it was made out of.

1956 Hall *Coll* [Quill Rose] asked [the revenuers] to take a picture of him. He was sittin' up on the still house—on his still.

2 *vb* To distill, make liquor (poteen in Ireland, illicit whiskey in the U.S.)

ULST.:   **c1910** Wier *Bab McKeen* 52 There wus a great dale o' stillin' in them days, an' the stuff wus made oot o' guid malt.

U.S.:   **1913** Kephart *Our Sthn High* 121 The big fellers that makes lots of money out o' stillin', and lives in luxury, ought to pay handsome for it.

1969 Hall *Coll* McCracken killed Joe Ray because Joe reported that McCracken was stillin'.

1975 Fink *Backpacking* 146 They had no hesitancy in telling us of various incidents in 'stillin' licker' and in offering to procure a supply for us.

stiller *n* A person who distills spirits (poteen in Ireland, illicit whiskey in the U.S.)

ULST.:   **c1910** Wier *Bab McKeen* 52 [He] had promised tae clear the decks o' cock-fechters, an' wee stillers, an' poachers.

1930 Shiels *Mt Dew* 28 Let every stiller pay his own fine or lie in gaol for it.

1956 Bell *Orange Lily* 50–51 In a society where the cottier farming six to ten acres of indifferent soil was as likely as not to open a bare cupboard in the morning, the liquor he made on the mountain was made to be sold. The purchasers were strong farmers and agents buying for the gentry 'who had a fancy, a sort of pride in saying to their guests, "I can give you a drop of the mountain dew."'

U.S.:   **1915** Bradley *Hobnobbing* 95 In places where the 'revenues' are 'raidin' around right smart, even men known personally to the 'stillers' are not allowed to visit the 'stills'.

1922 Dyer *Tenn Civil War Ques* 53 He was a farmer wrote no books, but was an excelent stiller in his day.

1998 Ownby *Big Greenbrier* II:19 When a deputy and his helpers destroyed a still and the moonshine whiskey it would make the stillers angry.

stob, stab, stub *n* A stake or post, small broken stump, limb, or root. [OED *stob* n 1 'a stump, portion remaining after mutilation' c1420→, 2 'a stick, a twig broken off' 1321→, 3 'a stake, a post' 1530→, now only Scottish and dialect; DOST *stob* n[1] 1 'a stump of a tree or shrub; a broken-off twig' late 15th century→; SND *stob* n 1 'a prickle, thorn, spike of a bush; a splinter of wood', *stob* n 7 'a post or stake, especially one used for fencing']

ULST.:   **1891** Simmons *Armagh Words and Phrases* 16 *stab, stob* = a stake of wood driven into the ground.

1923 Lutton *Montiaghisms* 40 *stob* = a wooden peg or stake.
1930 O'Donnell *Knife* 38 Breslin was driving paling stabs preparing for wiring.
1953 Traynor *Donegal Glossary* 280 *stab* = (1) a wooden post, stake; (2) a strong, woody thorn, spine. *Ibid.* 284 *stob* = a stake, post, stump of a tree. *Ibid.* 289 *stub* = a stake, post, a stump of a tree.
2000 Fenton *Hamely Tongue* 198 *stab* = a pointed wooden stake used in fencing, a splinter in one's finger, etc.

U.S.: **1891** Brown *Dial in Tenn* 175 A *stob* is a stake driven in the ground, or the tall stump of a tree.
1930 Shoemaker *1300 Penn Words* 58 *stob* = a dead hemlock tree, left standing by timbermen.
1939 Hall *Coll* We just went to cutting that old stob, you know, to start us a fire with.
1953 Randolph and Wilson *Down in Holler* 289 *stob* = a sharp or jagged stump, an irregular piece of dead timber standing upright.
1986 Ogle *Lucinda* 53 We called this riding the trees, swinging on grape vines about fifty feet out over the hollow with trees and cut off stobs beneath.

stog *vb* To move or go (around) in a heavy or clumsy manner, plod. [variant form of *stodge*; OED *stog* vb[2] 2 'to walk clumsily or heavily' 1818→; cf SND *stodge* vb 1 'to walk with a long, slow, heavy or deliberate step, plod, stump; to step uncertainly or unsteadily'; WEB3 Scottish, perhaps alteration of *stodge* 'to trudge through, or as if through muck and mire']
ULST.: c1910 Byers *Glossary* = to walk heavily or awkwardly.
U.S.: **1967** *DARE Coll* = to move around in a way that makes people take notice of you.
1997 Montgomery *Coll* He'd go stoggin' around the country.

streal, streel *vb* To trail along the ground, draggle; spread or trickle (as syrup on bread). [< Irish *sraoilleadh/sraoill* 'to drag, trail'; OED *streel* vb[2] 'to trail on the ground; to stream, float at length; also of persons, to stroll, wander aimlessly' 1805→, chiefly Anglo-Irish; cf SND *strule* 'a stream or steady trickle']
ULST.: **1881** Hart *Mere Irish* 124 Sthreeling right through Drumnakilleugh.
1910 Joyce *English in Ireland* 336 = a very common word all through Ireland to denote a lazy untidy woman ... 'Her dress was streeling in the mud'—a slattern ... as a verb *streel* is used in the sense of to drag along in an untidy way.
1953 Traynor *Donegal Glossary* 288 *streel* = to go about aimlessly.
1997 Share *Slanguage* 277 *streel* = to drag along untidily (of dress, etc.)
U.S.: **1992** Jones and Miller *Sthn Mt Speech* 111 *streal*.

strenth *n* Strength. Hence **strenthen** *vb* To strengthen.
ULST.: **1641** Montgomery *Letter* The strenthe of the rebels can not be known, nether doe they nor can they know ther owne strenthe.
1860 Patterson *Belfast Provincialisms* 10 = strength.
1885 Lyttle *Robin Gordon* 66 A'm jist tryin' the strenth o' my voice.
1897 MacManus *Dhroll Donegal* 41 Then we'll soon see his sthren'th, an' be the games, if he turns out the imposthore I believe him to be, we'll soon do for him then.

1920 McCallin *Fireside Tales* 23 She greatly feared that a turn among town's-ones wouldn't stren'then her daughter's love for home.

1920 McCallin *Ulster Plenishing* 16 With all the stren'th o' my position, in this corner, an' the care an' regard paid t'me ever since the day I came intil it, I'd a been all to pieces an' out of it long ago if I hadn't been specially made for oul' Jack Mucklewaite.

1959 Gregory *Ulster Ballads* 10 He jumps, an' he tummles, he romps, an' rowlls, / Till I wondher, whiles, where it is that he / Gits the stren'th tae keep on the go all day.

U.S.: **1753** McCullough *Journal* (21 June) Ezekel Strenth of y^e lord.

1829 Kirkham *English Grammar* 192 *strenth* = strength. Common ... in Pennsylvania.

1878 Burt *Dialects* 413 The Pennsylvanian says *strenth* and *lenth* for *strength* and *length*.

1905 Pound *Speech in Nebraska* 58 Sometimes [n] appears for [ŋ] in *strenth*, *lenth*, especially among those of Irish descent.

1913 Kephart *Our Sthn High* 299 I don't 'pear to have no stren'th left.

striffin, scriffin, striffan, striffen *n* A membrane, thin skin. [perhaps influenced by Scots *scruif* (cf SND n 4 'a thin layer on the skin of anything, a film'); cf Irish *s(t)reabhann* 'a membrane']

ULST.: **1891** Simmons *Armagh Words and Phrases* 16 *striffan* = a thin pellicle, the skin over an egg inside the shell.

1923 Lutton *Montiaghisms* 41 *striffen* = a very thin membrane.

1942 *Bangor Words* 76 *striffin* = the thin membrane between the shell and the white of an egg; any thin membrane.

1981 Pepper *Ulster-English Dict* 73 She spreads the butter thin as striffin.

U.S.: **c1926** Bird *Cullowhee Wordlist, striffin* = membrane: 'He cut away the striffin from the man's insides so as to be able to see what was wrong with him'.

1953 Randolph and Wilson *Down in Holler* 289 *striffin* = this name is applied to the membrane which lines an eggshell, also to the tough skin which protects the body of a mussel.

1978 Montgomery *White Pine Coll* They'd cut [the hog's] feet off, cut their feet off, and hang 'em. They'd hang 'em through these two front legs. There is a striffin that you, there's a certain place that you cut there.

1996–97 Montgomery *Coll* = also known as *scriffin*.

stripper *n* A cow not in calf and thus giving milk, though often in small quantities. [OED *stripper* n 'a cow not in calf, but giving very little milk'; SND *stripper* n perhaps influenced by Irish English; DHE *stripper* 'a cow giving little milk, so fit to be sold']

ULST.: **1829** McSparran *Irish Legend* 51 They asked him had he no kind of milk for the children, seeing that it would be so nourishing for them who fed almost continually on fish. Arrah! that's what we have, gragalmachree, and dwowl a better stripper than brawny in the barrantry; that is, I mane when she was a stripper.

1880 Patterson *Antrim/Down Glossary* 101 = a cow that is giving milk, but is not in calf.

1942 *Bangor Words* 76 = a cow that is not in calf, but is still giving milk.

1991 O'Kane *You Don't Say* 140 = a cow which has not conceived, so continues to be milked.

U.S.:   **1872** Schele de Vere *Americanisms* 554 = a cow which is nearly dry, and has to be stripped of the little milk she gives.
1993 Weaver *Scotch-Irish Speech* 14 'Shotes' (young pigs) and 'strippers' (cows with mature calves) might forage on the land but, on new grass, might eat too much and 'founder' (become bloated and die).
1995 Montgomery *Coll* = a cow not giving much milk, about to go dry.

stub See **stob**

stug See **stog**

suck See **sook**

suddent, suddint *n, adj, adv* Sudden; suddenly. Hence **suddenty** *n* Suddenness. [*suddent* Scottish form; OED *suddenty* n 1 'suddenness' 1388→, chiefly Scottish, obsolete except dialect; DOST *suddent* (at *suddan*/*suddand* adj) late 15th century→; SND *suddent* adj 1715→]

ULST.:   **1906** MacDermott *Foughilotra* 1 Then, suddent like, up jumps a big mon that was sittin' one side of me.
1920 Doyle *Ballygullion* 55 He lets go Mr Anthony's leg all av a suddint, an' turns sharp on me.
1930 McCurry *Ulster Village* 102 M'father himself was sittin' at the big turf fire with the rest of the boys when all of a suddent a han' come through the jamb hole, an' pitched him right into the fire.
1935 Megaw *Carragloon* 23 I hardly knew where I was standin'; it come so suddint, like.

U.S.:   **1909** Payne *Word-list East Alabama* 377 *suddent* = suddenly: 'She died sort of suddent-like'.
1913 Kephart *Our Sthn High* 277 The hillmen ... [insert] sounds where they do not belong. Sometimes it is only an added consonant: gyarden, acrost, corkus (caucus); sometimes a syllable: loaferer, musicianer, suddenty.
1940 Mathes *Jeff Howell* 21 A nice young man he was, Sir, an' we're sorry he had to go so suddent.

suggan, soogan, sugan, suggaun, suggin, sugin *n* In Ulster, a collar, saddle, or other seating of straw or rushes; in the U.S., a thick blanket or quilt suitable for camping out; a pouch, carryall. [< Irish *súgán* or Scottish Gaelic *sùgan* 'twisted rope of straw or heather'; OED *suggan* n 'a straw rope; a saddle; a coverlet' 1722→, Anglo-Irish; SND *suggan* n 'a coverlet for a horse's back used instead of a saddle; a bed cover']

ULST.:   **1829** McSparran *Irish Legend* 247 He mounted his capul bawn, accoutred in a straw saddle, or what the Irish call a sugan, with stirrups of gads or withes and a pair of branks.
1863 Hume *Rabbin's Ollminick* 15 Long sthroes is no motes, as the oul' woman sayd when she pulled the back saggaun out of the stirabout.
1880 Patterson *Antrim/Down Glossary* 95 *soogan* = a saddle of straw or rushes.
1888 O'Leary (in **1888** O"Leary *Legends of Tyrone* 133 She lulls them to rest in the low suggaun chair.
1904 Marshall *Dial of Ulster* 129 *soogan* = a straw collar, sometimes applied to a neckcloth.

1910 Joyce *English in Ireland* 330 *soogan* = a straw or hay rope twisted by the hand.
1923 Lutton *Montiaghisms* 41 *suggan* = a rustic saddle or collar, made of hay or straw, with which asses and horses are sometimes accoutred.
1953 Traynor *Donegal Glossary* 291 *suggin* = (1) a straw rope; (2) a straw pad, big enough to admit of two on it, on a horse's back.
1990 Todd *Words Apart* 153 *suggan* = hayrope used by farmworkers for tightening their trouser at the ankles to prevent fieldmice running up their legs during harvesting.
1991 O'Kane *You Don't Say* 134 *soogan* = a rope of hay or straw pulled and braided by hand and used for securing stacks.

U.S.:   **1904–07** Kephart *Notebooks* 4:749 Better put a ration in your suggin, Bob.
1915 Hayden *Wordlist Montana* 245 *soogan* = sheep herder's blanket: 'When they move, they just roll up the soogan and are off'.
1927 Mason *Lure of Smokies* 98 There was not a vanity case among the effects of his 'woman' except perhaps a 'sugin' of bear-oil with which, after Indian fashion, she anointed her hair and kept it sleek.
1952 Wilson *Folk Speech NC* 596 *suggin* = a bag, wallet; probably same word as *soogan*.

Sunday-go-to meeting *adj phr* Of clothes: one's finest set, suitable for wearing to church on Sunday. See also **meeting**.
ULST.:   **1920** McCallin *Fireside Tales* 102 There's nothin' to look forrit till but mopin' at a fire hid away in a range-grate, or wandtherin' about, roun' the street corners, like witless looneys, rigged out in a kind o' Sunday-go-to-Meetin' clothes every day.
1920 McCallin *Ulster Plenishing* 17 There was room for half a bushel of corn in each o' the pockets o' his Sunday-go-to-Meetin' coat.
U.S.:   **1946** Woodard *Word-list Virg/NC* 29 = best bib and tucker.
1967 *DARE Coll* = joking reference to one's best clothes.

swither *vb, n* [OED *swither* vb 'to be perplexed or undecided, hesitate' Scottish and dialect; n 1 'a state of agitation or excitement; a flurry, fluster' 1768→, 2 'a state of perplexity or indecision, or hesitation, doubt, uncertainty' 1719→, Scottish and dialect; DOST *swither* vb 'of a person: falter, hesitate' 16th century→; n 'agitation; doubt, hesitation; an instance of this']
1 *vb* To vacillate, hesitate, debate with oneself, be unsure or perplexed about.
ULST.:   **1801** Bruce *Poems* [Glossary 7] = to waver, to be in doubt what to choose.
1804 Orr *Poems* 36 Gif that's na done, whate'er ilk loun / May swear to, ne'er switherin', / In ev'ry pinch, he'll basely flinch – / 'Guidbye to ye, my brethren'.
1880 Patterson *Antrim/Down Glossary* 102 = to be in doubt, to hesitate.
1895 MacManus *Leadin' Road* 167 Between ourselves, I was long switherin' to go an' larn the thrade properly anyhow.
1983 Marshall *Drumlister* 33 So I swithered back an' forrit, / Till Margit got a man.
U.S.:   **1962** Thompson *Body & Britches* 21 Not an islet in the Sound but has its whispers and hopes of buried treasure, all planted by Kidd on those few nights when he hovered between Block Island and Gardiner's, swithering whether to trust a Royal Governor or to let his long, low, black sloop, the *Antonio*, slip away to Hispaniola.

2 *n* (often plural in form) Vacillation, doubt, a state of perplexity or uncertainty.

ULST.:   **1920** Doyle *Ballygullion* 28 Although she knowed fine what was comin' all along, she was still in a swither what to do.

1921 McCurry *Ballads Ballytumulty* 33 Poor Madge encouraged Hughy John / With many a word an' smile, / But cute or canny he sut on / In swithers all the while.

1932 Quinn *McConaghy's Money* 9 A'm in swithers what to do.

1933 Foster *Tyrone among Bushes* 31 Only last week I put on my weddin' dress to go to my niece's christenin', and as we were goin' along the road I was in swithers as to how it looked.

1991 O'Kane *You Don't Say* 141 = a state of uncertainty, a dilemma: 'Mary was in a terrible swither about whether to go to London or not'.

U.S.:   **1836** Smith *Exploits and Adventures* I ... laughed heartily to think what a swither I had left poor Job in, at not gratifying his curiosity.

1946 Woodard *Word-list Virg/NC* 29 *in a swither* = in an emotional storm; excited: 'He was all in a swither this morning'.

T

talk *vb*, **talk to** *vb phr* To court, discuss marriage with.

ULST.:   **c1895** (in **1898–1905** Wright *Engl Dial Dict*, s.v. *talk* 1 (8)) Pat is talking to
Kate this six months, they'll soon be married.
c1910 Byers *Glossary* = to court (a girl).

U.S.:   **1895** Edson and Fairchild *Tenn Mts* 374 Judge Jackson's son has been talkin' to
my daughter nigh on a year.
1921 Campbell *Sthn Highlanders* 145 A young man 'talking to' a young
woman in the Highlands is not giving her a scolding as he might be
understood to be doing, were he so rash.
1924 Raine *Saddlebags* 98 When young folk in love with each other make
serious plans, they are said to be *talking*. The same word is used by Regan in
King Lear.
1974 Fink *Bits Mt Speech* 26 *talking to* = courting: 'Jim's been *talking* to
Arminty nigh onto three years'.

teached *vb* (as both past-tense and past-participle forms) Taught. [OED (at **teach**
vb) 16th century→, Scottish and dialect; cf SND past-tense and past-participle form
teachit]

ULST.:   **1830** McMillan *Poems* D'ye no' mind, ye greedy clan, / What ye sae aften
teached – / The gospel to the needy man, / Should ai be freely preached.
1885 Lyttle *Robin Gordon* 16 'A'll send him tae skule', sez I, 'an' get him
teached tae read an' write an' dae a bit coontin', but that's a'.'
c1910 Byers *Glossary*.
2000 Fenton *Hamely Tongue* 210.
2005 McCullough *Ballyboley Schuil* 21 'Miss' McGilton teached the babby-
infants.

U.S.:   **1956** Hall *Coll* Miss Ogle teached school down there.
1982 Ginns *Snowbird Gravy* 58 I was teached to be calm, you know, by my
mother.

telled, teld, tellt, telt *vb* (as both past-tense and past-participle forms) Told. [DOST
telled (at *tell* vb) late 16th century→]

ULST.:   **1840** Bleakley *Poems* 97 I'm telt that women by themselves, / Maun live like
mules or dirty elves.
1885 Lyttle *Robin Gordon* 2 Betty set forrit a chair till the fire, an' tell't me tae
sit doon.
1901 Savage-Armstrong *Ballads of Down* 192 Kate, with a shiver, said, 'Doon
by the mill, / A'm tell't, a mon wuz murther'd yince, lang syne.'
c1910 Wier *Bab McKeen* 45 I tell't hir I wus ower busy makin' the breakfast
tae luck tha clock.
1953 Traynor *Donegal Glossary* 299 Ye telled me yer ain sel.
1981 Pepper *Ulster-English Dict* 74 Mary telt me about it and so did Aggy. It
must be right.
2000 Fenton *Hamely Tongue* 211 *telt*.
2005 McDonald *Wullie's New Claes* 28 'A fun this here pup', an tuk it in, oot o
tha guidness o ma hairt', he telt hur.

U.S.: **1882** Stowe *Fireside Stories* 234 I telled the deacon he was a gone hoss.
1899 Green *Virginia Word-Book* 386 *teld.*
1945 Botkin *Lay Burden Down* 117 Young Master's children ... telled me how they gitting 'long.

thae See **they**

that *adv* So, very (before adjs and advs and followed by a noun having a complement clause). [DOST *that* D adv 'to that extent, so much, so' 1559→; SND *that* III adv 'so, to such a degree; to that extent, very']

ULST.: **1880** Patterson *Antrim/Down Glossary* 104 = so: 'He was that heavy we couldn't lift him'.
1889 Hart *Derryreel* 145 Neil Gorman! Are ye that deef ye can't hear when ye're called?
1931 Bratton *Turf Fire* 88 She was that sour lookin' that you would think she was raired on butthermilk.
1935 Megaw *Carragloon* 153 I gives a yell after Archie, but he was travellin' that hard an' whistlin' that strong he never heard me.
1937 Fitzpatrick *Lived Co Down* 76 The poor soul got that thin that I'd be feared for you to see her.
1983 Pepper *Ulster Knowledge* 18 May you live that long that the skin of a gooseberry would make a skirt for you with seven flounces in it.
2000 Fenton *Hamely Tongue* 212 They wur fightin that wicked we could harly sinther them.
2004 Cromie *M'Craidy's Monkey* 112 Tha pair of them wus that fand o animals.

U.S.: **1903** Crumb *Dialect SE Missouri* 333 I was that tired I could hardly stand up.
1908 Payne *Word-list East Alabama* It was that late we never could 'a' got there.

thats *rel pron* Whose. [SND (at *that*) formed from contraction of *that* + *his*, the *-s* of *thats* later construed as a possessive ending as in *its*]

ULST.: **2000** Fenton *Hamely Tongue* 212 The boady thats cairt wuz taen.
U.S.: **1986** Montgomery *File* We need to remember a woman thats child has died.

that'un, that'n *pron* That one. See also **one.**

ULST.: **1861** Hume *Rabbin's Ollminick* 5 If that'un wos good, this is about ten times as good.
1990 Todd *Words Apart* 50 That'n is as conthrary as a bag o' wheezles.
U.S.: **1997** Landry *Coll* We'll try another'un, being that'un paid off.

the *def art* Used in many contexts in which English in general has no article or has a possessive pronoun. (Note: in Ulster, as elsewhere in Ireland, the article is used even more widely than in any variety of American English, as before placenames (*the County Armagh*) or actions and pastimes (*the dancing.*))

1 in a general indefinite sense.

ULST.: c**1910** Byers *Glossary* = used before certain words such as church, school, grace, bed, etc.: 'I found him in the school', 'lying in the bed', etc. *Ibid.* lying in the bed.

U.S.:   **1969** *GSMNP*-27:7 We was all in the bed asleep and he come up. He knocked
and knocked on the door and nobody answered him.

2 for possessive pronouns (as *the da, the dochter, the wife, the han, the heid, the
health, the bed*) In the U.S. this is common only to express familial relation
(thus, *the old lady, the old woman, the wife, the woman* = one's wife). [OED *the* 2
used instead of the possessive pronoun, with the names of relatives, 1816→]

ULST.:   **1931** Bratton *Turf Fire* 29 Don't listen to what the wife says to ye.
1983 Marshall *Drumlister* 32 The deil a man in this townlan' / Wos claner
raired nor me, / But I'm livin' in Drumlister / In clabber to the knee.
1983 Pepper *Ulster Knowledge* 72 He will refer to her as 'the wife' or 'the
missus', rarely 'my wife'.

U.S.:   **1913** Kephart *Our Sthn High* 257 'The woman', as every wife is called, has her
kingdom within the house.
c1951 Chapman *Speech Confusing* A mountain wife, though still in her teens,
is called 'the old woman' by her youthful husband.
1979 Carpenter *Walton War* 68 We've et, but the wife'll get you some supper.

3 in the phr *the both* = both. [SND *the* 8(1)]

ULST.:   **1920** Ervine *Mrs Martin's Man* 84 Will I make you a drop of tay, the both of
you?
1950 Mulcaghey *Harbison's Wake* 69 The both ov them shed tears galore sittin'
there by the bedside with the mortial remains of John Harbison.
2002 Sammon *Greenspeak* 38 = the definite article is always used in Irish, and
has transferred to Irish English.

U.S.:   **1940** Haun *Hawk's Done* 21 I can nigh see them now—the both of them
setting there, either one thinking of tothern.

4 in the phr *the most/maist* = most. [OED *the* 8(1), 1745→]

ULST.:   **1840** Bleakley *Poems* 101 I dealt in groceries and tea, / And could hae pleased
the maist o' nature.
1881 Hart *Mere Irish* The most of what they said was heerd by Shan
Whoriskey himself!
1886 Lyttle *Ballycuddy* 9 The maist o' my singin' is till wee Paddy here.
1936 White *Mrs Murphy* 143 The most of the people lets things go to the divil
because they won't take a hoult of them and do something.
2000 Fenton *Hamely Tongue* 213 the maist o yins.

U.S.:   **1939** Hall *Coll* I always made the feathers fly, but the trouble was the meat
went with it the most of the time.
1989 Landry *Smoky Mt Interviews* 194 Old man Sparks, he spent the most of
his life on that mountain.

5 in the phr *the best* = very well.

ULST.:   **2000** Fenton *Hamely Tongue* 14 = a very common reply to such enquiries as:
'Whut wie ir ye keepin?'; 'Hoo did ye get on?'

U.S.:   **1939** Hall *Coll* I always thought they got along the best ... I've enjoyed [my
job] the best so far.

6 with the names of diseases or ailments. [OED *the* demonstrative adj/def art 8a;
DOST *the* def art 10 c1420→; SND *the* 4]

ULST.:   **2000** Fenton *Hamely Tongue* 213 the jendies, the maisles, etc.

U.S.:   **1937** Hall *Coll* A sight of people died of the fever [= typhoid] on this branch
twenty-five or thirty year ago. *Ibid.* To cure the flux, drink a tea of sweet gum
bark or take some mutton taller melted.

1996 Cavender *Bold Hives* 18 It is common in parts of the American South, including Appalachia, to attach the definite article *the* to the descriptor. This grammatical form often appears today in illness discourse (e.g. My baby has *the* colic', 'He's got *the* cancer', 'She's just now getting over the measles'.)

them'uns, them'ns, them wans, them yins *pron* Those ones, 'them ones'.

ULST.: **1934** Cavanagh *Dunleary Legend* 17 Who'd wonder at that seein' the bad work some of them wans under him does be at.

1990 Todd *Words Apart* 131 Them'ns is all powerful smart.

2000 Fenton *Hamely Tongue* 240 *them yins* = those people, that crowd.

U.S.: **1918** Steadman *NC Word List* 19 *them-uns* = probably due to analogy with *we'uns, you'uns*, which are much commoner than *them-uns*.

thew See **thow**

they, thae *adv* There (to introduce clauses). [*they* Scottish form; cf SND (at *there*), possibly from false analysis of *there're* (pronounced as *there*) as being a contraction of *they* + *are*; citations for 1912, 1921 and 2002 reflect this reanalysis]

ULST.: **1912** O'Neill *Songs of Glens* 37 There' nobody can rightly tell the colour of his eyes, This Johneen.

1921 O'Neill *More Songs of Glens* 11 Never think I'm wantin' to miscall the race o' men, / There' not a taste o' harm in them, the cratures!

1953 Traynor *Donegal Glossary* 301 = the phrase *they are* means 'it is' ... : 'Is there a sitting room upstairs? They are'.

c1970 Gregg *Blaakberries* Thae wur yänst a wee gerrl wuz sweepin the fläer whun she fun a säxpenz.

2000 Fenton *Hamely Tongue* 213 Ir they oany left? If they wur naen tae be got whut wud ye dae?

2002 Gillen *Wizard's Quill* 29 There a lot o' trectors noo of course, / But I'm in no hurry to sell mae horse.

U.S.: **1871** Eggleston *Hoosier Schoolmaster* 146 They's always some sums too hard fer a feller.

1937 Hall *Coll* They used to be a puncheon floor in it, but my father tuck it up.

c1999 Sutton *Me and Likker* 31 I told him I couldn't do that or they would be a whole bunch of people after my ass for not saving them a jar of it.

tho See **thow**

thole *vb* To endure patiently, suffer. [OED *thole* vb 2 < Old English *?olian* 'to suffer, hold out, endure' (Sweet), now northern dialect or archaic; SND *thole* vb 'to suffer, undergo (pain, grief, vexation, etc.), to be subjected to or afflicted with, to have to bear or endure' 1718→]

ULST.: **1801** Hafiz *Winter Sketch* The cautious conie lea's her hole / To crap faint Nature's scanty dole / On bank or brae, / Doom'd hunger hard, puir beast! to thole / Now mony a day.

1831 McWilliams *Songs* 10 Would the great condescend but a day or an hour, / To thole the privations the poor must endure, / They surely would use every means in their power, / To Grant some relief to the Irish shore.

1861 Hume *Rabbin's Ollminick* 10 These bad times is tarrible hard for the poor t' thole.
1891 Simmons *Armagh Words and Phrases* 19 = to suffer or endure anything painful.
1910 Joyce *English in Ireland* 341 = to endure, to bear: 'I had to thole hardship and want while you were away'.
c1912 Byers *Characteristics of Ulsterman* 7 Sometimes the Ulsterman's bluntness of speech, his dislike of shams, his inability to 'thole' anyone who indulges in foolish and inappropriate remarks, and, especially, his disgust in his own judgment if he fails in 'sizing out' anyone, make him appear the reverse of pleasing to those who do not understand him.
1921 Doyle *Ulster Childhood* 15 When, for instance, he read in [Burns'] 'The Twa Dogs' of the 'poor tenant bodies, scant o' cash, How they maun thole a factor's snash', he paused to explain that a factor was, with us, a land-agent ... But I was rapt in the discovery that 'thole' and 'snash' were real words, and that I might use them in the future without shame-facedness.
1923 Lutton *Montiaghisms* 43 = to abstain from food and drink, to endure.
1935 Megaw *Carragloon* 15 So young Robert was gradually becoming an old Robert with little to say and much to thole.
1942 *Bangor Words* 79 = bear, suffer: 'I can't thole it any longer'.
1991 O'Kane *You Don't Say* 145 = to endure, to put up with: 'He's hard to thole when he starts boasting about his new car'.
2000 Fenton *Hamely Tongue* 214 = (1) endure pain: 'Ye may jaist thole tae it's better'; (2) stand: 'Boys but that boy's ill tae thole'; (3) bear: 'She cannae thole anither boady gettin a poun'.
U.S.:   **1916** Smith *Cape Cod Notes* 264 Since a thole-pin, unlike a metal row-lock, rarely breaks or groans, the figure indicates a survival of the root meaning of 'thole', 'to suffer'.
1940 Haun *Hawk's Done* 163 I thought I couldn't thole it when Ad and Linus first started selling off my stuff.

those ones See **one**

th'ough See **thu**

thow, tho *vb* Throw (past-tense and past-participle forms *thowed, thew*).
ULST.:   **1983** Pepper *Ulster Knowledge* 60 I thew it out.
1986 Pepper *Ulster Haunbook* 33 Get out the brush and map. It's tidying up time. Tho out all the junk you can get your hands on.
1997 Robinson *Grammar* 61 Particularly around Belfast, the letter 'r' is dropped after 'th' in words like 'throw', 'through', 'throttle' and 'three'.
U.S.:   **1801** Osborn *Diary* (7 Mar) I Thowed up my singlings in order for to Double.
1939 Hall *Coll* That's the nature of a turkey, to th'ow its head up.
1978 Montgomery *White Pine Coll* VIII-2 [The creature] has thowed a stick at us before, for disturbing it.

through-other, throoither *adj* (with stress on first syllable) Confused, disordered, in a mess. Hence *n* Confusion, disorder. [OED *throuither* adv/adj/n 1 '(as a phrase, originally of two words) mingled through each other or one another; promiscuously; indiscriminately; in disorder' 1596→, 2a 'in predicative use: mingled or mixed up; in a medley; in confusion, in disorder' 1630→, 3 'of persons or their attributes: disorderly; wild, reckless; disordered' 1813→, chiefly Scottish; SND *throuither* adj 'of persons: untidy, disorganised, unmethodical, slovenly, harum-scarum, unruly' 1801→; in the U.S. this usage has been reinforced, especially in Pennsylvania, by German *durcheinander* 'through one another']

ULST.: **1829** McSparran *Irish Legend* 84 Och, I believe nat, says she, for I'm some how or other all throughother, saving your presence.

1886 Lyttle *Ballycuddy* 28 A walkit oot then, an' went intil my sate in the meetin', but my heid wuz a' throoither, an' A got nae guid o' the sermun.

1901 Byers *Ulsterisms* 64 Unfortunately the wife may turn out to be a bad manager and the husband a failure, the house then gets a 'through-other' appearance.

1920 McCallin *Ulster Plenishing* 68 He was as through-other in his affairs at the en' of his career as when he started on it as the best han' at all in his thrade.

1921 Irvine *Poor Folk* 111 M' mind's all throughother wi' yer argymints, Anna.

1928 McKay *Oul' Town* 14–15 Biddy was just as 'throughother' as the place she lived in; she hardly iver washed her face, and when she did give it a wipe she maintained she looked handsomer than the young wans.

1993 Montgomery *Barnish* 51 = untidy, without order, disorganised.

2000 Fenton *Hamely Tongue* 216 *throughither* = confused: 'a' throughither wae bother'; = untidy: 'a throughither cretter'; = higgledy-piggledy: 'iverythin left throughither'.

U.S.: **1903** *Misc Word-list* 353 = confused, bothered: 'I feel all through-other'; 'the things in the drawer are all through-other'.

1929 Buxbaum *Iowa Locutions* 303 There, in *Sentimental Tommy*, for instance, was that curious 'through-each-other' which I had once heard from a neighbor who declared with exasperation that the children had left their playthings 'in a through-other'.

thu, th'ough *prep* Through.

ULST.: **1997** Robinson *Grammar* 61 Particularly around Belfast, the letter 'r' is dropped after 'th' in words like 'throw', 'through', 'throttle' and 'three'.

U.S.: **1905** Carr *Words NW Ark* I can't get th'ough.

1908 Payne *Word-list East Alabama* 300 She had a hard time, but she come thu at last.

till *prep, conj* [ultimately from Old Norse *til* 'to']

1 *prep* To (common in Ulster in infinitives (e.g. *till go*), but in the U.S. primarily used in expressing time (e.g. *quarter till two*).

ULST.: **1737** Murray *Letter* I was Cook till the Ship aw the Voyage.

1880 Patterson *Antrim/Down Glossary* 106 = used for *to*.

1920 McCallin *Ulster Plenishing* 56 When a bit o' that same luck does come till a body wanst in a while it's apt to be the cause of ill-luck till others.

1928 Ervine *Mountain* 153 If ye want to marry yer daughter til as fine a young fella as there is in this or anny other townlan' in county Donegal, ye'll have to give me the three cows an' the medda beyont Harrison's farm.

1935 Megaw *Carragloon* 101 It's not the newspaper he's at, but books, without a picture in them from one end till the tother.

1942 *Bangor Words* 80 = to: 'Add this one till it'.

1956 Bell *Orange Lily* 136 He was going to get married and had no house, nor habitation to take his wife till.
1969 Braidwood *Ulster Dial Lex* 32 *quarter till eleven.*
1997 Robinson *Grammar* 68 Telling the time in Ulster-Scots is much the same as in English, except that we have *ten efter* (rather than 'past') *echt,* and *ten til* or *aff* (rather than 'to') *echt.*
2000 Fenton *Hamely Tongue* 207 = to ('gan ower till Wattermoy'; 'gettin ready for till start the prootas'); towards ('Poo it till ye'); closed: ('Push the dorr till').

U.S.:   **1829** Kirkham *English Grammar* 207 Not here the day; he went till Pittsburg.
1868 Brackenridge *Recollections* 79 May it plase the coort, there is no jail at all till put him in.
1878 Burt *Dialects* 413 *Till* is often substituted for *to* in the Pennsylvania dialect. A horse comes *till* the stable, or a boy *till* the school-room.
1949 Kurath *Word Geog East US* 51 The greater part of ... the South Midland [area has] *till* [in expressions of telling time]. The Midland *till* has been carried seaward along the Cape Fear and the Peedee rivers and even competes with the Southern *to* along the Neuse.

2 *conj* In order that, with the result that, to the point that. [OED *till* conj B1g 'indicating purpose: in order that (one) may' Scottish and Irish; SND *till* conj II 3 'implying purpose: in order that']

ULST.:   **1824** McHenry *Insurgent Chief* 120 Peggy, bring here the wean till his lordship sees it.
1879 Lyttle *Paddy McQuillan* 10 Come awa wi' me till we get a snack, an' then if ye like A'll show ye a bit of Glesco.
1897 MacManus *Dhroll Donegal* 37 Bake me a bannock, cut me a callop, an' give me yer blissin' till I go away to push me fortune.
c1910 Byers *Glossary* = in order that: 'Come here till I see your eye'.
1910 Joyce *English in Ireland* 342 = used in many parts of Ireland in the sense of 'in order that': 'Come here Micky till I comb your hair'.
1917 Walsh *Guileless Saxon* 16 He says he 'ill come downstairs when he has had a smoke till he meets some of the people an' gets talkin' to them.
1921 Irvine *Poor Folk* 54 Come over here till I give ye a taste of me tongue.
1932 Quinn *McConaghy's Money* 19 Come on over here till A see ye.
1991 O'Kane *You Don't Say* 142 = so that, in order to: 'Hand me that spade till I clean out this drain'.
2004 *Ate Up* 32 Where's the han-churn til I get the soor dook made?

U.S.:   **1939** Hall *Coll* I'd have my mustache to freeze [in the cold weather] till I could hardly get my breath.
1956 Hall *Coll* The bean beetle got so bad till we stopped growing [beans] here.
1969 *GSMNP*-25:2:5 Most of the farms ... was straight up and down almost or just hillsidey, till it was actually hard farming.
1979 *GSMNP*-118:2 My mama had rheumatiz. She got till she couldn't walk and I was thirteen and I had to cook and wash.

t'other, tither, tother *pron, adj* The other (often used with the definite article: *the t'other*). [*the tother* represents a false division of Middle English *thet other* < Old English *ðæt oðer* 'the other'; OED *tother* pron/adj now Scottish, northern English; SND *t'ither* pron 2 'the other or second of two, frequently in opposition to *tane*', i.e. *the ane* 'the one']

ULST.: **1813** Porter *Poetical Attempts* Then twa-three steps before he falls, / He runs ram-stam, / Then down he goes, and out he bawls / The tither damn.

1861 Hume *Rabbin's Ollminick* 10 Mind I tell ye, it's no lie to say that one half o' the worl' disn't know how the tother half lives.

1903 Gwynn *Highways and Byways* 11 Maybe A vote for the one, maybe A vote for the tither.

1935 Megaw *Carragloon* 101 It's not the newspaper he's at, but books, without a picture in them from one end till the tother.

1953 Traynor *Donegal Glossary* 310 *tother* = a contraction of 'that one' or 'that other'.

2000 Fenton *Hamely Tongue* 218 = other: 'He towl me the tither day'; 'ether the yin or the tither'.

U.S.: **1834** Crockett *Narrative* 31 I was trying to get as far the t'other way as possible.

1871 Eggleston *Hoosier Schoolmaster* 15 As I pay the most taxes, t'others jist let me run the thing.

1924 Spring *Lydia Whaley* 3 There were two brothers in the Burg—one loafered, tother one was in a notion of marryin'.

1967 Hall *Coll* I remember him just the same as it a-being the tother day.

1976 Ogle and Nixon *If Only* We always called it this house and 'tother' house.

U

un- *prefix* This form and its variant *on-* are frequently used for *in-/im-*, as in **unconvenient, unpossible.** [SND *un-* prefix 'a negative prefix sometimes corresponding to English *dis-* or *in-*, and chiefly used before adjectives or adverbs']

ULST.:   **1838** McIlwham *McIlwham Papers* 11 Gie him a pail about the fifth rib o' his understandin' that'll steek his gab frae utterin' lies, tho' its fairly unpossible to gar him speak the truth.

        1906 MacDermott *Foughilotra* 4 It's a thing unpossible. They jes' des as they like.

        1921 Irvine *Poor Folk* 47 'It's undacent', says she to the king when she saw him, 'to be holdin' a colleen's clothes like that'.

        1978 Pepper *See Me* 16 And to emphasise how *on*-ward the people are, mention might be made of their insistence in substituting 'on' for 'in' at every opportunity.

U.S.:   **1801** Osborn *Diary* (24 Jun) I sot & Chated there a while but was unpatient for to go home.

        1916 Combs *Old Early English* 294 In, im, and un are often used interchangeably ... *ingrateful.*

        1971 Dwyer *Dict for Yankees* 32 I hope we didn't unconvenience you.

unbeknownst, onbeknownst *adj* Unknown, unperceived, without notice, knowledge or warning. [< OED *unbeknowins* adj/adv 1 'without the knowledge of' 1636→, 2 'unknown, lying outside of one's knowledge or acquaintance' 1824→]

ULST.:   **1904** Byers *Sayings of Ulster* 62 Such a person could not be deceived readily, unless it was 'unbeknownst' to him.

        1910 Joyce *English in Ireland* 344 *unbe-knownst* = unknown, secret.

        1920 Doyle *Ballygullion* 137 I Kep' a bit in the dhressin'-table unbeknownst to the docthor.

        1942 *Bangor Words* 83 *unbeknownst* = unknown, without one's knowledge: 'He did it unbeknownst till me'.

        1997 Share *Slanguage* 298 = unnoticed, unobserved.

U.S.:   **1909** Payne *Word-list East Alabama* 385 *unbeknownst* = without the knowledge of, secretly: 'He went into the house unbeknownst to me'.

        1939 Aurand *Idioms and Expressions* 27 UN-BEKNOWNST to her, I SNUCK up to her and gave her a big hug and kiss.

        1953 Randolph and Wilson *Down in Holler* 295 'She done it unbeknownst to me' means 'without my knowledge or consent'.

        1960 Hall *Smoky Mt Folks* 9 So [Boyd McClure] 'clim' the tree 'ferninst' the place where the animal was clinging, and 'onbeknownst' to the bear, prepared to shoot it.

        1974 Fink *Bits Mt Speech* 28 *unbeknownst* = without notice or warning: 'He left unbeknownst to anybody'.

unchancy See **chancy**

unconvenient *adj* Inconvenient. Hence **unconvenience** *n* Inconvenience; *vb* To inconvenience. [SND *unconvenient* adj Scottish form of English *inconvenient*]

ULST.: c1910 Byers *Glossary* = inconvenient.

U.S.: 1944 Wentworth *Amer Dial Dict* 672 *unconvenient*.

1971 Dwyer *Dict for Yankees* 32 I hope we didn't unconvenience you.

undecent, ondacent, ondaicent, ondecent, undacent *adj* Indecent, unfitting, disrespectful, improper, mean-spirited. [OED *undecent* adj 'unfitting, unbecoming, improper; offensive to propriety or moral feeling' 1563→, obsolete except dialect; DOST *undecent* adj 1 'unbecoming, unseemly, improper, indecent' late 16th century→]

ULST.: 1845 Carleton *Irish Peasantry* 54 Dick took Susy's advice, bekase, after all, his undacent drop was in him, or he'd never have brought the bottle out of the house at all.

1884 McFadyen and Hepburn *Lays and Legends* 6 It's rether ondacent to fecht wi' the clargy.

1895 MacManus *Leadin' Road* 43 I never yet in all my travels met with such ondaicent people.

1904 Marshall *Dial of Ulster* 128 *ondacent* = mean, disreputable.

c1910 Byers *Glossary*, *ondacent* = not decent, mean, disreputable, unfair.

1921 Irvine *Poor Folk* 47 'It's undacent', says she to the king when she saw him, 'to be holdin' a colleen's clothes like that.'

1948 Marshall *Planted by River* 93 Leave aff [the sword], ye ondacent vagabone, an' see if ye can bate a man with only one arm an' a bit o' cowl iron.

U.S.: 1909 Payne *Word-list East Alabama* 354 *ondecent* = indecent.

1934 *Web 2nd Intl Dict*, *undecent* = indecent.

unpossible, onpossible *adj* Impossible. [OED *unpossible* adj 1362→1866, now only dialect; DOST *unpossibil* adj 'not feasible, impossible'; SND *onpossible, unpossible* 1818→]

ULST.: 1838 McIlwham *McIlwham Papers* 11 Gie him a pail about the fifth rib o' his understandin' that'll steek his gab frae utterin' lies, tho' its fairly unpossible to gar him speak the truth.

1861 Hume *Rabbin's Ollminick* 11 When he was toul' that was unpossible complately, he said he had made it last March!

1942 *Bangor Words* 58 *onpossible*.

1953 Traynor *Donegal Glossary* 317 *unpossible*.

U.S.: 1813 Hartsell *Journal* 129 he Stated that it wold bee on posebele for beter meletials [= militias] to be maid then was haeve at this time.

1859 Taliaferro *Fisher's River* 89 I sha'n't try to describe her, for it is onpossible.

1942 Hall *Phonetics* 55 *onpossible*.

used to could *vb phr* Formerly was able to. Cf **used to would**.

ULST.: 1988 Braidwood *Notes* = used to be able to.

U.S.: 1891 Brown *Dial in Tenn* 174 *Could* is frequently used as an infinitive, as 'I can't play the fiddle now, but I used to could'.

1905 Carr *Words NW Ark* 99 *used to could, used to couldn't* = used to be able, did not use to be able.

1908 Heydrick *Provincialisms of SE Penn* 50 I used to could walk thirty miles a day.

1963 Edwards *Gravel* 122 I caint work like I used to could.

used to would *vb phr* Formerly would. Cf **used to could.**
ULST.:   **1988** Braidwood *Notes* = used to.
            2000 Fenton *Hamely Tongue* 224–25 She used tae wud'a ca'd whiles, but niver noo.
U.S.:   **1905** Carr *Words NW Ark* 99 *used to would, used to wouldn't* = used to, did not use to.
            1978 Montgomery *White Pine Coll* VI-3 The children used to would kind of stay in the background, you know.

us'uns, iz yins, us'ns *pron* Us. Cf **we'uns.** [SND *us yins* (at *yin* pron/adj 3)]
ULST.:   **2000** Fenton *Hamely Tongue* 110 *iz yins* = we, us.
U.S.:   **1863** Davis *Promise of Dawn* 13 The Church thinks it is Christ's body an' us uns is outsiders.
            1949 Webber *Backwoods Teacher* 75 Us'n don't like school.

V

vaunty, vauntie *adj* Boastful, vain, proud (Hence *vb* To boast). [< *vaunt* n + -*y* adj-forming suffix; OED *vaunty* adj 'proud, boastful' dialect except in Scotland; SND *vauntie* adj 'of persons: proud, boastful, vain; proud-looking, jaunty, ostentatious']

ULST.:   **1813** Porter *Poetical Attempts* A bottle o' the stoutest nappy, / That ever yet could boast the birth / O' either anger, wit, or mirth, / Cauldna hae made me half sae vauntie, / Or made me 'cock my crest' so cantie.

        c1955 Montgomery *Heard in Ulster* 145 = I heerd he was vauntin to all and sundry about the price he got for his pig.

        2000 Fenton *Hamely Tongue* 227 *vantie.*

U.S.:   **1930** Shoemaker *1300 Penn Words* 65 *vaunty* = boastful.

W

waddiner See **weddinger**

wait on *vb phr* To wait for. [OED (at *wait* vb 1 (3)); DARE (at *on* prep 3a) 'to wait for' more frequent South, Midland]

ULST.: **1932** Quinn *McConaghy's Money* 59 What are ye waitin' on?
   1936 White *Mrs Murphy* 79 I'm just waitin' on a letter from them.
   1979 Pepper *Quare Geg* 30 He said he got browned aff waitin' on a red bus and just tuk a black taxi.
   1997 Robinson *Grammar* 133 A waitit on him all day.
U.S.: **1908** Heydrick *Provincialisms of SE Penn* 50 I'll go along it you wait on me a few minutes.
   1909 Payne *Word-list East Alabama* 386 = to wait for.
   1969 *GSMNP*-27:8 They would follow us all day long, and we would have to stop and wait on them.
   1978 Montgomery *White Pine Coll* IV-4 I just didn't have time to wait on the sign ... If you're waiting on the moon, and you're needing to plant corn, it would probably be wet when the moon was right.
   1982 McCool *Pittsburghese* 37 = wait for, as in 'I had to wait on the bus for a half hour this morning'.

wan See **one**

wanchancy See **chancy**

want *vb*

 1 (+ *prep* or *adv*) with elliptical infinitive, as *want in, want off* = want (to come/get/go) in, off, etc. [OED *want* vb 5f, originally Scotland, northern Ireland, and U.S. colloquial; SND *want* 6; LAUSC Midland]

ULST.: **1953** Traynor *Donegal Glossary* 321 What do you want in for?
   2000 Fenton *Hamely Tongue* 227 *want hame* (*in, oot*, etc.) = wish to go home (in, out, etc.)
   2000 Graham *Slings and Arrows* Since mid-February republicans have given the impression that they want out.
U.S.: **1878** Burt *Dialects* 413 [The Pennsylvanian] says 'I want out' and 'I want down' for 'I want to get out' and 'I want to get down'.
   1914 Arthur *Western NC* 267 [We] claim that when we 'want in', we generally manage to 'get' in, whether we say 'get' or not.
   1939 Aurand *Idioms and Expressions* 25 I want OUT, or IN.
   1949 Kurath *Word Geog East US* 79 [I]n the common speech of the Midland, the shorter *I want off* is widely used. One hears it on the Susquehanna and from there westward to the Ohio Valley and southward all through the Appalachians. The preservation in the Midlands of this older English construction in which an adverb is joined directly to *want* may in part be due to German influence (cf *ich will hinaus*).
   1951 Barnwell *Our Mt Speech* He does not use come or go for entering or leaving a house, but, 'I want in, I want out'.
   1956 McAtee *Some Dial NC* 49 = with an understood verb omitted: 'That dog doesn't know whether he wants in or out'.

2 (+ *past participle*) with elliptical infinitive, as in *want done*, etc.

ULST.:   **1922** McKay *Mts of Mourne* 94 All the same, I wouldn't want redd of him for always, an' I wouldn't let anyone run him down.

1999 Kingsly *Protestant Speaks* Of course, the hard-liners on both sides want rid of the police.

2004 Graham *Government Nod* Alliance does not want subtle refinements of this system, but instead wants rid of these designations.

U.S.:   **1931** Maxfield *Speech SW Penn* 20 *Want* is used with certain preps. to replace infinitive. More rarely used with past ptcs.: 'The dog wants freed'.

1939 Hall *Coll* We set it on the fire and put our meat in it or beans or anything we wanted boiled.

1982 McCool *Pittsburghese* 37 *wants* = used for 'wants to be', as in 'The customer wants served'.

1999 McNeil *Purchase Knob* Just tell me what you want done.

3 Used as a progressive verb.

ULST.:   **1879** Lyttle *Paddy McQuillan* 47 A wuz wantin' Maggie tae gie ye a bowl, but she said that ye michtnae ken the odds atween it an' a cup.

1928 Ervine *Mountain* 150 You wurn't wantin' to be goin', I'd be thinkin'?

1937 Rowley *Tales of Mourne* 25 A young mother would be wantin' a bit of ribbon to tie on her baby's arm agin the enticements of the Wee People.

1948 Marshall *Planted by River* 248 What bothers me now is something I haven't said that I'm wanting to say.

U.S.:   **1939** Hall *Coll* Was you wantin' to go to town? *Ibid.* I'm wantin' to go to bed!

weddinger, waddiner, weddener, weddiner *n* A member of the wedding party; a wedding guest. [OED *weddinger* n 'a wedding-guest; plural, the whole wedding-party, including bride and bridegroom' 1802→, dialect]

ULST.:   **1902** McIlroy *Druid's Island* 114 Everything was in readiness, an' the minister in his place; but the waddiners wur late o' arrivin'.

1928 McKay *Oul' Town* 15 The weddiners walked two by two, and d'ye know, it was a purty sight; then after gettin' the knot tied in a church or chapel, they all proceeded to a public-house.

1953 Traynor *Donegal Glossary* 324 *weddinger* = a wedding guest.

1991 O'Kane *You Don't Say* 154 *weddener* = anyone who is 'on a wedding', i.e. prominently involved, particularly the bride and groom and their entourage, but sometimes extended to cover their families and other guests as well. A married couple on their first showing out as man and wife are still widely referred to as weddeners: 'Did you see the weddeners at mass this morning?'

U.S.:   **1895** Edson and Fairchild *Tenn Mts* 375 = the bride and the groom, with the wedding party.

1926 Randolph *Word-list from Ozarks* 404 *weddiner* = members of a wedding party: 'I heerd th' weddiners a-whoopin' an' a-hollerin' 'long bout sun-up'.

week *n* (also **a week**) One week from next (whichever day), as *Sunday week*.

ULST.:   **1895** MacManus *Leadin' Road* 65 ... if ye haven't yer rent paid up agane this day week.

1983 Marshall *Drumlister* 33 To Bridget I went back, / An' faced her for it that night week / Beside her own thurf-stack.

1991 Kirk *NITCS* We're practising for Children's Day, which is on Sunday week. *Ibid.* She's starting at Lisnaskea factory then, Monday week.
1997 Robinson *Grammar* 75 *Nix* or *neist Setterday*, which of course literally translated means 'next Saturday', actually means 'a week from Saturday', as, of course, does *Setterday week*.
1999 Devine and McVerry *SF Face Backlash* Political observers said this reaction is likely to be reflected in the polling booths on Friday week, when European and local elections are held in the South.

U.S.:   **1874** Swearingen *Letters* 165 our School for last year closed yesterday will reopen Sunday week.
1937 Hall *Coll* I reckon school commences next Monday a week.

we'uns, wee yins *pron* Both of us, all of us. Cf **us'uns**. See also **one**. [contraction of *we + ones*]

ULST.:   **c1910** Wier *Bab McKeen* 54 But afore that I micht tell't wee yins were sent tae different pairts o' the hill tae watch for the pleece.

U.S.:   **1913** Kephart *Our Sthn High* 286 Let's we-uns all go over to youerunses house.
1915 Bradley *Hobnobbing* 96 'The reason why we-uns knows so much more than you-uns', said an old mountain woman, 'is because we cain't *read* so much. So we *think* more.'
1973 *GSMNP*-76:22 Well, we ones [will] see you tomorrow.

wha a' See **who all**

whang *n* Rawhide, especially a shoelace made of such material. [< Middle English *thwang*, from which *thong* also derives; OED *whang* n (variant of *thwang/thong*) Scottish and dialect; SND *whang* n 'a thong, a long narrow strip of leather ... used in making shoes, as a band, strap, etc.']

ULST.:   **1880** Patterson *Antrim/Down Glossary* 114 = a thong, hence a shoe-tie.
1891 Simmons *Armagh Words and Phrases* 20 = a thong or boot-lace of leather.
1897 McIlroy *Lint in Bell* 10 Jamie Miskimmon's principal charm for us lay in his 'whangs'. We cannot recall a time when Jamie was so busy that he would not lay aise the work on hand, and taking up a piece of fresh leather, would proceed, after his own manner, to manufacture for us a pair of these useful accessories.
1904 Byers *Sayings of Ulster* 45 A boy with his 'galluses' (suspenders) broken, and no 'whang' in his boot (a variant of thwang, now thong) is very untidy.
1953 Traynor *Donegal Glossary* 326 = a leathern boot-lace.
1998 Daly *Pilgrim Journey* 19 Farmers' boots in Loughguile in those days were made for rough roads; they were hob-nailed or reinforced by sparables on the leather soles and iron protectors on the soles. They were laced with leather thongs or 'whangs'.

U.S.:   **1914** Arthur *Western NC* 265 Smaller skins were tanned in the same way, and those of dogs, coons, ground hogs, etc., were used for 'whang' leather—that is, they were cut into strings for sewing other leather with.
c1975 Lunsford *It Used To Be* 163 'Whang leather' is a tough rawhide leather suitable for making shoe strings. You cut it into fine strips for tying the rough boots or shoes.

what all *pron phr* All of what, exactly what.
ULST.:   1879 Lyttle *Paddy McQuillan* 40 A cudnae tell ye what a'.
          1991 Kirk *NITCS* What all goes on in Limavady? *Ibid.* They married cousins,
          and I don't know what all.
          2000 Fenton *Hamely Tongue* 234 Whut a' wuz taen?
U.S.:   1905 Miles *Spirit of Mts* 106 If the moon knowed what all you-uns hold hit
          responsible fur hit'd git scared and fall down out o' the sky.
          1956 Hall *Coll* What all kinds of herbs do you have on your porch?
          1973 *GSMNP*-5:8 I can play Oh My Darling, Nelly Gray, and I don't know
          what all, quite a few.
          1978 Montgomery *White Pine Coll* VI-3 They have a baby contest, and I don't
          remember what all they do have.
          1981 *GSMNP*-117:3 I don't know what all we didn't do.

what for *conj phr* (introducing a clause) Why, for what purpose, with what object.
[OED (at *what* pron 11c) Scottish and northern dialect; SND (at *what* pron V(5))
'why, for what reason' 1776→]
ULST.:   1921 Irvine *Poor Folk* 137 Whut fur shud he lave a shillin'?
          1934 Cavanagh *Dunleary Legend* 13 Ye did well, but what for did the king be
          after lockin' up the South wind?
          1936 White *Mrs Murphy* 232 And what for don't you think it?
          2005 Robinson *Alang Shore* 55 For pittin doon ma foes, whut-for / Shud A in
          moarnin be?
U.S.:   1931 Goodrich *Mt Homespun* 45 While Mrs. Fox had stepped outside on
          some errand, little Opal said to her sister, 'What for did you tell me Paw warn't
          at home?'
          1937 Thornborough *Great Smoky Mts* 134 I couldn't think what fur he's been
          talkin' to me about grasshoppers.

whenever, whaniver, whiniver, whuniver, whunävver *subordinating conj*
1 (usually in reference to a past event) Of a single point in time: when, at the
moment or very time that, as soon as. [OED *whenever* conj 2 'at the very time or
moment when, as soon as' now only Scottish and Irish use; SND *whanever* (at
whan conj) 'as soon as, at the very moment when']
ULST.:   1910 Joyce *English in Ireland* 348 = in general use in Ulster for *when*: 'I was in
          town this morning and whenever I came home I found the calf dead in the
          stable'.
          1920 Doyle *Ballygullion* 132 The day av the race came, an' whiniver I seen the
          boy passin' on the red bicycle, I down wi' my spade an' away to the big house.
          c1970 Gregg *Blaakberries* Thae wur yänst a wee gerrl wuz sweepin the fläer
          whun she fun a säxpenz. So whunävver she had redd up she went äntae the
          toon tae buy hersel a wee käd at the maarket.
          1975 Murphy *You're Talking* 82 'I have a horse in the stable', he says, 'and we'll
          put the crock of gold on him whenever you intend to go.'
          1990 McBride *Our Past* 51 The milkman grieved whenever Hamlet was
          replaced by a van sometime in the 1950s ... The milkman said his job became
          much more impersonal whenever his horse was replaced.
          1990 Todd *Words Apart* 168 Whenever he was in Belfast last week, he called to
          see us.

2002 Gillen *Wizard's Quill* 1 Whun iver I got near the hall I already hard the band / So I fired the oul bicycle ahint the cream'ry stan'.
2004 *No Photo?* How can they pretend that the thought of photographed decommissioning is a shock to them whenever the whole idea has been floating around for an age?
2005 Kennedy *SF Knew* This [happened] while the Government continued to treat them as phoney peacemakers and afforded them every courtesy of a democratic party whenever the opposite was patently the case.
2005 Robinson *Alang Shore* 68 A cudnae a bin more nor sax yeir oul whaniver A pit this strang memrie, like a poast-caird, in ma heid.
U.S.: **1878** Burt *Dialects* 413 The Pennsylvanians use *whenever* to signify 'as soon as'. Thus it will be said that '*whenever* the carriage came, the lady got in'.
1940 Haun *Hawk's Done* 88 Little Murf would be black too whenever he come into the world.
1973 *GSMNP*-86:5 Whenever I was about eight years old, when I got old enough to know where I was at, I left.
1974–75 McCracken *Logging* 3:9 Whenever he died, he had a spot about the size of a quarter right on the end of that bone.
1983 Pyle *CCC 50th Anniv* A:2:9 Whenever we come in, he said, 'Boy', he said, 'Am I glad to see you fellows.'
2 Of a process or extended period: through or during the time that.
ULST.: **1991** Kirk *NITCS* You don't seem to be as sleepy as you do whenever you're in your teens.
2002 Gillen *Wizard's Quill* 15 Mattha on the Fordson / Wus commin lik' a train, / It wus the nixt thing tae a circus, / Whuniver wae wur wains.
U.S.: **1973** *GSMNP*-4:1 Maybe one automobile in three months would go through that country whenever I was a boy.
1974–75 McCracken *Logging* 16:28 Whenever he was growing up, he said if he ever had any children, they would be named simple names.
1978 Montgomery *White Pine Coll* IV-2 My mother, whenever she was living, she just told you one time.

whinge *vb* To complain in a whining way. [< Old English *hwinsian*; OED *whinge* vb 'to whine, especially to complain peevishly' c1150→, originally Scottish and northern dialect; DOST *quhynge* vb 'to whine, complain'; SND *whinge* vb 'to whine, whimper, ... to complain or fret in a whining manner']
ULST.: **1880** Patterson *Antrim/Down Glossary* 115 = to whine, cry in a complaining way.
1953 Traynor *Donegal Glossary* 327 = to cry, especially in a fretful, peevish, complaining mannter.
U.S.: **1930** Shoemaker *1300 Penn Words* 68 *whingeing* = whining.

who all, wha a', who a' *pron phr* All of whom, exactly who. [OED *who-all* erroneously characterizes as U.S. dialect]
ULST.: **1989** Robinson *Scots in 17th Cent* 95 Non-standard English constructions are common in present-day Ulster-Scots such as 'it is *so*', 'who *all* is coming'.
1991 Kirk *NITCS* Who all was in that? Tell us about that.
2000 Fenton *Hamely Tongue* 231 Wha a' wuz there?; She towl me who a' wuz aksed.

U.S.:   1899 Green *Virginia Word-Book* 424 = all who, as '*who all* were there'.
1952 Wilson *Folk Speech NC* 607 = the use of *all* in this phrase is an attempt
to make an indefinite pronoun. It means 'who in general?'
1973 *GSMNP*-78:16 I know not too many, maybe one or two people that
could pretty well give you who all is buried here.

widow man, widder man, widdy man *n* A widower, man whose wife has died.
[DOST (at *widow* n 2b) 'a widower' 1643→]
ULST.:   1895 MacManus *Leadin' Road* 240 I'm a poor widdy woman—I mane to say
widdy man, your worship, with nine small childhre.
1904 Byers *Sayings of Ulster* 40 If a man has lost his wife he is a 'wida-man'.
1991 O'Kane *You Don't Say* 157 *widow man* = a widower (this expression is
quite widespread, as is 'widow-woman' for a widow).
U.S.:   1961 Murry *Salt* 20 He were a widder man, didn' have no woman, hunted an'
fished a heap, done a little farmin'.

widow woman *n* A widow, woman whose husband has died.
ULST.:   1895 MacManus *Leadin' Road* 150 I got an intherduction to Nelly Moriarty, a
widdy woman, with a snug sittin' down not far from me own townlan' at home.
1910 Joyce *English in Ireland* 350 = used for *widow*, ... especially in Ulster.
1920 Doyle *Ballygullion* 72 When a widow woman gets to her time av life, an'
no word av a second market, there's very little in breeches she'll not face.
1982 Glassie *Folk History* 50 They gave the money to poor men, widow
women, and orphans.
U.S.:   1937 Hall *Coll* An old widow woman lives at the Major Woody place.
1977 Weals *Cove Folk* We looked after them folks. If it was a widow woman,
she was took care of.

will can *vb phr* (usually in negative contexts and reduced to *'ll no* or *'ll not*) Will be
able to. Cf **might can.**
ULST.:   1886 Lyttle *Sons of Sod* 124 A'll no can stae oot lang.
1920 Gregory *Ulster Songs* 20 Yese neednae come pottherin' round my wee
farm—Ye'll can do my butther an' milk nae harm.
1959 Gregory *Ulster Ballads* 53 Now, beside the fire, / I'll can see an' spake /
Till my Heart's Desire.
2000 Fenton *Hamely Tongue* 237 A'll can dae that the morra; A'll naw can dae
it tae Monday.
U.S.:   1930 (in 1944 Wentworth *Amer Dial Dict* 92) 'She'll never kin catch a mouse
now' (said of a pet cat who became crippled).
1931 Maxfield *Speech SW Penn* 19 I don't think I will can go.
1982 Barrick *Coll* You won't can go.

without *conj* Unless. [OED *without* C1c 'if it be or were not the case that, unless'
c1200→, obsolete; DOST *without* conj C1c 'if it be or were not the case that, unless'
1500→; SND *without* conj 'unless, except that']
ULST.:   1861 Hume *Rabbin's Ollminick* 14 We used t' bathe at the Dhry Dock, but it
was dangersome t' jump in without ye cud swim.
1880 Patterson *Antrim/Down Glossary* 116 = unless: 'without you do it'.
1889 Hart *Derryreel* 86 He towld his wife she was never to pay away any of his
money again, without he would tell her what it was for.

U.S.:   1804 (in 1956 Eliason *Tarheel Talk* 304) They were as well done as thēy could
             be without you had been present.
             1937 Hall *Coll* You couldn't cow him without you whipped him.
             1973 *GSMNP*-88:94 I don't believe any of his children was married, without it
             was one.

withouten *prep* Without. [< Old English *wiputan* < from *wip* 'with' prep + *utan*
'outen' adv); OED *without* conj; DOST (at *without* conj C1) 'unless, except' 1520→]
    ULST.:   c1800 Thomson (in 1992 Scott and Robinson *Samuel Thomson* 7) But now ilk
             ane withouten fear / May to my door-step venture near.
             1997 Robinson *Grammar* 96 An alternative form of 'without' is *withouten* ... is
             only used in traditional literature with the 'doing without' or 'in the absense
             of' sense.
    U.S.:   1926 Roberts *Time of Man* 58 His pap come to this country withouten a cent.
             1939 Walker *Mtneer Looks* 9 An' I seed 'im throw a steer oncet an' tie 'm up
             withouten any help.

woman *n* One's wife (often used by a man in reference to his mate). Cf **man**. [OED
woman n 4a 'wife' 1450→, now only dialectal and U.S.; SND *woman* n 3(1) 'a wife'
1765→]
    ULST.:   1925 McKay *Mourne Folk* 109 His ould woman kept sayin', 'Didn't I tell ye,
             me man, what wud happen if ye offended the wee people?'
             1928 Ervine *Mountain* 97 What'll I do wi'out me wumman!
    U.S.:   1913 Kephart *Our Sthn High* 257 'The woman', as every wife is called, has her
             kingdom within the house.
             1939 Hall *Coll* We went over there a-chestnut hunting and took our women
             with us, leave them there.
             1979 Carpenter *Walton War* 69 'Now, Ellie', said Tome angrily, 'I ain't goin' to
             take that kind of talk from my woman.'

worm *n* The long, usually spiral-shaped metal tube attached to the cap of a **still** or
cooker and then submerged in cold water, in which vaporized alcohol condenses.
    ULST.:   1840 Boyce *Shandy Maguire* 13 Niver a minit at aze while there's a drap in the
             worm, or a grain in the kieve.
             1895 MacManus *Leadin' Road* 185 But it's seldom you were able to coax
             anything out of the worm to aiqual that.
             1920 Doyle *Ballygullion* 109 Big Billy Lenahan swore it was done like a worm
             in a still.
             1956 Bell *Orange Lily* 55 The lid of the creamery can was neatly drilled and a
             screw-fitting welded on for the attachment of the pipe and worm. The
             precious vapour rode along this pipe into the coils of the worm suspended in
             the cooling system, an old oil drum fed from a sluggish trinket that fed from
             the scrawbog further up the mountain.
             1978 McGuffin *Praise of Poteen* 14 A lateral tube was then luted into the
             worm, which was a copper tube of an inch and a half bore, coiled in a barrel
             for a flakestand (a worm tub). The tail of the worm where it emerged from the
             barrel was caulked with tow.
    U.S.:   1867 *Congressional Globe* 60 The singling tub is placed aside and the doubling
             tub put to the outlet of the worm.

1914 Arthur *Western NC* 273 When a sufficient quantity has been produced, the mash is removed from the still, and it is washed out, after which the 'singlings' are poured into the still and evaporated, passing through the worm a second time, thus becoming 'doublings', or high proof whiskey.

1967 Williams *Moonshining in Mts* 13 A copper coil made of tubing or retrieved from an old-fashioned water heater is a suitable 'worm'.

c1975 Lunsford *It Used To Be* 79 The worm is the copper pipe crooked around, possibly ten feet long. They bend it around a log or something to give it the proper curve. It's about eight to ten inches across and stands up about two and one-half feet high in a coil. The worm is put down in a keg and it is run out the bottom of the keg at the cover end. There is a spout that carries the water from a nearby branch or spring to pour into this keg to keep that worm cool. The worm is attached to the shank that's fastened to the cap of the still, and this cap is set on the still.

Y

yae See **ye**

y'all *pron* You (plural), all of you (the evidence for this form in Ulster is not altogether clear; documents have the spellings *ye aw* and *ye all*, which may represent contracted forms in speech). Cf **yous, your'uns, you'uns.**

ULST.:   1737 Murray *Letter* Now I beg of ye aw to come our here. *Ibid.* It shall be my earnest Request yence mere, to beg of ye aw to come here.
           1932 Quinn *McConaghy's Money* 72 What the hell's wrong with ye all?

U.S.:   1956 Hall *Coll* I played that night some for y'all and we went to bed.
           1993 Walker *Life History* 41 I don't want ya'll to think we are two bums.
           1994 Parton *Dolly* 14 Y'all get dressed. We're going over to Aunt Marth's house.

ye, yae *pron* You (singular and plural), in unstressed positions, especially as the direct object of a verb or the object of a preposition, less often as a subject. [OED *ye* pron 3 in objective case, c1449→; DOST *ye* pron 2 'in objective use as a direct object' c1550→; SND (at *ye* A) 'the original nominative has been retained in Scottish ... and has also been transferred to use as the objective case']

ULST.:   1737 Murray *Letter* Ye ken I had but sma Learning when I left ye.
           1840 Bleakley *Poems* 83 I ken the word yae aften read.
           1919 MacGill *Glenmornan* 190 'I suppose ye yerself was like me one time', said the girl.
           1936 White *Mrs Murphy* 162 You can't deny you were hidin' it from me, the both of ye.
           1964 Braidwood *Ulster/Elizabethan English* 88 The objective *ye* survives in Ulster *thankee.*
           1983 Marshall *Drumlister* 28 'I'll let ye know the reason', said John with scornful look.
           1983 Pepper *Ulster Knowledge* 18 May a doctor never earn a pound aff ye.
           2000 Fenton *Hamely Tongue* 239 *ye* = you (unstressed).

U.S.:   1913 Kephart *Our Sthn High* 84 I knowed I couldn't roust ye no other way.
           1939 Hall Coll If you call [a turkey] too much, you'll never get one to ye. *Ibid.* Get ye chairs. Git ye two moles.
           1957 *GSMNP*-23:2:28 [If] a neighbor wouldn't help ye, he wasn't considered a neighbor.
           1965 West *Git Tard in Hills* The 'ye' for 'you' is an interesting elision with such expressions as 'tell ye', 'see ye', 'tax ye'. The sound is not 'yee', but 'yi' (the 'i' pronounced as in 'it').

yees, yees, yeeze, ye's, yez See **yous**

yin See **one**

yinz See **you'uns**

yis, yiz See **yous**

yo, yow, yowe *n* A ewe. [OED (at *ewe* n) 14th century→; DOST *yow* n 'a female sheep, a ewe' 1474→; DARE (at *ewe* n) chiefly South, Midland]

ULST.: **1910** Russell *Language of Ulster* 26 A 'ewe' sheep is a 'yow'.

1937 Rowley *Tales of Mourne* 224 There's a couple o' oul' yowes, an' twa-three lambs is gone wandered in behin' Bernagh there, an' I'm for climbin' the Hare's gap an' goin' after them.

1983 Pepper *Ulster Knowledge* 14 'That's a fine yo' connotes a first class ewe 'worth a bit of money'.

2000 Fenton *Hamely Tongue* 240 = a ewe.

U.S.: **1961** Kurath and McDavid *Pron Engl Atl Sts* 157 Four types of pronouncing *ewe* are current in the Eastern states ... /ju/ is common in the North and in parts of the North Midland, especially in urbanized areas where the word is normally acquired in school or through reading ... /iu/ and /jiu/ are confined to the New England settlement area ... The type of /jo/ is heard in all parts of the Eastern States. In the South and South Midland it has rather general currency, except among the cultured; in the North Midland it is common in rural areas.

1980 *Smokies Heritage* 233 The ewe (pronounced yo in the Smokies) grazed in the Flanagan field for a while, but dogs began bothering her, and she had to be sold.

young one, young'n, young'un, young wan, young yin *n phr* A child, young person.

ULST.: **1863** Hume *Rabbin's Ollminick* 6 [Mon. Jennewerry 5] Oul' Chrissimis Day: They say it's more luckier nor the new one; but most o' the young ones knows nothin' about the oul' times afore the stile wos changed, an' the people lost their eleven days.

1920 McCallin *Fireside Tales* 183 As it sometimes happens with the oul' fellas like that, it was a young'n—only the slip of a girl not more than two or three and twenty—that took his fancy.

1928 McKay *Oul' Town* 14–15 Biddy was just as 'throughother' as the place she lived in; she hardly iver washed her face, and when she did give it a wipe she maintained she looked handsomer than the young wans.

2004 *Ate Up* 24 A guid run o hungerin thaa's whaat you yung yins need tae make them think mare o their mate.

U.S.: **1859** Taliaferro *Fisher's River* 114 With the 'young'uns' it was a generation from one Christmas to another.

1931 Goodrich *Mt Homespun* 63 [She was] quite unfit to take up the battle of life for herself and the three 'young-uns' clinging to her skirts.

1962 Dykeman *Tall Woman* 112 Go out and tend to the young'ns.

1997 Montgomery *Coll* He is forever talking about how sorry his young'uns are.

your ones, your uns *pron phr* Your family.

ULST.: **1880** Patterson *Antrim/Down Glossary* 118 *your uns* = your family.

1993 Montgomery *Barnish* 56 *your uns* = your family.

U.S.: **1993** Weaver *Scotch-Irish Speech* 14 With appropriate sons and daughters, sometimes 'your uns' become 'our uns', as 'we uns' become 'you uns'.

yous, yees, yeeze, ye's, yese, yez, yis, yiz, youse, yuhs *pron* You (plural). Cf **y'all, yous all, yous ones/yous'uns, you'uns.** [apparently a form arising in Ireland from Irish speakers attaching the plural suffix *-s* to *you* when used as a singular, reflecting a faulty learning of English]

ULST.:   **1829** McSparran *Irish Legend* 32 Bad luck to the sheep thief among yes.
1845 Carleton *Irish Peasantry* 22 Sure the life would be dhrownded out of both of ye, and yees might cotch a faver into the bargain ... as it's my turn to tell a story, I'll give yez something to amuse yez,—the best I can. *Ibid.* 35 A more faithful boy isn't alive this day nor I am to yez all, ye darlings of the world.
1880 Patterson *Antrim/Down Glossary* 118 Yous can't get commin' through this way.
1893 Bullock *Awkward Squad* 128 'Yis may laugh', shouted Terry, 'laugh till yi're blue.'
1895 MacManus *Leadin' Road* 197 I would give yez a dhrop would warmed yez down to the exthraymities of yer big toes.
1920 Gregory *Ulster Songs* 20 Yese neednae come pottherin' round my wee farm—Ye'll can do my butther an' milk nae harm.
1925 Hayward *Ulster Songs* 58 Come all yeeze airy bachelors / And a warning take by me, / Give over your wild ram-bell-in / And shun bad companee.
1933 MacNeill *Reverence Listens* 43 'I seen ye', says I, 'comin' home from the Soiree, the two o' yees, and there wasn't a patch of moonshine atween ye'.
1939 Paterson *Country Cracks* 52 I cud niver thole the whole winter through without news of ye's.
1953 Traynor *Donegal Glossary* 334 *yees, yez, yiz.*
1990 Todd *Words Apart* 172 *Yiz* is quare and crafty.
1997 Robinson *Grammar* 65 I'll see yis aa themoarra. *Ibid.* 72 Exactly the same situation [i.e. between emphasised and unstressed words] exists with the plural forms of 'you' in Ulster-Scots – *yiz* and *yous. Yiz see yous boys – qu'she – yiz ir aa daft.*
1998 Dolan *Dict Hiberno-English* 292 *yous* = plural of 'you'.

U.S.:   **1890** Davis *Disreputable Friend* 686 'Ah!' snarled Raegen ... 'you'se think you have me now, sure, don't you?'
1908 Heydrick *Provincialisms of SE Penn* 52 Did youse see them yesterday?
1932 Farrell *Young Lonigan* 138 Now shut up, and shake hands; if yuh don't, I'll fight the both of yuhs, said the dick.

yous'uns, yous ones, yousens, yousins, yuz yins *pron* You (plural). [This form is not attested in the U.S., but both **you'uns** and **yous** are; which show that it is produced by the same grammatical system]

ULST.:   **1955** Murphy *Culprit of Shadows* 6 Yous ones will have to brerr an' fence the garden ditch, the fowl may break out into the oats.
1978 Pepper *See Me* 30 If yousins don't get up I'll knock ye down.
1979 Pepper *Quare Geg* 33 Not always, however, are the younger generation unaware of the fact that there are precepts in speech that should be observed. A Belfast boy was heard telling a companion, 'It's not yousens. It's yous.'
2000 Fenton *Hamely Tongue* 240 *yous/yuz yins* = you people, you lot.

you'uns, yinz, yunz *pron* You (plural), all of you. Cf **y'all, yous, yous'uns**. [SND *you yins* (at *yin* pron/adj 3); LAUSC Midland]

ULST.: **1936** White *Mrs Murphy* 143 I wouldn't say but the hangman's rope might have been the end of Teddy if it hadn't been for you'uns.

1953 Traynor *Donegal Glossary* 335 Will you'uns stay long at Glenalla?

U.S.: **1810** Bell *Journey to Ohio* 37 Youns is a word I have heard several times, but what it means I don't know.

1862 (in **1999** Davis *Civil War Letters*) 77 I recived a letter from awl of younes the other day.

1939 Aurand *Idioms and Expressions* 25 YOU'NS ain't the only PEPPLES (pebbles) on the PEACH (beach).

1949 Kurath *Word Geog East US* 67 You'ns is the Midland form and occurs in the folk speech in Pennsylvania west of the Susquehanna, in large parts of West Virginia, and in the westernmost parts of Virginia and North Carolina.

1956 *GSMNP*-22:17 I was just scared, afraid some of you'uns would get bit.

1982 McCool *Pittsburghese* 39 = all of you, literally 'you ones': 'Are yunz going to the game?'

2004 *Yunzonics, yunz* = Possibly a shortening of you'uns, or a shorterning, or an attempt to make up a different, unique word for the plural form of the second-person of the pronoun you ... People who make fun of it draw attention to it locally by saying something like 'yunzes' or 'yinziz'.

yow, yowe See **yo**

yuhs See **yous**

yunz See **you'uns**

yuz yins See **yous ones**

SOURCES FOR CITATIONS

(Note: Citations in this volume are drawn from the following sources. After each item below is indicated the abbreviated information by which it is identified in the text.)

Adams, Frazier B. 1970. *Appalachia Revisited: How People Lived Fifty Years Ago*. Ashland, Ky.: Economy. (**1970** Adams *Appal Revisit*)

Adams, G. B. 1965. [Miscellaneous slip file, on deposit at Ulster Folk and Transport Museum, Cultra, Northern Ireland]. (**1965** Adams *File*)

Adams, G. B. 1975/76. 'The Diamonds of Ulster and Pennsylvania', *Ulster Folk and Transport Museum Yearbook*, pp 18–20. (**1975/76** Adams *Diamonds*)

Adams, G. B. 1980/81. 'Animal Call-Words', *Ulster Folk and Transport Museum Yearbook*, pp 26–27. (**1980/81** Adams *Call-Words*)

Adams, Sheila Kay. 1995. *Come Go Home with Me*. Chapel Hill, N.C.: University of North Carolina Press. (**1995** Adams *Come Go Home*)

Adamson, Ian. 1981. *The Identity of Ulster*. Bangor: Pretani.

Andrews, Scottie. 1997. *Dude's Mountain Vittles: Country Food Mountain Style*. Waynesville, N.C.: Old Style Printing. (**1997** Andrews *Mt Vittles*)

Anonymous. 1863. 'My Uncle Flatback's Plantation', *Southern Literary Messenger* 37 (Oct):590–604. (**1863** Anonymous *Flatback's Plantation*)

Anonymous. 1931. 'My Holiday in the Country: A Philological Essay', *Derry and Antrim Yearbook*, pp 30–32. (**1931** Anonymous *Holiday*)

Arthur, John Preston. 1914. *Western North Carolina: A History*. Raleigh, N.C.: Edwards & Broughton. (**1914** Arthur *Western NC*)

Ashcom, B. B. 1953. 'Notes on the Language of the Bedford, Pennsylvania, Subarea', *American Speech* 28:241–55. (**1953** Ashcom *Lg Bedford Penn*)

Aswell, James. c1940. 'Brief Glossary of Tennessee Idiom'. [Typescript prepared under auspices of the W.P.A., on deposit at the Tennessee State Library, Nashville]. (**c1940** Aswell *Glossary Tenn Idiom*)

Atkinson, A. 1823. *Ireland Exhibited to England*. Vol. 1. London: Baldwin, Cradock & Joy. (**1823** Atkinson *Ireland Exhibited*)

Atwood, E. Bagby. 1953. *A Survey of Verb Forms in the Eastern United States*. Ann Arbor: University of Michigan Press. (**1953** Atwood *Verbs East US*)

Aurand, A. Monroe, Jr. 1939. *Quaint Idioms and Expressions of the Pennsylvania Germans*. Lancaster, Pa.: Aurand Press. (**1939** Aurand *Idioms and Expressions*)

Bailey, Louise Howe. 1990. *Draw Up a Chair*. Skyland, N.C.: Hickory Printing. (**1990** Bailey *Draw Up Chair*)

Baldwin, Joseph Glover. 1853. 'Sketches of the Flush Times of Alabama and Mississippi, Part II', *Southern Literary Messenger* 19 (Feb):86–90. (**1853** Baldwin *Flush Times*)

Ballymena Observer. 1892. [Selected citations in the *English Dialect Dictionary*, ed. Joseph Wright. 1898–1905. London: Henry Frowde.] (**1892** *Ballymena Observer*)

'Bangor Words'. 1942. [Typescript on deposit at Ulster Folk and Transport Museum, Cultra, Northern Ireland]. (**1942** *Bangor Words*)

Barnwell, Lila Ripley. 1951. 'Our Mountain Speech', *Asheville Citizen* (4 Jan). (**1951** Barnwell *Our Mt Speech*)

Barrick, Mac E. 1982. [Collection of material from North-Central Pennsylvania, on deposit at *Dictionary of American Regional English* editorial office, Madison, Wisc.] (**1982** Barrick *Coll*)

Bartlett, John Russell. 1848. *Dictionary of Americanisms: A Glossary of Words and Phrases Usually Considered Peculiar to the United States*. Boston: Little, Brown. (**1848** Bartlett *Americanisms*)

Bartlett, John Russell. 1859. *Dictionary of Americanisms: A Glossary of Words and Phrases Usually Considered Peculiar to the United States*. Boston: Little, Brown. (**1859** Bartlett *Americanisms*)

Beggs, Thomas. 1834. *A Minstrel's Offering: Original Poems and Songs*. Belfast: Hugh Clark. (**1834** Beggs *Minstrel's Offering*)

Bell, Jonathan, and Mervyn Watson. 1988. *Farming in Ulster: Historic Photographs of Ulster Farming and Food*. Belfast: Friar's Bush. (**1988** Bell and Watson *Farming in Ulster*)

Bell, Margaret Van Horn Dwight. 1912. *A Journey to Ohio in 1810 as Recorded in the Journal of Margaret Van Horn Dwight*. New Haven, Conn.: Yale University Press. (**1810** Bell *Journey to Ohio*)

Bell, Sam Hanna. 1956. *Erin's Orange Lily*. London: Dobson. (**1956** Bell *Orange Lily*)

Berrey, Lester. 1940. 'Southern Mountain Dialect', *American Speech* 15:45–54. (**1940** Berrey *Sthn Mt Dialect*)

Berry, Pearlleen D., and Mary Eva Repass. n.d. *Granpa Says ... Superstitions and Sayings from Eastern Kentucky*. Fredericksburg, Va.: Foxhound Enterprises. (**n.d.** Berry and Repass *Granpa Says*)

Betts, Leonidas, and Richard Walser. 1974. *Gateway to North Carolina Folklore*. Raleigh: North Carolina State University. (**1974** Betts and Walser *NC Folklore*)

Bewley, Irene. 1943. 'Picturesque Speech', *Tennessee Folklore Society Bulletin* 9 (3); 4. (**1943** Bewley *Picturesque Speech*)

Bird, William. c1926. 'Wordlist Compiled at Cullowhee, North Carolina'. [Typescript in Horace Kephart Collection, Hunter Library, Western Carolina University, Cullowhee, N.C.] (**c1926** Bird *Cullowhee Wordlist*)

Black, George Fraser. 1921. *Scotland's Mark on America*. New York: America's Making. (**1921** Black *Scotland's Mark*)

Bleakley, William. 1840. *Moral and Religious Poems*. Belfast: James Wilson. (**1840** Bleakley *Poems*)

Botkin, B. A. 1945. *Lay My Burden Down*. Chicago: University of Chicago Press. (**1945** Botkin *Lay Burden Down*)

Bowden, Hugh. 1901. 'The Presbyterian Congregation at Portaferry, in the Ardes in the County of Down, about the Year 1825', *Ulster Journal of Archaeology*, 2nd series, 7:7–8. (**1825** Bowden *Portaferry Congregation*)

Bowman, Elizabeth Skaggs. 1938. *Land of High Horizons: An Intimate Interpretation of the Great Smokies*. Kingsport: Southern. (**1938** Bowman *High Horizons*)

Boyle, Francis. 1811. *Miscellaneous Poems*. Belfast: Lyons. (**1811** Boyle *Poems*)

Boyce, John ('Paul Peppergrass'). 1840. *Shandy Maguire; or, Tricks upon Travellers*. New York: Pratt. (**1840** Boyce *Shandy Maguire*)

Boyle, Francis. 1811. *Miscellaneous Poems*. Belfast: Lyons. (**1811** Boyle *Poems*)

Brackenridge, Henry Marie. 1868. *Recollections of Persons and Places in the West*. Philadelphia: Lippincott. (**1868** Brackenridge *Recollections*)

Brackenridge, Hugh Henry. 1815. *Modern Chivalry*. Edited for the Modern Reader by Lewis Leary. Schenectady: New College and University Press. (**1815** Brackenridge *Modern Chivalry*)

Bradley, Francis Aspenwall. 1915. 'Hobnobbing with Hill-billies', *Harper's* 93 (Dec):91–103. (**1915** Bradley *Hobnobbing*)

Bradley, Francis W. 1950. 'A Word-list from South Carolina', *Publication of the American Dialect Society* 14:3–73. (**1950** Bradley *Word-list from SC*)

Braidwood, John. 1964. 'Ulster and Elizabethan English', *Ulster Dialects: An Introductory Symposium*, ed. G. B. Adams, 5–110. Holywood, Northern Ireland: Ulster Folk Museum. (**1964** Braidwood *Ulster/Elizabethan English*)

Braidwood, John. 1965. 'Towards an Ulster Dialect Dictionary', *Ulster Dialect Archive Bulletin* 4:3–14. (**1965** Braidwood *Ulster Dial Dict*)

Braidwood, John. 1969. *The Ulster Dialect Lexicon*. Belfast: Queen's University Belfast. (**1969** Braidwood *Ulster Dial Lex*)

Braidwood, John. 1974. 'Crowls and Runts: Ulster Dialect Terms for the Runt of the Litter', *Ulster Folklife* 20:71–84. (**1974** Braidwood *Crowls and Runts*)

Braidwood, John. 1977. 'The Brogue on the Tongue (Poor English – Good Irish)', *Queen's University Association Annual Report*, 67–74. Belfast. (**1977** Braidwood *Brogue on Tongue*)

Braidwood, John. 1988. [Notes shared with the editor]. (**1988** Braidwood *Notes*)

Bratton, Robert. 1931. *Round the Turf Fire: Humourous Sketches of Ulster Country Life*. Dublin: Talbot. (**1931** Bratton *Turf Fire*)

Briggs, Charles F. 1840–47. *The Trippings of Tom Pepper, or, The Results of Romancing*. 2 vols. New York: Burgess, Stringer & Co. (**1847** Briggs *Tom Pepper*)

Broaddus, James, and W. L. McAtee. 1983. 'An Annotated Estill County, Kentucky Word List', *Midwestern Journal of Language and Folklore* 9:24–62. (**1983** Broaddus and McAtee *Estill Co Word List*)

Broome, Harvey. 1970. *Harvey Broome, Earth Man: Some Miscellaneous Writings.* Knoxville, Tenn.: Greenbrier. (**1970** Broome *Earth Man*)

Brown, Calvin S. 1891. 'Dialectal Forms in Tennessee', *Publications of the Modern Language Association* 6:171–75. (**1891** Brown *Dial in Tenn*)

Brown, John. 1795. 'John Brown's Journal of Travels in Western North Carolina in 1795. Edited by A. R. Newsome', *North Carolina Historical Review* 11:284–313. (**1795** Brown *Journal*)

Bruce, David. 1801. *Poems Chiefly in the Scottish Dialect, Originally Written under the Signature of the Scots-Irishman.* Washington, Pa.: J. Colerick. (**1801** Bruce *Poems*)

Bullock, Shan F. 1893. *The Awkward Squad and Other Stories.* London: Cassell. (**1893** Bullock *Awkward Squad*)

Burnett, G. L. 1939. *Gap o' the Mountains.* Knoxville, Tenn.: Newman. (**1939** Burnett *Gap o' Mts*)

Burt, N. C. 1878. 'The Dialects of Our Country', *Appleton's Journal*, new series, 5:411–17. (**1878** Burt *Dialects*)

Bush, Florence Cope. 1992. *Dorie: Woman of the Mountains.* Knoxville: University of Tennessee Press. (**1992** Bush *Dorie*)

Buxbaum, Katherine. 1929. 'Some Iowa Locutions', *American Speech* 4:302–04. (**1929** Buxbaum *Iowa Locutions*)

Byers, John W. 1901. 'Ulsterisms', *Northern Whig* (6 May). (**1901** Byers *Ulsterisms*)

Byers, John W. 1904. *Sayings, Proverbs, and Humour of Ulster.* Belfast: Wm Strain & Sons. (**1904** Byers *Sayings of Ulster*)

Byers, John W. c1910. 'Glossary'. [Typescript on deposit at Ulster Folk and Transport Museum, Cultra, Northern Ireland]. (**c1910** Byers *Glossary*)

Byers, John W. c1912. 'The Characteristics of the Ulsterman'. Privately published. (**c1912** Byers *Characteristics of Ulsterman*)

Calhoun, John C. 1851–56 [1816]. *The Works of John C. Calhoun.* 6 vols. New York: Appleton. (**1816** Calhoun *Works*)

Campbell, Carlos C. 1960. *Birth of a National Park in the Great Smoky Mountains.* Knoxville, Tenn.: University of Tennessee Press. (**1960** Campbell *Birth Natl Park*)

Campbell, John C. 1921. *The Southern Highlander and His Homeland.* New York: Russell Sage. (**1921** Campbell *Sthn Highlander*)

Carleton, William. 1845. *Traits and Stories of the Irish Peasantry.* 2 vols. Reprinted in 1990, Savage, Md.: Barnes & Noble. (**1845** Carleton *Irish Peasantry*)

Carpenter, Cal. 1979. *The Walton War and Tales of the Great Smoky Mountains.* Lakemont, Ga.: Copple House. (**1979** Carpenter *Walton War*)

Carpenter, Jacob. c1845–1920. [Diary, excerpted in Alberta Pierson Hannum. 1943. *The Mountain People: The Great Smokies and the Blue Ridge*, ed. Roderick Peattie, 73–151. New York: Vanguard. (**1868** Carpenter *Diary*)

Carr, Joseph William. 1905. 'A List of Words from Northwest Arkansas', *Dialect Notes* 3:68–103. (**1905** Carr *Words NW Ark*)

Carson, Joseph. 1831. *Poems, Odes, Songs and Satires*. Newry: Morgan & Stevenson. (**1831** Carson *Poems*)

Carter, Forrest. 1976. *The Education of Little Tree*. New York: Delacorte. (**1976** Carter *Little Tree*)

Carter, Ted. 1975. 'It's the Gospel Truth', *Asheville Times* (11 Dec). (**1975** Carter *Gospel Truth*)

Cavanagh, Kit. 1934. *A Dunleary Legend and Other Tales*. Belfast: Quota. (**1934** Cavanagh *Dunleary Legend*)

Cavender, Anthony. 1990. *A Folk Medical Lexicon of South Central Appalachia*. Johnson City, Tenn.: East Tennessee State University. (**1990** Cavender *Folk Medical Lex*)

Cavender, Anthony. 1996. 'A Note on the Origin and Meaning of Bold Hives in the American South', *Southern Folklore* 53:17–24. (**1996** Cavender *Bold Hives*)

Cerello, James. 1967. 'A Preliminary Lexical Survey of Certain Dialect Peculiarities Found among Elderly Residents of the Eastern Central and Southern Districts of Dakota County, Minnesota'. River Falls, Wisc.: University of Wisconsin Master's thesis. (**1967** Cerello *Dakota Co*)

Chalmers, Marjorie. 1975. *'Better I Stay': An Invitation in the Great Smokies*. Gatlinburg, Tenn.: Crescent. (**1975** Chalmers *Better*)

Chapman, Ashton. c1951. 'Speech of WNC Mountain People Is Often Confusing to Newcomers', *Asheville Citizen*. (**c1951** Chapman *Speech Confusing*)

Chapman, Maristan. 1928. *The Happy Mountain*. New York: Literary Guild. (**1928** Chapman *Happy Mt*)

Chase, Richard. 1942. *The Jack Tales*. Boston: Houghton Mifflin. (**1942** Chase *Jack Tales*)

Clapin, Sylva. 1902. *A New Dictionary of Americanisms: Being a Glossary of Words Supposed to be Peculiar to the United States and the Dominion of Canada*. New York: Louis Weiss. (**1902** Clapin *Americanisms*)

Clifford, John. c1982. *Poems of John Clifford*. Larne: Larne and District Folklore Society. (**c1982** Clifford *Poems*)

Cobb, Collier. 1910. 'Early English Survivals on the Outer Banks', *University of North Carolina Magazine* 40 (Feb):3–10. (**1910** Cobb *Early English*)

Cochrane, Gavin. 1766. [Letter of June 27 to the Earl of Dartmouth. Cited in M. M. Mathews. 1959. 'Of Matters Lexicographical', *American Speech* 34:126–30.] (**1766** Cochrane *Letter*)

Colcord, Joanna. 1945. *Sea Language Comes Ashore*. New York: Cornell Maritime
  Press. (**1945** Colcord *Sea Language*)

Combs, Josiah [H.] 1916. 'Old, Early and Elizabethan English in the Southern
  Mountains', *Dialect Notes* 4:283–97. (**1916** Combs *Old Early English*)

Combs, Josiah H. 1919. 'A Word-list from the South', *Dialect Notes* 5:31–40. (**1919**
  Combs *Word-list South*)

'Contributions of the Cornell University Dialect Society'. 1901. *Dialect Notes*
  2:135–50. (**1901** *Contrib Cornell Univ*)

Cooper, Horton. 1972. *North Carolina Mountain Folklore and Miscellany*.
  Murfreesboro, N.C.: Johnson. (**1972** Cooper *NC Mt Folklore*)

Cooper, James Fenimore. 1823. *The Pioneers*. 2 vols. New York: Wiley. (**1823**
  Cooper *Pioneers*)

'Cracker'. 1921. *South Carolina Historical and Genealogical Magazine* 22:99–100.
  (**1921** *Cracker*)

Craig, John. c1750. [Diary]. See Robert Davidson. (**c1750** Craig *Diary*)

Crane, Stephen. 1895. *Red Badge of Courage: An Episode in the American Civil War*.
  New York: Appleton. (**1895** Crane *Badge of Courage*)

Crockett, David. 1834. *Narrative of the Life of David Crockett of the State of
  Tennessee*. Baltimore: Carey, Hart. Facsimile edition published 1973, Knoxville,
  Tenn.:University of Tennessee Press. (**1834** Crockett *Narrative*)

Crockett, David. 1835. *An Account of Col. Crockett's Tour to the North and Down
  East, in the Year of Our Lord One Thousand Eight Hundred Thirty-Four*.
  Philadelphia: Carey & Hart. (**1835** Crockett *Account*)

Cromie, Will. 2004. 'A Byre o a Hoose', *Ullans: The Magazine for Ulster-Scots*
  9/10:116–17. (**2004** Cromie *Byre*)

Cromie, Will. 2004. 'M'Craidy's Monkey', *Ullans: The Magazine for Ulster-Scots*
  9/10:112–15. (**2004** Cromie *M'Craidy's Monkey*)

Crozier, Alan S. 1984. 'The Scotch-Irish Influence on American English', *American
  Speech* 59:310–31. (**1984** Crozier *Scotch-Irish Influence*)

Crumb, D. S. 1903. 'The Dialect of Southeastern Missouri', *Dialect Notes* 2:304–37.
  (**1903** Crumb *Dialect SE Missouri*)

Dalton, Alford P. 1950. 'A Wordlist from Southern Kentucky', *Publication of the
  American Dialect Society* 15:22–23. (**1950** Dalton *Wordlist*)

Daly, Cahal. 1998. *Steps on My Pilgrim Journey: Memories and Reflections*. Dublin:
  Veritas. (**1998** Daly *Pilgrim Journey*)

Dargan, Olive Tilford. 1925. *Highland Annals*. New York: Scribner's Sons. (**1925**
  Dargan *Highland Annals*)

Davidson, Robert. 1847. *A History of the Presbyterian Church in the State of Kentucky,
  with a Preliminary Sketch of the Churches in the Valley of Virginia*. New York:
  Davidson. (**1847** Davidson *Presby Church in Kentucky*)

Davis, Hattie Caldwell. 1999. *Civil War Letters and Memories from the Great Smoky Mountains*. Maggie Valley, N.C.: privately published. (**1999** Davis *Civil War Letters*)

Davis, Hubert. 1973. 'Glossary', *'Pon My Honor Hit's the Truth: Tall Tales from the Mountains*, 93–102. Murfreesboro, N.C.: Johnson. (**1973** Davis *'Pon My Honor*)

Davis, Rebecca Harding. 1863. 'The Promise of the Dawn', *Atlantic Monthly* 11 (Jan):10–25. (**1863** Davis *Promise of Dawn*)

Davis, Richard Harding. 1890. 'My Disreputable Friend, Mr. Raegen', *Scribner's Magazine* 8 (Dec):685–695. (**1890** Davis *Disreputable Friend*)

De Armond, Nora. 1982. *So High the Sun*. Knoxville, Tenn.: Jostens. (**1982** De Armond *So High*)

Devine, Michael, and Peter McVerry. 1999. 'SF Face Backlash on Bodies', *Belfast Telegraph* (6 Feb). (**1999** Devine and McVerry *SF Face Backlash*)

Dictionary of American Regional English. 1965–84. [Responses to nation-wide interviews and miscellaneous submissions in project files, Madison, Wisc.] (**1966–84** *DARE Coll*)

A Dictionary of the Queen's English. 1965. Raleigh: North Carolina Department of Natural and Economic Resources. (**1965** *Dict Queen's English*)

Dingus, L. R. 1927. 'Appalachian Mountain Words', *Dialect Notes* 5:468–71. (**1927** Dingus *Mt Words*)

Dodds, Brian. 2003. 'The Newry Nyuck'. (<http//: www.geocities.com/briaind/nyuck2.htm>) (**2003** Dodds *Newry Nyuck*)

Dolan, Terence P., ed. 1998. *Dictionary of Hiberno-English*. Dublin: Gill & McMillan. (**1998** Dolan *Dict Hiberno-English*)

Downing, Jack. 1834. *The Life of Andrew Jackson, President of the United States*. Philadelphia: Greenbank. (**1834** Downing *Life Andrew Jackson*)

Doyle, Lynn. 1920. *Ballygullion*. Dublin: Maunsel. (**1920** Doyle *Ballygullion*)

Doyle, Lynn. 1921. *An Ulster Childhood*. Dublin: Maunsel. (**1921** Doyle *Ulster Childhood*)

Doyle, Lynn. c1950. 'Polis Protection', *Brave Crack! An Anthology of Ulster Wit and Humour*, 9–27. Belfast: Carter. (**c1950** Doyle *Polis Protection*)

Dunglison, Robley. 1931 [1829]. 'Americanisms from *Virginia Literary Museum and Journal of Belle-Lettres, Arts, Sciences, &c*', *The Beginnings of American English: Texts and Essays*, ed. Mitford M. Mathews, 99–112. Chicago: University of Chicago Press. (**1829** Dunglison *Virginia Museum*)

Dwyer, Paul. 1971. *Dictionary for Yankees and Other Uneducated People*. Highlands, N.C.: Merry Mountaineers. (**1971** Dwyer *Dict for Yankees*)

Dyer, Gustavus W. et al., eds. 1985 [1922]. *Tennessee Civil War Veterans Questionnaire*. 5 vols. Easley, S.C.: Southern Historical Press. (**1922** Dyer *Tenn Civil War Ques*)

Dykeman, Wilma. 1955. *The French Broad*. New York: Holt, Rinehart & Winston. (**1955** Dykeman *French Broad*)

Dykeman, Wilma. 1962. *The Tall Woman*. Newport, Tenn.: Wakestone. (**1962** Dykeman *Tall Woman*)

Eaton, Allen. 1937. *Handicrafts of the Southern Highlands*. New York: Russell Sage. (**1937** Eaton *Handicrafts*)

Edson, H. A., and Edith M. Fairchild. 1895. 'Tennessee Mountains in Word Lists', *Dialect Notes* 1:370–77. (**1895** Edson and Fairchild *Tenn Mts*)

Edwards, Lawrence. 1963. *Gravel in My Shoe*. Montevallo, Ala.: Times. (**1963** Edwards *Gravel*)

Eggleston, Edward. 1871. *The Hoosier Schoolmaster*. New York: J. B. Ford. (**1871** Eggleston *Hoosier Schoolmaster*)

Eggleston, Edward. 1874. *The Circuit Rider: A Tale of the Heroic Age*. New York: J. B. Ford. (**1874** Eggleston *Circuit Rider*)

'An Elegy on the Late Revd Mess Sawney Sinkler, Teacher of Plunket-Street Meeting-House, Dublin, wha departed out o' this Warld the first o' April, the Year o' our Lord 1722'. 1733. *The Humble Remonstrance of the Five-Foot-Highians against the AntiChristian Practice of Using a Standard in Enlisting of Soldiers ...*, 19–23.Dublin: Roberts. (**1733** *Sawney Sinkler*)

Eliason, Norman E. 1956. *Tarheel Talk: An Historical Study of the English Language in North Carolina to 1860*. Chapel Hill, N.C.: University of North Carolina Press. (**1956** Eliason *Tarheel Talk*)

'Elijoy Church (Baptist) – Blount County ("Arm of Miller's Cove Church on Elijoy") Records, 1818–1878, Transcribed by Betty R. Davis'. 1989. [On deposit in McClung Collection, Knox County Public Library, Knoxville, Tenn.] (**1856** *Elijoy Minutes*)

England, George Allan. 1914. 'Rural Locutions of Maine and Northern New Hampshire', *Dialect Notes* 4:67–83. (**1914** England *Rural Locutions*)

Enslow, Ella. 1935. *Schoolhouse in the Foothills*. New York: Simon & Schuster. (**1935** Enslow *Schoolhouse*)

Erskine, Ralph. 1943. 'Adventures among the Mountain Craftsmen', *The Great Smokies and the Blue Ridge*, ed. Roderick Peattie, 201–16. New York: Vanguard. (**1943** Erskine *Adventures*)

Ervine, St John G. 1920. *Mrs Martin's Man*. New York: Macmillan. (**1920** Ervine *Mrs Martin's Man*)

Ervine, St John G. 1928. *The Mountain and Other Stories*. London: Allen & Unwin. (**1928** Ervine *Mountain*)

Erwin, Alan. 2003. 'Pressure Grows on Human Rights Boss to Quit Job', *Belfast Telegraph* (31 July). (**2003** Erwin *Pressure Grows*)

Evans, E. Estyn. 1957. *Irish Folk-Ways*. London: Routledge & Kegan Paul. (**1957** Evans *Irish Folk-Ways*)

Evans, E. Estyn. 1965. 'Cultural Relics of the Ulster-Scots in the Old West of North America', *Ulster Folklife* 11:33–38. (**1965** Evans *Cultural Relics*)

Evans, E. Estyn. 1969. 'The Scotch-Irish: Their Cultural Adaptation and Heritage in the American Old West', *Essays in Scotch-Irish History*, ed. E. R. R. Green, 69–86. London: Routledge & Kegan Paul. (**1969** Evans *Cultural Adaptation*)

Farmer, John. 1889. *Americanisms – Old and New; A Dictionary of Words, Phrases, and Colloquialisms Peculiar to the United States, British America, etc.* London: Poulter. (**1889** Farmer *Americanisms*)

Farrell, James. 1932. *Young Lonigan.* New York: Vanguard. (**1932** Farrell *Young Lonigan*)

Federal Writers' Project. 1938. *The Ocean Highway: New Brunswick, New Jersey, to Jacksonville, Florida.* New York: Modern Age. (**1938** FWP *Ocean Highway*)

Federal Writers' Project. 1939. *A Guide to Tennessee.* New York: Viking. (**1939** FWP *Guide Tenn*)

Fenton, James. 2000. *The Hamely Tongue: A Personal Record of Ulster-Scots in County Antrim.* Belfast: Ullans Press for the Ulster-Scots Language Society. (**2000** Fenton *Hamely Tongue*)

Fenton, James. 2000. *Thonner and Thon: An Ulster-Scots Collection.* Belfast: Ullans Press. (**2000** Fenton *Thonner and Thon*)

Fenton, James. 2004. 'Slaimish'. Unpublished poem. (**2004** Fenton *Slaimish*)

Fenton, James. 2004–05. [Notes to the editor, personal communication]. (**2004/2005** Fenton *Notes*)

Fink, Paul [M.] 1974. *Bits of Mountain Speech.* Boone, N.C.: Appalachian Consortium. (**1974** Fink *Bits Mt Speech*)

Fink, Paul [M.] 1975. *Backpacking Was the Only Way.* Johnson City, Tenn.: East Tennessee State University. (**1975** Fink *Backpacking*)

Fisher, Ben C. 1990. *Mountain Preacher Stories: Laughter among the Trumpets.* Boone, N.C.: Appalachian Consortium. (**1990** Fisher *Preacher Stories*)

Fithian, Philip Vickers. 1773. *Journal of Philip Vickers Fithian, 1773–74, a Plantation Tutor of the Old Dominion*, ed. with an introduction by Hunter Dickson Farish. Charlottesville: University Press of Virginia. (**1774** Fithian *Journal*)

Fitzpatrick, Kathleen. 1937. *They Lived in County Down.* London: Chatto & Windus. (**1937** Fitzpatrick *Lived Co Down*)

Flecher, Henry McD. 1866. *Poems, Songs and Ballads.* Belfast: Reed. (**1866** Flecher *Poems*)

Flint, Timothy. 1826. *Recollections of the Last Ten Years, Passed in Occasional Residences and Journeyings in the Valley of the Mississippi.* Boston: Cummings, Hilliard. (**1826** Flint *Recollections*)

Foster, Lloyd. 1970. 'History of Walker Valley'. [Typescript of his interviews transcribed by Mary Ruth Chiles, on deposit in Library, Great Smoky Mountains National Park, Gatlinburg, Tenn.] (**1970** Foster *Walker Valley*)

Foster, Lydia M. 1933. *Tyrone among the Bushes*. Belfast: Quota. (**1933** Foster *Tyrone among Bushes*)

Frome, Michael. 1966. *Strangers in High Places: The Story of the Great Smoky Mountains*. Garden City, N.Y.: Doubleday. (**1966** Frome *Strangers*)

Fruit, John P. 1890. 'Kentucky Words and Phrases', *Dialect Notes* 1:63–69. (**1890** Fruit *Kentucky Words/Phrases*)

Fruit, John P. 1892. 'Kentucky Words', *Dialect Notes* 1:229–34. (**1892** Fruit *Kentucky Words*)

Gabbard, Alex. 1992. *Return to Thunder Road: The Story behind the Legend*. Lenoir City, Tenn.: Gabbard. (**1992** Gabbard *Thunder Road*)

Gailey, Alan. 1984. 'Scotland, Ireland, and America: Migrant Culture in the 17th and 18th Centuries', *Irish Studies Working Papers* 84–1. (**1984** Gailey *Migrant Culture*)

Gainer, Patrick W. 1975. 'Speech of the Mountaineers', *Witches Ghosts and Signs: Folklore of the Southern Appalachians*, 1–18. Morgantown, W.V.: Seneca. (**1975** Gainer *Speech Mtneer*)

Gallagher, Patrick. 1939. *My Story*. London: Cape. (**1939** Gallagher *My Story*)

Garber, Aubrey. 1976. *Mountain-ese: Basic Grammar for Appalachia*. Radford, Va.: Commonwealth. (**1976** Garber *Mountain-ese*)

Garland, Hamlin. 1917. *A Son of the Middle Border*. New York: Macmillan. (**1917** Garland *Son of Border*)

Gibbons, Phebe Earle. 1869. 'Pennsylvania Dutch', *Atlantic Monthly* 29 (Oct):473–87. (**1869** Gibbons *Pennsylvania Dutch*)

Gillen, Charlie. 2002. *From the Wizard's Quill*. N.p.: n.p. (**2002** Gillen *Wizard's Quill*)

Ginns, Patsy Moore. 1982. *Snowbird Gravy and Dishpan Pie: Mountain People Recall*. Chapel Hill, N.C.: University of North Carolina Press. (**1982** Ginns *Snowbird Gravy*)

Given, Thomas. 1900. *Poems from College and Country, by Three Brothers*. Belfast: Baird. (**1900** Given *Poems*)

Glassie, Henry. 1965. 'Old Barns of Appalachia', *Mountain Life and Work* 40 (summer):21–30. (**1965** Glassie *Old Barns*)

Glassie, Henry, 1982. *Irish Folk History: Texts from the North*. Philadelphia: University of Pennsylvania Press. (**1982** Glassie *Folk History*)

G. M. M. 1839. 'The Bachelor Beset; or, the Rival Candidates', *Southern Literary Messenger* 5 (Nov):751–57. (**1839** M.G.M. *Bachelor Beset*)

Goodrich, Frances Louisa. 1931. *Mountain Homespun*. New Haven, Conn.: Yale University Press. (**1931** Goodrich *Mt Homespun*)

Gould, John. 1975. *Maine Lingo*. Camden, Me.: Down East Magazine. (**1975** Gould *Maine Lingo*)

Graham, William. 2000. 'Bread and Butter Back on the Menu', *Irish News* (6 Jan). (**2000** Graham *Bread and Butter*)

Graham, William. 2000. 'Political Slings and Arrows in America', *Irish News* (17 Mar). (**2000** Graham *Slings and Arrows*)

Graham, William. 2004. '"Government Nod" to the DUP and Alliance', *Irish News* (22 June):8. (**2004** Graham *Government Nod*)

Grant, William, and David Murison, eds. 1931–76. *Scottish National Dictionary*. 10 vols. Edinburgh: Scottish National Dictionary Association. (**1931–76** Grant and Murison *SND*)

Great Smoky Mountains National Park Golden Anniversary Commemorative Book: 1934–1984. 1985. Gatlinburg, Tenn.: Oakley Enterprises. (**1956–84** *GSMNP*)

Green, Bennett Wood. 1899. *Word-Book of Virginia Folk-Speech*. Richmond, Va.: Jones. (**1899** Green *Virginia Word-Book*)

Gregg, Robert J. 1958. 'Notes on the Phonology of a County Antrim Scotch-Irish Dialect'. *Orbis* 7:392–406. (**1958** Gregg *Phonology*)

Gregg, Robert J. 1959. 'Notes on the Phonology of a County Antrim Scotch-Irish Dialect', *Orbis* 8:400–24. (**1959** Gregg *Phonology*)

Gregg, Robert J. c1970. 'The Boany Wee Bunch o Blaakberries'. [Transcription of traditional anecdote, deposited in the Ulster Folk and Transport Museum, Cultra, Northern Ireland.] (**c1970** Gregg *Blaakberries*)

Gregg, Robert J. 1985. *The Scotch-Irish Dialect Boundaries in the Province of Ulster*. CFH/FCEH no. 6. [Port Credit, Ontario]: Canadian Federation for the Humanities. (**1985** Gregg *Scotch-Irish*)

Gregory, Pádraic. 1912. *The Ulster Folk*. London: David Nutt. (**1912** Gregory *Ulster Folk*)

Gregory, Pádraic. 1920. *Ulster Songs and Ballads*. Dublin: Talbot. (**1920** Gregory *Ulster Songs*)

Gregory, Pádraic. 1959. *Complete Collected Ulster Ballads*. Belfast: Mullan & Son. (**1959** Gregory *Ulster Ballads*)

Gwynn, Stephen. 1903. *Highways and Byways in Donegal and Antrim*. London: Macmillan. (**1903** Gwynn *Highways and Byways*)

Hafiz. 1801. 'A Winter Sketch (in the Scotch Dialect)', *Belfast News-Letter* (10 Nov):2. (**1801** Hafiz *Winter Sketch*)

Haldane, Isabel, Lady Duntreath. 1630. '[Letter] to Her Son, Archibald Edmonstone, Laird of Duntreath'. *Historical Manuscripts Commission Report on Manuscripts in Various Collections. Volume V.: The Manuscripts of Col. Mordaunt-Hay, of Duns Castle; Sir Archibald Edmonstone of Duntreath; Sir John James Graham, of Fintry, K.C.M.G., etc.*, 135–37. Hereford: HMSO, 1909. (**1630** Haldane *Letter*)

Hall, Bayard Rush. 1843. *The New Purchase: or, Seven and a Half Years in the Far West*. New York: Appleton. (**1843** Hall *New Purchase*)

Hall, Joseph S. 1937–67. [Interviews and other material collected by Joseph Sargent Hall, on deposit in Library, Great Smoky Mountains National Park, Gatlinburg, Tenn., and at Archives of Appalachia, East Tennessee State University, Johnson City, Tenn.] (**1937–67** Hall *Coll*)

Hall, Joseph S. 1937–39. [Notebooks, on deposit at Archive of Folk Culture, Library of Congress, Washington, D.C., and at Archives of Appalachia, East Tennessee State University, Johnson City, Tenn.] (**1939** Hall *Notebook*)

Hall, Joseph S. 1942. *The Phonetics of Great Smoky Mountain Speech*. American Speech Reprints and Monographs no. 4. New York: King's Crown. (**1942** Hall *Phonetics*)

Hall, Joseph S. 1960. *Smoky Mountain Folks and Their Lore*. Asheville, N.C.: Cataloochee. (**1960** Hall *Smoky Mt Folks*)

Hamilton, Alice McGuire. 1977. *Blue Ridge Mountain Memories: The True Story of a Mountain Girl at the Turn of the Century*. Atlanta: Conger. (**1977** Hamilton *Mt Memories*)

Hamilton, Hugh. 1774. [Estate inventory, Mecklenburg County, N.C., in North Carolina State Archives, Raleigh, C.R.065.508.104]

Hamilton, Alexander. 1863. *Memoirs of the Maxwells of Pollok*, ed. William Fraser, 256. Edinburgh, 1863. (**1635** Hamilton *Letter*)

Hannum, Alberta Pierson. 1943. 'The Mountain People', *The Great Smokies and the Blue Ridge*, ed. Roderick Peattie, 73–151. New York: Vanguard. (**1943** Hannum *Mt People*)

Harder, Kelsie. 1954. [Miscellaneous notes and citations compiled by Kelsie B. Harder from central Tennessee, on deposit at Dictionary of American Regional English office, Madison, Wisc.]. (**1954** Harder *Coll*)

Harris, George Washington. 1867. *Sut Lovingood: Yarns Spun by a 'Nat'ral Born, Durn'd Fool'*. Facsimile edition, ed. M. Thomas Inge and reprinted in 1987, Memphis: St Lukes Press. (**1867** Harris *Sut Lovingood*)

Harris, Joel Chandler. 1883. *Nights with Uncle Remus: Myths and Legends of the Old Plantation*. Boston: Houghton, Mifflin. (**1883** Harris *Nights with Remus*)

Harrison, James A. 1884. 'Negro English', *Anglia* 7:232–79. (**1884** Harrison *Negro English*)

Hart, William ('W. H. Floredice'). 1881. *Memories of a Month among the 'Mere Irish'*. London: Kegan Paul. (**1881** Hart *Mere Irish*)

Hart, William ('W. H. Floredice'). 1889. *Derryreel: Collection of Stories from Northwest Donegal*. London: Hamilton, Adams. (**1889** Hart *Derryreel*)

Hartley, Alan H. 2004. *Lewis and Clark Lexicon of Discovery*. Pullman, Wash.: Washington State University Press. (**2004** Hartley *Lewis and Clark Lexicon*)

Hartsell, Jacob. 1939–40 [1813–14]. 'The "J. Hartsell Memora": The Journal of a Tennessee Captain in the War of 1812, ed. Mary Harden McCown', *East Tennessee Historical Society Publications* 11:93–115; 12:118–46. (**1813–14** Hartsell *Journal*)

Harvey, Karen J. 2001. 'Diamonds in the Rough: Scotch-Irish Town Planning in Northern Appalachia during the Early Republic', *Journal of Scotch-Irish Studies* 1 (2):107–24. (**2001** Harvey *Diamonds in Rough*)

Haun, Mildred. 1937. 'Cocke County Ballads and Songs'. Nashville, Tenn.: George Peabody College Master's thesis. (**1937** Haun *Cocke Co*)

Haun, Mildred. 1968. *The Hawk's Done Gone and Other Stories*, ed. Hershel Gower. Nashville, Tenn.: Vanderbilt University Press. [pp 1–197 originally published in 1940 edition, pp 201–354 previously unpublished stories written in the early 1940s dated in this dictionary as 'c1945']. (**1940** Haun *Hawk's Done*; **c1945** Haun *Hawk's Done*)

Hayden, Marie Gladys. 1915. 'A Wordlist from Montana', *Dialect Notes* 4:43–45. (**1915** Hayden *Wordlist Montana*)

Haynes, Alice Hawkins. 1991. *Haywood Home: Memories of a Mountain Woman*. Tallahassee, Fla.: Rose. (**1991** Haynes *Haywood Home*)

Hayward, Richard. 1925. *Ulster Songs and Ballads*. London: Duckworth. (**1925** Hayward *Ulster Songs*)

Heap, Norman A. 1983. 'A Word List from Bucks County, Pennsylvania, 1850–1876', *Publication of the American Dialect Society* 70. (**1983** Heap *Bucks Co Word List*)

Henry, Sam, ed. 1933. *Rowlock Rhymes and Songs of Exile by 'North Antrim'*. Jersey: Bigwood. (**1933** *North Antrim*)

Herbison, David. 1848. *Midnight Musings; or, Thoughts from the Loom*. Belfast: Mullan, McComb & Henderson. (**1848** Herbison *Midnight Musings*)

Herbison, David. 1853. *My Ain Native Toun by David Herbison: The Bard of Dunclug*, ed. with an introduction by Ivan Herbison. Ballymena: Dunclug. (**1853** Herbison *My Ain Native Toun*)

Heydrick, B. A. 1907. 'Provincialisms of Southeastern Pennsylvania', *German American Annals* 9, new series 5:307–81. (**1907** Heydrick *Provincialisms of SE Penn*)

Heydrick, B. A. 1908. 'Provincialisms of Southeastern Pennsylvania', *German American Annals* 10, new series 6:32–52. (**1908** Heydrick *Provincialisms of SE Penn*)

Heydrick, B. A. 1916. 'Pennsylvania', *Dialect Notes* 4:337–39. (**1916** Heydrick *Pennsylvania*)

Hoffman, Charles Fenno. 1835. *A Winter in the West*. New York: Harper & Brothers. (**1835** Hoffman *Winter in West*)

Holmes, Mary Jane Hawes. 1923 [1854]. *Tempest and Sunshine*. New York: Sears. (**1854** Holmes *Tempest and Sunshine*)

Hooper, Ben W. 1963. *The Unwanted Boy: The Autobiography of Governor Ben W. Hooper*, ed. Everett Robert Boyce. Knoxville, Tenn.: University of Tennessee Press. (**1963** Hooper *Unwanted Boy*)

Huddleston, Robert. 1844. *A Collection of Poems and Songs, on Rural Subjects.* Belfast: J. Smyth. (**1844** Huddleston *Poems and Songs*)

Hume, Abraham ['Billy McCart']. 1861. *Poor Rabbin's Ollminick for the Town o' Bilfawst: Containing Various Different Things Which Ivvery Parson Ought t'be Acquentit with.* Belfast: Henderson. (**1861** Hume *Rabbin's Ollminick*)

Hume, Abraham ['Billy McCart']. 1863. *Poor Rabbin's Ollminick for the Town o' Bilfawst ... 1863.* Belfast: Henderson. (**1863** Hume *Rabbin's Ollminick*)

Humphreys, David. 1815. *The Yankey in England: A Drama in Five Acts.* N.p.: n.p. (**1815** Humphreys *Yankey in England*)

Huskey, Charles Aaron. 1986. 'Life in the Sugarlands', *Sugarlands: A Lost Community of Sevier County*, ed. Jerry L. Wear, 2–9. Sevierville, Tenn.: Sevierville Heritage Committee. (**1986** Huskey *Sugarlands*)

Hutson, Arthur. 1947. 'Gaelic Loan-Words in American', *American Speech* 22:18–23. (**1947** Hutson *Gaelic Loan-Words*)

Irvine, Alexander. 1900. *My Lady of the Chimney Corner.* London: Collins Clear-Type. (**1900** Irvine *Lady Chimney Corner*)

Irvine, Alexander. 1921. *The Souls of Poor Folk.* London: Collins. (**1921** Irvine *Poor Folk*)

Ison, Isaac, and Anna H. Ison. 1993. *A Whole 'Nother Language: Our Personal Collection of Appalachian Expressions.* N.p.: n.p. (**1993** Ison and Ison *Whole Nother Lg*)

Jackson, Sarah E. 1975. 'Unusual Words, Expressions, and Pronunciations in a North Carolina Mountain Community', *Appalachian Journal* 2:148–60. (**1975** Jackson *Unusual Words*)

Janson, Charles William. 1807. *The Stranger in America: Containing Observations Made during a Long Residence in That Country.* London: Cundee. (**1807** Janson *Stranger in America*)

'Jefferson County, Tennessee, Will Book 1, 1792–1810'. 2001. *East Tennessee Roots* 9 (1):35–49. (**1793** *Jefferson Co Wills*)

Johnson, Clifton. 1913. *Highways and Byways from the St. Lawrence.* New York: Macmillan. (**1913** Johnson *Highways and Byways*)

Jones, Loyal, and Jim Wayne Miller. 1992. 'Glossary of Mountain Speech', *Southern Mountain Speech*, 63–120. Berea, Ky.: Berea College Press. (**1992** Jones and Miller *Sthn Mt Speech*)

Joyce, Patrick W. 1910. *English as We Speak It in Ireland.* London: Longmans, Green. (**1910** Joyce *English in Ireland*)

Justus, May. 1938. *The House in No-End Hollow.* Garden City, N.Y.: Doubleday. (**1938** Justus *No-End Hollow*)

Justus, May. 1943. *Bluebird, Fly Up!* New York: Lippincott. (**1943** Justus *Bluebird*)

Justus, May. 1952. *Children of the Great Smoky Mountains*. New York: Dutton. (**1952** Justus *Children*)

Justus, May. 1957. *The Other Side of the Mountain*. New York: Hastings House. (**1957** Justus *Other Side*)

Justus, May. 1970. *Tales from Near-Side and Far*. Champaign, Ill.: Garrard. (**1970** Justus *Tales*)

Kemble, Frances Anne. 1863. *Journal of a Residence on a Georgia Plantation in 1838–1839*. New York: Harper & Brothers. (1863 Kemble *Journal Georgian*)

Kemper, Jackson. 1925 [1838]. 'A Trip through Wisconsin in 1838'. *Wisconsin Magazine of History* 8:423–45. (**1838** Kemper *Trip Wisconsin*)

Kennedy, Billy. 2005. 'SF Knew about Provo Raids as Talks Went on', *Belfast News-Letter* (3 Feb). (**2005** Kennedy *SF Knew*)

Kephart, Horace. 1904–07. [Notebooks (unpaginated), on deposit at Manuscripts Division, Hunter Library, Western Carolina University, Cullowhee, N.C.] (**1904–07** Kephart *Notebooks*)

Kephart, Horace. 1913. *Our Southern Highlanders*. New York: Macmillan. (**1913** Kephart *Our Sthn High*)

Kephart, Horace. 1917. 'A Word-list from the Mountains of Western North Carolina', *Dialect Notes* 4:407–19. (**1917** Kephart *Word-list*)

Kilpatrick, Lewis H. 1921. 'The Journal of William Calk, Kentucky Pioneer', *Mississippi Valley Historical Review* 7:363–77. (**1921** Kilpatrick *Journal William Calk*)

King, Edward. 1875. *The Great South*. Hartford, Conn.: American Publishing. Edited by W. McGruder Drake and Robert R. Jones and republished in 1975, Baton Rouge, La.: Louisiana State University Press. (**1875** King *Great South*)

Kingsly, Stephen. 1999. 'Northern Protestant Speaks to Irish America', *Irish Echo* (2–8 Mar). (**1999** Kingsly *Protestant Speaks*)

Kirk, John M. 1991. *Northern Ireland Transcribed Corpus of Speech* [Transcriptions of Tape-Recorded Survey of Hiberno-English Speech]. Colchester: Economic and Social Research Council. (**1991** Kirk *NITCS*)

Kirkham, Samuel. 1829. *English Grammar in Familiar Lectures*. Albany, N.Y.: Steele. (**1829** Kirkham *English Grammar*)

Knight, Henry Cogswell. *Letters from the South and West*. Boston: Richardson and Lord. (**1824** Knight *Letters*)

Kosier, Patty Pylant. 1988. *Maggie of Maggie Valley, N.C.* Corpus Christi, Tex.: privately published. (**1988** Kosier *Maggie*)

Kurath, Hans. 1939–43. *Linguistic Atlas of New England*. Providence, R.I.: Brown University Press. (**1943** Kurath *LANE*)

Kurath, Hans. 1949. *Word Geography of the Eastern United States*. Ann Arbor: University of Michigan Press. (**1949** Kurath *Word Geog East US*)

Kurath, Hans, and Raven I. McDavid, Jr. 1961. *The Pronunciation of English in the Atlantic States*. Ann Arbor: University of Michigan Press. (**1961** Kurath and McDavid *Pron Engl Atl Sts*)

Landry, Bill. 1989. [Interviews conducted under the auspices of the Great Smoky Mountains National Park, on deposit in Library, Great Smoky Mountains National Park, Gatlinburg, Tenn.] (**1989** Landry *Smoky Mt Interviews*)

Landry, Bill. 1988–97. [Interviews conducted for the *Heartland* television series, on deposit at WBIR-TV, Knoxville, Tenn.] (**1988–97** Landry *Coll*)

Lanham, Charles. 1849. *Letters from the Allegheny Mountains*. New York: Putnam. (**1849** Lanham *Allegheny Mts*)

Laughlin, Hugh C. 1944. 'A Word-list from Buncombe County, North Carolina', *Publication of the American Dialect Society* 2:24–27. (**1944** Laughlin *Word-list Buncombe Co*)

Lipscomb, John. 1928 [1784]. *Early Travels in the Tennessee Country, 1540–1800*, ed. Samuel Cole Williams, 269–79. Johnson City, Tenn.: Watauga Press. (**1784** *Lipscomb's Journal*)

Logan, James. 1924. *Ulster in the X-Rays*. London: Stockwell. (**1924** Logan *Ulster in X-Rays*)

Longstreet, Augustus Baldwin. 1835. *Georgia Scenes, Characters, Incidents, &c.: in the First Half Century of the Republic, by a Native Georgian*. August: Sentinel. (**1835** Longstreet *Georgia Scenes*)

Lowell, James Russell. 1867. *The Biglow Papers*, 2nd series. Boston: Ticknor & Fields. (**1867** Lowell *Biglow Papers*)

Lowry, Houston. 2000. 'Folk Medical Terminology as Remembered from My Practice'. [Typescript]. (**2000** Lowry *Folk Medical Term*)

Lowry, Houston. 2001. 'Expressions, Sayings, Descriptions of Patients in My Practice: Notes Sporadically Made from about 1965 through 1998'. [Typescript]. (**2001** Lowry *Expressions*)

Lunsford, Bascom Lamar. c1975. 'It Used To Be: Memories of Bascom Lamar Lunsford', ed. Mildred Frances Thomas. [Typescript on deposit at Appalachian Library, Appalachian State University, Boone, N.C.] (**c1975** Lunsford *It Used To Be*)

Lutton, William. 1923. *Montiaghisms – Ulster Words and Phrases*. ed. F. J. Bigger. Armagh. n.p. Reprinted in 1976, Belfast: Linen Hall Library. (**1923** Lutton *Montiaghisms*)

Lyttle, Wesley Guard. 1879. *Robin's Readings, Vol. 1: The Adventures of Paddy M'Quillan*. Bangor: Herald. (**1879** Lyttle *Paddy McQuillan*)

Lyttle, Wesley Guard. 1885. *Robin's Readings, Vol. 2: The Adventures of Robin Gordon*. Bangor: Herald. (**1885** Lyttle *Robin Gordon*)

Lyttle, Wesley Guard. 1886. *Robin's Readings, Vol. 3: Life in Ballycuddy, County Down*. Bangor: Herald. (**1886** Lyttle *Ballycuddy*)

Lyttle, Wesley Guard. 1886. *Sons of the Sod: A Tale of County Down*. Bangor: Herald. (**1886** Lyttle *Sons of Sod*)

Lyttle, W[esley] G[uard]. c1890. *Daft Eddie or The Smugglers of Strangford Lough*. Bangor: North Down Herald. Reprinted in 1979, Newcastle: Mourne Observer. (**c1890** Lyttle *Daft Eddie*)

Mac Airt, Sean. 1949. 'Tyrone Folktales,' *Bealoideas* 19:29–72. (**1949** Mac Airt *Tyrone Folktales*)

McAtee, W. L. 1956. *Some Dialect of North Carolina*. Chapel Hill, N.C.: privately published. (**1956** McAtee *Some Dial NC*)

McBride, Doreen. 1990. *We Are Our Past*. Banbridge: Adare Press. (**1990** McBride *Our Past*)

McBride, Doreen. 2000. *Ulster Scots as She Tummels*. Banbridge: Adare Press. (**2000** McBride *Ulster Scots*)

McCallin, William. 1920. *Cracks from Old-Fashioned Ulster Plenishing*. Belfast: W. McCallin. (**1920** McCallin *Ulster Plenishing*)

McCallin, William. 1920. *Ulster Fireside Tales*. London: Heath Cranton. (**1920** McCallin *Fireside Tales*)

McCallin, William. 1938. *The Braes o' Killywhapple and Other Tales*. Belfast: Quota. (**1938** McCallin *Killywhapple*)

McClean, Oonagh. 1980. 'Ulster Words and Their Meaning', *The Curran* 14 (spring):2–3. (**1980** McClean *Ulster Words I*)

McClean, Oonagh. 1980. 'Ulster Words and Their Meaning', *The Curran* 15 (summer):2. (**1980** McClean *Ulster Words II*)

McClean, Oonagh. 1980. 'Ulster Words and Their Meaning', *The Curran* 16 (autumn):2. (**1980** McClean *Ulster Words III*)

McClean, Oonagh. 1980/81. 'Ulster Words and Their Meaning', *The Curran* 18 (winter):2. (**1980/81** McClean *Ulster Words IV*)

McClean, Oonagh. 1981. 'Ulster Words and Their Meaning', *The Curran* 21 (spring):2. (**1981** McClean *Ulster Words V*)

McClellan, Robert. c1614. 'Assignment of 240a. of "Happerdascher's Portioun of Londary"'. [Legal Documents (1614–17) from McClellan Family Papers, Collection T 640, Public Record Office of Northern Ireland, Belfast.] (**c1614** McClellan *Assignment*)

McCool, Sam. 1982. *Sam McCool's New Pittsburghese: How to Speak like a Pittsburgher*. Pittsburgh, Pa.: Goodwill. (**1982** McCool *Pittsburghese*)

McCracken, Weaver H., III. 1974–75. 'Interviews about Logging in Great Smoky Mountains National Park'. [24+ vols. of transcripts made by Mary Ruth Chiles and deposited in Library, Great Smoky Mountains National Park, Gatlinburg, Tenn.] (**1974–75** McCracken *Logging*)

McCullough, James. 1748–58. [Journal, typescript given to the author by Kerby A. Miller]. (**1753–55** McCullough *Journal*)

McCullough, Sheena. 2005. 'Ballyboley Schuil', *Hamewarks fae Ballyboley: Tha Cless o 2004*, 21. Belfast: Ullans Press. (**2005** McCullough *Ballyboley Schuil*)

McCurry, Samuel S. 1921. *The Ballads of Ballytumulty*. Belfast: Carsell & Sons. (**1921** McCurry *Ballads Ballytumulty*)

McCurry, Samuel S. 1930. *Stories of an Ulster Village*. Belfast: Adams. (**1930** McCurry *Ulster Village*)

McDavid, Raven I., Jr. 1949. 'Grist from an Atlas Mill', *American Speech* 24:105–14. (**1949** McDavid *Atlas Mill*)

McDermott, W. R. 1906. *Foughilotra: A Forbye Story*. Dublin: Sealy, Bryers & Walker. (**1906** McDermott *Foughilotra*)

McDonald, Fiona. 2005. 'Wullie's New Claes', *Hamewarks fae Ballyboley: Tha Cless o 2004*, 25–29. Belfast: Ullans Press. (**2005** McDonald *Wullie's New Claes*)

McFadyen, Dugald ['Cruck-a-Leaghan'] and David Hepburn ['Slieve Gallion']. 1884. *Lays and Legends of the North of Ireland*. London: Houlston & Sons. (**1884** McFadyen and Hepburn *Lays and Legends*)

MacGill, Patrick. 1915. *The Rat Pit*. London: Jenkins. (**1915** MacGill *Rat Pit*)

MacGill, Patrick. 1919. *Glenmornan*. London: Jenkins. (**1919** MacGill *Glenmornan*)

MacGill, Patrick. 1928. *Black Bonar*. London: Jenkins. (**1928** MacGill *Black Bonar*)

MacGill, Patrick. 1934. *The Glen of Carra*. London: Jenkins. (**1934** MacGill *Glen of Carra*)

McGuffin, John. 1978. *In Praise of Poteen*. Belfast: Appletree. (**1978** McGuffin *Praise of Poteen*)

McHenry, James. 1824. *O'Halloran: or, The Insurgent Chief*. London. (**1824** McHenry *Insurgent Chief*)

McHenry, James. 1825. *The Hearts of Steel*. Philadelphia: Poole. (**1825** McHenry *Hearts of Steel*)

McIlhatton, James. 2004. 'The Old Whin Bush', *The Ulster-Scot* (Oct):3. (**2004** McIlhatton *Whin Bush*)

McIlroy, Archibald. 1897. *When Lint was in the Bell*. Belfast: McCaw, Stevenson & Orr. (**1897** McIlroy *Lint in Bell*)

McIlroy, Archibald. 1900. *By Lone Craig-Linnie Burn*. London: T. Fisher Unwin. (**1900** McIlroy *Craig-Linnie Burn*)

McIlroy, Archibald. 1902. *The Humour of Druid's Island*. Dublin: Hodges, Figgis. (**1902** McIlroy *Druid's Island*)

'McIlwham, Thomas'. 1838. *The McIlwham Papers: In Two Letters from Thomas McIlwham, Weaver, to His Friend, Mr. James McNeight*. Belfast: McComb. (**1838** McIlwham *McIlwham Papers*)

McIntyre, Rae. 1990. *Some Handlin': The Dialect Heritage of North Ulster, Collected by Pupils and Friends of Ballyrashane Primary School*. 2nd ed. Limavady: North-West Books. (**1990** McIntyre *Some Handlin'*)

McKay, Louise. 1922. *The Mountains of Mourne: Their Charm and Their People*. London: Jarrolds. (**1922** McKay *Mts of Mourne*)

McKay, Louise. 1925. *Mourne Folk*. London: Stanley Paul. (**1925** McKay *Mourne Folk*)

McKay, Louise. 1928. *My Oul' Town*. London: Stanley Paul. (**1928** McKay *Oul' Town*)

McKenzie, Andrew. 1832. *The Masonic Chaplet, with a Few Other Poems*. Belfast: Hugh Clark. (**1832** McKenzie *Masonic Chaplet*)

MacManus, Seumas. 1895. *The Leadin' Road to Donegal: and Other Stories*. London: Digby, Long. (**1895** MacManus *Leadin' Road*)

MacManus, Seumas. 1897. *Twas in Dhroll Donegal*. London: Downey. (**1897** MacManus *Dhroll Donegal*)

MacManus, Seumas. 1898. *The Bend of the Road*. London: Downey. (**1898** MacManus *Bend of Road*)

MacManus, Seumas. 1898. *The Humours of Donegal*. London: Unwin. (**1898** MacManus *Humours of Donegal*)

MacManus, Seumas. 1899. *In Chimney Corners: Merry Tales of Irish Folklore*. New York: Harper. (**1899** MacManus *Chimney Corners*)

MacManus, Seumas. 1903. *A Lad of the O'Friels*. London: Ibister. (**1903** MacManus *Lad of O'Friels*)

MacManus, Seumus. 1935. *Bold Blades of Donegal*. New York: Stokes. (**1935** MacManus *Bold Blades*)

McMillan, George. 1830. *Poems Satirical and Moral*. Belfast: Smyth. (**1830** McMillan *Poems*)

McNeil, Kathryn K. 1999. *Purchase Knob: Essays from a Mountain Notebook*. Santa Barbara, Cal.: Fithian. (**1999** McNeil *Purchase Knob*)

MacNeill, W. 1930. *Told to His Reverence: County Down Sketches*. Dublin: Talbot. (**1930** McNeill *Told to Reverence*)

MacNeill, W. 1933. *His Reverence Listens Again: County Down Sketches*. Dublin: Talbot. (**1933** McNeill *Reverence Listens*)

McSparran, Archibald. 1829. *An Irish Legend: or, McDonnell, and the Norman de Borgos: A Biographical Tale*. Belfast: Smyth. (**1829** McSparran *Irish Legend*)

McWilliams, Hugh, 1992. *Songs of Hugh McWilliams, Schoolmaster, 1831*, ed. John Moulden. Portrush: Ulstersongs. (**1831** McWilliams *Songs*)

Malone, Kemp. 1931. 'Any More in the Affirmative', *American Speech* 6:460. (**1931** Malone *Any More in Affirm*)

Malone, Kemp. 1960. 'Bonnyclabber', *Celtica* 5:142. (**1960** Malone *Bonnyclabber*)

Maples, Alie Newman. 1982. *Memories of My Mountains*. N.p.: n.p. (**1982** Maples *Memories*)

Marshall, John J. 1904–06. 'The Dialect of Ulster: A Glossary of Words in the
    Ulster Dialect, Chiefly Used in the Midland and North-western Counties', *Ulster
    Journal of Archaeology*, new series 10:121–30; 11:64–70,122–25,175–79;
    12:18–21. (**1904–06** Marshall *Dial of Ulster*)

Marshall, W. F. 1936. *Ulster Speaks*. London: British Broadcasting Corporation.
    (**1936** Marshall *Ulster Speaks*)

Marshall, W. F. 1948. *Planted by a River*. Belfast: Mullan. (**1948** Marshall *Planted by
    River*)

Marshall, W. F. 1983. *Livin' in Drumlister: The Collected Ballads and Verses of W. F.
    Marshall, the Bard of Tyrone*. Belfast: Blackstaff. (**1983** Marshall *Drumlister*)

Mason, Robert Lindsay. 1912. 'Raiding Moonshiners in Tennessee', *Recreation* 35
    (5):197–99. (**1912** Mason *Raiding Moonshiners*)

Mason, Robert [Lindsay]. 1927. *Lure of the Great Smokies*. Boston, Mass.: Houghton
    Mifflin. (**1927** Mason *Lure of Smokies*)

Massey, Ellen Grey. 1978. *Bittersweet Country*. Garden City, N.Y.:
    Anchor/Doubleday. (**1978** Massey *Bittersweet Country*)

Mathes, C. Hodge. 1940. 'Jeff Howell's Buryin'', *Tennessee Folklore Society Bulletin* 7
    (2):19–22. (**1940** Mathes *Jeff Howell*)

Mathes, C. Hodge. 1952. *Tall Tales from Old Smoky*. Kingsport, Tenn.: Southern.
    (**1952** Mathes *Tall Tales*)

Maurer, David W. 1930. 'Schoonerisms: Some Speech-Peculiarities of North-
    Atlantic Fishermen', *American Speech* 5:387–95. (**1930** Maurer *Schoonerisms*)

Maurer, David W. 1949. 'The Argot of the Moonshiner', *American Speech* 24:3–13.
    (**1949** Maurer *Argot of Moonshiner*)

Maxfield, E. K. 1931. 'The Speech of South-Western Pennsylvania', *American Speech*
    7:18–20. (**1931** Maxfield *Speech SW Penn*)

May, John. 1873. *Journal and Letters of Col. John May, of Boston, Relative of Two
    Journeys to the Ohio Country in 1788 and '89*. Cincinnati: Clarke. (**1789** May
    Journal)

Medford, W. Clark. 1961. *The Early History of Haywood County*. Asheville, N.C.:
    Miller. (**1961** Medford *History Haywood Co*)

Medford, W. Clark. 1966. *Great Smoky Mountain Stories and Sun over Ol' Starlin*.
    Waynesville, N.C.: Miller. (**1966** Medford *Ol' Starlin*)

Megaw, W. R. 1935. *Carragloon: Tales of Our Townlands*. Belfast: Quota. (**1935**
    Megaw *Carragloon*)

Miles, Emma Bell. 1905. *The Spirit of the Mountains*. New York: Pott. Reprinted in
    1975, Knoxville, Tenn.: University of Tennessee Press. (**1905** Miles *Spirit of Mts*)

Miller, Jim Wayne. 1969. 'The Vocabulary and Methods of Raising Burley Tobacco
    in Western North Carolina', *North Carolina Folklore* 17:27–38. (**1969** Miller
    Raising Tobacco)

'Minutes of the Big Pigeon Baptist Church [Cocke County], 1787–1874. Transcribed by the Works Progress Administration'. [On deposit in McClung Collection, Knox County Public Library, Knoxville, Tenn.] (**1789–94** *Big Pigeon Minutes*)

'Miscellaneous Word-list'. 1903. *Dialect Notes* 2:349–53. (**1903** *Misc Word-list*)

Montgomery, Hugh. 1641. '[Letter] to Alexander, Sixth of Earl of Eglintoun, 17th December 1641'. *Memorials of the Montgomeries*, ed. William Fraser, 242=44. Edinburgh, 1859. (**1641** Montgomery *Letter*)

Montgomery, May, and Francis Montgomery. 1993. *Barnish, Co. Antrim Dialect Dictionary: Local Sayings Words and Phrases, etc.*. Barnish: privately published. (**1993** Montgomery *Barnish*)

Montgomery, Michael. 1975–99. [Miscellaneous observations on mountain speech]. (**1975** Montgomery *File*)

Montgomery, Michael. 1978. [Interviews conducted in White Pine, Tennessee, analyzed in the author's 1979 University of Florida Ph.D. dissertation 'A Discourse Analysis of Appalachian English' and referenced according to the list of speakers on p. 163 of that work.] (**1978** Montgomery *White Pine Coll*)

Montgomery, Michael. 1992–99. [Observations and responses by consultants to queries for the *Dictionary of Smoky Mountain English*, ed. Michael B. Montgomery and Joseph S. Hall. 2004. Knoxville: University of Tennessee Press.].(**1992–99** Montgomery *Coll*)

Montgomery, Michael. 1995–97. [Miscellaneous observations and examples collected in Northern Ireland]. (**1995–97** Montgomery *Ulster File*)

Montgomery, R. H. c1955. 'Heard in Ulster'. [Manuscript on deposit at Ulster Folk and Transport Museum, Cultra, Northern Ireland]. (**c1955** Montgomery *Heard in Ulster*)

Morley, Margaret. 1913. *The Carolina Mountains*. Boston: Houghton Mifflin. (**1913** Morley *Carolina Mts*)

Morrison, H. S. 1929. *Modern Ulster: Its Character, Customs, Politics, and Industries*. London: Allenson. (**1929** Morrison *Modern Ulster*)

Motte, Jacob Rhett. 1940. *Charleston Goes to Harvard: The Diary of a Harvard Student of 1831*, ed. Arthur H. Cole. Cambridge: Harvard University Press. (**1940** Motte *Charleston to Harvard*)

Mulcaghey, Matt. 1950. 'John Harbison's Wake', *Brave Crack! An Anthology of Ulster Wit and Humour*, 67–73. Belfast: Carter. (**1950** Mulcaghey *Harbison's Wake*)

Murfree, Mary. 1884. *In the Tennessee Mountains*. Boston, Mass.: Houghton Mifflin. (**1884** Murfree *In Tenn Mts*)

Murfree, Mary. 1885. *The Prophet of the Great Smoky Mountains*. Boston, Mass.: Houghton Mifflin. (**1885** Murfree *Prophet*)

Murphy, Michael J. 1945. *At Slieve Gullion's Foot*. Dundalk: Dundalgan. (**1945** Murphy *Gullion's Foot*)

Murphy, Michael J. 1955. *Culprit of the Shadows*. Belfast: Carter. (**1955** Murphy *Culprit of Shadows*)

Murphy, Michael J. 1975. *Now You're Talking*. Belfast: Blackstaff. (**1975** Murphy *You're Talking*)

Murphy, Michael J. 1976. *Mountainy Crack*. Belfast: Blackstaff. (**1976** Murphy *Mountainy Crack*)

Murray, James. 1737. [Letter]. *Philadelphia Gazette* 464 (27 Oct–3 Nov):1. (**1737** Murray *Letter*)

Murray, Thomas E., and Beth Lee Simon. 2002. 'At the Intersection of Regional and Social Dialects: The Case of *like* + Past Participle in American English', *American Speech* 77:32–69. (**2002** Murray and Simon *Intersection of Dialects*)

Murry, Howard. 1961. *Salt o' Life*. Winston-Salem, N.C.: Blair. (**1961** Murry *Salt*)

Nelson, Louise K. 1997. *Country Folklore 1920s & 1930s and That's the Way It Was*. Alexander, N.C.: WorldComm. (**1997** Nelson *Country Folklore*)

Nelson, Louise K. 1999. *Aroma and Memories of Grandma's and Mama's Kitchen*. Alexander, N.C.: WorldComm. (**1999** Nelson *Aroma and Memories*)

New Haven Register. 1978 (30 Nov):68. (**1978** *New Haven Register*)

New Orleans Daily Picayune. 1840. (30 Aug):2. (**1840** *New Orleans Picayune*)

'A North-Country Grace'. 1733. *The Humble Remonstrance of the Five-Foot-Highians against the AntiChristian Practice of Using a Standard in Enlisting of Soldiers ...*, 29–31. Dublin: Roberts. (**1733** *North Country Grace*)

'The North Country-Man's Description of Christ's-Church, Dublin; in a Letter to a Friend'. 1733. *The Humble Remonstrance of the Five-Foot-Highians against the AntiChristian Practice of Using a Standard in Enlisting of Soldiers ...*, 24–28. Dublin: Roberts. (**1733** *North Country Description*)

'No Photo? Then Reply in the Negative'. 2004. *Belfast Telegraph* (10 Dec). (**2004** *No Photo?*)

Northern Bard. 1734. *Elegy on the Much Lamented Death of Quarter-Master Brice Blare; Who Died at Strabane*. Dublin: Coghill's Court. Reprinted in 1907, *Ulster Journal of Archaeology*, 2nd series 13:160–61. (**1734** *Northern Bard*)

'Notes'. 1870. *The Nation* (28 July):55–57. (**1870** *Notes*)

Nuhan, Erchie. 2004. 'Memories', *Ullans: The Magazine for Ulster-Scots* 9/10:68–70. (**2004** Nuhan *Memories*)

O'Donnell, Peadar. 1929. *Adrigoole*. London: Cape. (**1929** O'Donnell *Adrigoole*)

O'Donnell, Peadar. 1930. *The Knife*. London: Cape. (**1930** O'Donnell *Knife*)

Ogle, Lucinda. 1986. 'Lucinda Oakley Ogle and Early Settlers', *Sugarlands: A Lost Community of Sevier County*, ed. Jerry L. Wear, 37–77. Sevierville, Tenn.: Sevierville Heritage Committee. (**1986** Ogle *Lucinda*)

Ogle, Lucinda. 1986. 'My Valley ... in the Smokies', *In the Smokies* 4 (2):39. (**1986** Ogle *My Valley*)

Ogle, Lucinda, and Emily Nixon. 1976. 'If Only These Walls Could Talk', *Sevier County Times* (26 Sept):B7. (**1976** Ogle and Nixon *If Only*)

O'Kane, William. 1991. *You Don't Say?: The Tyrone Crystal Book of Ulster Dialect.* Dungannon: Irish World. (**1991** O'Kane *You Don't Say*)

O'Leary, Ellen. 1888. *A Legend of Tyrone: Fairy and Folk Tales of the Irish Peasantry*, ed. and selected by W. B. Yeats, 132–34. London: Scott. (**1888** O'Leary *Legend of Tyrone*)

Oliver, Duane. 1989. *Hazel Creek from Then to Now.* N.p: privately published. (**1989** Oliver *Hazel Creek*)

Olmsted, Frederick Law. 1857. *A Journey through Texas, or, A Saddle-Trip on the Western Frontier.* New York: Mason Brothers. (**1857** Olmsted *Journey Texas*)

O'Neill, Moira. 1893. 'The Glens and Their Speech', *Blackwood's Magazine* 154:367–76. (**1893** O'Neill *Glens and Speech*)

O'Neill, Moira. 1912. *Songs of the Glens of Antrim.* Edinburgh: Blackwood. (**1912** O'Neill *Songs of Glens*)

O'Neill, Moira. 1921. *More Songs of the Glens of Antrim.* Edinburgh: Blackwood. (**1921** O'Neill *More Songs of Glens*)

Orr, James. 1804. *Poems, on Various Subjects.* Belfast: Smyth & Lyons. [Selected in Philip Robinson, ed. 1992. *The Country Rhymes of James Orr, the Bard of Ballycarry*. Folk Poets of Ulster Series, Vol. 2. Bangor: Pretani]. (**1804** Orr *Poems*)

Orr, James. 1817. *Posthumous Works ... with a Sketch of His Life.* Belfast: Smyth & Lyons. [Selected in Philip Robinson, ed. 1992. *The Country Rhymes of James Orr, the Bard of Ballycarry*. Folk Poets of Ulster Series, Vol. 2. Bangor: Pretani]. (**1817** Orr *Posthumous Works*)

Osborn, John. 1800–01. *John Osborn Diary January 1, 1800 – October 2, 1802.* <http: freepages.history.rootsweb.com/~helmsnc/osborndiary> (**1800–01** Osborn *Diary*)

Otto, John Solomon. 1987. 'Cracker: The History of a Southeastern Ethnic, Economic, and Racial Epithet', *Names* 35:28–39. (**1987** Otto *Cracker*)

'Our Cabin; or, Life in the Woods'. 1843. *American Pioneer* 2 (10):435–59. (**1843** *Our Cabin*)

Our Smokies Heritage Book 1. 1982. Gatlinburg, Tenn.: Crescent. (**1982** *Smokies Heritage*)

Ownby, Evolena. 1998. 'Memories of Big Greenbrier, Sevier County, Tennessee', *Smoky Mountain Historical Society Journal* 23(3):10–19. (**1998** Ownby *Big Greenbrier*)

Parris, John. 1955. *Roaming the Mountains with John Parris.* Asheville, N.C.: Citizen-Times. (**1955** Parris *Roaming Mts*)

Parris, John. 1957. *My Mountains, My People.* Asheville, N.C.: Citizen-Times. (**1957** Parris *My Mts*)

Parris, John. 1982. 'Here's How to Understand Mountain Folks', *Asheville Citizen-Times* (18 July). (**1982** Parris *Here's How*)

Parton, Dolly. 1994. *Dolly: My Life and Other Unfinished Business*. New York: HarperCollins. (**1994** Parton *Dolly*)

Paterson, T. G. F., ed. 1939. *Country Cracks: Old Tales from the County of Armagh*. Dundalk: Tempest. (**1939** Paterson *Country Cracks*)

Patterson, David. 1860. *The Provincialisms of Belfast and the Surrounding Districts pointed out and corrected: to which is added an Essay on Mutual Improvement Societies*. Belfast: Alex. Mayne. (**1860** Patterson *Belfast Provincialisms*)

Patterson, William H. 1880. *A Glossary of Words in Use in the Counties of Antrim and Down*. London: English Dialect Society. (**1880** Patterson *Antrim/Down Glossary*)

'Pawpaw Hollow [Sevier County] Minutes. 1803–1870'. [Transcribed copy on deposit in McClung Collection, Knox County Public Library, Knoxville, Tenn.] (**1836–55** *Pawpaw Hollow Minutes*)

Payne, L[eonidas] W. 1908–09. 'A Word-list from East Alabama', *Dialect Notes* 3:279–328, 343–91. (**1908–09** Payne *Word-list East Alabama*)

Pearsall, Marion. 1959. *Little Smoky Ridge: The Natural History of a Southern Appalachian Neighborhood*. Tuscaloosa: University of Alabama Press. (**1959** Pearsall *Little Smoky*)

Peattie, Daniel Culross. 1943. 'Indian Days and the Coming of the White Man', *The Great Smokies and the Blue Ridge*, ed. Roderick Peattie, 15–72. New York: Vanguard. (**1943** Peattie *Indian Days*)

Pederson, D. L. 1897. 'The Mountaineers of Madison County, North Carolina', *Missionary Review of the World* 20 (Nov):821–31. (**1897** Pederson *Mtneers Madison Co*)

Pepper, John. 1978. *See Me, See Her?* Belfast: Blackstaff. (**1978** Pepper *See Me*)

Pepper, John. 1979. *A Quare Geg*. Belfast: Blackstaff. (**1979** Pepper *Quare Geg*)

Pepper, John. 1981. *Ulster-English Dictionary*. Belfast: Blackstaff. (**1981** Pepper *Ulster-English Dict*)

Pepper, John. 1983. *Encyclopedia of Ulster Knowledge*. Belfast: Blackstaff. (**1983** Pepper *Ulster Knowledge*)

Pepper, John. 1986. *John Pepper's Ulster Haunbook*. Belfast: Blackstaff. (**1986** Pepper *Ulster Haunbook*)

'Petitions to the North Carolina General Assembly from Inhabitants South of the French Broad'. 2001 [1784–89]. Transcribed by Cherel Bolin Henderson. *Tennessee Ancestors* 17:208–27. (**1784–88** *Petitions French Broad*)

Pickering, John. 1816. *A Vocabulary or Collection of Words and Phrases Which have been Supposed to be Peculiar to the United States of America*. Boston: Cummings and Hilliard. (**1816** Pickering *American Vocabulary*)

'Pioneer Dialect of Southern Illinois'. 1902. *Dialect Notes* 2:225–49. (**1902** *Pioneer Dial*)

Pittsburgh Dictionary. 2004. <http//: www.geocities.com/SouthBeach/Port/ 9832/pittsburgh.html>. (**2004** *Pittsburgh Dictionary*)

Pittsburghese. 2004. <http//: www.pittsburghese.com>. (**2004** *Pittsburghese*)

Porter, Hugh. 1813. *Poetical Attempts*. Belfast: Simms & McIntyre. [Selected in Amber Adams and J. R. R. Adams, eds. 1992. *The Country Rhymes of Hugh Porter, the Bard of Moneyslane*. Folk Poets of Ulster Series, Vol. 1. Bangor: Pretani]. (**1813** Porter *Poetical Attempts*)

Porter, Hugh. 1813. 'Glossary', *Poetical Attempts*. Belfast: Simms & McIntyre. (**1813** Porter *Glossary Poetical Attempts*)

Porter, Tom, and Charles Cunningham. 1987. 'Mourne Dialect', *12 Miles of Mourne: Journal of the Mourne Local Studies Group* 1:26–29. (**1987** Porter and Cunningham *Mourne Dialect*)

Pound, Louise. 1905. 'Dialect Speech of Nebraska', *Dialect Notes* 3:55–67. (**1905** Pound *Speech in Nebraska*)

Pound, Louise. 1916. 'Wordlist from Nebraska', *Dialect Notes* 3:271–82. (**1916** Pound *Wordlist Nebraska*)

Powell, William S. 1968. *A North Carolina Gazetteer*. Chapel Hill, N.C.: University of North Carolina Press. (**1968** Powell *NC Gazetteer*)

Powers, Elizabeth D., and Mark E. Hannah. 1982. *Cataloochee: Lost Settlement of the Smokies*. Charleston, S.C.: Blazer. (**1982** Powers and Hannah *Cataloochee*)

Purkey, Lena. 1975. *Home in Madison County*. Johnson City, Tenn.: East Tennessee State University. (**1975** Purkey *Madison Co*)

Pyle, Charlotte. 1983. 'CCC Fiftieth Anniversary Interviews'. 3 vols. [Typescript on deposit in Library, Great Smoky Mountains National Park, Gatlinburg, Tenn.] (**1983** Pyle *CCC 50th Anniv*)

Quinn, Hugh. 1932. *Collecting the Rent*. London: Constable. (**1932** Quinn *Collecting Rent*)

Quinn, Hugh. 1932. *Mrs McConaghy's Money*. London: Constable. (**1932** Quinn *McConaghy's Money*)

Quinn, Hugh. 1932. *A Quiet Twelfth*. London: Constable. (**1932** Quinn *Quiet Twelfth*)

Raine, James Watt. 1924. *Land of Saddle-Bags: A Study of the Mountain People of Appalachia*. New York: Council of the Women for Home Missions and Missionary Education Movement of the United States and Canada. (**1924** Raine *Saddlebags*)

Randolph, Vance. 1926. 'A Word-list from the Ozarks', *Dialect Notes* 5:397–405. (**1926** Randolph *Word-list from Ozarks*)

Randolph, Vance, and George Wilson. 1953. *Down in the Holler: A Gallery of Ozark Folk Speech*. Norman: University of Oklahoma Press. (**1953** Randolph and Wilson *Down in Holler*)

Rawlings, Marjorie Kinnan. 1931. 'Jacob's Ladder', *Scribner's Magazine* 89 (Apr). (**1931** Rawlings *Jacob's Ladder*)

Rawlings, Marjorie Kinnan. 1938. *The Yearling*. New York: Scribner's Sons. (**1938** Rawlings *Yearling*)

Ray, John. 1738. 'A Letter from John Ray of New York, to Peter Ennis of Colraine, in Ireland, Pedlar'. *American Weekly Mercury*, October 5–12. (**1738** Ray *Letter*)

Reid, Mayne. 1856. *The Scalp Hunters*. London: Hyde. (**1856** Reid *Scalp Hunters*)

Reynolds, Charlie. 2002. *My Granfeyther's Tunge*. N.p.: privately published. (**2002** Reynolds *Granfeyther's Tunge*)

Riley, James Whitcomb. 1941. 'Little Mock-Man', *The Collected Poems of James Whitcomb Riley*. Garden City, N.Y.: Doubleday. (**1894** Riley *Little Mock-Man*)

Ritchie, Jean. 1955. *Singing Family of the Cumberlands*. New York: Oxford University Press. (**1955** Ritchie *Singing Family*)

Roberts, Elizabeth Madox. 1926. *The Time of Man, a Novel*. New York: Viking. (**1926** Roberts *Time of Man*)

Robinson, Philip. 1989. 'The Scots Language in Seventeenth-Century Ulster', *Ulster Folklife* 35:86–99. (**1989** Robinson *Scots in 17th Cent*)

Robinson, Philip. 1994. *Diamonds in Stone: 21 Years of Conservation Area Designation in Northern Ireland*. Antrim: Greystone. (**1994** Robinson *Diamonds in Stone*)

Robinson, Philip. 1997. *Ulster-Scots: A Grammar of the Traditional Written and Spoken Language*. Belfast: Ullans Press. (**1997** Robinson *Grammar*)

Robinson, Philip. 2004. 'Prugh', *Ullans: The Magazine for Ulster-Scots* 9/10:125–27. (**2004** Robinson *Prugh*)

Rollins, Philip Ashton. 1922. *The Cowboy*. New York: Scribner's Sons. (**1922** Rollins *Cowboy*)

Rowley, Richard. 1937. *Tales of Mourne*. London: Duckworth. (**1937** Rowley *Tales of Mourne*)

Royall, Anne. 1829. *Mrs. Royall's Pennsylvania, or Travels Continued in the United States*. Washington, D.C.: privately published. (**1829** Royall *Pennsylvania*)

Royall, Anne. 1931 [1826]. 'Grison Republic', *The Beginnings of American English: Texts and Essays*, ed. Mitford M. Mathews, 88–98. Chicago: University of Chicago Press. (**1826** Royall *Grison Republic*)

Russell, Charles C. 1910. *The People and Language of Ulster*. Belfast: M'Caw, Stevenson & Orr. (**1910** Russell *Language of Ulster*)

Sackett, Samuel, and William E. Koch, eds. 1961. *Kansas Folklore*. Lincoln: University of Nebraska Press. (**1961** Sackett and Koch *Kansas Folklore*)

St Clair, Sheila. 1971. *The Folklore of Ulster*. Cork: Mercier. (**1971** St Clair *Folklore Ulster*)

Sammon, Paddy. 2002. *Greenspeak: Ireland in Her Own Words*. Dublin: Town House. (**2002** Sammon *Greenspeak*)

Savage-Armstrong, George Francis. 1901. *Ballads of Down*. London: Longman's, Green. (**1901** Savage-Armstrong *Ballads of Down*)

Schele de Vere, Maximilian. 1872. *Americanisms*. New York: Scribner. (**1872** Schele de Vere *Americanisms*)

'Schools Competition: Ate Up, Ye'r at Yer Grannie's'. 2004. *Ullans: The Magazine for Ulster-Scots* 9/10:20–35. (**2004** *Ate Up*)

'Scotch Poems'. 1753. *The Ulster Miscellany*, 369–86. [Dublin?: n.p.] (**1753** *Scotch Poems*)

Scott, Ernest McA., and Philip S. Robinson, eds. 1992. *The Country Rhymes of Samuel Thomson, the Bard of Carngranny*. Folk Poets of Ulster Series, Vol. 3. Bangor: Pretani. (**1992** Scott and Robinson *Samuel Thomson*)

Settle, Mary Lee. 1956. *O Beulah Land*. New York: Viking. (**1956** Settle *Beulah Land*)

Share, Bernard. 1997. *Slanguage: A Dictionary of Irish Slang*. 2nd ed. 2004. Dublin: Gill & Macmillan. (**1997** Share *Slanguage*)

Shearin, Hubert G. 1911. 'An Eastern Kentucky Dialect Word-list'. *Dialect Notes* 3:537–40. (**1911** Shearin *East Kentucky Dialect*)

Sheppard, Muriel E. 1935. *Cabins in the Laurel*. Chapel Hill, N.C.: University of North Carolina Press. (**1935** Sheppard *Cabins in Laurel*)

Sherwood, Adiel. 1931 [1837]. [Word-list from *Gazetteer of the State of Georgia*]. *The Beginnings of American English: Texts and Essays*, ed. Mitford M. Mathews, 117–21. Chicago: University of Chicago Press. (**1837** Sherwood *Georgia Provincialisms*)

Shields, A. Randolph. 1977. *The Cades Cove Story*. Gatlinburg, Tenn.: Great Smoky Mountains Natural History Association. (**1977** Shields *Cades Cove*)

Shiels, George. 1930. *Mountain Dew*. London: Macmillan. (**1930** Shiels *Mt Dew*)

Shoemaker, Henry W. 1930. *Thirteen Hundred Old Time Words of British, Continental or Aboriginal Origins, Still or Recently in Use among the Pennsylvania Mountain People*. Altoona, Pa.: Times Tribune. (**1930** Shoemaker *1300 Penn Words*)

'Shore Sign: A Play Based on the Superstitions of the Cumberland Mountain Folk'. 1946. *Tennessee Folklore Society Bulletin* 12 (4):3–7. (**1946** *Shore Sign*)

Shute, Henry Augustus. 1911. *Plupy, 'the Real Boy'*. Boston: Gorham. (**1911** Shute *Plupy*)

Simmons, D. A. 1891. *A List of Peculiar Words and Phrases Formerly in Common Use in the County Armagh, Together with Expressions at One Time Current in South Donegal*. Dublin: Freeman's Journal. (**1891** Simmons *Armagh Words and Phrases*)

Simms, Edna Lynn. 1934–40. [Collection of note cards on deposit at Berea College, Berea, Kentucky,] (**1940** Simms *Coll*)

Slone, Verna Mae. 1982. *How We Talked*. Pippa Passes, Ky.: Pippa Valley Printing. (**1982** Slone *How We Talked*)

Smith, Charles Forster. 1883. 'On Southernisms', *Transactions of the American Philological Association* 14:42–56. (**1883** Smith *Southernisms*)

Smith, Charles Forster. 1886. 'On Southernisms', *Transactions of the American Philological Association* 17:34–46. (**1886** Smith *Southernisms*)

Smith, Charles F. 1886. 'Southern Dialect in Life and Literature'. *Southern Bivouac* 4:343–50. (**1886** Smith *Southern Dialect*)

Smith, Ersa Rhea Noland. 1989. *Flyin' Bullets and Resplendent Badge*. Sevierville, Tenn.: Nandel. (**1989** Smith *Flyin' Bullets*)

Smith, Herbert W. 1916. 'Notes from Cape Cod', *Dialect Notes* 4:263–67. (**1916** Smith *Cape Cod Notes*)

Smith, Joseph, and Elizabeth Smith. 1795. [Letter to 'Loving Son' from Chester County, Pennsylvania, manuscript in Campbell Family Collection, McClung Historical Collection of Knox County Public Library, Knoxville, Tenn.] (**1795** Smith *Letter*)

Smith, Richard Penn. 1836. *Colonel Crockett's Exploits and Adventures in Texas*. Philadelphia: Collins. (**1836** Smith *Exploits and Adventures*)

Smith, Seba. 1834. *The Life and Writing of Major Jack Downing of Downingville*. Boston: Lily, Wait, Colman & Holden. (**1834** Smith *Life Jack Downing*)

Smokies Heritage. 1978–82. [Published monthly by Crescent Printing, Gatlinburg, Tenn.] (**1980–82** *Smokies Heritage*)

Smyth, Clifford. 2004. 'Tartan and Kilt in Ulster', *The Ulster-Scot* (Nov):14. (**2004** Smyth *Tartan in Ulster*)

Spencer, Ezalee Kear. 1999–2000. 'Down Memory Lane'. *Smoky Mountain Historical Society Journal,* Part I:25.3.6–10; Part II:25.4.2–11; Part III:26.1.2–8. (**1999–2000** Spencer *Memory Lane*)

Spring, Agnes Wright. 1924. 'Rough Outline of Visit with Aunt Lydia Whaley'. [Typescript on deposit in Library, Great Smoky Mountains National Park, Gatlinburg, Tenn.] (**1924** Spring *Lydia Whaley*)

Sproule Family. 1845–90. [Letters to and from County Tyrone, manuscripts on deposit at University of North Carolina Library, Chapel Hill.] (**1851–61** Sproule *Letters*)

Stanley, Oma. 1936. 'The Speech of East Texas', *American Speech* 11:145–66. (**1936** Stanley *Speech East Texas*)

Starratt, William. 1722. [Epistle]. *The Works of Allan Ramsay*, ed. Oliver Burns and John W. Ramsay, 70–72. Edinburgh: Blackwood & Sons, 1953. (**1722** Starrat *Epistle*)

Steadman, John M., Jr. 1918. 'A North Carolina Word List', *Dialect Notes* 5:18–21. (**1918** Steadman *NC Word List*)

Stewardson, Thomas. 1870. '"Kesh", "Neb", "Butty"'. *Notes and Queries* 143 (24 Sept):389. (**1870** Stewardson *Kesh Neb Butty*)

Stowe, Harriet. 1882. *Sam Lawson's Old Fireside Stories*. Boston: Houghton, Mifflin. (**1882** Stowe *Fireside Stories*)

Sutton, Popcorn. c1999. *Me and My Likker*. Maggie Valley, N.C.: privately published. (**c1999** Sutton *Me and Likker*)

Swearingen, Janelle. 1994 [1874–96]. 'Letters from Home', *Tennessee Ancestors* 10:163–68. (**1874** Swearingen *Letters*)

Taliaferro, H[arden E.] 1859. *Fisher's River (North Carolina) Scenes and Characters*. New York: Harper & Brothers. (**1859** Taliaferro *Fisher's River*)

Taliaferro, Harden E. 1938. *Carolina Humor: Sketches by Harden E. Taliaferro*. Richmond, Va.: Dietz. [Stories from *The Southern Literary Messenger*, published originally 1860–63]. (**1938** Taliaferro *Carolina Humor*)

Taylor, Jay L. B. 1923. 'Snake County Talk', *Dialect Notes* 5:197–225. (**1923** Taylor *Snake Co Talk*)

Thomas, Jean. 1942. *Blue Ridge Country*. New York: Duell, Sloan & Pearce. (**1942** Thomas *Blue Ridge*)

Thompson, Harold William. 1962. *Body, Boots & Britches: Folktales, Ballads, and Speech from Country New York*. New York: Dover. (**1962** Thompson *Body & Britches*)

Thompson, Maurice. 1889. 'Ben and Judas', *Century Illustrated Monthly* 38 (May–Oct):893–902. (**1889** Thompson *Ben and Judas*)

Thompson, William Tappan. 1844. *Major Jones' Courtship*. Philadelphia: Carey & Hart. (**1844** Thompson *Major Jones' Courtship*)

Thompson, William Tappan. 1845. *Chronicles of Pineville*. Philadelphia: Carey & Hart. (**1845** Thompson *Pineville*)

Thomson, Samuel. See Scott, Ernest McA., and Philip S. Robinson.

Thornborough, Laura. 1937. *The Great Smoky Mountains*. New York: Crowell. Revised ed. published in 1956, Knoxville, Tenn.: University of Tennessee Press. (**1937** Thornborough *Great Smoky Mts*)

Thornton, Richard. 1912. *An American Glossary*. London: Francis. (**1912** Thornton *American Glossary*)

Todd, Loreto. 1990. *Words Apart: A Dictionary of Northern Ireland English*. Gerrards Cross: Smythe. (**1990** Todd *Words Apart*)

'Tourist Board Fighting a Losing Battle'. 2003. *Belfast Telegraph* (3 Aug):12. (**2003** *Tourist Board*)

Traynor, Michael. 1953. *The English Dialect of Donegal: A Glossary, Incorporating the Collections of H. C. Hart, etc*. Dublin: Royal Irish Academy. (**1953** Traynor *Donegal Glossary*)

Trent, Emma Deane Smith. 1987. *East Tennessee's Lore of Yesteryear*. Whitesburg, Tenn.: privately published. (**1987** Trent *Lore Yesteryear*)

Trout, Ed, and Olin Watson. c1978. *A Piece of the Smokies: A Pictorial History of Life in the Smoky Mountains*. Maryville, Tenn.: n.p. (**c1978** Trout and Watson *Piece of Smokies*)

Ulster Folk Ways. 1978. Cultra: Ulster Folk and Transport Museum. (**1978** Ulster *Folk Ways*)

United States Congress. 1867. *Congressional Globe*, 39th Congress, 2nd Session (21 Jan):60. (**1867** *Congressional Globe*)

University of Tennessee/Great Smoky Mountains National Park Cooperative Oral History Project. 1996–99. [Taped interviews on deposit in Library, Great Smoky Mountains National Park, Gatlinburg, Tenn.] (**1996–99** *GSMNPOHP*)

'Various Contributions'. 1890. *Dialect Notes* 1:72–76. (**1890** *Various Contrib*)

Vincent, Bert. 1968. *The Best Stories of Bert Vincent*. Maryville, Tenn.: Brazos. (**1968** Vincent *Best Stories*)

Vincent, Bert. 1970. *More of the Best Stories of Bert Vincent*. Maryville, Tenn.: Mangrum. (**1970** Vincent *More of Best*)

Walker, Cas. 1993. *My Life History: 'A Book of True Stories'*. N.p.: privately published. (**1993** Walker *Life History*)

Walker, Raphy S. 1939. 'A Mountaineer Looks at His Own Speech', *Tennessee Folklore Society Bulletin* 5:1–13. (**1939** Walker *Mtneer Looks*)

Walsh, Louis. 1917. *The Guileless Saxon: An Ulster Comedy in Three Acts*. Dublin: Gill and Son. (**1917** Walsh *Guileless Saxon*)

Weals, Vic. 1977. 'Cove Folk Knew a Stranger by His Factory-Made Track'. *Knoxville Journal* (17 Jan), 7. (**1977** Weals *Cove Folk*)

Weals, Vic. c1959. *Hillbilly Dictionary: An Edifying Collection of Mountain Expressions*. Gatlinburg, Tenn.: Weals. (**c1959** Weals *Hillbilly Dict*)

Weals, Vic. 1976. 'Words Stay "Alive" with Oldtimers', *Knoxville Journal* (26 July):7. (**1976** Weals *Words Stay*)

Weaver, Jack. 1993. 'Sociolinguistics of Scotch-Irish Speech in Appalachia'. *Irish Studies Working Papers* 93:12–19. (**1993** Weaver *Scotch-Irish Speech*)

Webber, Everett. 1949. *Backwoods Teacher*. Philadelphia: Lippincott. (**1949** Webber *Backwoods Teacher*)

Webster, Noah. 1847. *American Dictionary*. Springfield, Mass.: Merriam. (**1847** Webster *American Dictionary*)

Webster's New International Dictionary, 2nd ed. 1934. Springfield, Mass.: Merriam-Webster. (**1934** *Web 2nd Intl Dict*)

'A Week in the Smoky Mountains'. 1860. *Southern Literary Messenger* 31 (Aug):117–31. (**1860** *Week*)

Wellman, Judith. 2004. [Remarks at Symposium on the Underground Railroad, 1 Jan]. C-SPAN Television. (**2004** Wellman *Underground Railroad*)

Wentworth, Harold, ed. 1944. *American Dialect Dictionary*. New York: Crowell. (**1944** Wentworth *Amer Dial Dict*)

West, John Foster. 1965. 'They Git Tard in the Hills but Hit ain't from Talkin'', *Charlotte Observer* (21 March). (**1965** West *Git Tard in Hills*)

White, Agnes Romilly. 1934. *Gape Row*. London: Selwyn & Blount. Reprinted in 1989, Belfast: White Row Press. (**1934** White *Gape Row*)

White, Agnes Romilly. 1936. *Mrs Murphy Buries the Hatchet*. London: Selwyn & Blount. Reprinted in 1988, Belfast: White Row Press. (**1936** White *Mrs Murphy*)

White, Henry Adelbert. 1912. 'A Word-list from Central New York', *Dialect Notes* 3:565–69. (**1912** White *Word-list Cent NY*)

White, Richard Grant. 1868. 'Words and Their Uses', *Galaxy* 5 (Apr):191–99. (**1868** White *Words and Uses*)

Whitener, Rogers. 1981. 'Selections from "Folk-Ways and Folk Speech"'. *North Carolina Folklore Journal* 29:1–86. (**1981** Whitener *Folk-Ways*)

Wier, John. 2002. *Bab McKeen: The Wit and Wisdom of an Ulster Scot*, ed. Jack Adams. Ballymena: Mid-Antrim Ulster-Scots Society. (**c1910** Wier *Bab McKeen*)

Wilburn, Hiram C. c1950. 'Quern, a Grinding Device, Dates from Ancient Days', *Asheville Citizen*. (**c1950** Wilburn *Quern*)

Wilder, Roy. 1984. *You All Spoken Here*. New York: Viking. (**1984** Wilder *You All Spoken*)

Williams, Cratis D. 1944. 'A Word-list from the Mountains of Kentucky and North Carolina', *Publication of the American Dialect Society* 2:28–31. (**1944** Williams *Word-list Mts*)

Williams, Cratis D. 1961. 'The Content of Mountain Speech', *Mountain Life and Work* 37(4):13–17. (**1961** Williams *Content Mt Speech*)

Williams, Cratis D. 1962. 'Metaphor in Mountain Speech', *Mountain Life and Work* 38(4):9, 11–12. (**1962** Williams *Metaphor Mt Speech*)

Williams, Cratis D. 1967. 'Moonshining in the Mountains', *North Carolina Folklore* 15:11–17. (**1967** Williams *Moonshining in Mts*)

Williams, Cratis D. 1967. 'Subtlety in Mountain Speech', *Mountain Life and Work* 43(1):14–16. (**1967** Williams *Subtlety Mt Speech*)

Wilson, George. 1944. 'A Word-list from Virginia and North Carolina', *Publication of the American Dialect Society* 2:38–52. (**1944** Wilson *Word-list*)

Wilson, George. 1952. 'Folk Speech', *The Frank C. Brown Collection of North Carolina Folklore*, ed. Newman Ivey White et al. Vol. 1:505–618. Durham, N.C.: Duke University Press. (**1952** Wilson *Folk Speech NC*)

Wood, Gordon [R]. 1958. 'A List of Words from Tennessee', *Publication of the American Dialect Society* 29:3–18. (**1958** Wood *Words from Tenn*)

Wood, Gordon R. 1971. *Vocabulary Change*. Carbondale: Southern Illinois University Press. (**1971** Wood *Vocabulary Change*)

Woodard, C. M. 1946. 'A Word-list from Virginia and North Carolina', *Dialect Notes* 6:4–43. (**1946** Woodard *Word-list Virg/NC*)

Woodmason, Charles. c1765. *The Carolina Backcountry on the Eve of the Revolution*. Edited and introduced in 1953 by Richard J. Hooker, 150–61. Chapel Hill, N.C.: University of North Carolina Press. (**c1765** Woodmason *Carolina Backcountry*)

Woofter, Carey. 1927. 'Dialect Words and Phrases from West-Central West Virginia'. *American Speech* 2:347–67. (**1927** Woofter *Dialect West Virginia*)

'Word-list'. 1896. *Dialect Notes* 1:411–27. (**1896** *Word-list*)

'Word-lists'. 1895. *Dialect Notes* 1:368–400. (**1895** *Word-lists*)

Wright, John. 2005. 'A'm No Sae Bad', *Hamewarks fae Ballyboley: Tha Cless o 2004*, 14–17. Belfast: Ullans Press. (**2005** Wright *No Sae Bad*)

Wright, Joseph, ed. 1898–1905. *English Dialect Dictionary*. London: Henry Frowde. (**1898–1905** Wright *Engl Dial Dict*)

Yunzonics: Translating Pennsylvanian. 2004. <http//: www.tomtwine.com/pa.html> (**2004** *Yunzonics*)

Zeigler, Wilbur Gleason and Benn S. Grosscup. 1883. *The Heart of the Alleghanies: or, Western North Carolina; Comprising its Topography, History, Resources, People, Narratives, Incidents, and Pictures in Travel, Hunting and Fishing, and Legends of Its Wildernesses*. Raleigh, N.C.: Williams. (**1883** Zeigler and Grosscup *Heart of Alleghanies*)